EDUCATION IN A COMPETITIVE AND GLOBALIZING WORLD SERIES

LEARNING IN THE NETWORK SOCIETY AND THE DIGITIZED SCHOOL

EDUCATION IN A COMPETITIVE AND GLOBALIZING WORLD SERIES

Motivation in Education
Desmond H. Elsworth (Editor)
2009. ISBN: 978-1-60692-234-7

**The Reading Literacy of U.S. Fourth-Grade
Students in an International Context**
Justin Baer, Stéphane Baldi, Kaylin Ayotte,Patricia J. Green and Daniel McGrath
2009 ISBN: 978-1-60692-138-3

Teacher Qualifications and Kindergartners Achievements
*Cassandra M. Guarino, Laura S. Hamilton, J.R. Lockwood,Amy H. Rathbun and Elvira
Germino Hausken*
2009 ISBN: 978-1-60741-180-2

**Effects of Family Literacy Interventions
on Children's Acquisition of Reading**
Ana Carolina Pena (Editor)
2009 ISBN: 978-1-60741-236-6

Nutrition Education and Change
Beatra F. Realine (Editor)
2009. ISBN: 978-1-60692-983-4

Reading at Risk: A Survey of Literary Reading in America
Rainer D. Ivanov
2009. ISBN: 978-1-60692-582-9

Evaluating Online Learning: Challenges and Strategies for Success
Arthur T. Weston (Editor)
2009. ISBN: 978-1-60741-107-9

Learning in the Network Society and the Digitized School
Rune Krumsvik (Editor)
2009. ISBN: 978-1-60741-172-7

EDUCATION IN A COMPETITIVE AND GLOBALIZING WORLD SERIES

LEARNING IN THE NETWORK SOCIETY AND THE DIGITIZED SCHOOL

RUNE KRUMSVIK
EDITOR

Nova Science Publishers, Inc.
New York

LIBRARY OF CONGRESS CATALOGING-IN-PUBLICATION DATA

Learning in the network society and the digitized school / editor, Rune Krumsvik.
    p. cm. -- (Education in a competitive and globalizing world)
  Includes bibliographical references and index.
  ISBN 978-1-60741-172-7 (hardcover : alk. paper)
  1. Computer-assisted instruction. 2. Web-based instruction. 3. Information technology. 4. Education--Effect of technological innovations on. I. Krumsvik, Rune J.
  LB1028.5.L386   2009
  371.33'44678--dc22   2009004633

Published by Nova Science Publishers, Inc. ✦ *New York*

CONTENTS

PREFACE

Rune Krumsvik

Learning in the Network Society and the Digitized School is a refereed research anthology focusing on how digitization of society and school influence communities of practise, pedagogy, didactics, ICT and learning in the 21st century. This has become increasingly important during the digital revolution the last ten years and e.g. in Norway digital literacy have enjoyed a historic rise in their academic status, becoming the fifth core competence to be incorporated in all subjects at all age levels (6-19 years) under the new national curriculum (KD 2006). This digitization of society and school presents opportunities, challenges and dilemmas in the running of schools and the question that arises is to what extent this has any impact on young people's learning as well as students in higher education. The anthology aims to examine these issues from different methodological and theoretical perspectives, based on the overall theme "research meets practise – practise meets research". The anthology consists of 16 chapters with thematic areas as: ICT and personalisation, ICT and creativity, ICT and dialogical approaches, ICT and school development, Digital divides, Situated learning in the Network society, ICT in English-teaching, collaboration in virtual student-settings, ICT and learning, Digital didactics, Adapted education and ICT, and ICT and Pedagogy. The anthology aims to reflect ongoing educational research within these areas in Sweden, Norway and United Kingdom, but the anthology is highly relevant for all other countries dealing with implementation of ICT in education. A referee committee consisting of 18 referees from different countries has carried out a blind review of the chapters in the anthology.

The main thread through the anthology is the challenges and opportunities in regard to handle the digitization of society and school in the digital era. One of the main reason for focusing on this area is that the digital revolution and the ever increasing digitalisation of school life have altered some of the conditions under which our educational system operate compared to before the digital revolution in the beginning of the 1990's (Krumsvik 2006). Several of the chapters in this anthology examine this situation and the need to reconsider what the terms *knowledge, knowing* and *know-how* are in 2008. Therefore some of the chapters discuss if there is a need to develop a digital epistemology which can capture a broader view of knowledge to encapsulate the impact of the latest digital trends on the underlying conditions applicable to our universities, schools, pedagogy, didactic and subjects.

The anthology also set out to discuss how digital literacy can create new approaches to how we view and assess knowledge in the digital age. For example, in relation to the new national curriculum in Norway, ICT and digital literacy occupy a prominent position and enshrining this area so clearly in the curriculum puts Norway in a unique position internationally with digital literacy as the fifth basic competence in all subjects at all levels. This makes for a situation in which digital trends and new learning spaces are paving the way for new educational approaches and assessment forms, while a number of apparent obstacles prevent these approaches from becoming a reality.

From a Norwegian perspective, the digital revolution has produced radical changes in the Norwegian society since the mid-1990s, and the school system too has been affected by these developments. A British study, *Personalisation and Digital Technologies* (Green, Facer, Rudd, Dillon & Humphreys 2006), provides an insight into the extent of this digital revolution. The study forecasts that today's average British school-age child will, by the age of 21, have spent 15,000 hours in formal education, 20,000 hours watching television and 50,000 hours in front of a computer screen. Although this is merely a prediction, it nevertheless provides an indication of the extent to which today's "screenagers" (Rushkoff 1996) or "millennium learners" (Pedro 2006) use the media. Much of this media use is entertainment-focused (which makes it difficult to distinguish between entertainment and learning), but several of the chapters are asking whether any of it might be relevant to school activities. The basis of this notion is that pupils are acquiring digital self-confidence through frequent use, and that such aspects are important for their transcontextual learning (learning that takes place in and between multiple contexts, Lave & Wenger 2003). "Digitized", situated learning may represent a new form of knowledge building that may be relevant in a school context, both as a theoretical lens to understand this digitization of society and school and for developing a new, broader digital epistemology which have to reflect this new digitized, knowledge building.

However, the question that arises in several of the chapters is to what extent this broader digital epistemology has any impact on young people's learning, and whether we really know enough about what constitutes knowledge accumulation among digital natives today. A number of previous studies showed that ICT had had little demonstrable effect on young people's learning (Cuban 2001), so there is reason to be sceptical of simple conclusions in this regard. At the same time we are seeing the digital revolution and the massive transcontextual use of media by young people paving the way for different, indirect approaches to learning than under the previous curricula in different countries. Although we can identify only a vague outline of what this might imply, the British report mentions that schools must show "[…] an awareness that many learners today are already creating personalised environments for themselves outside school using digital resources" (Green et al. 2006:4). Looking at this in the context of the previous curricula in the Nordic countries, we have to consider the extent to which schools should take more account of the digital world inhabited by today's "screenagers" outside of school. In contrast to mid 1990's, pupils in 2008 move in digital fields comprising a number of digital and multimodal learning resources, networks, a user-friendly Web 2.0, online communities, new forms of communication, etc. that did not exist when the previous curricula was introduced. As a consequence of this (and the digitization of society in general), *participation* in the Network society in 2008 means that the majority of e.g. Norwegian citizens are able to obtain almost all the services from public authorities through the Net (e.g. www.norge.no, www.minside.no, www.skatteetaten.no), communicate in new ways through the Net (Skype, chat, SMS, E-mail, etc.), has access to enormous sources of information and knowledge through the Net (e.g. www.wikipedia.org, www.naturfag.no, www.skolenettet.no, www.utdanning.no, www.viten.no) and at the same can present themselves through the Net (e.g. www.facebook.com, www.twitter.com,), have a "voice" in the public room through the Net (e.g. Internet blogs, discussion forums) and participate in Net societies (www.myspace.com, www.youtube.com). This establishes a lot of possibilities that we never has seen before and the majority of the screenagers have already constituted this on-line existence in this digital landscape as part of their *Bildung*-journey (Krumsvik & Støbakk 2007). This might also have impact in how these screenagers learn and therefore I will claim that that never before has our Network society been so prepared for a "digitized" situated learning than in 2008. With a swarm of digital learning resources, digital communities and people a "mouse click" away this constitutes a very good starting point to capture the informal learning that occurs for screenagers, even if we not today value it as "knowledge" defined from a traditional perception of knowledge.

However, the question one have to ask is if the rapidly digitization of society and school establish a gap between the majority of digital natives (the "Haves", screenagers) and digital immigrants (the "Have-Not's") , and if so, how do this influence human development for the digital illiterates, as well as teaching and learning in our contemporary society? Previous studies from the US showed that implementation of ICT in the USA has created an unexpected side-effect: "(…) the creation of a technological underclass in America's public schools" (Cuban & Tyack, 1998, p. 125). This digital diversity followed traditional socio-economic and cultural "trails" and created new problems for already vulnerable schools and pupil-groups. Another study from the US *"Computer and Internet Use by Students in 2003"* revealed the same tendency as before and found that digital divides was closely tied to socioeconomic status of the pupils parents, their family income and by ethnicity (DeBell & Chapman 2006). And in a report from Organisation for Economic Co-operation and Development [OECD], *Understanding the Digital Divide* (2001), the same dilemma is highlighted for European conditions, where "falling through the Net" threatens certain groups. As a consequence of this we can ask if *access* and *participation* has become so important ground pillars in our Network society, that the citizens and pupils who do not have necessary access to technology at home, at school and in spare time, actually experiences that they are digital illiterates and in many ways are segregated from the mainstream society. As a consequence of this they are also hindered to participate in the "digitized" situated learning which occurs "anytime, anywhere and with anyone" because of the digitization of society and school, as well as peoples in general on-line existence. In e.g. Norway this situation is quite common among minority pupils in school (Frønes, 2002), but we also see special kind of digital inequality (in frequency and how they use technology) among parents and youngsters from lower socioeconomic family status (Vaage 2008). Several teacher educators and teachers state that the Mathew effect (Merton 1973) is already possible to observe among pupils even if this digitized society is only "ten years old": pupils who are doing well in school in general are using the technology to more subject-related activities; pupils who achieves rather bad in school are using the technology more to entertainment. This might be the "back side of the medallion" of the digitization of society and school and needs to be considered seriously if we mean something with the ground pillars in almost all countries: Inclusion and adapted education for the pupils. Therefore some chapters in the anthology are mentioning if we see the contours of that our schools need to be aware of that they can equalise some of the digital divides with e.g. a strategy of increasing the subject-use of ICT in the subjects, relate adapted education to such issues and give access to school computers after school time for vulnerable pupil groups.

As a summary of this preface I will claim that this anthology tries to communicate that we face a number of possibilities, challenges and dilemmas in this new digital educational landscape in our Network society and where both the need for a digital epistemology, increased digital literacy among teachers, digital didactics and awareness for digital divides has to be considered in light of the digital revolution. If one considers these issues more seriously we might be able to realize the main topic for the anthology: establish new practices for teachers and pupils based on collaboration, sharing and feedback across formal – and informal learning spaces. In that case "Learning in the Network society and the digitized school" becomes more than good intentions – it might be a useful lens to understand "how teachers teach and learners learn" in a digitized society.

REFERENCES

Castells, M. (2001). *The Internet Galaxy*. New York: Oxford University Press.

Cuban, L. (2001). *Oversold and Underused. Computers in the Classroom*. Cambridge: Harvard University Press.

Cuban, L., & Tyack D. (1998). Tinkering Toward Utopia. Cambridge: Harvard University Press.

DeBell, M., and Chapman, C. (2006). *Computer and Internet Use by Students in 2003* (NCES 2006–065). U.S. Department of Education. Washington, DC: National Center for Education Statistics.

Frønes, I. (2002). *Digitale skiller* [Digital divides; in Norwegian]. Bergen: Fagbokforlaget.

Green, H., Facer, K., Rudd, T., Dillon, P. & Humphreys, P. (2006). *Personalisation and Digital Technologies*. London: Futurelab.

KD (Ministry of Education and Research) (2006). Prinsipper for opplæringen [The quality framework]. Oslo: Government Administration Services.

Knobel, M. (1999). *Everyday literacies*. New York: Peter Lang.

Krumsvik, R. (2006). *ICT-initiated school development in lower secondary school*. Doctoral thesis, dr.philos. The University of Bergen. Bergen: Allkopi.

Krumsvik, R. (2007a). *Skulen og den digitale læringsrevolusjonen* [The school and the digital learning revolution; in Norwegian]. Oslo: Universitetsforlaget

Krumsvik, R. & Støbakk, Å. (2007a). Digital danning [Digital Bildung]. In R. Krumsvik (Ed.), *Skulen og den digitale læringsrevolusjon* [The school and the digital learning revolution; in Norwegian]. Oslo: Universitetsforlaget.

KUF (Ministry of Education and Research) (1996). *Læreplanverket for den 10-årige grunnskolen.*[The national curriculum for elementary school; in Norwegian]. Oslo: Nasjonalt Læremiddelsenter.

Lave, J., & Wenger, E. (1991). *Situated Learning. Legitimate peripheral participation.* Cambridge: Cambridge University Press.

Merton, R. K. (1973). *The Sociology of Science: Theoretical and Empirical Investigations.* Chicago, IL: University of Chicago Press.

OECD (Organisation for Economic Co-operation and Development) (2001). *Understanding the digital divide.* Access date: 20.02.2003, from http://www.oecd.org/dataoecd/38/57/1888451.pdf.

Pedro, F. (2006). The new millennium learners: challenging our Views on ICT and Learning. OECD-CERI. Paris. Retrieved from: http://www.oecd.org/dataoecd/1/1/38358359.pdf 20.10.08.

Rushkoff, D. (1996). *Playing the Future: What We Can Learn From Digital Kids – Children of Chaos in the UK.* New York: Riverhead Books.

Vaage, O.F. (2008). *Norsk Mediebarometer 2007* [The Norwegian Media Statistics; in Norwegian]. Oslo: Statistisk Sentralbyrå.

PREFACE: EDUCATING WORLD CITIZENS: LEVERAGING THE POTENTIAL OF ICT

Etienne Wenger

Something exciting is happening in the world of learning. The complex challenges we face today urgently call for new models of how we can learn individually and collectively. Communities of practice can serve as one such model. They are as ancient as human kind; yet they represent a model of learning that is extraordinarily aligned with the new geographies of connectivity and identity emerging at the dawn of the 21st century.

In this essay I explore the potential of ICT for enabling new roles for schools in educating our students to become world citizens. These roles are suggested by looking at schooling from the perspective of social learning theory. I start with a very brief summary of some elements of social learning theory. Then I look at the convergence of two interrelated sets of trends—in learning and in technology—that are put into relief when looked at from a social perspective on learning (Wenger, 2006). I start with trends in learning and follow with trends in technology, but this is for presentation purposes only. In reality these two sets of trends shape each other so closely that they are not so easily distinguishable. Certainly one does not cause the other in any simple way. Finally I explore the implications for schools in two ways: how these trends are changing the position of the school in a digitized society and how schools can leverage current trends to renew their function in the lives of students.

A SOCIAL PERSPECTIVE ON LEARNING

A social theory of learning takes as its fundamental axiom that we are social beings and explores the implications of this axiom for how we can both understand and support learning. Of course, our social nature is most obvious when we are interacting with others, but we are social beings even when we are by ourselves, because the concepts, words, and other artifacts we use reflect our participation in social communities. Hence, learning has a social dimension whether or not it takes place in interactions with others at any given time.

Knowledge as Practice

From this perspective, knowledge is embedded in social practice. The world of human knowledge is composed of a huge collection of practices. The living communities that develop, share, and refine these practices then become central to social learning theory. It makes sense to call them "communities of practice." They are a key element of learning. And so are the boundaries between these communities—boundaries where misunderstandings are easy but also where new possibilities can be negotiated. From this perspective, a body of knowledge becomes a constellation of interrelated practices that contribute to defining what knowing is—whether it is a science, an art, a profession, or a hobby. As we enter, engage with, and leave these communities, learning is a social journey as well as a cognitive process. It entails becoming a participant in the social body of knowledge as well as in the cognitive curriculum.

Learning and Identity

Each step changes our ability to engage in human practices—and to make sense of our world and our lives. The learning that members of communities of practice do together does not separate the "content" from the formation of the person for whom knowledge is a meaningful way of being. Learning entails new ways of being in the world. It transforms both our participation and our identity—it is a social journey of the self.

Focus on Learning in Organizations

While as old as human societies, communities of practice have recently attracted increasing interest in organizations trying to manage knowledge as a strategic asset—in the private, public, and professional sectors. The concept of community of practice has helped these organizations in two ways. At a conceptual level, it has given managers a perspective to see where knowledge "lives" in their organizations. And at a practical level, it has helped them figure out what to do about it—cultivate communities of practice and integrate them in the functioning of the organization. As a medium for peer-to-peer learning, communities put the responsibility for managing knowledge where it belongs: in the hands of practitioners who use this knowledge in the performance of their tasks.

Communities, Learning and Technology

It would have been hard to imagine that the technologies introduced over the last two decades would have the profound effect they have had on communities of practice. The concept was proposed as a way to understand something fundamental about human learning, not technology. Yet technological developments have both confirmed the importance of this perspective and affected the way it is understood. There is something about the web that fits really well with the pervasiveness of peer-to-peer learning processes typical of communities of practice. In retrospect, looking back at the development of the internet, it makes sense that such technology would profoundly affect the potential of communities because the interactivity and connectivity it enables are so aligned with the ways communities of practice function as a context for learning (Wenger et al., 2009).

LEARNING IMPERATIVES

A number of developments in learning imperatives create new conditions for the world that our students are entering as present and future contributors. By learning imperatives here I mean some of the driving forces that shape the learning that will be required of our students as citizens of the world.

Partialization

The increasing complexity and diversity of knowledge today mean that nobody can claim full mastery of any domain of interest (Gibbons et al, 1994). Even within a specialized domain, there is too much to know, too much new knowledge being produced too fast for any one participant to claim exclusive ownership or full mastery of the domain. This makes social participation all the more critical to the possibility of significant and sustained knowing. Learning is learning to take part in communities and networks where the knowledge of the domain is distributed.

Globalization

Today, when members of a community consider what learning partners and resources they need, they are considering individuals, groups, and organizations from all over the world. They see their community as integrally connected with global systems of practices that are potentially relevant to their learning. Their emerging identity is defined for them through a process that reaches across the planet (Ryberg, 2007).

Horizontalization

At the same time as we are witnessing increased processes of verticalization through institutions that attempt to standardize knowledge (Giddens, 1991), we are witnessing a process of horizontalization through a new emphasis on peer-to-peer learning, both in organizations and in society more generally. This has led to the proliferation of communities of practice. When brought together members of a community of practice quickly realize how much they can learn from each other. They want to hear each other's stories and discuss each other's experience. From a vertical relationship between a provider and a recipient of knowledge, communities of practice represent a horizontal relationship among people negotiating how their respective experience can be relevant to each other. The horizontal nature of these learning processes does not deny a role for experts. Experts have much to contribute, but in the context of a community, they still have to negotiate the mutual relevance of what they know to what others know from their perspectives. Practice remains a collective achievement. It is quite a significant development that institutions see as one of their key learning strategy to cultivate peer-to-peer communities, rather than the more traditional, vertical processes of creating training courses and procedures that instruct people what to do.

Personalization of Value Creation

The creation of value in knowledge-based services depends on personal engagement with challenges. Such an experience of meaningfulness is a key source of creativity. When I work with organizations, I see that the people who are creating high value are not those who comply but those who are personally involved in what they do and engage their own identities in taking on challenges and inventing new solutions. In an industrial context, you might be able to expect that people will withdraw their personal sense of engagement and meaningfulness to comply with the design of the process, which is the main source of value creation. But in a knowledge-intensive context, it is the opposite. When meaning-making, creative use of knowledge, and innovation are key, it is above all the engagement of a personal sense of meaningfulness in the work that will create value.

TECHNOLOGY AFFORDANCES

New technologies like the web have enabled people to interact in new ways across time and space and find learning partners independently of geography and affiliation. This has led to new breeds of distributed yet interactive communities of practice, with more dynamic and fluid boundaries and accelerated formation of new communities in the interstices.

Access to Information

New technologies are enabling ubiquitous access to information in two ways. On the one hand, the internet frontier is being settled by traditional contributors as well as non-traditional entrants with exploding information resources, including websites about everything imaginable and even course offerings. On the other hand, a collection of emerging technologies are providing instant access to information across time and space, both through a variety of access devices and through improved search capabilities and social computing (e.g., tagging, social links).

Peripherality

Technology is affording an exploding ability to belong peripherally, to be "lurkers" as peripheral participants are called in web lingo. We are able to become involved with countless practices without being a member of the community. We have countless service encounters, in which we witness practices as customers of our lawyers, doctors, financial advisors, hairdressers, specialized stores, etc. Films and television give us insights into exotic practices such as open-heart surgery, emergency rooms, courtrooms, and police watch. We lurk on web-based conversations among aficionados. This generalized peripherality affects the proportion of deep to peripheral participation as constituents of our identities.

Expression

At the same time as it provides access to information, the web facilitates expression in ways unimaginable a few years ago. Blogs, pages in social networking systems, and public spaces for commentaries enable a generalized capability for self-expression. Furthermore, the malleability of digital content with hypertext means that it can be reappropriated, reused, remixed, and linked as a form of self-expression, for instance, through collections such as lists of favorites that come to represent our experience. Finally, wikis and open-source processes enable mass collaboration on a planetary scale (Tapscott and Williams, 2006).

New Geographies of Community and Identity

The reach and interactivity of the web has given rise to an explosion of possibility for communities as people can find learning partners all over the world. As everyone belongs to many communities, groups, and networks over the course of a lifetime and at any given time, dynamic multi-membership becomes a way of life and a pervasive characteristic of post-modern identity. As a consequence of this generalized multimembership, each person is a unique intersection of connections, which gives rise to very individualized trajectories of identity.

CHALLENGES TO THE ROLE OF SCHOOLS

In what ways do the trends outlined above challenge the role of school in a globalized, digitized society? The following are a few factors that suggest that a transformation is necessary.

Access to Information

Access to information was a key service and a central challenge for earlier institutions of learning. This is less and less a problem and certainly no longer a unique service of schools.

A generalized increase in access to information and peripherality allows students to find sources of content other than educational institutions. If anything, there is an overwhelming plethora of information. The more salient issue now is how to forge an identity that can navigate productively a growing sea of information. We need well-developed identities to guide our choices of focus and our accountability to the knowledge of myriad of communities we enter in contact with.

The Shelf Life of Knowledge

The shelf life of knowledge is becoming shorter. On the one hand, human knowledge is evolving very fast as the world, our societies, and technology keep changing. On the other hand, students are not likely to have a simple life trajectory or a single career, as human trajectories move fast and go through rapid transformations (McCracken, 2008). As a result, much of what we learn will be relevant for only a limited time. This makes it less likely that what a student learns in school beyond the very early years of "basics" remains relevant later in life. As much as *what* we know, it is *how* we know that matters—knowing with an identity that is ready to unlearn and relearn constantly in order to move on.

Cultural Canons

Even as globalization creates homogenizing trends, it also brings into contact a great diversity of cultures, values, and educational canons. Within cultures as well new voices are struggling to make themselves heard, creating a more complex chorus. What constitutes our cultural common ground is less and less obvious, but increasingly contestable and contested. Holding such a diversified society together requires less a common heritage than a willingness to engage and learn across boundaries. The destabilization of cultural canons makes curricular decisions less obvious and indeed divisive. It entails that the pursuit of common ground is receding as the main source of social cohesion to be replaced by boundary crossing. Again, this bridging ability depends on identities able to manage the insider/outsider tensions of boundary experiences.

Sequestration from the Rest of Life

The sequestration of schools and other educational institutions from the rest of society was once very important to protect children from rapacious child labor, and remains so in a number of countries. But it makes less sense in many societies today if we consider the price of the separation: that education has to forego using participation in the world as primary curricular material. The walls of the school that were supposed to shelter learning have become an obstacle. They create a self-referential world where students build local identities that do not necessarily articulate well with the rest of their lives.

Together, these factors suggest that, beyond a few basic skills of literacy that can be taught in self-standing institutions, it is going to be increasingly difficult and less and less useful to find a universal curriculum. Rather it is going to become more important to devise educational experiences that can transform students' broader experience of who they are in the world. This realization challenges us to place participation, meaningfulness, and identity at the center of learning issues, and thus of schooling, in the 21st century.

THE PEDAGOGICAL POTENTIAL OF TECHNOLOGY

If our students already have access to a world of information, if the school is no longer a privileged locus of access to codified knowledge, then what can the school contribute to the challenge of learning? It from this perspective, I would suggest, that a key preoccupation in our schools today needs to be a deep understanding and judicious leverage of the pedagogical potential of technology. The questions that are often asked about ICT concern its place in the curriculum or its role in enabling curriculum delivery. I am suggesting that a more challenging question would be how we can use ICT to help our schools go beyond the typically narrow focus on learning as acquiring a curriculum: how we can use ICT to implement a view of learning as developing new ways of engaging in the world, that is, new identities.

Educate World Citizens

Schools need the pedagogical wherewithal to create learning experiences toward the formation of world citizenship. Students are coming to our schools with an experience of the world and technology that is transforming their expectations about learning (Ryberg, 2007). Most of them already see the planet as the stage for their learning—with a mix of excitement and apprehension. They come with a sense of personal reach that sends tentacles around the world. They build their identities as individualized trajectories that are ready to travel far and wide, both culturally and literally. They are budding world citizens. The use of ICT in education must respond or become irrelevant.

Use the World as a Curriculum

Perhaps one of the most interesting pedagogical promises of ICT is to break the walls of the school and to discover new ways to leverage the world itself as a living curriculum. The connective nature of ICT has this potential, whether it lets students take their learning into the world or bring the world into the classroom. In both cases the point is to use technology to expand the students' horizon and experience of the world and themselves in it. For instance, ICT is already used in some schools to connect students with peers in other places and cultures, so they can discover and engage with new learning partners. Other projects connect them as contributors to large scientific data-collection processes. We need to explore more systematically this potential to cross boundaries, leverage new forms of peripherality, visit various communities of practice and explore otherness through various channels.

Make Learning Meaningful through Acts of Engagement

A lot of instruction and assessment today focuses on the mechanics of learning—skills, techniques, and information that can be readily tested. But if students are going to put their educational experience in the service of true world citizenship, it is their ability to engage meaningfully with what they are learning that will drive their development. We must explore the potential of ICT to bring the experience of schooling closer to student's experience of their own lives so they can engage in learning as a personal journey into new meanings. This question shifts the focus from what we put in students' heads to what we do to increase their ability to contribute to the world in their own ways.

Use Your Identity as an Invitation

As teachers we can invite students into our own identity of participation and thus open their experience to a new world. When I remember those teachers who had a significant impact on my life, I notice that they all did this. At a deep level, this invitation into one's identity is the essence of teaching. This is an aspiration that goes beyond ICT, but to which ICT can contribute by enabling teachers to bring more of themselves into their teaching. More pragmatically, this suggests that the teachers themselves need meaningful experiences of engagement with the technology as an opening to the world, so they can invite students into their own identities as digital denizens.

REFERENCES

Gibbons, Michael; Limoges, Camilles; Nowotny, Helga; Schwartzman, Simon; Scott, Peter; and Trow, Martin (1994) *The new production of knowledge: the dynamics of science and research in contemporary societies*. London: Sage Publications.

Giddens, Anthony (1991) *Modernity and self-identity: self and society in the late modern age*. Stanford, CA: Stanford University Press.

McCracken, Grant (2008) *Transformations: identity construction in contemporary cultures*. Indiana University Press.

Ryberg, Thomas (2007) *Patchworking as a Metaphor for Learning: Understanding youth, learning and technology*. Unpublished Ph.D. dissertation. University of Aalborg, Denmark.

Tapscott, Don, and Williams, Anthony (2006) *Wikinomics: how mass collaboration changes everything*. New York: Penguin Publishers.

Wenger, Etienne (2006) *Learning for a small planet*. Available at www.ewenger.com/research.

Wenger, Etienne, White, Nancy and Smith, John (2009) *Digital habitats: stewarding technology for communities*.CreateSpace.

THE REFEREES IN THE ANTHOLOGY

The Editor would like to thank the following referees for their blind review of the chapters in this anthology:

Professor Yngve Nordkvelle
Lillehammer University College, Norway

Associate professor Yvonne Fritze
Lillehammer University College, Norway

Professor Arne Krokan
Norwegian University of Science and Technology, Norway

Associate professor Andreas Lund
University of Oslo, Norway

Professor Trond Eiliv Hauge
University of Oslo, Norway

Professor Staffan Selander
University of Stockholm, Sweden

Research leader Hans C. Arnseth
ITU, University of Oslo, Norway

Professor Barbara Wasson
University of Bergen, Norway

Associate professor Frode Guribye
University of Bergen, Norway

Research leader Morten Søby
ITU, University of Oslo, Norway

Associate professor Gunilla Jedeskog
University of Lindköping, Sweden

Professor Anton Havnes
University of Bergen, Norway

Associate professor Laurence Habib
Oslo University College

Professor Sølvi Lillejord
University of Bergen, Norway

Dr. David Benzie
Marjon University College, Great Britain

Professor Olga Dysthe
University of Bergen, Norway

Associate professor Knut S. Engelsen
Stord/Haugesund University College, Norway

Associate professor Carl Fredrik Dons
Sør-Trøndelag University College

Associate professor Bjarne Købmand Pedersen
University College Sjælland, Denmark

In: Learning in the Network Society and the Digitized School   ISBN 978-1-60741-172-7
Editor: Rune Krumsvik   © 2009 Nova Science Publishers, Inc.

Chapter 1

Transforming Students' Learning: How Digital Technologies Could Be Used to Change the Social Practices of Schools

Bridget Somekh[1] and Cathy Lewin[2]
Manchester Metropolitan University, UK

Abstract

This chapter looks at the transformative potential of digital technologies for learning in formal educational settings. It draws upon research into pedagogy and learning with ICT that we have carried out over twenty-five years: initially Bridget's work in the 1980s when the first 'microcomputers' arrived in schools in England, and over the last ten years our collaborative work at the Centre of ICT, Pedagogy and Learning at Manchester Metropolitan University. Our focus is on how changes in pedagogy and learning have taken place in formal education, why there are barriers to these changes and how they can be overcome.

Introduction

Do we have evidence to suggest that digital technologies have the power to change the social practices of schools? … that is, the power to change the pedagogic process, adult-student relationships, and the cultural-cognitive process of knowledge acquisition? Vygotsky showed us that human capabilities are shaped through the use of cultural tools and artefacts (Vygotsky, 1978). Of these, language is the most extraordinary and complex, enabling us to interact socially with others and laying the foundations for the development of mind: that is, the conscious being (self, identity) that is capable of complex reasoning and imagination – the ability to shape and express thoughts; and reflexivity to enable us to explore, and perhaps to understand, our own emotions through introspection. Digital technologies are a new kind of cultural tool. Their transformative potential has been compared to that of the discovery of writing by the ancient Greeks or the development of the printing press by Johannes Gutenberg in the fifteenth century. They are adjuncts to human intelligence. Other comparisons, say with the discovery of the wheel or the motor car, have less resonance because the transformative potential of digital technologies lies in their power for storing, searching, accessing, and creating knowledge and information. Digital technologies replace manual labour not through mechanical advantage, but because they allow humans to develop complex systems of control capable of carrying out numerous inter-linking procedures with exact precision measured in fractions of a millimetre. To clarify McLuhan's metaphor of the telegraph as 'an extension of the self' (McLuhan, 1964), digital technologies provide us with extensions to the human mind, they make global communication immediate; they even shift our reliance upon the written word by enabling us to communicate easily, both locally and globally, through still and moving images; more than that, they enable different communication media to merge and hybridise, offering us new affordances for social transformation.

This chapter looks at the transformative potential of digital technologies for learning in formal educational settings. It draws upon research into pedagogy and learning with ICT that we have carried out over twenty-five years: initially Bridget's work in the 1980s when the first 'microcomputers' arrived in schools in England, and over the last ten years our collaborative work at the Centre of ICT, Pedagogy and Learning at Manchester Metropolitan University. Our focus is on how changes in pedagogy and learning have taken place in formal education, why there are barriers to these changes and how they can be overcome. We illustrate our argument almost entirely from our own work in the UK, but our thinking has been strongly influenced by a review of the international literature, particularly a small number of cases of radical pedagogical change. For example, through sustained action research, the way children and teachers develop and use online resources at the Godoy island school in Norway has transformed learning (Krumsvik, 2006); and computers and communication technologies have empowered children to generate knowledge that contributes to development in their communities in the Knowledge Producing Schools in Australia (Bigum, 2002). We write in the knowledge that young people in countries across the world are now routinely using digital technologies extensively in out-of-school environments; and that, as a result, their social practices for communicating with their peers, accessing popular culture, and finding out what they decide they need to know, are transformed by comparison with the social practices of our own generations back in the 1960s and 1980s (Lewin, 2004). We know too that equivalent transformations have not occurred in schools in the great majority of countries. Indeed, the most ubiquitous of digital technologies, the cell phone, is often banned in schools. The key issue for education is, of course, the purposes for which technology is used, but it has become clear that schools are constrained by very narrow perceptions of the value of technology for learning. Resources like Wikipedia and electronic texts are not always understood to be richly extending traditional books rather than replacing them. Social networking sites may at first be used frivolously, but frivolity can merge imperceptibly into a more subtle, sensitive and reflective communication. Yet our research has shown us that the potential for transformation of learning in formal educational settings is great; and that participatory action research with teachers can play a role in changing the social practices of classrooms and schools to enable this to occur. We see working in this way as part of our remit as researchers.

LESSONS LEARNED IN THE 1980S

In 1984 when I (Bridget) was a teacher of English language and literature in a secondary school in the UK, I took an Acorn computer into my classroom to explore how I could use it to teach writing to eleven year old students. At the time I was using Graves' approach which emphasised drafting and re-drafting of text as a core principle (Graves, 1983). My students used this method to write poetry, producing many drafts before they completed their work. But I was not happy with using the same approach in teaching them story writing, because of the inauthentic labour of copying out long texts 'in best'. Would writing on a computer (as I had just begun to do myself for my Masters' degree assignments) enable them to use the powers of a word processor to draft and re-draft on screen, writing experimentally and creatively, improving their successive drafts until they were ready to print out their final copy? My research into students' writing with a word processor did not progress far since I only had one computer to use with my 32 students in five 40 minute periods each week. Instead, I learnt many unexpected things about the social practices of classrooms: that the presence of a computer shifted the focus of students' attention away from me to the computer screen; that students' motivation to use the computer was very high and this reduced the time I needed to spend on managing their behaviour; that my relationship with my students changed because some of them knew more about how to operate the computer than I did, making me less of an authority on skills and knowledge and more of a co-learner and facilitator of their learning. I also learnt many unexpected things about the social practices of the school: that by bringing a computer into my classroom, as an English teacher, I was crossing boundaries and could not necessarily expect support (the mathematics department 'owned' the existing computers and one of the maths teachers took home the computer I wanted to borrow for the summer holidays without any negotiation); that I needed to take action myself (making small purchases, seeking external advice) to sort problems out quickly, as there were no systems in place to provide me with technical support; and that I would have been unable even to begin my research without external support from a local education authority adviser, who gave me good advice and money for the computer and printer, and the university that gave me justification for carrying out this innovatory project as part of my Masters degree.

By 1988 I was a researcher at the University of East Anglia, about to start work on my Ph D, when I secured funding for the Pupil Autonomy in Learning with Microcomputers Project (PALM). 'Autonomy' was a policy buzz word at the time and was interpreted by the project as 'autonomy from teacher control, often involving collaborative work with other students' (with the shortage of computers at the time individual use by students was a rarity). Working in my new role from outside the classroom, carrying out action research in partnership with around 100 teachers in 24 schools in East Anglia, I could scale up my research to focus on students' learning across the whole curriculum in both primary and secondary schools. Could a computer assist teachers in encouraging and enabling students to become more autonomous learners? And would action research be an effective way of giving teachers professional development in the use of digital technologies (then called IT)? One of the main outcomes of the PALM project was an empirically-derived model of 'a transforming pedagogy for information technology' (Bridget Somekh & Davies, 1991). It was developed from an analysis of 40 teachers' case studies of their action research published in the PALM Teachers'

Voices series (PALM, 1988-90) and encapsulates what they had learnt from exploratory, developmental use of IT in their teaching over a period of between one and two years. The model adopts a definition of pedagogy that assumes that learning derives from 'active engagement of the learner' and that both teachers and learners have 'cognitively active roles, since knowledge is constructed through heuristic processes of creative thinking and interaction, as well as the acquisition of appropriate information'.

In terms of students' learning, PALM research showed that teachers used information technology best when:

- the computer became a third partner in their pedagogic interactions with students;
- teachers embedded a computer-based task in a 'framing task' which integrated it with students' other on-going curriculum work.
- teachers and students worked together as co-learners without any anxiety on the teacher's part of needing to 'stay ahead' of the students in their mastery of computer skills.

And that:

- when computer-based production replaced labour-intensive tasks, such as drawing graphs, this required a shift in the focus of the lesson to more cognitively demanding tasks, such as interpreting graphs, and resulted in new demands being made on the teacher to sustain students' motivation at this level over a longer period of time. Students could potentially gain a much deeper level of understanding of the use and interpretation of graphs, but the teacher could no longer rely on them spending most of the lesson on an absorbing lower level task. This was a shift to 'learning tasks' as opposed to 'busy tasks' (Doyle, 1979).
- when students were engaged in collaborative computer-based tasks, teachers needed to learn the art of what Beverly Labbett (1988) called 'skilful neglect' to avoid interrupting their collaborative decision-making (which often wrongly gave the impression of being 'a hiatus' period).
- students were able to be more autonomous from the teacher when engaged in exploratory project work, but this kind of learning was considerably easier to achieve with longer time-frames rather than the 40 minute period typical of the secondary school time-table.

LESSONS LEARNED DURING 1999-2004

The ImpaCT2 Evaluation

Post the introduction of the national curriculum, which was phased in between 1988 and 1990, there has been a shift in UK policy-makers' interest away from how computers might make students' learning more autonomous of teacher's control to whether they can raise the level of students' attainment in formal national tests. In the ImpaCT2 evaluation of the government's National Grid for Learning programme in 2000-2002, in which we first worked together, one of the main aims was to measure gains in attainment in English, Maths and Science by comparing the actual national test scores of students in NGfL schools with their 'expected' scores. 'Statistically significant positive associations' were shown between ICT and national tests in English at age 11, science at age 14 and science and Design and Technology at age   16. There were also 'strong indications of a positive association' (although not statistically significant) between ICT and Maths at age 11, and Modern Foreign Languages and Geography at age 16 (Harrison et al., 2002, p. 2-3), A striking – and unexpected – finding of ImpaCT2, however, was the very low level of use of ICT for teaching curriculum subjects in either primary or secondary schools. Students regularly ticked 'never or hardly ever' when asked how often they used computers in English, maths or science lessons. It became apparent that whereas policy-makers had assumed that computers paid for by NGfL money would be used to teach subjects, they were overwhelmingly being used to teach ICT skills in specialist ICT lessons. Lesson plans designed by the Qualifications and Curriculum Authority (QCA) which embedded skills acquisition in 'real tasks' were being taught by ICT teachers so that newly acquired skills were rarely subsequently used for subject learning. However, ImpaCT2 also found compelling evidence of students' frequent, extensive and creative use of powerful ICT equipment out of school, typically in their homes. This use was 'sustained' and students were 'discriminating in use of the internet, which [was] enabling them to develop skills and literacies in networked ICT, confidence in its use, and a range of on-line social and communication skills.' (B Somekh et al., 2002, p. 2-3),

Using Concept Mapping to Explore Children's Awareness of Technology

From 1999 onwards there had been rapid penetration of the internet into homes in the UK and a large number of businesses developed websites, enabling online shopping to develop rapidly. To find out what impact this had had on young people's awareness of ICT, we used a concept mapping task, adapted to invite students to use drawings rather than words to 'tell the researcher what you know about Computers in My World' (CIMW). This task took 30 minutes to complete and was administered on two occasions to the full sample of 2,000 students across the age ranges 10-16. These maps provided us with a record of each child's thinking about CIMW on that day. They were representations of children's impressions and ideas, rather than an exact record of children's knowledge of ICTs and their uses. For this reason our analysis did not focus on how the maps illustrated correct or incorrect knowledge; instead we adopted a phenomenagraphic approach to identify students' 'kinds of awareness' of ICT. Phenomenography suggests that among a group working in a similar socio-cultural context there are usually four or five different kinds of awareness of any phenomena. These 'kinds of awareness' are normally organised as a 'focal awareness', surrounded by a 'field of awareness' in which other features are less well defined. Finally, there are 'fringe' awarenesses which are there in the background but may be only half-remembered (Marton & Booth, 1997). We focused on identifying these different kinds of awareness of Computers in My World for the children in our sample.

Analysis of One Concept Map: An Example

The concept map by Liz, aged 13 (see Fig 1), suggests wide-ranging knowledge of computers in the year 2000. Our analytic method categorised nodes into Spheres of Thinking – i.e. ways of thinking about ICT (SoTs) and Zones of Use – i.e. places where ICT is used (ZoUs). Liz's map includes eight SoTs and nine ZoUs including the Millenium Dome in

London. The arrangement of the nodes on the page suggests that after the starting point of the computer itself in the top left hand corner, *the internet is the focal awareness,* linking to travel, home, school (indirectly), shops, workplaces and banks, as well as to the millenium dome via a branching link. From the number of objects in the map, there appears also to be *a field of awareness of the use of computers to control things* such as services ('controls important things' is linked to 'fire brigade', 'police', 'insurance' and 'traffic lights'). The follow-up interview with Liz six months later suggested that her knowledge of the role of computers in today's world was extensive and that she was an experienced user. She confirmed that the computer and its printer were drawn first and next came the internet 'because that's the main reason that I use the computer at home.' Phone lines, on-line shopping, banking and email came next, with the locations of home and school, computer games and other entertainment. *The internet is confirmed as the focal awareness but is defined to include communications*: 'Is there any part of your map that's particularly important to you?' asks the interviewer. 'Probably the internet, because I spend ages on the internet and I'm always on it. I really like hotmail, MSN messenger and email. That's what I usually spend my time on.' *There is a wide range of fringe awareness*, which includes use of computers for control but without this having any greater prominence than many other things. The emphasis in drawing the map seems to have been on trying to think of 'loads of different ideas'. The 'bug' was included because 'there was a bug going round at the time, I think the "I love you one" that had everything going down.'

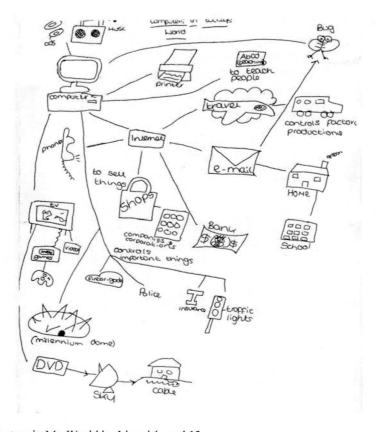

Figure 1. Computers in My World by Liz, girl aged 13.

What Children Told Us about their Learning at Home through 'Playing Games'

ImpaCT2 found evidence that young people made a strong discursive separation between their use of digital technologies at home and at school, counting whatever they did on computers at home as 'games' and understanding the term 'learning' to refer only to what they were formally taught in schools. This led to misunderstandings among both teachers and parents, who routinely discounted what students did with ICT at home as 'playing games' and by definition of no value for learning. In fact, in logs of their computer use kept for the evaluators, students recorded a wide range of uses likely in the opinion of the evaluators to have led to learning. For example:

> One Year 11 girl recorded brief use (five minutes) of word processing in an English lesson. All other use for both schoolwork and leisure work took place out of school. (…) Out of school use for school work totalled nine hours and consisted of word processing, CD-ROMs and surfing the Internet. For leisure use, she indicated that she had used the following resources for a total of 25 hours: word processing (4 hours), art packages (2 hours), CD-rewriter (2 hours), CD-ROM (2 hours), email (6 hours), surfing the internet (3 hours), creating web pages (2 hours) and [a messenger service]' (4 hours). (B Somekh et al., 2002, p. 11)

Pupils consistently recorded more use of ICT outside school than in school, and in most cases this seemed to be because of poor access to ICT at school. This effect was particularly marked in secondary schools where, despite the large amount of new ICT equipment purchased through the NGfL, students who were not studying an examination subject that required the use of ICT were likely to have only very occasional access to the internet or computer resources. ImpaCT2 told us a lot about young people's use of ICT outside school and showed us the effect of barriers to ICT's effective uptake for teaching and learning in school.

The Evaluation of the Gridclub 'Edutainment' Website

In the evaluation of the GridClub website service, which we undertook in 2002-03, we were able to build on this work by focusing more specifically on children's learning with ICT. GridClub was an 'edutainment' website for 7-11 year old children comprising a suite of online games covering all areas of the national curriculum and a club site, Oracle's Think.com. The club allowed children to communicate with one another through email and sending 'stickies', develop their own web pages, and engage in online tasks involving producing various kinds of writing with opportunities to enter competitions and win certificates or badges. GridClub was developed, in a public-private partnership between government and Channel4 Television, for use by children at home. It was intended to complement formal learning at school, as a means of breaking down the barriers between home and school and encouraging parents to become more involved in their children's learning. However, ironically, whereas in ImpaCT2 which was intended to be mainly focused on formal learning in schools we learnt a great deal about students' use of ICT at home; in the GridClub evaluation which was intended to be focused on children's informal learning in homes we ended up learning a great deal about how children's use of ICT is shaped and constrained by the socio-cultural practices of the classroom.

The Social Construction of Online Learning – Merging of Physical and Virtual Contexts

In designing the evaluation of this virtual space for informal learning – GridClub – we immediately faced the problem of collecting data from the children who were using it and their parents. A research design that relied on collecting data online seemed risky (and indeed it subsequently proved difficult to get responses to our online questionnaire) so we decided to approach schools, not as 'case studies,' but as 'key informant' schools. Through these schools we would be able to meet children using GridClub and their parents, as well as interviewing their teachers to gain insights on how use of GridClub at home might be having an impact on their learning in school. However, our work did not progress quite as we had expected. Socio-cultural factors immediately strongly shaped GridClub's positioning between home and school. Proud of its reputation as 'a safe site' Think.com imposed a requirement for schools to register children as 'authentic' 7-11 year olds, rather than children being registered by their parents at home. In an age when adopting alternative online 'identities' is commonplace (Turkle, 1995) this is perfectly understandable, but it served to turn teachers into 'gatekeepers' of children's access to GridClub, with responsibility for registering their class as members and issuing individual children with passwords. Typically, children's access to GridClub was provided first in ICT lessons at school or in the school's computer club. Some children then went on to access it at home. The existing separation between home and school – the very gulf that government policy-makers were hoping to bridge – led to considerable variation between schools in the extent to which they suggested to children that they could access GridClub from home. Interviewing teachers in our 'key informant schools' about their impressions of what children were learning from GridClub we found evidence of another systemic barrier to its wider use: typically only one teacher in each school was promoting GridClub, the one who was using it regularly in either ICT lessons or computer club, while the other teachers seemed to regard it as 'not theirs' (memories from Bridget's own teaching surfaced here, the need to always have new material to offer in lessons or children would complain - 'Miss, miss, we've done this with Mr X.'). So our research led to the systematic collection of evidence of GridClub being socio-culturally positioned, to fit tradition and 'due process,' as a resource for use in the subject ICT (or the related computer club) in schools, rather than a resource for children to use in their own homes. We also found evidence of extensive, creative use of GridClub, including use at home, by children in some classrooms. The questions was, why these classrooms and not others?

Using 'Learning Indicators' to Generate Knowledge about Learning with ICT

The evaluation of GridClub provided us with a unique opportunity to explore the nature of children's learning with ICT, and the crucially important role of the teacher in shaping children's experiences of online learning. Since GridClub set out to provide informal learning experiences we were able to set aside, for research purposes, the whole paraphernalia of targets and levels of attainment which dominated teachers' lesson planning and curriculum 'delivery' in England at the time. Rather than adopting this kind of linear model of learning we turned to the research literature on learning over the previous ten years. What was the current knowledge of the learning process? Could we draw on this literature to identify a set of behavioural criteria that would indicate that children were learning? What kinds of things would children do and say as a result of learning? Could we track them? We developed criteria which we called 'learning indicators' as a discursive shift from the 'performance indicators' so often used in outcomes-based approaches to evaluation. Learning indicators, which relied on collecting and interpreting qualitative evidence of social practices rather than measuring knowledge and skills by means of test scores, fitted well with our approach of 'supportive evaluation' (B Somekh, 2007, chapter 8). Our six learning indicators were:

1. A 'whole being' model which gave priority to 'Learning to Learn' rather than learning of specific knowledge and information (Claxton, 2002)
2. The 'Developmental Assets' that primary children need to flourish as creative, independent, human beings (SearchInstitute, 1998)
3. The 'Communities of Practice' in which learning is situated, which enable learning through a process of 'legitimate peripheral participation' (Lave & Wenger, 1991; Wenger, 1998)
4. Fun and Play, through which children are motivated to learn, and may have opportunities to engage in creative, imaginative, self-regulated but rule-governed behaviours (Vygotsky, 1978).
5. The construction of childhood by adults as either a state of preparation for adulthood or a state of full personhood, in other words full, autonomous human *beings* who are capable of taking responsibility, or dependents only *becoming* human beings through upbringing and training (James & Prout, 1997).
6. The experience of intensive engagement in a task or experience, known as 'Flow', which Csikszentmihalyi (1996) has shown is indicative of the 'highly focused state of consciousness' leading to learning and creativity.

To track the learning indicators we developed a range of data collection methods, targeting each learning indicator with at least one method. These were 'flow' interviews (LI 4 and 6); concept mapping (LI 2, 3, 4 and 5); video-observations of children using GridClub (LI 1, 2 and 4); analysis of online interactions (LI 1, 2, 3 and 5); and analysis of online games (mainly to help us focus video-observations) (LIs 2 and 4). In 'flow' interviews we asked small groups of children if they could remember a time when they were using GridClub and they 'forgot the time', and followed up their almost universally affirmative responses with the question, 'tell me about what you were doing when that happened?' From this we learnt that children frequently became totally immersed in the experience of GridClub and could tell us vivid stories of when it happened and what feature of GridClub they were using at the time. Their stories divided into two distinct categories: experiences of 'flow' when using GridClub at home, typically finding that they had missed doing something else they had planned, like watching their favourite TV programme; and stories of 'broken flow' when using GridClub at school, invariably running out of time because the time allotted to them had come to an end. Two kinds of GridClub activity gave rise to 'flow' experiences: playing games that involved solving a problem/answering questions with the reward of getting to a new 'level'; and, for those who had accessed Think.com (by no means all), working on developing their own web pages.

Using Concept Mapping to Explore Children's Experience of 'Being in Gridclub'
In the concept mapping task we asked children to draw maps of 'Being in GridClub' from which we learnt surprising information about the extreme variation in their experience,

not merely between using GridClub at home or at school, but between using GridClub in different classrooms. The critical factor was the teacher's pedagogy and the relationship between the teacher and the children. Classrooms in which teachers constructed children as 'Beings', providing positive developmental assets and giving high priority to fun and play, elicited exploratory engagement in GridClub from children and enabled them to access the full range of its affordances, often using it frequently at home as well as at school. This is clearly shown in Imogen's concept map:

Figure 2. Imogen, aged 10.10 – Concept Map of Being in the Grid Club."

By contrast, Kevin who was in a different classroom in another school shows a much narrower range of awareness of the affordance of GridClub. Only one boy in his class (not him) had accessed GridClub at home and learnt to use Think.com to send stickies and emails. Kevin's map contains mainly drawings of himself *in the classroom*, with several portrayals of the teacher, and he portrays himself in all cases except possibly one in a subservient position, obeying instructions rather than engaging in exploratory online learning. When asked whether he had sent an email to anyone outside the school, Kevin used the teacher's exact words, 'We're only using it to send emails to people in our class "till we get the hang of it".' His use of GridClub appeared to be constrained by a 'learned dependency' that characterised pedagogy in this classroom.

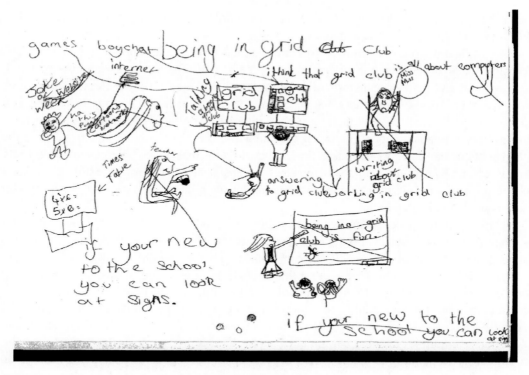

Figure 3. Kevin, aged 8.4 – Concept map of 'Being in GridClub.'

Learning How the Affordances of Technologies are Mediated by Activity Systems

What we learnt from our research on GridClub was that children's experience of learning in a virtual environment is far more strongly shaped by the location in which they are physically situated that we had previously imagined. Through this research we came to understand that to speak of a digital technology's affordances makes little sense unless one understands an affordance to be *a latent possibility*, the utilisation of which is entirely contingent upon the mediating factors of the activity system in which we are situated – in this case a classroom, with a particular teacher, within a school, in the English education system.

A THEORETICAL FRAMEWORK FOR INTERVENTIONS AND PARTICIPATORY RESEARCH

Our understanding of how digital technologies can be used to change the social practices of schools has developed through interpreting these empirical data in the light of theories of social practice as a cultural performance. A meta-analysis of these theories, including for example Wertsch's theory of mediated activity (Wertsch, 1998), Lave and Wenger's 'legitimate peripheral participation' (Lave & Wenger, 1991) and Engestrom's 'expansive learning' (Engestrom, 1987), was used to develop a framework for planning and analysing research interventions (B Somekh, 2007, pp. Chapters 1-3). Rather than focusing on one theory only, we discovered how insights from one theory inform and strengthen insights from other theories. The resulting framework became a heuristic tool to inform our analysis of data from research with teachers and students.

As we learnt from our GridClub research, digital technologies cannot of themselves be transformative of human behaviours. A technology's affordances can only be explored, appropriated and realised transformatively in relation to the specific practices of the people who use them, or as Wertsch (1998, p.25) puts it, research needs to examine 'agent and cultural tools in mediated action (…) as they interact'. The tool – if used skilfully – is an integral part of human capability, rather than an add-on: the pole vaulter cannot perform the jump without the pole. At the same time, what the tool makes possible cannot be entirely predicted in advance, for who could foresee the transformative impact of texting with a cell phone on young people's social lives in England, or the relative absence of this impact with their peers in the United States?

Humans are inter-dependent with other humans, so that they seldom engage in activities on their own. This is particularly true of learning activities, since the early development of the mind is shaped through the interactive communication of young child and adult (Vygotsky, 1986). This process continues into adult life through the stimulation of original thinking and the development of persuasive arguments in dialogue (Prawat, 1991). In this sense the social community also has a mediating role in shaping an individual's ability to use digital tools skilfully and creatively for learning. If we add to this a concept of the self as fluid rather than essentialist, multiple rather than unique, with the actor ('I') and the reflective 'me' continuously responding to the patterned expectations of the 'generalised other' of the group (Mead, 1934), we can begin to understand a social practice as a kind of choreographed performance. What children do with digital technologies in a classroom is not a matter of their choice, but their participatory engagement in a performance in which the rules governing behaviour have been culturally-historically constructed (Langemeyer & Nissen, 2005). Moreover, the classroom is itself enmeshed in regulatory frameworks established by the school and the larger education system, giving each participant a recognised role in the division of labour (teacher, student, teaching assistant etc.) (Engeström, 1999).

All of this makes it difficult for digital technologies to have the same kind of impact in schools as they have had in the wider community. The compulsory nature of schooling and the power play inherent in an institution where over 90% of the participants are conscripts rather than volunteers, makes a school a special kind of organisation, peculiarly resilient in maintaining the status quo (Bidwell, 2001). Innovations in social practices, such as classroom pedagogy, require all participants to be consciously engaged in envisioning doing things differently and trying out the innovation through a process of cyclical exploration. It is only when digital technologies offer a good fit with the aims, values and practices of the existing activity system that they are embraced with enthusiasm without meeting systemic barriers to change. They can then become embedded in pedagogic practices in a way that leads to real changes over a period of, say, two years as in the case of the introduction of interactive whiteboards into English primary schools between 2004 and 2006 (see Lewin, Somekh and Steadman, 2008). In most cases digital technologies do not offer this kind of good 'fit', rather their transformative power lies in their capacity to disrupt current practices and offer possibilities of doing things in new ways. How, then, could we research this process of transformation?

TOWARDS THE TRANSFORMATION OF STUDENTS' LEARNING WITH DIGITAL TECHNOLOGIES

Developing Pedagogies with E-Learning Resources: The PELRS Project

During 2002-03, we began to use these theories as the basis for designing research which would combine participatory action research with setting up and testing a prototype of innovative pedagogy with ICT. This was to be the Pedagogies with E-Learning (PELRS) Project, co-sponsored by the General Teaching Council for England and Manchester Metropolitan University (www.pelrs.org.uk). PELRS worked with teachers and students in four schools for the first two years, focusing on the question, 'Could we teach and learn in radically different ways now we have the internet, internet-look-alike CD/DVD materials, digital imaging and video etc?' In the first three months case studies were carried out in the four schools and these confirmed that they were already engaged in using ICT innovatively within the teaching of ICT itself and occasionally in special project work with a curriculum focus. However, in none of the schools was ICT integrated with teaching and learning across all curriculum subjects. The focus of activity in the first two years was on developing examples of new pedagogic practices with ICT starting with a process of brainstorming and visioning. In year 3 PELRS worked with a further 12 schools to trial and customise the PELRS pedagogic model and explore the extent to which it could be scaled up for wider use in the education system.

Representing a Theoretical Framework for Pedagogy Semiotically

Participatory action research with the teachers began in the second term of the first year with development of a generic pedagogic framework (GPF) for use in planning learning events. The intention was to represent the theories underpinning the research design semiotically, so that teachers' planning of day-to-day activities could be informed by theory. In practice, the GPF became the focus for discussion between teachers and university-based researchers. We produced a draft diagram, incorporating what we saw as the key features of the theoretical framework that had practical power that could be translated into actions (see Fig. 4). The teachers used this diagram as the basis for devising four specific strategies for innovative pedagogies with ICT. The design of the diagram evokes Engestrom's triangual representation of the human activity system (1999), but draws equally upon the finding from the PALM project, discussed earlier in this chapter, that ICT needs to be understood as a third partner in the pedagogic interactions between teachers and pupils.

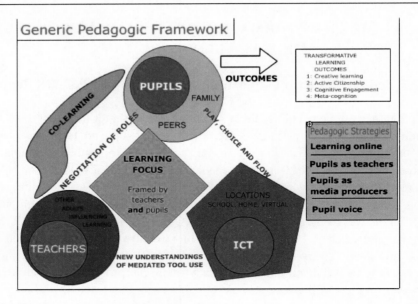

Figure 4. The PELRS Generic Pedagogic Framework.

Teachers' Role as Co-Researchers in PELRS Action Research

The focus of the action research in PELRS was agreed in advance by approaching teachers known to have an interest in using ICT for innovative teaching, in schools which were well equipped at the time (e.g. with wireless networks, 'banks' of laptops for use during lessons, and in some cases well developed websites). Teachers participated in the whole research process – deciding what data should be collected, discussing and interpreting selections from the data (for example episodes from video-recordings) and commenting on draft writing. They also participated in presenting PELRS work at public events such as workshops and conferences. The intention was to involve them as full participants in establishing and exploring the prototype practices without burdening them with an additional workload, for which they had no time allocation. Support was provided for release from teaching and refreshments at after-school meetings but in practice teachers saw the main advantage of the project as the regular in-classroom support from our colleague, Matthew Pearson, who shared their enthusiasm for teaching and learning in new ways and was able to help them overcome technical problems when they arose.

Towards Transformative Learning with Digital Technologies

The PELRS pedagogic framework was intentionally expressed in discourse that signalled a break with current practice, embedded in a socio-culturally mediated epistemology and a student-centred educational philosophy. Teachers chose the focus of the lesson, drawing on the national curriculum, but through discussion in an introductory plenary session students had real choices of how they would organise their learning and the resources they would use. The traditional roles of teachers and pupils were negotiated with an emphasis on learning taking place in three locations: school, home and virtual. Pupils were given choices about their learning, opportunities to learn through play, and learning contexts which would enable them to experience 'flow'. Teachers were cast in the role of co-learners with their students and there was an emphasis on them gaining new understandings of how ICT could mediate the learning process through their conscious interventions. At the heart of PELRS was the goal of transformative learning, located in the two dimensional diagram in a white box at the top right hand corner, but in fact envisaged as emerging directly from the learning focus in a three-dimensional representation. It was agreed that our working definition of transformative learning was when pupils were able to:

- achieve specified learning outcomes (e.g. normally from the national curriculum)
- learn creatively (e.g. contributing, experimenting, solving problems,
- learn as active citizens (e.g. acting autonomously, taking responsibility),
- engage intellectually with powerful ideas (e.g. using thinking skills, grappling with ideas/concepts)
- reflect on their own learning (e.g. evaluating own learning through metacognition)

The four themed PELRS strategies were, in fact, no more than variations of the generic framework but they all had resonance with teachers' vision for their students' learning building on newly emerging policy initiatives. Educational policies in England at the time were beginning to develop as two parallel strands, somewhat in conflict with one another: on the one hand the core policies of the tightly specified national curriculum, attainment levels and targets, and public profiling of schools' standards through published inspection reports and league tables of test scores; on the other hand new policies encouraging pupils to be given real choices and a 'voice', and the transformation of learning through pupils' access to technologies. The strategies were intentionally in harmony with these new policies. They all involved radical changes in the traditional classroom roles – for example, 'pupils as teachers' signalled strongly to both teachers and pupils that they were expected to abandon the traditional divisions of labour.

PELRS student-researchers focused on the question: 'How could what we do with ICT at school be more like what we do at home.' Their role was to participate in analysis of selected extracts of video data, take on occasional new responsibilities in teaching their peers how to use ICT equipment, and act as advisers to the teachers and university-based-researchers. Around six student-researchers were selected from each participating class, on the basis of their demonstrable ICT skills acquired from using ICT at home. They were drawn as far as possible from both genders and a cross-section of socio-economic home backgrounds, although in practice two of the four PELRS schools were located in an area of profound socio-economic disadvantage. In addition to working with the student-researchers, all students in the PELRS classes experienced new learning opportunities through their participation in PELRS learning events designed around innovative pedagogies.

PELRS achieved a considerable shift in students' learning experiences, and in some cases transformative learning outcomes. For example, five year old children worked with their teacher to produce an instructional video, using digital cameras designed for use in schools, to teach other children how to make a paper windmill. They worked in groups, taking on the roles of director, cameraman, presenter and editor, writing their own script which included designing and building a paper windmill while video-recording the process. The headteacher felt that the children's learning was unusually deep because the work had allowed the teacher to 'stop trying to get through the curriculum,' and focus on learning per se. The children were clearly proud of their achievement. In another school, children aged 9-10 chose to work in groups and use the internet, as well as the school library, to research the growth and reproduction of plants. Each group took responsibility for learning one aspect of the topic and preparing a presentation to teach it to their peers. Video data recorded before and during this project captured a major shift in classroom discourse, with more student-initiated questions and a marked reduction in administrative and disciplinary utterances by the teacher, showing that these young children were taking responsibility for their own learning. In a secondary school, a teacher of German found that students, aged 13-14, were more highly motivated to speak German, and took more care to use the right words with the correct pronunciation, when she asked them to record their group work and play it back to the class. This also allowed students to learn by informally assessing each other's work, and helped her to plan follow-up teaching. All this work focused on topics specified in the national curriculum, and formal tests administered by their teachers at a later date confirmed that students had not only learnt as much as they would have done from formal methods, but had retained knowledge of key concepts and terminology over several months. It became clear from this work that learning transformation does not happen through student-computer interaction alone; it does not take place through a cognitive process occurring in isolation in a student's head, but through interaction and dialogue with other students (Pearson & Somekh, 2006).

Systemic Barriers to Learning with Digital Technologies in Secondary Schools

Nevertheless, PELRS also showed that some barriers to transforming students' learning were extremely difficult to overcome, because they were endemic to aspects of the education system over which teachers had little or no control. They were particularly in evidence in secondary schools with the result that although PELRS worked successfully with the whole age range, 5-16, much more innovative and successful work took place in primary schools. In secondary schools the main barriers to transforming learning with technology were: short time frames for learning due to the organisation of the school day in periods of typically an hour or less; aggressive filters on internet access put in place by technicians, creating major problems for students' exploratory project work ; and major logistical problems in giving students access to digital technologies (moving them to specialist ICT rooms, or loaning laptops to students for single lessons and collecting them again at the end). It became clear that we needed next to design a prototype intervention study working with teacher-researchers in a secondary school.

THE NEXT STEPS: TRANSFORMING PEDAGOGY WITH DIGITAL LEARNING COMPANIONS

In 2006 we began to develop ideas for a research project with secondary schools building on the findings of the PELRS project. Preliminary work for the Secondary Personalised E-Learning Project (SEPEL) with two schools took place between January and June 2007, with start-up funding from Becta and the General Teaching Council for England. SEPEL was designed to set up prototype practices which might overcome the barriers to learning with ICT identified by PELRS. Its vision was of teacher-researchers, student-researchers and university-based researchers exploring how pedagogy and learning could be transformed if students had their own personal 'digital learning companions' (DLCs) and were able to use them as and when needed in an environment with wireless networking. Its focus was on using digital technologies as a tool for students' learning across the whole curriculum of the school. The DLCs would remove the logistical barriers that make it so difficult to use technology for learning with continuous movements between lessons; and they would integrate learning at school and technology-use at home because they would physically   accompany the students home.

The SEPEL project aimed to transform the teaching and learning of an entire year group, by providing all students in Year 7 (the first year of secondary school) with a DLC and to re-design the curriculum and pedagogy to make good use of its affordances. Teachers and senior leaders embarked on preparatory work during the spring of 2007, at the same time as we investigated possible machines to use as DLCs. No light weight, inexpensive machine was available at that time, although several manufacturers appeared to have machines at the development stage. In the absence of anything ideal, it seemed that a tablet-PC would provide the best solution because of its easy adaptability for use in science and mathematics. As development work continued, however, it became clear that SEPEL needed a financial model which could be used not just for this one year group, but sustained in future years with other year groups. Hence the project would only be able to go ahead if parents were willing to contribute to the cost of the DLC. Tablet PCs were expensive and the costs of SEPEL as we planned it in the spring of 2007 were too great. Support was available from the E-Learning Foundation (http://www.e-learningfoundation.com/) and a manufacturer was prepared to provide machines at discount prices, but the headteachers of the schools decided they were not prepared to approach parents to make financial contributions. We had to put our plans on hold.

However, a third school with whom we began exploring ideas when the other two withdrew, was determined to find a way. The headteacher was inspired by an article in the Times Educational Supplement in the autumn of 2007 suggesting that schools in Wales (where the school is located) were not accessing funding available to support pupil ownership of personal laptops. Meanwhile, the technology was advancing rapidly. By the spring of 2008 a number of small, light-weight, low cost, machines had come onto the market. Staff at the school discovered a piece of technology that was low cost yet with adequate functionality (including the facility to audio record and video record) to meet the needs of learners in schools. They were also drawn to a high specification PDA and one or two other possible machines. A group of young people from year 7 (aged 11-12) were asked to spend two hours playing with four devices and assessing them and then to recommend to the headteacher which should be chosen as the DLC for their entire year group from September 2008.

The school's plans are going ahead. This time the school, rather than the university, is leading the design of the project, but many of the features of SEPEL are being incorporated.

In an interview just before this article went to press, the headteacher described the progress to date: there has been an assembly where the students who assessed the different technologies talked about the devices and how they could be used; the tutors have all been given the chosen technology to show the learners in their classes and promote feelings of excitement about the future development; the parents have attended a parents evening and had an opportunity to try out the technology; those parents expressing concerns have been dealt with on a one-to-one basis to put their minds at ease and the school has been proactive in securing agreements from parents to engage in the hire purchase arrangement (a nominal monthly amount). All of these strategies have been put in place to generate interest from the learners and support from the parents. The response to date has been extremely positive.

The headteacher's vision is that "young people in this school will no longer be constrained to using technology in rooms designed for computers and not for learning, which can only be accessed if the timetable allows and for limited periods of time." Building on the SEPEL development work, students will be asked to draw up rules for use of the DLC and how it might best support their learning, as well as how it might be used in their homes by themselves and their family. These will be discussed with teachers to come to a negotiated agreement, so that the same machines can be used both for school work, and for accessing music and popular culture at home, as well as for email and social networking. The headteacher recognises that learners may have useful and productive ideas, drawing on their personal experiences outside school, about how pedagogies can be transformed. He is encouraged by teachers' positive attitudes and believes they will be better placed to consider how technology can make learning more effective, and more enjoyable for the learners and themselves, because they will no longer be constrained by limited access. He has established 'innovation teams' of teachers to develop new pedagogies. These groups are required to develop ideas, techniques and strategies for taking teaching and learning forward and one will focus particularly on ways of making the best use of the DLCs in the classroom so that "the teachers own that really." The DLCs will be used (initially by one entire year group in the school) as another learning tool alongside traditional tools such as books and pencils. It will be used when learners feel it is appropriate. It will support learning beyond the school day and informal as well as formal learning. His vision is that, "Teachers and learners will enjoy learning together. The traditional boundaries of teaching and learning will be pushed and reshaped collaboratively, leading to radically new social practices, making the school a 'buzzier place' and putting teachers and learners, as one learning community, at its heart."

Our role as researchers will be to work alongside this school, supporting the development of their use of the DLCs by involving teachers and students in a process of action research. The shift in leadership of the project from the university to the school, and the new products that have become available in the market place over the last year, are both significant developments. Our exploration of how digital technologies could be used to radically change the social practices of schools continues with some justifiable optimism.

ACKNOWLEDGEMENTS

We would like to thank the British Educational and Communications Technolgy Agency (Becta) which funded ImpaCT2 and the start-up phase of SEPEL; the National Council for Educational Technology (forerunner to Becta) which funded the PALM project; the Department for Education and Skills which funded the GridClub Evaluation, and the General Teaching Council for England which co-funded the PELRS project with Manchester Metropolitan University and the SEPEL project. We would also like to thank the schools and their teachers and students who have contributed so much to this research over many years. Finally, we would like to thank our research colleagues at the Centre for Applied Research in Education, University of East Anglia (1986-95) and the Centre for ICT, Pedagogy and Learning at Manchester Metropolitan University (2000-2008).

REFERENCES

Bidwell, C. E. (2001). Analyzing Schools as Organizations: Long-Term Permanence and Short-Term Change. *Sociology of Education, 74*(Extra Issue: Current of Thought: Sociology of Education at the Dawn of the 21st Century.), 100-114.

Bigum, C. (2002). Design sensibilities, schools and the new computing and communication technologies. In I. Snyder (Ed.), *Silicon Literacies: communication, Innovation and Education in the Electronic Age* (pp. 130-140). London and New York: Routledge.

Claxton, G. (2002). Education for the Learning Age: a sociocultural approach to learning to learn. In G. Wells & G. Claxton (Eds.), *Learning for Life in the 21st Century*. Oxford and Malden MA: Blackwell Publishing.

Csikszentmihalyi, M. (1996). *Creativity: Flow and the Psychology of Discovery and Invention*. New York: Harper Perennial.

Doyle, W. (1979). Classroom tasks and student abilities. In P.L.Peterson & H.J.Walberg (Eds.), *Research on Teaching: concepts, findings and implications*. National Society for the Study of Education, Berkeley, CA: McCutchan.

Engestrom, Y. (1987). *Learning by Expanding: An Activity-Theoretical Approach to Developmental Research*. Helsinki: Orienta-Konsultit Oy.

Engeström, Y. (1999). Activity theory and individual and social transformation. In Y. Engeström, M. Reijo & R.-L. Punamäki (Eds.), *Perspectives on Acitivity Theory* (pp. 19-38). Cambridge UK, New York and Melbourne: Cambridge University Press.

Graves, D. H. (1983). *Writing: teachers and children at work*. London: Heinemann Education.

Harrison, C., Fisher, T., Haw, K., Lewin, C., Lunzer, E., Mavers, D., et al. (2002). *ImpaCT2: the Impact of Information and Communication Technologies on Pupils' Learning and Attainment*. Coventry: Department for Education and Skills.

James, A., & Prout, A. (Eds.). (1997). *Constructing and Reconstructing Childhood*. London: Falmer Press.

Krumsvik, R. J. (2006). *ICT in the School; ICT-initiated school development in lower secondary school*. University of Bergen, Norway.

Labbett, B. (1988). Skilful neglect. In J. Schostak (Ed.), *Breaking into the Curriculum. The impact of information technology on schooling*. London and New York: Methuen.

Langemeyer, I., & Nissen, M. (2005). Activity Theory. In B. Somekh & C. Lewin (Eds.), *Research Methods in the Social Sciences* (pp. 188-196). London and Thousand Islands CA: Sage.

Lave, J. & Wenger, E. (1991). *Situated Learning: Legitimate peripheral participation*. Cambridge, New York and Melbourne: Cambridge University Press.

Lewin, C. (2004). Access and use of technologies in the home in the UK: implications for the curriculum. *The Curriculum Journal, 15*(2), 139-154.

Lewin, C., Somekh, B. & Steadman, S. (2008) Embedding interactive whiteboards in teaching and learning: The process of change in pedagogic practice, Special Issue on Valuing Individual and Shared Learning: the role of ICT, *Education and Information Technologies,* 13(4) 291-303.

Marton, F. & Booth, S. (1997). *Learning and Awareness*. Mahwah NJ: Lawrence Erlbaum Associates.

McLuhan, M. (1964). *Understanding Media*. London and New York: Routledge and Kegan Paul.

Mead, G. H. (1934). *Mind, Self and Society* (Vol. 1). Chicago: University of Chicago Press.

PALM. (1988-90). *Teachers' Voices Series*. Norwich: CARE, University of East Anglia.

Pearson, M. & Somekh, B. (2006). Learning Transformation with Technology: a question of socio-cultural contexts? *International Journal for Qualitative Studies in Education, 19*(4), 519-539.

Prawat, R. S. (1991). The Value of Ideas: The Immersion Approach to the Development of Thinking. *Educational Researcher, 20*(2), 3-10.

SearchInstitute. (1998). *Healthy Communities, Healthy Youth Took Kit*. Minneapolis, MN: Search Institute.

Somekh, B. (2007). *Pedagogy and Learning with ICT: Researching the Art of Innovation*. London and New York: Routledge.

Somekh, B. & Davies, R. (1991). Towards a Pedagogy for Information Technology. *The Curriculum Journal, 2*(2), 153-170.

Somekh, B., Lewin, C., Mavers, D., Fisher, T., Harrison, C., Haw, K., et al. (2002). *ImpaCT2: Pupils' and Teachers' Perceptions of ICT in the Home, School and Community*. London: Department for Education and Skills.

Turkle, S. (1995). *Life on the Screen: Identity in the Age of the Internet*. London and New York: Phoenix.

Vygotsky, L. (1978). *Mind in Society: The Development of Higher Psychological Processes*. Cambridge MA: Harvard University Press.

Vygotsky, L. (1986). *Thought and Language. (Original Russian edition, 1934)*. Cambridge MA and London: MIT Press.

Wenger, E. (1998). *Communities of Practice: learning, meaning and identity*. Cambridge UK, New York and Melbourne: Cambridge University Press.

Wertsch, J. V. (1998). *Mind as Action*. New York and Oxford: Oxford University Press.

In: Learning in the Network Society and the Digitized School   ISBN 978-1-60741-172-7
Editor: Rune Krumsvik   © 2009 Nova Science Publishers, Inc.

Chapter 2

MEANING-MAKING AND THE APPROPRIATION OF GEOMETRIC REASONING: COMPUTER MEDIATED SUPPORT FOR UNDERSTANDING THE RELATIONSHIP BETWEEN AREA AND PERIMETER OF PARALLELOGRAMS

Jan Wyndhamn[1] and Roger Säljö[2]
1) Linköping University, Sweden
2) University of Gothenburg, Sweden

ABSTRACT

The study reported concerns issues of meaning-making and mediation in the context of collaborative learning in early geometry instruction. Collaborative learning is not one type of activity or method, rather it is an approach which may unfold differently in the classroom. In this study, we conceive of collaborative learning as interesting both as a process and in terms of its products, i.e. learning outcomes. This implies that through collaboration, students have possibilities to interact with fellow students in order to explore mathematical ideas, and the activities may result in individual learning. However, there is no guarantee that collaborative modes of learning necessarily result in better learning. The critical issue is what kind of activity and meaning-making students engage in. Whether the outcome of the activities is some kind of learning or not is an empirical question.

INTRODUCTION

A mathematics classroom is characterized by different communicative patterns (Cobb, Wood, Yackel, & McNeal, 1992). Using established teacher jargon, these activities, in a highly stylized manner, can be summarized in two different images. The most common pattern has been, and maybe still is, that the teacher, using the whiteboard and in a presentational manner, "goes through" the subject matter to be learned. The teacher "explains" the mathematical concepts covered, and she then, in a stepwise fashion, "instructs" the students on how to deal with the type of problem that is in focus. As a next step, the teacher in this mode of teaching often "gives" the students a number of similar problems from the text book as "exercises" to "practise" on individually. During this phase of "silent" individual problem solving, the teacher walks around in the classroom and attends to the questions raised by individual students on how to solve problems. As a part of this supervision and monitoring, the teacher may show the student "how to go about solving the problem" or "how one can think" when encountering problems of this kind. A different image of mathematics learning in classrooms is that the students are divided into groups of different sizes, usually two or three children in each. In this teaching style, the students are engaged in "talking mathematics", and through their "collaboration" they solve the problems assigned to them. Collaboratively they "discuss" the possible strategies for solving problems, or they engage in "inquiry" in order to find out what the problem is all about (Carlsen, 2008; Jaworski, 2006). By working in a "student active" and "laboratory" like framing with activities such as making drawings, measuring and comparing objects, the students are expected to "discover" and "understand" how specific mathematical principles and models function. Today tools such as a mini-calculator and "interactive" computer software would also often be part of this kind of setting.

The terms quoted testify to the discourses that surround mathematics teaching and learning. In spite of the apparent variation in how to categorize activities in the mathematics classroom, and the many pedagogical ideologies on offer, the discourses originate in a limited number of perspectives on learning. The terms indicate that they draw on behaviourist, cognitive and constructivist perspectives, respectively. The activities in the classroom are initiated by the teacher, who designs them so as to enable students to "learn" mathematics, "acquire" or "appropriate" knowledge and skills, and "reach the goals" of instruction. The general idea behind the activities that the teacher designs is that they should facilitate learning. What design or instructional approach the teacher decides on reflects the particular view of learning that he or she represents. Different theoretical perspectives generate different alternatives for how to organize the teaching and learning, and each perspective builds on specific assumptions about the nature of learning.

The study to be reported here concerns issues of meaning-making, learning and mediation in the context of what is generally referred to as collaborative learning (Bjuland, 2004; Springer, Stanne, & Donovan, 1999). The idea of promoting collaborative learning is not tied to one specific learning theory or instructional approach, even though there is perhaps a tendency to associate it with constructivist, pragmatist and sociocultural perspectives. Collaborative learning cannot be conceived as one type of activity or method, rather it is an approach which may unfold differently in the classroom. In this study, we conceive of collaborative learning as interesting both as a process and in terms of its products, i.e. learning outcomes. This implies that through collaboration, students have possibilities to interact with fellow students in order to explore mathematical ideas, and the activities are expected to result in individual learning. However, there is no guarantee that collaborative modes of learning necessarily result in better learning. The critical issue is what kind of activity and meaning-making students engage in. Whether the outcome of the activities is some kind of learning or not is an empirical question.

MEDIATION AND LEARNING OF ELEMENTARY GEOMETRY

The focus of the present study is on the role of mediation in learning and understanding. Mediation is a fundamental concept in a sociocultural perspective. The basic assumption is that people think by means of cultural tools (Vygotsky, 1986, 1981). Cultural tools emerge in social practices, and they are of different kinds: linguistic (or intellectual/mental) tools such as the alphabet, measurement systems and conceptual constructions, and physical tools (artefacts) such as hammers, knives and computers. But cultural tools are often simultaneously intellectual and physical, a ruler is a physical artefact with measurement units as inscriptions and a mini-calculator is a device which operates on the basis of the number system and various symbolic mathematical operations; thus, cultural tools are simultaneously ideational and physical as Cole (1996; Cole & Derry, 2005) emphasizes.

Human reasoning, remembering and perception take place through the use of cultural tools. Many, even most, of the tools we use are appropriated through our everyday communication with other people, and they are not necessarily visible to us. They are part of a conceptual (and physical) world that we have come to take for granted through socialization. This is a kind of indirect or implicit mediation (Wertsch, 2007). In other cases, such as when encountering what Vygotsky (1986) refers to as "scientific concepts", the manner in which the world is mediated is more abstract, and the concepts may be more difficult to appropriate. In such settings, some form of instruction or guidance will be necessary in order for a person to understand how to use a specific intellectual tool for meaning-making.

Early mathematics learning is full of experiences of this kind where the nature of the mediation is a problem for the learner (Wyndhamn & Säljö, 1997). Children encounter symbolic systems, concepts and operations that require instruction, since the tools are not part of our everyday experiences. Thus, children have few, if any, opportunities to develop "ownership" of such resources for meaning-making in their daily activities. The field of geometry is one such area, where a rich number of concepts are used to describe and analyse objects and relationships in the world. Even though the terminology of geometry may overlap with everyday language, geometric concepts such as base, side, area, angle and others are defined within the particular discursive constructions of geometry. In scientific languages, unlike everyday language, concepts are explicitly defined so as to be as clear as possible within the universe of meaning that defines a particular domain. This implies that there are restrictions on how concepts should be used if one is going to be successful at "talking science" (Lemke, 1990).

The background of the present study is an interest in issues of mediation in early geometry learning. More specifically, we will focus on how pupils appropriate a basic understanding of how to calculate the area and perimeter of parallelograms, and how they construe the relationships between these variables/quantities. The introduction to these types of problems usually takes place through teaching about squares and rectangles. Thus, in the case of squares the area is the product of the side-lengths, $l \times l = l^2$, and in the case of the rectangle the area is the product of the side-length of the base and the width/height. The more challenging problems occur when the parallelogram has another shape, i.e. when the angles are not 90 degrees as is illustrated in Figure 1.

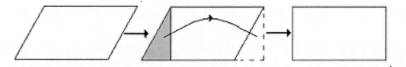

Figure 1. Parallelogram and illustration of "cut and paste" (or "paper cut") model for transforming parallelogram to rectangle.

The customary manner of explaining how to calculate the area in this case is illustrated in the figure (cf., e.g., www.mathleague/help/com/area.htm). The transformation shown implies that a right-angled triangle is cut out from the parallelogram and moved to the other side. In this graphical manner, the parallelogram is transformed into a rectangle. The area may then be calculated as the product of the base and height, $b \times h$. This approach to calculating the area can be referred to as a "cut and paste" (or "paper cut") method.

The transformation of a rectangle into a parallelogram metaphorically speaking takes place by 'tilting' the rectangle. The interesting issue is what the relationship is between the area and the perimeter of the rectangle and the parallelogram. For many pupils, such transformations are often difficult to grasp (cf. Sayeki, Ueno, & Nagasaka, 1991). For instance, pupils might think the area stays the same in the case of the "tilted" parallelogram, since nothing is added or taken away. This is a kind of conservation attitude in the Piagetian sense in which the children argue that the rectangle is restored to its original form when "tilted" back. Thus, children (and probably many adults, too) interpret the side of the parallelogram as equal to the height (cf. Hart, 1981). In Vygotskian parlance, this can be seen as a problem of mediation in the sense that these two concepts – side and height – are perceived as identical, while in the scientific language of geometry they are not.

Rectangles, Parallelograms and Forms of Mediation

In the model in Figure 2 below, the rectangle is transformed into a parallelogram through what one one can refer to as a "hinge" or "frame" model. The rectangle, may be seen as "tilted" in the sense the "frame" is pushed to the side so that it, in the language of the pupils we have studied, "leans" in a particular direction which results in a parallelogram. The area can then be calculated through the customary "cut and paste" method.

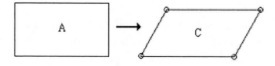

Figure 2. Transformation through the "hinge" or "frame" model.

From a historical perspective, however, there is a different transformation which is relevant in this situation, and which is interesting from the point of view of the mediation it implies. In 1629, Cavalieri, who was a student of Galilei, made an attempt to alleviate this particular misunderstanding of the relationship between areas and perimeters of rectangles and parallelograms. He suggested an alternative principle which may be used as a tool for illustrating the fact that the area of the parallelogram is a product of the base and the height. He argued that every solid body, irrespective of its shape, can be seen as a pile or stack of thin slices or sheets analogous to a deck of cards. If the deck of cards is tilted or displaced, the volume of the object will not change as long as the height remains the same (Cavalieri's principle). If one looks at the deck of cards from one side, this transformation from a rectangle to a parallelogram is easily visible as is shown in Figure 3.

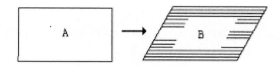

Figure 3. Transformation of rectangle into parallelogram following the "deck of cards" model (Cavalieri's principle).

What is interesting when seeing these two different ways of estimating the area of a parallelogram is that they imply different modes of reasoning in terms of the logic used. Arguing along the lines of the "frame" or "hinge" model, and using the "cut and paste" method, comes close to a deductive mode of thinking in which the reasoning is based on some assumed logical fundamentals applicable to the situation: since nothing is taken away or added, the area stays the same, or, alternatively, since the figure can be restored to a rectangle, the area must be the same. The "deck of cards" model, on the other hand, comes closer to induction in the sense that it implies drawing conclusions from series of observations. Comparing all the transformations possible with the deck of cards, one can infer that the area stays the same as long as no cards are taken away (or added). The "thickness" of the deck of cards is not changed, which implies that the height stays the same. And so, of course, does the base.

Thus, these two models imply that the premises for the meaning-making are different, or, in Vygotskian language, the conceptual mediation is different. When using the "deck of cards" model as a tool for mediation, the area will stay the same, while the perimeter will change. With the "frame" or "hinge" model, and the "cut and paste" method for calculation, the area will change, while the perimeter stays the same. The core of the dilemma of understanding these relationships is the abstract nature of the concept of area. An area has to be calculated by using certain intellectual procedures; it is a secondary quality, as it were. "If the area gets smaller when the rectangle is tilted, where has the rest of it gone?" is a question that is tricky for many pupils. Such a comment illustrates the difficulties for students of understanding the nature of these transformations.

An additional problem when it comes to meaning-making procedures in this context is that when the rectangle is only slightly "tilted" as in Figure 2, the visual impression may lead to the conclusion that the area stays the same between A and C. Thus, the visual impression will support a more deductive form of thinking in which the assumption that nothing is "taken away" or "added" is confirmed. If the height of the parallelogram would be further reduced, the visual impression would make it more difficult to keep to the assumption of the constancy of the area.

What is interesting about these intellectual problems as cognitive challenges is that theoretical assumptions and visual impressions come into conflict, and so do deductive and inductive forms of reasoning (Parzysz, 1988; Schoenfeld, 1986). In order to successfully solve these kinds of problems, pupils have to consider both empirical observations and the relevance of specific intellectual tools, and they have to combine these sources of information into a procedure that is functional. In Popper's (1959) terms, they have to operate both within the "context of discovery" by deciding on what kind of figure they are seeing, and in the "context of justification" by realizing what is a relevant manner of proving how the area should be calculated.

EMPIRICAL OBSERVATION AND DEDUCTION: AN INSTRUCTIONAL APPROACH

Van Hiele (1986) designed a model for teaching in situations of this kind. The model is progressive in nature and takes into account the tensions for pupils (or any novice) between, on the one hand, perception and, on the other hand, deductive reasoning on the basis of specific "scientific" premises. The model contains different levels and can briefly be described as follows:

Level 0.   The visualization level. The pupil works with and recognizes different geometric figures and shapes such as triangles and squares. The geometric objects are perceived as wholes rather than as combinations of identifiable elements.

Level 1.   An elementary analytical level. Recognition of different figures and shapes and their characteristics. This knowledge is grounded in empirical observations and facts. No linkages between different features of figures are made.

Level 2.   Informal deductive work takes place. One starts to work with definitions, deducing simple characteristics of geometric figures, and there is a beginning analysis of relationships between different characteristics.

Level 3.   Deductive reasoning in a more formal sense is employed. Definitions, axioms and theorems are used as elements of geometric theorizing.

Level 4.   At this level, the work takes place at a theoretical level, and there is no need to refer to concrete instances or situations.

Since the formula for the area of the parallelogram is possible to deduce in a logical manner, the nature of the work expected by students would be at level 2, where the calculation of the area follows from the realization of the relationship between the base and height of the figure.

In the van Hiele-model, it is argued that the manner in which a pupil progresses through these steps is a result of teaching and not of age or maturity. Working one's way up through the levels implies appropriating specific "scientific concepts" in Vygotskian terms, i.e. this kind of development is very much a product of schooling in which the individual becomes familiar with the cultural tools of geometry (Säljö, 2005). Based on this assumption, van Hiele suggests sequences of activities that will take the pupil from one level to the next. The experiences from lower levels are necessary for successful appropriation of the cultural tools and concepts that have to be used at the higher levels. An important element of the argumentation is that it is possible to engage in forms of logical reasoning that are productive for development long before one masters the concepts at the higher levels. In this sense, van Hiele's didactic conclusions have elements of a Piagetian view of development in which concrete observations and experiences pave the way for the pupil's ability to accommodate to more abstract forms of deductive reasoning (Piaget, 1970). This also raises the important instructional question of how the pupil's current level of mastery can be matched with teaching and learning experiences that promote development "upwards."

MEDIATION: AN INSPIRING EXPERIMENT

The study that serves as a background for the work to be reported here was carried out by Sayeki, Ueno and Nagasaki (1991). In this study, the authors demonstrate that when students are introduced to the problems of the area of the parallelogram through the "deck of cards" model and the Cavalieri principle, their performance is much better than when the mediation takes place through the "frame" or "hinge" model of Figure 2 (which is referred to as the "paper cut" model in the study). The study was performed as a teaching experiment with three groups taught by means of these two models; one experimental group working with the "deck of cards" model and two control groups using the "paper cut" method for calculating the area. This "paper cut" (or "cut and paste") method is the traditional approach in Japanese schools according to the authors.

Basically, what the results show is that the "deck of cards" model was a more efficient tool for mediating the understanding that the area stays the same irrespective of the transformations made as long as the base and the height are the same. Most pupils taught in this manner understood this principle, and they discovered it rather quickly. The teacher who used the "paper cut" approach to calculating the area, on the other hand, had to spend much more time explaining the relationship between the transformations and the area of the parallelogram. The authors made a delayed retention test after a week, and the pupils in the experimental group were much better at remembering the formula and at calculating the area.

The study also shows that irrespective of what group the students belonged to, they had difficulties predicting what happens to the area in the case of the "frame" model. Again this testifies to the conflict between perception and logical reasoning in this particular situation. The students were convinced that the area stayed the same, and the authors claim that students were surprised when they were shown by means of a "frame" (the outside part of a matchbox) how the area decreases as the frame is "tilted."

In the study, the experimental group was first introduced to the "deck of cards" model and then to the flexible "frame" model. In spite of the good results when it comes to understanding that the area remained constant in spite of the transformations in the case of the "deck of cards" model, this group, too, had difficulties understanding what happens to the area in the case of the "frame" model. Thus, there is something conflictual about such transformations for pupils, and they become uncertain of how to reason in spite of the fact that they have shown that they master the principles of how to calculate the area.

This observation formed the background of the present study in which this problem of the relationships between area and perimeter was incorporated into a simple computer program. The point of this program was to give pupils the possibility to manipulate the geometric figures in accordance with both of these models in order to ascertain if they understood the differences between the "deck of cards" and the "frame" model. The basic question is if pupils will discover the logic of what varies and what remains constant when transforming the figures in accordance with the two models. Is it possible to use a computer tool which allows for manipulation of visual representations to crystallize the thinking of the pupils so that they realize the principles involved?

RESEARCH QUESTIONS AND METHOD

The basic questions of the present study are:

1. How is the thinking of the pupils regarding the area of parallelograms co-determined by a computer mediated presentation of the two different models ("deck of cards" and "frame" model, respectively)?
2. How do the pupils talk about the geometric objects when working with them on the screen? Or, expressed differently, to what extent are there signs that the pupils can articulate the differences between the two models in geometrically relevant terms?
3. How do the pupils solve this kind of problems after having worked with the software?

Questions 1 or 2 thus concern what the collaborating pupils appropriate while working with the computer program (i.e. the focus is on the process), while the third question concerns what they may have appropriated from interacting with the program (outcome of learning).

Participants

Nine pairs of pupils participated in this exploratory study. They were 12 years of age and participation was voluntary. The participants were divided into three groups on the basis of their achievements in mathematics: high, medium and low achievers. This division into groups was done by the teacher who were instructed to form homogeneous pairs. Thus, there are three pairs at each level.

Table 1. Groups and participants in empirical study

Achievement Level in Mathematics		
High	**Average**	**Low**
11 Alice, Anna	21 Diana, Doris	31 Gisela, Glenn
12 Bodil, Britta	22 Erik, Eva	32 Harry, Helge
13 Carola, Conny	23 Frank, Frida	33 Ingrid, Irene

The pupils previously had had some teaching about the rectangle and the area. This implies that they had some familiarity with basic concepts such as base, height and side.

Data Collection

All groups worked in front of a computer in the regular computer room in the school. The pupils were told that after working with the computer program they would be required to solve a problem with parallelograms. All groups worked independently of each other, and they used a mouse to manipulate the objects on the screen. All these activities were saved in a file. The program started when the pupils wrote their names. The interaction between the pupils was audio recorded and later transcribed.

The Program

The computer program was specifically designed for this study, and it is divided into four parts.

Part 1

It presented a family of parallelograms, and the members square and rectangle were represented as coloured images. The concepts of area and perimeter were explained in text and with illustrations. After this, it was shown, both in text and through images, how a parallelogram can be transformed either in accordance with the "deck of cards" model or the "frame" model. One of the authors (JW) read the text, and the pupils were given the opportunity to ask questions. No further information was given.

Part 2

Through the program the pupils were given instructions on how the shape and the size of the parallelograms shown could be changed. Through the mouse, the pupils could move the cursor and click on any of four small "buttons" on the screen, and in this manner they could manipulate four different parameters.

Table 2. Parameters that could be manipulated

Parameter	Indicated by
Length (base) with constant angles	red button
Height with constant angles	green button
Perimeter with constant area ("deck of cards" model)	yellow button
Area with constant perimeter ("frame" model)	blue button

It should be observed that no geometric terms (except area and perimeter) were mentioned in the program or in the oral introduction to the task. The pupils had eight possible ways of manipulating the figures. The measures (areas and perimeters) were shown on the screen as the pupils manipulated the shapes. When changing the figure, the measurements were changed. The pupils were given time to practise how to change the figures.

Part 3

This particular part is the most important one for the present study. On the screen a parallelogram of 210 area units and 62,6 length units was shown to the pupils. In five consecutive tasks the pupils were told to adjust the parallelogram to the following measurements:

Area	225	100	150	320	100
Perimeter	80	50	100	86	40

When the pupils had arrived at a parallelogram with the given measurements, the next task followed automatically. Every task started with 210 and 62,6. When the correct values were reached – either for the area or the perimeter – the colour of the numbers changed so that the pupils could see when the measurements they had given were correct. All attempts made by the pupils were stored on a file.

Part 4

Before the pupils started working on the final target task, they were given the opportunity to repeat what they had been through, and they could also return to images that illustrated the models.

After this computer training session, the target task was presented. This task was to be solved using paper and pencil. On the first paper, a picture with the two models, the "deck of cards" and "frame" model respectively, was shown. The pupils were asked a) to identify them in terms of whether they represented a "deck of cards" or "frame" model (task 1), b) to explain the differences between them and to give motives for their explanations of the transformations (task 2). On a second paper, a parallelogram was shown. The sides were 7 and 10 centimetres, and the height from the longest side 6 centimetres. There were no measurements given on the paper, and the paper was blank with no lines or any other markings. The pupils were asked to draw a rectangle with the same area as the parallelogram (task 3, which is the task that corresponds to the third research question). They used a pencil and a ruler with centimetres for the measuring. The conversations were recorded and field notes were made of the work.

It should be pointed out that the computer program followed the intentions behind the van Hiele model. The program is sequential and makes it possible for the pupils first to recognize the geometric shapes and then to reflect and discuss what characterizes them. It should also be pointed out that the groups were working independently and without teacher support, which was the case in the Japanese study by Sayeki et al. (1991).

RESULTS

The time the groups devoted to the tasks varied between 26 and 33 minutes, and there are no significant differences in this respect between the groups.

Identification of the Geometric Figures and Transformations

In response to the first problem of identifying the transformations (task 1), all the groups were successful, i.e. they could distinguish between the two models. All pairs, except group

21 with Diana and Doris, managed to describe the characteristics of the transformations (task 2) and to draw a rectangle which accommodated to either model. An excerpt from group 21 illustrates the problems the girls had with task 2 of identifying the characteristics of the transformations and the difference between the two models:

> Diana: There is no difference between the deck of cards and the hinges. Area and perimeter stay the same. It should be like that.

Diana then draws a rectangle (task 3) which is 10 centimetres in length and 7 centimetres in height, i.e. she used the measurements given for the sides of the oblique-angled parallelogram. In other words, neither in her explanation nor in her drawing is there any evidence that she understands the differences between the two models (even though she uses the terms deck of cards and hinges).

The most common way of drawing the rectangle was to draw it on the paper next to the parallelogrammen given, and then to use the ruler to make the relevant measurements. Two pairs (12 and 31) made their drawing on top of the parallelogram given. By using this strategy, they did not have to use the ruler for measuring; rather they argued on the basis of the constancy of the height and the length of the original parallelogram given.

Carola and Conny of pair 13 were the only ones to place the rectangle next to the given parallelogram. For Conny it was obvious that the height would stay the same:

> Conny: The deck of cards neither gets higher nor lower but longer, drawn out (illustrates with gestures)

The features and arguments that the pupils refer to for characterizing the two models and the differences between them are summarized in Table 3.

Table 3. Categorization of arguments given by the pupils

Referring to...	Examples of utterances
Appearance	It looks like the deck of cards.
	The deck of cards is thick and it stands upright.
	This one is like the hinges.
Differences	The hinges press down more than the deck of cards.
	The hinges tilt quicker. (with gestures)
Constancy of height (implicitly expressed)	It is the same ... (points to the height)
	The deck of cards stays ... (uses thumb and index finger to show constancy of height by moving the hand over the figure)

The accounts given by each of the pairs in some cases fall into more than one category. Pairs 13, 23, 31, 32 and 33 referred to the appearance. Pairs 11, 12, 13 and 21 focussed on the differences as the important characteristic to pay attention to. Pairs 13, 22 and 33 referred to the constancy of the height. There is a tendency that low achieving pairs focus on the appearance, while the high achievers focussed on the differences between the models.

Turning to the nature of the interaction with the computer, there are some initial quantitative observations that can be made. Table 5 shows the total number of times the pupils clicked with the mouse.

Table 4. Number of mouse clicks per pair

Achievement Level				Sum	Mean
High	70	42	23	135	45
Average	39	63	53	155	52
Low	81	47	51	179	60
				469	**52**

There is a slight indication that the higher the achievement level of the student pair, the fewer the number of mouse clicks (although this difference does not reach statistical significance). The variation within competence levels in this respect is high, which makes this variable ambiguous when it comes to predicting its role in the problem solving process. Table 5 shows the outcome in terms of the distribution of mouse clicks across the four parameters that could be manipulated through the technology to change the area and the perimeter.

Table 5. Number of mouse clicks to change parameters

Parameter	Achievement Level			
	High	Average	Low	Sum
Length (base)	26	45	45	116
Height	38	49	42	129
Perimeter	37	38	47	122
Area	34	23	45	102
	135	**155**	**179**	**469**

The distribution over the cells does not show any statistically significant differences. The computer registered in which order the parameters were changed by the pupils so that the intended areas and parameters would be reached. The analyses of the 45 (9 groups and 5 tasks) computer registrations show that four different types of strategies emerge. The dominant strategy is that the pairs first adjust the base and height of the parallelogram so that the size of the area desired "can be fixed" – an expression frequently used by the pupils. Then one used the "deck of cards" model to reach the intended perimeter. This strategy was systematically used by pairs 11, 12, 22, 23 and 32.

On some occasions the intended perimeter seems to have been arrived at more or less by chance. The correct area could then be arrived at by means of the "frame" model. Pair 21 was consistent in using this second type of strategy. Pair 13 shows a third and more flexible strategy. Carola and Conny throughout their work tried to minimize the number of trials. This group was the only one to use the graded co-ordinate axes which appeard on the screen. They considered every parallelogram as an approximate rectangle. Pairs 31 and 33 worked in a random manner testing out different opportunities until they finished the program.

Mediating Talk in Front of the Computer

From the learning point of view, an interesting aspect of the collaborative situation in front of the computer is how the students communicated when they worked with the program. An analysis of the conversations shows that four different types of utterances appear.

Table 6. Types of utterances during the conversation at the computer

Category	Illustrating examples
Deictic level	(Pupils pointing to the screen while talking)
	Take this one. Put the mouse here.
	Increase this one.
	More here.
	Try this one first.
Visual level	Take the blue button, I think.
	Reduce with the yellow one.
	Use red.
Metaphorical level	Change with the deck of cards.
	Try with the hinges.
Formal level	We try to mark the area first.
	Change both the area and the perimeter at the same time.
	The perimeter is far from correct. Add to it.

At the deictic level, which is interesting from the point of view of learning, all talk is totally dependent on the pointing to the screen. Expressions such as this one and more here are only possible to understand in the presence of non-verbal cues and the screen. At the visual level, the students refer to features of what appears on the screen; features which are arbitrary from the point of view of learning geometry. At the metaphorical level, the two types of mediating models are used, and at the formal level geometric concepts appear as part of the discussion. These differences in how pupils talk are significant when it comes to understand what they may appropriate from the activity, and we will return to this.

The pairs are not consistent in how they talk and refer to what they see on the screen. The first category of utterances is used by groups 21, 31 and 33, the second one by 21, 21, 22, 23, 31, 32 and 33. the third one by groups 12 and 23, and the fourth one by 11, 13 and 22. An interesting, and important, observation is that a situation of this kind with a computer screen seems to invite talking about the colours and other concrete features of what appears on the screen. This implies that the mediation is dominated by visual features on the screen which have little to do with geometry.

Transforming a Parallelogram into a Rectangle Using Paper and Pencil

In this final task, the pupils were supposed to transform a parallelogram (with sides 10 and 7 centimetres and a height of 6 centimetres) to a rectangle with the same area using paper and pencil. The performance of this task can be seen as one criterion for how successful the groups were in appropriating the conceptual differences between the two models. It is not possible to go into great detail about these nine conversations, as they developed quite differently. Five of the groups, however, in their discussions used the "deck of cards" model as a mediating tool; 12, 13, 22, 23 and 31.

Group 21, which we have commented on earlier, did not engage in much discussion. This was also the only group which did not manage to explain the differences between the two models. Diana solved most of the tasks, and Doris either confirmed by saying "yes" or by being silent. If Diana could not find the expected measurements, she simply handed the mouse over to Doris saying: Now you can try! They did not discuss while attempting to make the transformation on paper. Diana started by making a rectangle with the sides 10 and 7 centimetres, and Doris agreed to this solution. Thus, the conclusion with respect to this group seems obvious; the girls did not grasp the differences between the two models and the manners in which they indicate the relationships between area and perimeter. In this sense, there is no evidence of appropriation.

Two other pairs, 22 and 23, started in the same manner by measuring the sides of the parallelogram. Then they made a rectangle with the base 10 centimetres and a height of 7 centimetres. In both these cases, however, the figures were corrected during the collaboration when students started discussing and arguing in order to reach consensus.

<u>Group 23</u>

Frank:	Will the sides really be the same here (while pointing to the parallelogram given and the rectangle they had just produced)
Frida:	Do you mean 10 centimetres and 7 centimetres?
Frank:	It must sort of be shorter straight up
Frida:	Yes, but how long then?
Frank:	It must be ...
Frida:	But think of the deck of cards ... These lines must be shorter (points to the shorter sides of the rectangle)
Frank:	Yes, the same measurements as here ... between (points to the height of the parallelogram).
Frida:	Reduce ... (erases parts of the shorter sides of the rectangle)
Frank:	The same space in between ... 6 centimetres (uses the ruler to measure the height of the parallelogram)
Frida:	Mm (completes the rectangle so that the area is correct)

The essential point is to realize that the heights must be the same. No pupil used the term "height" though, but there were other ways to describe the "space in between" as Frank refers to it towards the end of the discussion. Already in his second utterance, "It must sort of be shorter straight up", Frank introduces the difference between the side of the parallelogram and its height (which he refers to as "straight up"). Frida picks this comment up in her response: "Yes, but how long then?" Her formulation implies that she accepts that there is a difference between the side and the height, and she wants to know how big this difference is. Frank and Frida then go on to solve the problem by referring to the deck of cards metaphor. Group 13 below comes closest to a mathematical terminology by talking about "how high" the figures were, but, still, the concept of height is not explicitly singled out as the variable to be attended to.

It is obvious that the situation changes when the groups move from the computer mediated representations to the paper and pencil task. In order to deal with the latter problem, the pupils have to create a new context in which they have to co-ordinate their reasoning and their "inter-thinking" as Mercer (2000) refers to such dialogical activities. The pupils must establish a discourse which can guide their activities, and an interesting point is to what extent there is evidence of transfer from the computer mediated activities.

Pair 13

Carola:	Think of the deck of cards.
Conny:	(measures the sides of the parallelogram with the ruler) 10 centimetres … 7 centimetres … 10 times 7 is 70, but … (measures the height of the parallelogram)
Carola:	Is is like that?
Conny:	With the deck of cards …
Carola:	… it's the same … (pointing to the height)
Conny:	10 is the same … 6 centimetres … it should be 6
Carola:	But … Does the area become smaller now? … 7 …
Conny:	No, the perimeter gets longer … or shorter
Carola:	Mm. How long is … (points to the height)? This was difficult …
Conny:	Yes, 10 times … how high … 10 times 6 is it.
Carola:	Mm.
Conny:	The deck of cards neither gets higher nor lower … but longer … (gesturing)
Carola:	Yes. (draws a rectangle next to the given parallelogram on the paper in order to get the correct height. She does this without measuring the 6 centimetres)

This rather elaborate and focussed discussion is interesting from several points of view. It illustrates the difficulties the participants have in maintaining a consistent discourse. Everyday discursive constructions of how high or long an object is are mixed with attempts to engage in mathematical meaning-making. Carola and Conny manage to move ahead in the discussion and draw a rectangle, but it is still obvious that what is lacking in this conversation is the geometric concept of "height." In the absence of this distinctive term, they use everyday expressions and pointing and gesturing as resources for meaning-making. But, and this is our point, in this case the concept of height needs to be invoked in order to create a satisfactory conceptual ordering, and it needs to be used if the exercise is to be conducive to learning something that is more general than what is presented in this particular exercise. Thus, and as is shown, the participants manage to provide a solution to the task, but they do this by using local resources in the example rather than by introducing the general concept of height. In this case, a concept – such as height – must be introduced in order to extend – or even liberate – the understanding from the local setting of producing a rectangle here-and-now, to become a generalized understanding of a concept that has many instantiations.

It is obvious that it is just at this point that the presence of a teacher could make an important difference. What happens in the situations we have observed is that the pupils are very happy with manipulating the figures, and they go along with the intentions of the designer of the program. However, the critical point is taking one's reasoning to a conceptual level, where the manipulations performed are seen as instances of certain geometric relationships and patterns. We will return to this.

Another point that is interesting about this example is that it illustrates the dynamic features of joint reasoning or "inter-thinking", to use Mercer's expression. Thus, it is impossible to localize the reasoning either within the minds of Carola or Conny as individual participants in this practice; rather it is "distributed" between them. Both contribute to building an intermental platform of temporarily shared concerns and understandings which moves the discussion forwards. One person uses the utterances by the other to continue reasoning and to come up with new proposals or ideas. Language very clearly serves as "the vehicle of thought" (Wittgenstein, 1953, §329) which makes it possible for the participants "to go on" with their activity to continue in Wittgenstein's (1980, § 875) suggestive language.

DISCUSSION AND CONCLUSIONS

To return to our initial problem of how the two models function as mediational means in this situation, our study illustrates how the computer program and the screen serve as mediating tools that the participants use as resources for meaning-making. Through their computer mediated activities, the pupils obviously managed to identify several important aspects of parallelograms. After only 20 minutes of co-operation in the computer context, all groups (except 21) managed to find out the principles of how to calculate the area of the parallelogram. The two models obviously were very helpful as conceptual constructions, and they made what is otherwise abstract and difficult to realize understandable. At a general level, the study therefore confirms the Japanese experiment by Sayeki et al (1991), with the notable exception that in this case the parallelograms were computer representations rather than concrete objects. The objects, thus, do not have to be physically present and the pupils do not have to work "hands on"; rather the strength of the situation from the point of view of mediation lies in the power of the two metaphorical constructions of the "deck of cards" and the "frame" model to make pupils discover differences in the transformations in the images on the screen in front of them.

A metaphor can be expressed in terms of 'X is Y', 'X is like Y' and 'X is as if Y' (cf. Pramling, 2006). In the present study, X is a parallelogram and Y a deck of cards or a frame. The metaphor in this sense carries information regarding characteristics of a shape. It makes it possible to talk about X as a familiar phenomenon and to discuss novel ideas about something which is already well known (Y). The metaphors serve as linguistic vehicles for seeing what is important, general and distinctive about geometric shapes and their characteristics, but at the same time they make it possible to see something new in what is already familiar. Using the program, the pupils – while "learning while doing" to use Dewey's expression – have appropriated something about how a parallelogram can be transformed and what characteristics that are relevant to attend to.

Our documentation of the results indicates that the pupils in their conversations to a large extent do not talk about the parallelogram X as such. Rather, they first and foremost focus on the comparison with Y (i.e. the metaphorical illustration). In other words, they seem to stay in the metaphorical construction or analogy between two shapes or objects. They do not to any significant extent talk about the characteristics that the models are intended to illustrate. However, there are two groups (13 and 23) where the participants perceive the "deck of cards" model as a metaphor for the geometric principle, even if the members of these groups still tend to think with the metaphors as entities in their own right. To be able to interpret something as a metaphor requires some familiarity with not only the picture itself, but also with relevant objects and events in the physical reality and one must also develop a sense of how models are structured or designed (cf. Stålhammar, 1997). For Diana in group 21, the models did not function as cognitive tools in any apparent manner. In her remarks, she seems to assume that there is one basic order of things and there is no need for recontextualizing what one sees – "it should be like that" is her comment. The work with the computer modelling did not create any new experiences or reactions for her. She seemed to be searching for confirmations of what she already assumed to be true.

In the sociocultural perspective, mediation is closely linked to appropriation. Appropriation implies taking over and using cultural tools that are new to the individual but which exist in society. Thus, what is present inter-mentally between people is taken over and becomes part of the intra-mental repertoire of a person. The point of the program was to create a situation in which the participants in interaction and in co-operation with the software appropriate elements of a geometric discourse. What we have seen in this study is that there are indeed such observations of signs of appropriation, but that the depth of the appropriation from similar experiences varies. This indicates that appropriation is relative to activities and not merely to the stimulus material provided or the particular pedagogical situation organized.

In this context, the appropriation process can be linked to the progression described in the van Hiele model presented earlier. The first level implies that there were no signs of appropriation. One pair (group 21) did not in any visible manner profit from the program or the activities they engaged in. A second level implies the appropriation of terminology. In the present case, the pupils quickly start using the term deck of cards, but without necessarily appropriating the conceptual features at any depth. At the next level, there are signs of appropriating some features of the surface structure of the figures and shapes but they do not necessarily understand how they relate to each other or form part of a coherent system. At a more advanced level, the pupils appropriate insights into when, why and how a cognitive/cultural tool functions. A conceptual and theoretical platform is created making it possible for the individual to use the tool in new contexts and for new problems. In our data, some of the pupils realized the relevance of height when estimating the area of a parallelogram, but the concept had not been crystallized so as to be available for "voluntary use" in Vygotsky's terms. At the highest level, the individual has appropriated a specific kind of discourse as a coherent mode of reasoning in mathematical settings. This implies that one can think and communicate relatively freely within the frames defined by this particular social or professional language and use its discursive conventions.

An interesting feature of the nature of the activities that students developed in this study is the reliance on what is referred to as deictic language. In the transcripts, words such as this, this one, here, there, now, first etc. appear frequently. For their interpretation these expressions are dependent on the co-presence of two actors focussing the same visual field.

The words are highly context dependent and they are often accompanied by gestures. The pupils temporarily share a focus of attention, which makes it possible for the discussion to continue in a co-ordinated manner. The colour terms function as efficient interactive resources when the partners share a visual field. In this case, green, red, blue and yellow can be used unequivocally to move the discussion forward. From the appropriation point of view, however, such deictic resources are not linked to the terms and concepts of geometric reasoning. Conversations where the metaphors ("deck of cards", "frame" etc.) were used, however, contain elements which provide a specific, conceptual premise structuring the discussion and which may lead to appropriation of geometric concepts. This applies also to discussions that had sequences where the pupils discussed on the formal level using concepts such as area and perimeter. In these two latter cases, the discourse of the students is conducive to appropriation in the direction of increasing mastery of geometric reasoning.

In the present case, most of the discussion took place at a relatively superficial level if we use the model by van Hiele as a frame of reference. The contributions of the students generally stayed at Level 1, even though they occasionally were at Level 2. It is obvious that the program was not sufficient to produce other activities and conceptualizations. The students stayed fairly close to the visual impressions, and they to a large extent used deictic language. To reach higher levels of reasoning in the van Hiele model, it is likely that other activities have to be included in the didactic situation. For instance, the program could be made more advanced in terms of the variations in illustrations and exercises offered. But an even better way, in our opinion, would be to involve teachers in processes of learning of this kind. The teacher would be able to raise questions at appropriate points and to introduce links to what has already been attended to in the curriculum. In order to appropriate "scientific concepts" in situations of this kind, the pupils have to oscillate between the concrete and the conceptual/theoretical level. They have to confront their situated experiences with the objectified concepts of geometry, and then go back again to what they see in front of them. In other words, they have to generalize and particularize (Billig, 1996) repeatedly in order to appropriate abstract concepts of the kind that were learning targets here. It seems likely that a teacher has a unique role in providing the kinds of provocations and scaffolds that are conducive to developing and overcoming such tensions between what is observed and some abstract, as yet not mastered, conceptualization. The provocations have to be there interactively and inter-mentally for the students to appropriate them as part of their intra-mental repertoire. The powerful contributions by teachers will lie precisely in the manner in which they manage to focus students' attention on the conceptual implications of the two mediating tools used in this study. And in this case they must also provide interactive support that allows students to realize what is generic from a conceptual point of view in what is visually present here-and-now on the screen.

ACKNOWLEDGEMENT

The research reported here has been funded by The Swedish Research Council and the Knowledge Foundation. This chapter was written while the second author was a Finland Distinguished Professor at the Centre for Learning Research, University of Turku.

REFERENCES

Billig, M. (1996). *Arguing and thinking* (2nd Ed.). Cambridge, England: Cambridge University Press.

Bjuland, R. (2004). Student teachers' reflections on their learning process through collaborative problem solving in geometry. *Educational Studies in Mathematics, 55,* 199-225.

Carlsen, M. (2008). *Appropriating mathematical tools through problem solving in collaborative smallgroup settings.* Kristiansand: Doctoral Dissertations of University of Agder.

Cobb, P., Wood, T., Yackel, E., & McNeal, B. (1992). Characteristics of classroom mathematics traditions: An interactional analysis. *American Educational Research Journal, 29*(3), 573-604.

Cole, M. (1996). *Cultural psychology: A once and future discipline.* Cambridge, MA: The Belknap Press.

Cole, M. & Derry, J. (2005). We have met technology and it is us. In R. J. Sternberg & D. D. Preiss (Eds.), *Intelligence and technology. The impact of tools on the nature and development of human abilities.* (pp. 209-227). Mahwah, NJ: Erlbaum.

Hart, K. M. (1981). *Children's understanding of mathematics: 11-16.* London: John Murray.

Jaworski, B. (2006). Theory and practice in mathematics teaching development: Critical inquiry as a mode of learning in teaching. *Journal of Mathematics Teacher Education, 9*(2), 187-211.

Lemke, J. L. (1990). *Talking science. Language, learning and values.* Norwood, NJ: Ablex.

Mercer, N. (2000). *Minds and words: how we use language to think together.* London: Routledge.

Parzysz, B. (1988). Knowing vs. seeing. Problems of plane representation of space geometry figures. *Educational Studies in Mathematics, 19*(1), 79-92.

Piaget, J. (1970). Piaget's theory. In P. H. Mussen (Ed.), *Manual of child psychology* (pp. 703-732). London: Wiley.

Popper, K. (1959). *The logic of scientific discovery.* London: Hutchinson.

Pramling, N. (2006). *Minding metaphors: Using figurative language in learning to represent.* Göteborg: Acta Universitatis Gothoburgensis.

Säljö, R. (2005). *Lärande och kulturella redskap. Om lärprocesser och det kollektiva minnet* [Learning and cultural tools. On processes of learning and the collective memory]. Stockholm: Norstedts Akademiska Förlag.

Sayeki, Y., Ueno, N. & Nagasaka, T. (1991). Mediation as a generative model for obtaining area. *Learning and Instruction, 1*(3), 229-242.

Schoenfeld, A. (1986). On having and using geometric knowledge. In J. Hiebert (Ed.), *Conceptual and procedural knowledge. The case of mathematics.* (pp. 225-264). Hillsdale, NJ: Erlbaum.

Springer, L., Stanne, M. E. & Donovan, S. S. (1999). Effects of small group learning on undergraduates in science, mathematics, engineering, and technology: A meta-analysis. *Review of Educational Research, 69,* 21-51.

Stålhammar, M. (1997). Metaforernas mönster i fackspråk och allmänspråk [The patterns of metaphors in professional language and general language]. Stockholm: Carlssons.

van Hiele, P. M. (1986). *Structure and insight. A theory of mathematics instruction.* London: Academic Press.

Wertsch, J. (2007). Mediation. In H. Daniels, M. Cole & J. Wertsch (Eds.), *The Cambridge companion to Vygotsky* (pp. 178-192). New York, NY: Cambridge University Press.

Wittgenstein, L. (1953). *Philosophical investigations.* Oxford, England: Blackwell.

Wittgenstein, L. (1980). *Culture and value.* Oxford, England: Blackwell.

Vygotsky, L. S. (1986). *Thought and language* (A. Kozulin, Trans.). Cambridge, MA: MIT-Press.

Vygotsky, L. S. (1981). The instrumental method in psychology. In J. V. Wertsch (Ed.), *The concept of activity in Soviet psychology* (pp. 134-143). Armonk, NY: M. E. Sharpe.

Wyndhamn, J., & Säljö, R. (1997). Word problems and mathematical reasoning-a study of children's mastery of reference and meaning in textual realities. *Learning and Instruction, 7*(4), 361-382.

Internet source: www.mathleague/help/com/area.htm.

In: Learning in the Network Society and the Digitized School   ISBN 978-1-60741-172-7
Editor: Rune Krumsvik   © 2009 Nova Science Publishers, Inc.

Chapter 3

WHAT COULD BE? CREATIVITY IN DIGITISED CLASSROOMS

Avril Loveless
University of Brighton, UK

ABSTRACT

The question 'What could be?' in this article relates to how teachers might work in digitised classrooms to foster creativity. In the UK there are debates about how curriculum reform and technology might meet the future challenges of the network society, and education policies for creativity in schools focus on the benefits of creative experiences to individuals, as well as benefits to society and the economy in preparing participants in the creative and cultural industries. The discussion focuses on two themes: digital movies as tools for learning; and pedagogy for creativity which includes improvisation and skilful neglect. The discussion is supported and illustrated by an account of Creativity and Teacher Education (CREATE), a four year project with student teachers working with digital video technologies in English Primary schools. The project enabled the student teachers to reflect on their own understandings of creativity and creative teaching, and informed the teacher educators in the research, design and development of the undergraduate BA (Qualified Teacher Status).

Keywords: creativity, digital technologies, teacher education, pedagogy.

INTRODUCTION

As this article is being written early in 2008, policy makers and practitioners in the UK are engaged in discussions of a vision for education in the context of socio-technological change to 2025 and beyond. The programme, 'Beyond Current Horizons', is an attempt to identify the broad fields and questions with which education will need to engage in relation to social and technological change in government, industry, education, not for profit sectors and international sectors (DCSF, 2008a). A preliminary discussion paper highlights three categories of activity in which technology might have an impact on society and education, and then poses a question for further discussion (DCSF, 2008b). The first category is automation and artificial intelligence and the practical application of machine intelligence; the second is ubiquitous computing, where information processing is integrated into everyday objects, locations and activities; and the third is the brain/world interface, and how the relationship between the mind and the external world is mediated by technology. The questions that are then posed include two that are of particular interest in the focus of this article: 'To what extent should education 'inherit' its futures from other interests such as business, defence or international development, for example?', and 'To what extent is education about constructing futures and building the contexts in which society, economy and politics develop?' The themes and case studies of this anthology - networked society and the digitized classroom - also embrace these questions about how technologies in educational experiences and purposes are placed in the wider community, society and international dimensions.

Creativity is encouraged and supported in the curriculum and practice of schools yet is a field which holds a number of these tensions of inheritance or shaping. Is the development of creativity in schools to equip learners for participation in the creative industries and knowledge economy, or to foster a quality of creative learning through imagination and experience for its own sake? Is the focus on creativity inherited from the economic demands of a networked, globalised society, or might creative learners play a role in shaping the wider social and economic contexts in the future? How might these different perspectives on creativity be understood and worked through in practice? Do digital technologies make a distinctive contribution as tools and media in creative activity, and how might this challenge pedagogy and the design of learning environments in school traditions? The CREATE project, which is the focus of this article, engages with questions of the affordances of digital technologies for creativity, pedagogy in classroom environments and the role of initial teacher education in the development of the professional knowledge which underpins pedagogy for creativity with digital technologies.

CREATIVITY IN EDUCATION

Creativity can be understood as an interaction between the characteristics and resources of individuals; subject domains; communities; environments; and the affordances of mediating tools and technologies (Csikszentmihalyi, 1996; Loveless, 2002; Sternberg & Lubart, 1999). Definitions of creativity, such as 'imaginative activity fashioned so as to produce outcomes that are original and of value' (NACCCE, 1999 p29) draw attention to concepts; purpose; context; culture; evaluation; and the skills, techniques and expertise required to design and make artefacts, outcomes and experiences for other audiences and participants. Approaching creativity as emerging in interaction has enabled us to pay attention to a number of dimensions: the characteristics, dispositions and processes of individuals and groups; the subject domains in which conceptual connections are made and new knowledge constructed; the places or 'niches' where creativity can flourish or decline; the tools and technologies that shape the creative activities; and the wider social and cultural influences that provide contexts for judgements of originality, purpose and value. These dimensions cannot be easily separated or isolated from the others.

Early interest in creativity in the West tended to be focused around psychological areas relating to personality, cognition and the stimulation of creativity in individuals, but in the last few decades, awareness of the influence of social contexts and environments on the creativity of individuals, groups and organisations has developed (Baer & Kaufman, 2006; Rhyammar & Brolin, 1999; Sternberg & Lubart, 1999). The focus on individuals described characteristics such as openness to experience; independence; self-confidence; willingness to take risk; sense of humour or playfulness; enjoyment of experimentation; sensitivity; lack of a feeling of being threatened; personal courage; unconventionality; flexibility; preference for complexity; goal orientation; internal control; originality; self-reliance; and persistence (Shallcross 1981, cited in Craft, 2000, p13). More recent theories have drawn attention to the multiple factors which influence creative activity and expression, such as motivation and skills (Amabile 1996); the interrelationship of intellectual abilities, knowledge, styles of thinking, personality, motivation and environment (Sternberg & Lubart, 1999); and the interaction between individuals, subject domains and society (Csikszentmihalyi, 1996; Gardner, 1988). It is also useful to think about individuals being actively creative within a medium, in which they have control, and are able to play, take risks, and exercise critical judgement (Robinson, 2001).

Creativity in educational contexts has been approached in different ways, including focussing on creative teaching, teaching for creativity, and creative learning (Craft, 2005), and a number of recent national educational policy developments in the UK have attempted to promote creativity. For example, the 1999 NACCCE report 'All our futures' had considerable influence in the shaping of policy for creative and cultural education. More recent developments include a website of knowledge and practice to inform creative activity in the curriculum (QCA, 2004); a national scheme for Creative Partnerships in which schools work with creative practitioners for curriculum innovation (Creative-Partnerships, 2003); and a framework for 'Nurturing Creativity in Young People' in the use of creative portfolios (Roberts, 2006). These initiatives are put forward in the context of wider debates about innovation in a growing market for creative industries (NESTA, 2006a), and concerns about an 'innovation gap' in the skills and attributes required to create and exploit economic innovation (NESTA, 2006b). There are many issues associated with creativity which our society and education system need to address, not only recognising the influence of economic development, but also of globalisation, community development, social justice, and wisdom (Craft, 2005; Craft, Claxton, & Gardner, 2008).

DIGITAL TECHNOLOGIES AS TOOLS FOR CREATIVITY

The contribution of digital tools to creative endeavour has been reviewed and discussed for some years (see for example, Loveless, 2002, 2007a), and indeed it is interesting to note the attention that they are given in contrast to other media and tools such as paint and brushes in the visual arts, for example. The creative activities which are afforded by digital tools also take place in a wider cultural context in which digital technologies have an impact and influence, recognised in the debates in programmes such as 'Beyond Current Horizons'. Two approaches to the potential of digital tools in activities for creativity can be considered in the context of this case study in teacher education, firstly in capabilities for active learning processes, and secondly in creative endeavour and outcomes.

One way of looking at digital technologies in use is to focus on 'ICT capability' of learner, (where ICT is the acronym for information and communications technology). This relates to understanding and competence with digital technologies in the general processes of dealing with information. The word 'capability' carries the meanings of having power or fitness for a task, being qualified and able, being open to or susceptible to development. It implies a knowledge or skill being turned to use, an ability which is used actively, involving understanding and choice (Loveless, 2003). ICT capability includes the recognition and exploitation of the affordances of the technologies for learning. Digital technologies can be tools which offer learners the potential to extend or enhance their abilities; allow users to create novel ways of dealing with tasks which might then change the nature of the activity itself; or provide limitations and structure which influence the nature and boundaries of the activity. The potential lies not in the technologies themselves, but in the interaction with human intention, activity and tools. Conole and Dyke discuss a taxonomy of the affordances of ICT as: accessibility; speed of change; diversity; communication and collaboration; reflection; multimodality and non-linearity; risk, fragility and uncertainty; immediacy; monopolization and surveillance (Conole & Dyke, 2004). Fisher et al (2006) identified clusters of purposeful approaches to learning with digital technologies, in which there are a number of connections with ideas of creativity, imagination and experience:

- Knowledge building: adapting and developing ideas; modelling; representing understanding in multimodal and dynamic ways;
- Distributed cognition: accessing resources; finding things out; writing, composing and presenting with mediating artefacts and tools;
- Community and communication: exchanging and sharing communication; extending the context of activity; extending the participating community at local and global levels;
- Engagement: exploring and playing; acknowledging risk and uncertainty; working with different dimensions of interactivity; responding to immediacy.

In reviewing and describing the use of digital tools in creative endeavour and outcomes in physical and virtual learning environments, five aspects of process and activity can be identified:

- developing ideas: supporting imaginative conjecture, exploration and representation of ideas;
- making connections: supporting, challenging, informing and developing ideas by making connections with information, people, projects and resources;
- creating and making: engaging in making meanings though fashioning processes of capture, manipulation and transformation of media;
- collaboration: working with others in immediate and dynamic ways to collaborate on outcomes and construct shared knowledge;
- communication and evaluation: publishing and communicating outcomes for evaluation and critique from a range of audiences. (Loveless, 2007a)

The range of creative activity with digital technologies is wide. Creative imagination not only generates ideas, but also discerns those with potential for growth, and there are many examples of digital tools for conjectural play, exploration and developing ideas, from programming in Logo to multi-player online games. Network technologies offer opportunities for making connections with information, case studies, exemplar materials, and creative practitioners. Social software enables users to connect, categorise and retrieve web content, tracing the links made by others. Digital technologies have long been used to create and make meaning, from early manipulations of text and image with word processors and painting programmes to the composition and presentation of multimedia, music and digital movies. Creative collaborations are possible in the networks and exchange of material, and the use of virtual 'space' to create and share work offers a distinctive contribution to collaborations across time and place, often disrupting traditional structures and commercial interests. Digital tools are used to communicate and publish creative outcomes, through showcasing, feedback, tagging, and networking. Mobile and context-aware technologies can bring together experiences of physical and virtual spaces in which people interact with the environments, each other and information sources associated with a particular location. There is a wide scope of creative activity with digital tools in education, through the enthusiasm of pupils and teachers engaging with a variety of technologies as well as through partnerships with experienced creative practitioners. Digital technologies in classrooms can therefore shape creative experience, which will raise challenges to pedagogy and curriculum. Digital video in particular, can offer opportunities for representations of self, yet also challenge pupils' and teachers' expectations and behaviours in classrooms (Pearson, 2005; Potter, 2005).

CREATE: A CASE STUDY OF CREATIVITY AND TEACHER EDUCATION

The case study encompasses activity with four cohorts of student teachers in an English initial teacher education programme, between 2004 and 2007. The research was carried out by a team of three university tutors, and the study was supported in two phases by research grants from the Teacher Training Agency (TTA), and the Creativity Development Fund from the Centre for Excellence in Teaching and Learning in Creativity (CETL-Creativity) in the Universities of Brighton and Sussex. The research questions at the core of the study focused on:

(i)   student teachers' understandings of creativity and reflections on their own creative experiences;
(ii) the contribution of the digital technologies to creative practices;
(iii) developments in professional knowledge and pedagogy in schools and in the University.

The study took place within a taught module called 'Creativity and Digital Technologies', in the BA(QTS) programme at the University of Brighton with four cohorts of student teachers between 2004 and 2006. 60 student teachers were involved over the four years. They were all studying ICT as a specialist subject on either Key Stages 1 & 2 age phase (5-11yrs) or Key Stages 2 & 3 age phase (7 – 14yrs). The module was taught in the final semester of the four year course, after the student teachers had completed all their school placements and most of their undergraduate assignments. They were therefore confident in their experience and expertise as classroom teachers, aware that they had met the national Department for Education and Schools Standards for 'Qualifying to Teach', and were preparing for the final university assessments before graduation. The projects were therefore designed to challenge some of the usual ways of working in university taught modules, in order to provoke new ways of thinking about teaching for creativity with digital media technologies. In the first two years of the study a small group of students who were appointed to jobs local to the university, were included in the study in the first six months of their Newly Qualified Teacher (NQT) year, but this aspect of the project is not considered in this article which focuses on the initial teacher education phase.

Creating, capturing, editing, presenting and evaluating digital movies was the main purpose in the activities, and the work was done in three different contexts: (i) student teachers working together in the University; (ii) student teachers working together with pupils and teachers in local primary schools; (iii) student teachers returning to the University for reflection on and critique of the outcomes. The University provided digital media kits for each phase of the activities: laptops with media manipulation software, digital video cameras, digital cameras and webcams. In the University, the student teachers worked in groups to play with digital video, music, editing and presentation technologies in order to make digital movies and then relate their experiences to recent research and policy initiatives for creativity. Pairs of student teachers then worked intensively with small groups of pupils in schools to create and present digital movies. The topics of these movies drew on a range of subject content areas and included narratives from popular children's books; original narratives; reflections on themes such as 'friendship' or 'bullying'; and mimics of news, sports or documentary programmes on school-based topics. The students later spent time in the schools and University reflecting on the experience and outcomes in relation to developments in their understandings of creativity, the affordances of the activities with digital technologies and challenges to pedagogy. It was recognised that the making of digital movies per se was not necessarily creative, but that the activity offered opportunities to reflect upon and analyse the experience in terms of the conceptual understanding of creativity as interactive, as discussed earlier in this article.

A case study methodology and qualitative data collection methods were used: concept mapping, group and individual interviews, paired 'video diaries', observations, group feedback, analysis of digital movie outcomes, and student teacher reflections. Video materials of both 'work in progress' and the final movies from the students and the children were also collected, viewed and discussed in the groups. Digital technologies were used to represent the data in varied ways, and the data analysis was used to inform the development of the curriculum and pedagogy in successive years of the project. The ethical issues and challenges associated with working with our own students were discussed with the cohorts and permissions were given to use data collected from the different activities. Confidentiality and personal anonymity were guaranteed, although institutional anonymity was not possible, given the reporting requirements of the project funders. The data collected through the variety of methods were analysed independently by the three tutor researchers, who categorised initial emergent themes which were then discussed, modified and agreed. These themes were then used for further analysis of the range of data. Different stages and aspects of the study were reported and disseminated throughout the period of the project (Loveless, 2005; Loveless, Burton, & Turvey, 2006; Loveless, Turvey, & Burton, 2006, 2007; Turvey, Loveless, & Burton, in preparation). Two particular themes emerging from the study will be discussed in this article: digital movies as tools for learning; and pedagogy for creativity.

DIGITAL MOVIES AS TOOLS FOR LEARNING

The range of data identified three aspects of the digital movie making which contributed to the interactive creative experience of the activities: 'Hard Fun', 'Lights, Camera and Action', and 'Mirrors and Traces'.

'Hard Fun' - a term borrowed from Papert's work with Logo (Papert, 1980) - captures the descriptions and observations of the students and children's engagement with the work in progress to capture, compose, edit and project the final movies. The challenge of making the movie itself was demanding, and the capacity of the digital tools, such as the video cameras, editing software and projection facilities, for capture, storage, provisional editing and sharing supported the groups' engagement with the variety of tasks, and focused the concentration required to refine and realise imaginative ideas. These experiences were observed and evaluated as demonstrating the characteristics of 'flow' in creative activity (Csikszentmihalyi, 1996).

'Lights, Camera and Action' was the phrase coined to describe the combination of roles which students and children adopted and developed in order to get the job of movie making done. This ranged from discussing ideas to scripting, designing sets and props, directing, filming, acting, composing, editing, evaluating and promoting. A fluidity in these roles was observed, where the movie-makers changed and moved between roles at different times in the process, taking turns with different technical skills and discussing approaches to solving the problems raised by the variety of tasks. Each of these descriptions can also be related to experiences with drama and film in education, and it might be argued that the digital technologies were merely different tools in familiar contexts. We would suggest, however, that the features of the technologies for these activities were distinctive, not only in making film and media literacy techniques more accessible, but also in shaping the nature of the processes themselves. 'Mirrors and Traces' was used as a category to describe and explain these more distinctive contributions of the digital movie technologies, through the immediacy of feedback on the ideas captured – more colloquially described as 'holding up a mirror to ourselves in the film', and the opportunities for composing, editing and evaluating – or 'leaving traces that we can return to and think about'. Creative learning has been characterised by the qualities of imagination and experience, and the use of digital tools in these activities drew upon and shaped the learners' ideas and activities. After a day's work completing a movie, one child suggested that 'the editing was hard, annoying, frustrating and it got on my nerves sometimes…..but if we didn't do that it would have been a rubbish movie'. Recognising the potential of these digital tools for realizing and fashioning imaginative ideas requires not only a capability with digital techniques, but also an understanding of the connections between them and the purpose and context of those ideas.

PEDAGOGY FOR CREATIVITY: IMPROVISATION AND 'SKILFUL NEGLECT'

The student teachers were aware of, and discussed the differences between creative teaching and teaching for creativity, and how these two approaches interacted with each other. They used their own personal and group experiences of creative work with digital video in order to prepare and plan imaginatively for the activities with children in school, yet found themselves having to draw upon a range of teaching strategies in the immediacy of the activities which challenged two particular aspects of their practice: improvisation in response to the requirements of the moment; and offering space for learners through 'skilful neglect' (Labett, 1988; Loveless, 2007b).

Teachers are expected to demonstrate understanding and capability in planning clear learning objectives and teaching strategies in lessons and schemes of work. Student teachers were therefore experienced in detailed planning and design of activities, yet they encountered some challenges in working on extended and intensive tasks with the children that demanded a more open-ended design. They recognised that they needed room for response to children's imaginative ideas for creating movies which were often also ambitious in meaning and scope. The differences between being well planned and being well-prepared were noted and discussed in the reflections on the work in progress and final outcomes. Being prepared is 'draft' in character; engaging in the design of opportunities and possibilities for pupils; and requiring an openness of mind about the relationship between the subject content, the pupils' response and needs, and the teacher's pedagogical strategies. Such openness of mind helps to make a link between the careful, organized preparation and planning, and the unscripted interactions in the moments of teaching. These moments are similar to experiences of improvisation in which the artistry of teaching is expressed and performed. Student teachers making digital movies with children remarked that they hadn't realised 'how much they knew', until they were able to draw upon their understandings of the potential and constraints of the digital tools, conventions of film and media literacy, and their knowledge of conceptual meanings being expressed in the movies. They also recognised that they needed to be confident enough to be flexible in departing from their initial plans in response to the pupils' conceptual, technical and organisational needs.

'Skilful neglect' is a term used twenty years ago by Labbett writing of her observations of teaching with Logo, and developing strategies for stepping back and offering a safe space for learners to explore, make mistakes, and solve problems. The observations of the cohorts in the CREATE projects recognised these strategies of skilful neglect in some, but not all, of the groups of student teachers and children. Some student teachers worked in quite careful and controlled ways, directing the activities closely and providing technical support and suggestions whenever the children encountered a problem. Others followed the ideas of the children, yet provided few suggestions for refining or shaping them. Some, however, responded in an open way to the children's ideas, but offered a light touch in discussion, questions and technical hints when the children were stuck, or lacking particular skills and knowledge to realise their ideas. They stepped back to let the children explore different possibilities with the digital equipment and the ideas that they wanted to portray, yet were able to step forward when the children found themselves in a cul-de-sac in need of a different approach to the challenge. Such 'skilful neglect' demonstrated degrees of confidence in expertise with the topic and the digital tools, as well as a commitment to supporting active, creative learning for the pupils. Such a pedagogic approach was more comfortable with the disruption to more familiar models of organising time, groupings and resources and indicated an understanding of the benefits of loosening up, slowing down and creating space both for initial exploration and studied fashioning of ideas.

WHAT COULD BE......?

How then do these themes of digital tools, pedagogy for creativity and assessment inform the wider discussion of 'what could be' in digitised classrooms within a networked society? The CREATE project provided the cohorts of student teachers with intensive experiences of creative activity in familiar school classrooms. These experiences involved disruption of the usual timetables and groupings and immersion in closely focused activities from initial planning to public projection, but offered opportunities for detailed reflections on 'making the familiar strange'.

The creative use of digital tools cannot be taken for granted, but requires an understanding of the affordances of the activities with particular technologies to realise imaginative ideas through fashioning with the medium, purposefully and with value. The student teachers needed direct experience for themselves and with children in order to make conceptual connections between the digital tools and the nature of the activity, and move beyond capturing and recording, to manipulating and making meaning with digital resources. Familiar teaching strategies for developing this work were challenged. Not only did the management of the activities need to be reworked in order to provide the children with time and space for immersive, focused experiences, but the pedagogical strategies also needed to reflect changes in time and space. Appropriate preparation reflected the depth of teacher knowledge required to support learning with digital technologies in a curriculum context, and the need for open mindedness and improvisation in response to the children's imagination and creative aspirations. Such knowledge was also drawn upon when making decisions about the safe distance of 'skilful neglect' between pupils and teachers, enabling creative exploration with supported techniques for fashioning and critical evaluation of ideas and outcomes.

These experiences were explored in the context of an Initial Teacher Education course which encouraged student teachers to engage in direct experience whilst developing awareness of the wider policy issues. Initial Teacher Education can play a role in developing understanding by offering opportunities for intensive, focused experiences which disrupt and challenge familiar practices and provide time and space for reflection. An increased focus on creativity in schools, whether for construction of creative expression or reproduction of participation in creative industries, demands an understanding of the complexity of the interactions between creativity, digital tools, learners, teachers and the subject contexts. 'What could be?' might therefore be answered in classrooms which reflect this complexity in the time and space given to learners to engage with digital technologies in focused, authentic activities, and the prepared, responsive pedagogy of teachers with confidence in their learners and in the tools they use to express their creativity.

ACKNOWLEDGEMENTS

The CREATE project was supported by funding from the Teacher Training Agency, and the Creativity Development Fund from the Creativity Centre for Excellence in Teaching and Learning.

REFERENCES

Baer, J. & Kaufman, J. C. (2006). Creativity Research in English-Speaking Countries. In J. C. Kaufman & R. J. Sternberg (Eds.), *The International Handbook of Creativity*. New York: Cambridge University Press.

Conole, G. & Dyke, M. (2004). What are the affordances of information and communication technologies? *ALT-J, Research in Learning Technology, 12*(2), 113 - 124.

Craft, A. (2005). *Creativity in Schools: Tensions and Dilemmas*. London: Routledge.

Craft, A., Claxton, G. & Gardner, H. (Eds.). (2008). *Creativity, Wisdom, and Trusteeship*. Thousand Oaks, California: Corwin Press.

Creative-Partnerships. (2003). *What is Creative Partnerships?* Retrieved 25th August, 2006, from http://www.creative-partnerships.com/aboutcp/

Csikszentmihalyi, M. (1996). *Creativity: Flow and the Psychology of Discovery and Invention*. New York: HarperCollins.

DCSF. (2008a). *Beyond Current Horizons*. Retrieved 24th February 2008, from http://www.beyondcurrenthorizons.org.uk/

DCSF. (2008b). *Previous global futures, technology futures and questions for education: a provocation paper*. London: Department for Children, Schools and Families.

Fisher, T., Higgins, C., & Loveless, A. (2006). *Teachers Learning with Digital Technologies: A review of research and projects*. Bristol: Futurelab.

Gardner, H. (1988). Creative lives and creative works: A synthetic scientific approach. In R. J. Sternberg (Ed.), *The nature of creativity* (pp. 298-321). New York: Cambridge University Press.

Labett, B. (1988). Skilful neglect. In J. Schostak (Ed.), *Breaking into the Curricuulum*. London: Methuen & Co. Ltd.

Loveless, A. (2002). *A Literature Review in Creativity, New Technologies and Learning: A Report for NESTA Futurelab*. Bristol: NESTA Futurelab Available On-line [http://www.nestafuturelab.org.uk].

Loveless, A. (2003). The interaction between primary teachers' perceptions of ICT and their pedagogy. *Education and Information Technologies, 8*(4), 313-326.

Loveless, A. (2005). *Creativity and ICT as Catalysts for Change in Teacher Education*. Paper presented at the World Conference for Computers in Education, Stellenbosch, South Africa.

Loveless, A. (2007a). *Creativity, technology and learning: a review of recent literature (Update)*. Bristol: Futurelab.

Loveless, A. (2007b). Preparing to teach with ICT: subject knowledge, Didaktik and improvisation. *The Curriculum Journal, 18*(4).

Loveless, A., Burton, J., & Turvey, K. (2006). Developing conceptual frameworks for creativity, ICT and teacher education. *Thinking Skills and Creativity, 1*(1), 3-13.

Loveless, A., Turvey, K. & Burton, J. (2006). *Conceptual frameworks for creativity, teacher professional knowledge and digital technologies: a two year study with student teachers and primary school pupils working creatively with DV resources.* Paper presented at the British Educational Research Association Conference, Warwick.

Loveless, A., Turvey, K., & Burton, J. (2007). *Didaktik and Creativity.* Paper presented at the ECER 2007, 'Contested Qualities of Educational Research', Ghent, Belgium.

NACCCE. (1999). *All Our Futures:Creativity, Culture and Education.* Sudbury: National Advisory Committee on Creative and Cultural Education: DfEE and DCMS.

NESTA. (2006a). *Creating growth: How the UK can develop world class creative businesses.* London: National Endowment for Science, Technology and the Arts.

NESTA. (2006b). *The Innovation Gap: Why policy needs to reflect the reality of innovation in the UK.* London: National Endowment for Science, Technology and the Arts.

Papert, S. (1980). *Mindstorms.* Brighton: Harvester.

Pearson, M. (2005). Splitting Clips and Telling Tales: Students Interaction with Digital Video. *Education and Information Technologies, 10*(3), 189 - 205.

Potter, J. (2005). 'This Brings Back a Lot of Memories' - a case study in the analysis of digital video production by young learners. *Education, Communication and Information, 5*(1), 5 - 23.

QCA. (2004). *Creativity: find it, promote it.* Retrieved 22nd January 2005, from http://www.ncaction.org.uk/creativity

Rhyammar, L. & Brolin, C. (1999). Creativity research: historical considerations and main lines of development. *Scandinavian Journal of Educational Research, 43*(3), 259-273.

Roberts, P. (2006). *Nurturing Creativity in Young People.* London: Department for culture, media and sport; Department for education and skills.

Robinson, K. (2001). *Out of our minds: learning to be creative.* Chichester: Capstone Publishing Ltd.

Sternberg, R. J. & Lubart, T. I. (1999). The concept of creativity: prospects and paradigms. In R. J. Sternberg (Ed.), *Handbook of Creativity.* Cambridge, UK: Cambridge University Press.

Turvey, K., Loveless, A. & Burton, J. (in preparation). Recognising value in children's creative engagement with digital video editing and production.

In: Learning in the Network Society and the Digitized School   ISBN 978-1-60741-172-7
Editor: Rune Krumsvik

Chapter 4

DISTRIBUTED TEACHER COLLABORATION: ORGANIZATIONAL TENSIONS AND INNOVATIONS MEDIATED BY INSTANT MESSAGING

Thomas de Lange[1] and Sten Ludvigsen[2]
University of Oslo, Norway

ABSTRACT

This chapter is about a teacher-team using instant messaging in a professional working context. Our empirical case displays a situation in which the teachers are co-writing a *subject report*, which is a document that is providing course information to external examiners. Our study observes how the teacher team uses instant messaging as an embedded communicative tool in the process of writing this report. Our case represents a common situation and the conversations occur naturally as a part of the organized work in the teacher team. The selected empirical case describes and highlights an activity in which the teachers identify a discrepancy not only in the report but also in their teaching practice. The case therefore contains a principal discussion about deeper institutional problems. Our aim is to show how the teachers encounter these problems during the instant messaging and how they follow up their online contributions in a long-term perspective.

INTRODUCTION

This chapter is about a teacher team using instant messaging (IM) in a professional working context. Our empirical case displays a situation in which the teachers are co-writing a *subject report*, which is a document that is providing course information to external examiners. Our study observes how the teacher team uses IM as an embedded communicative tool in the process of writing this report. Our case represents a common situation and the conversations occur naturally as a part of the organized work of the teacher team. The selected empirical case describes and highlights an activity in which the teachers identify a discrepancy between reporting and their teaching practice. The case therefore contains a principal discussion about institutional problems. Our aim is to show how the teachers encounter these problems during the IM and how they follow up their online contributions in a long-term perspective.

The context of our study is vocational media and communication studies at the upper secondary level in Norway. The teacher team we are observing have been working together for almost three years. IM has been a natural and consistent practice of this teacher team and has been used regularly, not only in reporting but also in instructional planning, coordination and other teaching-related work. In these IM conversations, the teachers use several additional electronic resources such as the Internet; electronic files such as documents, pictures, student web-site productions; as well as diverse resources from the local schools learning management system, etc. The team is therefore used to combining several ICT-resources in team-based IM conversations.

The main data in our study is taken from online conversations, supported by reporting documents, instructional plans and a follow-up interview. Theoretically our study is based on cultural-historical activity theory which affords a focus on institutionalized practices.

Subject reporting is in this school context a formal documentation of course contents during a whole school year. The intention of such reports is to provide external examiners with relevant course information before the final course exams. For the teachers at our particular school, subject reporting is generally based on the teachers' own instructional plans. Our analysis will focus explicitly on how the teachers use IM as a tool in the reporting process. They hardly ever discussed their use of this tool during the working process, which they generally used effortlessly during the conversations. However, the teachers do address how their instructional plans are maladjusted toward subject reporting and the course syllabus. In this situation the teachers are describing their own instructional plans, syllabus goals and subject reporting form, etc., as tools guiding essential parts of their professional practice.

Our conception of course syllabus and instructional plans as tools is here especially relevant in relation to conceptions in cultural-historical activity theory (CHAT). In our analysis we introduce core concepts in CHAT in order to understand how the teachers approach the reporting process by using and adjusting various instruments and tools that are part of their professional context. CHAT is here used to identify underlying breakdowns and clashes between the teachers' practice versus official documents and reporting routines. Tensions are here seen as natural features in social activities which hold a potential for productive modification and organizational improvements (Barab, Schatz, & Scheckler, 2004; Yamagata-Lynch, 2003). IM will be seen as an expressive device for a particular type of institutional discourse within the teacher community. The main focus on tensions in our study is based on the discrepancies and frustrations the teachers are describing during these conversations when co-writing the subject report. We will approach this situation by posing the following research questions:

- What outcomes follow from the online discussions and co-writing of the subject report?
- What part does IM play in the process of co-writing the subject report?

The first question focuses on identifying institutional characteristics and tracing the consequences and outcomes following IM interactions. The second question focuses directly on the use of IM as a part of the teachers' professional practice.

Following this introduction, we present a brief review on research on IM in professional contexts. This section is followed by a theoretical outline of CHAT and an explanation of how we are using this theory in our analysis. After presenting the theoretical concepts we will concentrate on our empirical case. This empirical section starts with a broad context description and is followed by presenting the authentic online conversations of the teacher team. The analyses of conversational data are further supported by data from our follow-up interviews, where we outline the more longitudinal outcomes of the issues addressed in the IM dialogue. Finally we will present our findings and draw some conclusions regarding IM as a working tool in our particular context.

INSTANT MESSAGING IN PROFESSIONAL SETTINGS

Instant messaging (IM) is a quick exchange of text-based communication which during the last ten years has become a commonly used resource in diverse social settings (Shin-Yuan, Albert, Yen, & Chang, 2007). The growing use of IM is often explained by the easy access and user friendliness of IM software. IM also holds an appealing quality in its combined synchronous and a-synchronous features: It gives the user a sense of immediacy as a receiver and sender as well as flexibility in when to respond. In this way IM draws on both direct verbal communication (such as face-to-face and phone conversations) and more formal conventions in writing such as in e-mail (Educause, 2005; Aasgaard & Marksten, 2007).

Isaacs and colleagues report that research on IM in professional work generally falls into three categories: A) properties of IM conventions, B) functions and tasks in which IM is used to support, and C) frequency/patterns of IM use (Isaacs, Walendowski, Whittaker, Schiano, & Kamm, 2002). Isaacs' research findings point out that IM essentially takes place over shorter periods of time, that multitasking is frequent and that the participants often switch to other communication media when the conversations run into complex issues and discussions. These findings are confirmed by Lovejoy and Grudin, who in their research point out the informal characteristics in most IM conversations (Lovejoy & Grudin, 2003). Similar findings are unveiled by Nardi and Bradner, who claim that IM usually appears in informal communication, such as quick questioning, organizing social meetings and scheduling (Nardi & Bradner, 2000). General research within this area therefore suggests that IM is successfully used in establishing social bonds, while in professional contexts it functions mainly as a medium for simple task coordination (Contreras-Castillo, Pérez-Fragoso, & Favela, 2006).

Voida and colleagues (Voida, Newstetter, & Mynatt, 2002) have contributed with research that describes structures and conventions in IM as a mixture of written and verbal communication. They emphasise that IM on the one hand refers to text based communication as a-synchronous, edited and hierarchically structured communication; on the other hand, IM resembles face-to-face communication as being synchronous, sequentially structured into clauses and contextually shared in a specific moment. Based on comprehensive interaction analysis, Voida and colleagues conclude that even extensive use of IM has not led to any adequate conventional structures by the users. Rather, their findings imply a general lack of structure and coordination. Their main explanation for this characteristic is the absence of a stable shared forum, which they see as essential for establishing conversational conventions (p. 193).

Research on IM usage leaves us with some concern. Shin-Yuan and colleagues (2007) suggest that IM usage might be suitable for handling quite complex work tasks (Shin-Yuan et al., 2007). In an experimental study conducted on students using either IM or e-mail, Shin-Hung et al. imply that IM was more successfully used than e-mailing in solving both practical tasks and sophisticated problem solving and thereby contradicts Nardi and Bradner's conclusions as well as Voida's findings.

Our own study explores mainly how a teacher team uses IM as one of several tools in writing a subject report. The task of subject reporting is here to be considered as fairly complex inasmuch as it involves putting together a coherent written text on a basis of instructional plans, teaching experiences and completed school projects during a course year. Our study aims partly at understanding how the teachers solve this task by using IM. But in order to understand how this interactional tool is integrated into the teachers' professional practice, we need to see their actions in a closer relation to the institutional context.

USING ACTIVITY THEORY TO CHARACTERIZE THE TEACHER TEAM

Conceptualizing the teacher team as a group commits us to define what this sort of social entity means in reference to our analysis. A basic assumption in our study is the socio-cultural understanding of individual actions mediated through cultural artefacts originally based on Vygotsky's account of artefact-mediated actions:

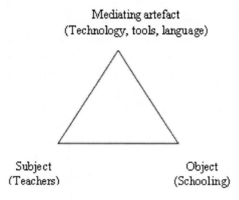

Figure 1. Vygotsky's mediational model (Cole, 1996).

The model above consists of a subject relating to an object by means of mediating artefacts (Vygotskij, 1978; Wertsch, 1998). This implies that the subject is approaching an object (either an entity or a goal) by using various tools and mediational means which influence how the objective is accomplished. The teacher team we are observing has existed for almost three years and has during this time generated a pattern of interaction, negotiations and a joint repertoire of tools, words, experiences and routines. The teacher team also relates to an institutional establishment with diverse roles, rules and community members. Hence, belonging to a teacher team necessarily means that work activities are connected to a domain with certain members and criteria for membership.

Understanding this social practice as a whole means understanding what happens in light not only of actions in the moment but also of the social boundaries, rules and the history of the social group (Cole, 1996; Cole & Engeström, 1993; Engeström, 1994, 1999; Miettinen, 1999, 2005). Engeström's extension of Vygotsy's triangle illustrates how these extensive social features are incorporated into an analytic model:

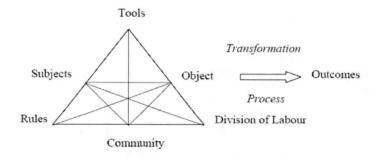

Figure 2. Engeström's extended mediational structure of an activity system.

The activity triangle above represents an extended view of mediated action which incorporates multiple components, such as tools, rules, other members and diverse roles into the analysis of a systemic whole (Foot, 2001). In this way the subject's actions are analytically connected to the community. For our particular case, the term activity implies that the teachers' actions take place within certain social boundaries with a specific history of how tasks have been solved and how tools have been used earlier.

The empirical data used to describe the teacher team as a collaborative practice is in our case based mainly on online interactions, interviews, how they use artefacts and, finally, the outcome of the subject report. These data represent evidence for describing the teachers' activity as a collective, mediational structure. The team is here seen as a community that produces events, actions and outcomes over a lengthy period of time. The following figure depicts the main features that are relevant in the particular collaborative situation which we are observing:

A central aspect in our study is to encapsulate how the teacher team relates to the formal task of subject reporting. The teacher team is here analyzed mainly on the basis of the teachers' online conversations. Our aim is to understand this relation between the teachers' approach toward the object and their use of tools and instruments in creating the outcome of the externally given task of subject reporting.

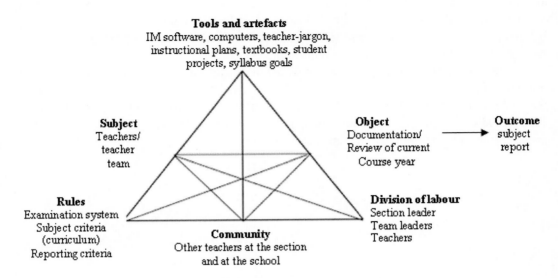

Figure 3. An image of the teacher team engaged in writing a subject report.

Imbalance between elements in social practices is a central feature in CHAT analysis (Engeström & Miettinen, 1999; Miettinen, 1999). Analyzing imbalances and what they cause is a door opener to understand how an activity proceeds and evolves. In our teacher team the subject report is an externally given element. In solving this task, the teachers are basically using the same resources as they use in instructional planning and teaching. Reporting therefore mirrors their teaching practice, but the object of reporting is still very different from the teachers' school activities such as classroom teaching. Here rests a potential imbalance between the externally given object of reporting versus the practice of everyday schooling. This discrepancy is in CHAT termed as a contradiction. Kuutti (1996) explains what this theoretical concept means:

> Activity theory uses the term contradiction to indicate a misfit within elements, between them, between different activities or between different developmental phases of a single activity. Contradictions manifest themselves as problems, ruptures, breakdowns and clashes. Activity theory sees contradictions as sources of development; activities are virtually always in the process of working through contradictions (p. 34).

Contradictions are not to be understood as failures or obstacles, but reveal the "growing edges" or the starting point of development of the activity system (Foot, 2001; 2002). The analysis of contradictions therefore holds the potential of understanding how an organization, institution or work group develops. Contradictions are empirically exposed as tensions or conflicting incidents and always consist of two related coexisting forces. In our case this tension is set in motion by the teacher team using internally created instructional experiences and resources in order to write an externally demanded subject report. In this sense the contradiction is located between the two points of inner practice and external demand.

A second aspect in the concept of contradiction relates to the potential development of a community. Yrjö Engeström describes this as a space of possible change, which is closely related to the Vygotskian notion of proximal development:

The zone of proximal development may be depicted as [an] ... area between actions embedded in the current activity with its historical roots and contradictions, the foreseeable activity in which the contradictions are expansively resolved, and the foreseeable activity in which the contradictions have led to contradiction and destruction of opportunities (Engeström, 1999).

The processes Engeström refers to as contradictory may occur in different events and levels of activity or between different activity systems. Contradictions can trigger changes that consolidate into new practices or turn into nothing. This interpretation of the proximal zone of development is not limited to discrete skills or actions but also refers to emergence of long-lasting changes in social practices (Engeström, 1987).

It is important in the forthcoming analysis of the teacher team to observe tensions that indicate coexisting but contradictive forces in the teachers' course of action. In doing so we wish to examine how the teachers handle these tensions and determine whether it creates a space of proximal development that affects future teaching practice. Our analysis is therefore based on three main aspects:

First, to identify the object that gives direction to the subject reporting. Secondly, to determine how the teachers proceed and accomplish this object by using diverse tools and instruments from their established teaching practice. Here, we will dedicate some of our analysis to the teachers' use of IM in the process of writing the report. Finally, we discuss whether the effort of reporting opens a proximal zone of development for the teachers' own teaching practice.

STUDY DESCRIPTION

Our particular case takes place at "Longhill"[1] Upper Secondary which is a school located in the outer regions of Oslo. The school has approximately 520 learners and 45 staff. The school started offering a course in vocational Media and Communication studies in 2002, and the teachers we observed have been working together since 2003. The Media and Communication course at "Longhill" is organized in a separate section at the school where teachers work in course teams organized around each course level. In the classroom the teachers always work in pairs.

Vocational media and communication is a course that emphasises digitalized media production (Erstad, Gilje, & De Lange, 2007, 2007b). This course includes four main subjects: 1) digital production, 2) visual design, 3) communication and 4) history of expression. The course as a whole strongly emphasises digital production and stresses project work as a principal working method in the classroom (Ministry of Education, 2000, 2001). Consequently all the above-mentioned subjects are integrated into several media projects. In our case at "Longhill", the teachers writing the report have been teaching six projects during the course year, each lasting between 3-7 weeks: 1) photo, 2) sound-production (radio), 3) movie and fiction-production, 4) documentary, 5) advertisement and 6) web-design. All course subjects are integrated into these projects and are assessed on the basis of the students'

---

[1] "Longhill" is a fictional name given to preserve the anonymity of the school.

total achievements in the project periods. The report-writing we are observing is therefore based on projects, taking all four course subjects into account.

There is an established practice at "Longhill" that involves several procedures for instructional planning and documentation. There are, first of all, three local plans (strategic, periodic and year). In addition each teacher has to write a subject report which documents the course contents during a school year. The following table gives an overview of the plans and documentation procedures used at "Longhill" upper secondary:

Table 1. Plans and documentation procedures at "Longhill"

Subject report	Strategic plans	Periodic plans	Year plans
Intention: Providing inform to external examiner about course content/focus through the school year. *Responsibility:* Course teachers/teacher teams	*Intention:* Overarching view of pedagogical and instructional focus at "Longhill" *Responsibility:* School management	*Intention:* Providing a quarterly instructional plan over course year *Responsibility:* Course teachers/teacher teams	*Intention:* Providing and overarching plan for each course year (also used to inform strategic plans) *Responsibility:* Course teachers/teacher teams
External task given by local school authorities	Task given by the local school management	Local teachers' own planning resources	

The subject report (left column) is an official documentation of a course year. This reporting routine is a procedure for giving course-information to both local school administrators and course examiners before the final exams. The reporting procedure is required by local authorities and is monitored and implemented by the local school leaderships. Subject reporting is consequently a standard part of the reporting system in Norwegian upper secondary education (Directorate for Education and Training, 2005).

The subject reports are made available for examiners before the final exams. The main information sources the teachers are using when writing the subject report are their own instructional plans. At "Longhill" the writing of subject reports is based mainly on information from periodic plans (second column from the right). The periodic plans contain detailed descriptions of the classroom instruction and are frequently edited and updated during the quarterly periods. The updating process involves filling in experiences, accomplishments and instructional outcomes during the course year. The teachers also use many additional resources in their subject reports such as diverse textbooks, syllabus goals, school projects, student hand-ins, assignments and graded tests. These are more or less implicit resources that contribute to forming the contents of the subject reports.

The objective with the subject report is to give a content review and account of a whole course year. The teachers are requested to relate the passages in the report directly to the subject syllabus. The subject report is also supposed to contain specific topics presented in class, working methods used in teaching and assessment strategies used both for grading and for supervision of students. In order to avoid a range of different accounts in these reports, the school authorities have provided a standardized and "easy-to-follow" grid-sheet as illustrated below:

Table 2. Standardized form[2] for subject-reporting

Fagrapport - skjema A

Hovedområder i læreplanen/ læreplanmål	Spesielt vektlagte hovedmomenter/ læringsmål (Tema/emner)	Lærestoff/læremidler	Arbeidsmåter/ Organisering av læringsarbeidet	Vurderingsform/ vurderingskriterier	Merknader

Syllabus goals — Emphasised themes/topic — Resources/ Remedies — Working methods — Assessment — Comments

The figure above displays the standardized form of the subject report, where the intention is to give a review of the subject lessons during a whole school year. The grid-sheet framework is divided into note-boxes that specify the use of learning resources, teaching methods, themes/topics and how these aspects are related to the syllabus goals. When filled out, these reports usually stretch over several pages.

The local school management is responsible for distributing these subject reports to the oral examiners in the subject. Our approach in this study is essentially about the process by which a teacher team at "Longhill" is working out how to fill in the grids in the above model for the second year of vocational media and communication studies. The teacher team is doing so mainly on the basis of their periodic plans, but they are also using other instructional resources which they have been using during the course year. Before analysing our data we will give a short description of the course subject on which our teachers report.

The media teachers we observe are writing the subject report at the end of May in 2005, a few weeks before the oral exams. The co-writing process of this report is taking place in the evening. The teachers are sitting in front of their own computers in their respective homes. Their writing of the report is accompanied by an IM conversation in Windows Messenger which has the following user interface:

---

[2]   Form downloaded from the official web-site of the Education Authorities in Oslo: http://www.utdanningsetaten.oslo.kommune.no/getfile.php/utdanningsetaten%20%28UDE%29/Internett%20 %28UDE%29/Skjema/gs/02_Fagrap_2003_2004.pdf.

Figure 4. MSN-Messenger[3] service interface used by the teacher team.

The data from the online conversations involves two teachers and covers a period of about 2.5 hours. The following analysis is shown in four extracts. These extracts are presented chronologically and exhibit only input related to the subject-reporting. The extracts below are therefore purified in the sense that they leave out irrelevant and non-professional comments. On the one hand this conversation as a whole represents a selected slice from the teachers' team-practice of using IM. On the other hand the conversation highlights a tension in the teachers' professional practice.

DATA PRESENTATION

The data in this section are presented in a two-fold structure: The first part contains four extracts from the IM conversation, and starts with extract 1 where the teachers discuss how to coordinate the report writing. In extract 2 the teachers are downloading relevant documents from a shared database. This extract displays how the teachers converse on IM while simultaneously working on electronic files with the subject report. Extract 3 displays how the teachers experience a conflict between the teachers' local periodic plans and the subject syllabus. This conflict is made visible in the writing process of the subject report. At this stage we present a synthesised analysis of the first three extracts in relation to Engeström's activity model. After this we present a fourth extract where the teachers come up with a possible solution to the conflict which illustrates a possible zone of development for the teacher team. In the second part we present interview data one year after the IM conversations. This follow-up interview was a planned continuation of a larger ethnographic study in the same teaching context. The interview was therefore carried out in order to underpin and elaborate on both the IM conversations as well as a larger empirical corpus of video data. These interviews display the long-term measures taken by the teachers and how

---

[3] MSN (**M**icrosoft **N**etwork) Messenger Service is equivalent to Windows Live Messenger today.

they used the IM conversation to improve their teaching practice. In excerpt 1 the teachers start their work on the report.

Extract 1: Coordinating the Work-Flow

4.	M: (20:19:28)	Ready for the subject report?
6.	J: (20:19:42)	Well. Fairly ready
8.	J: (20:20:07)	Downloading all the periodic plans now.
15.	J: (20:24:20)	It'll mostly be about deleting dates, keeping week numbers and adjust a bit on the content, and then it should be fine. The most important things are the main components they (students) have been touching on. We could add a little section on gained competence after each period?
18.	J: (20:25:28)	We have so much material that no one will bother reading it anyway...
19.	M: (20:26:03)	Yeah. That's a smart strategy. So, should we distribute (split) the strategic plans (between us) then. By the way, I don't want to sound
20.	J: (20:26:41)	Distribute is fine. I know I'm going to put less effort into this than you.
21.	M: (20:28:07)	No, no. I have become lazy and I'm not feeling well. No prestige in it for me. They are fine (the strategic plans) as they are I think. What we need, but probably don't need anyway, is to make visible the workbooks – maybe on a separate sheet.
22.	J: (20:29:04)	The workbooks are important. IF we do that, we also have to attach all the handouts that aren't part of the workbooks.
23.	J: (20:29:15)	Or isn't it a point to it?
24.	J: (20:29:21)	Thinking about the external examiners...
25.	M: (20:29:43)	No, we'll just write "divers handouts" and leave it to them to look it up in the strategic plan
26.	M: (20:29:58)	...or?
27.	J: (20:30:06)	Ok
28.	M: (20:30:44)	They didn't ask for it last year.
29.	M: (20:31:29)	How about you starting with the fall (term), and I'll start with the west (wordplay) ehh! Spring
30.	J: (20:32:01)	Yeah, already started with sound (topic in media education)

These conversations go on for about 13 minutes and are mainly about how they will distribute the workload. In line 8 teacher J expresses that he is "downloading" the periodic plans. This clearly indicates that the teachers are using their own instructional plans in this working process. Further, the extract shows how the teachers discuss the level of detail they should provide in their report. A main problem addressed by teacher M seems to be the heavy workload in writing this report and she tries to limit the extent of informational details. This is expressed in lines 21, 25 and 28. The extract ends with a distribution of work, where teacher J already has started with "Sound", which is one of several topics in the media and communication course.

Extract 2: Exchanging Working Material

This extract displays a new stage where the teachers have produced text and start to exchange these report-outlines for feedback. The conversation stretches over a period of almost 20 minutes:

52	M: (20:52:46)	Soon finished with documentary film. I'll send it over so that we'll get an overview. And loud music helps
53	J: (20:53:32)	Send it over. I still have a lot to do on SOUND. A lot of strange things happened in this period… OD (One-day charity work), social science etc. Have to sort out what's relevant.
54	J: (21:04:27)	Received, viewed, read
55	M: (21:04:56)	To much, too little, just right
56	M: (21:07:49)	Proposal for delivery. We hand in a subject report for each project. Then we write in the responsible teachers. In that way we yet again stress that we work project-based
57	J: (21:08:24)	Each project instead of each subject
68	M: (21:08:50)	Good idea?
59	J: (21:09:10)	Yes, it's easier to follow for those who might read this
60	M: (21:09:57)	Waiting for documentary film. Too much, too little, completely horrible objectionable?
61	J: (21:10:56)	Sorry. I think its fine. Think I suddenly became more of a pedant than you regarding SOUND, but it's more incomplete in the first place.
62	M: (21:11:46)	More illuminating feedback please. What can be improved? Don't have to be sorry. Have just deleted a lot of nonsense

The above extract starts with teacher M stating that she is sending over a draft of her report on "Documentary". Teacher J verifies receiving the draft and in line 54 he confirms having read it. This is followed by M asking for feedback on her text in line 55. In line 56 teacher M is then proposing a different structure in their reports. This utterance refers directly to the report draft that recently was sent to teacher J. Teacher M's proposal here is aiming at not filling in reports for each subject but merging the subject reports into project reports together in project periods. Teacher J confirms this proposal in line 57 by saying: "Each project instead of each subject". Lines 60-62 are comments about the contents in the reporting drafts.

A closer look at this extract shows that the teachers' utterances are about exchanging outlines of their reports. They are exchanging electronic files with filled-in grid-sheets and are giving feedback on both the contents and the structure of these written drafts. The utterances are therefore closely connected to a content analysis of electronically exchanged files. The IM conversations and utterances are therefore directly related to the content of their written work.

The teachers also raise principal issues such as the restructuring of the reports. The suggestion to incorporate all subjects into project-period reports diverges from the standardized grid-sheet form. The reasoning for this re-structuring is that the reporting system is based mainly on the differentiation between independent academic subjects as in traditional schooling. Vocational education is based on the project methods which assume that several subjects are integrated into a common problem or theme. This means that teacher M's comments on restructuring the reports (line 56) also are a declaration of principles.

This proposal of restructuring the report indicates a tension between academic and vocational courses at the local school. Initially, all teachers are asked to fill in an identical standardized form divided into separate subjects. By pointing out "…that we yet again stress that we work project-based", teacher M indicates that reporting of separate subjects is unreasonable in their teaching context. This extract also demonstrates how IM is used as an effective tool to accentuate and emphasize problematic elements not only in reporting as such, but also in the teachers' professional practice. These conversations make apparent the underlying tension between the teacher's commitments to a vocational and project-based teaching practice in media studies and the traditional academic focus on divided subjects.

Extract 3: Syllabus Goals versus Teaching Practice

The next extract follows two minutes later. This sequence pictures how the teachers discuss the above-mentioned tensions between academic versus vocational teaching, in relation to syllabus goals:

68	J: (21:13:03)	Think that the learning goals should be more specific.
69	M: (21:14:01)	Oh no, have the energy to write zip and nothing (?). I'm just going to check how thorough Siv is (head of the section). I won't struggle with this any further. Extremely unmotivated (?). Refuse to put anything in there.
71	J: (21:15:18)	What are they supposed to go through regarding learning goals? It's important to emphasise the main points we have been working with. What learning goals in the period have contributed to the attainment of syllabus goals?
72	J: (21:15:58)	Siv has been clear on that in her example. It's the column she's been filling in for the most part…
73	M: (21:16:21)	I don't care, refuse. Next year.
74	M: (21:16:35)	Don't get paid for working that much.
75	J: (21:17:54)	No, I agree. This is a lot of work, and we know that it won't be used in the way it is supposed to. As I mentioned, better to sum up the competence they are supposed to attain?
76	J: (21:18:31)	Or just leave it as it is….
77	M: (21:18:47)	REFUSE AGAIN. I JUST DON'T HAVE THE ENERGY AND ESPECIALLY NOT WORKING THIS MUCH. AND I'M BEING HONEST WITH THIS. I'M SICK AND TIRED OF DOING THINGS THAT ARE OF NO IMPORTANCE REGARDING OUR

		TEACHING.
78	J: (21:19:21)	…!
79	M: (21:20:55)	Its no use including all of the syllabus goals, in project-based work the reasoning is that the students just as much take part by setting goals
80	M: (21:21:44)	I see your point, but if one wants do this, it needs to be done from the beginning. It's impossible to do it in a couple of evenings

In the extract above the teachers are discussing how to integrate the learning goals defined in the subject syllabus into the subject report. This integration of goals into the subject report is a standard directive given by the predefined grid-sheet in the reporting form[4]. The teachers are thereby requested to connect the contents in their classroom lessons to specific curricular goals. What teacher J is pointing out in lines 68 and 71 is that this connection seems to be weak in their reports. Teacher M responds with a rather heated comment and refuses to spend more time on working out this connection (lines 69, 73 and 74). In lines 75 and 76 teacher J is accepting this rather passive approach to the problem, for one thing by pointing out that the report "… won't be used in the way it's supposed to…". The teachers do not go thoroughly into what this discrepancy really means. But in the following three utterances in lines 77, 79 and 80, the tension from extract two arises yet again and is very explicitly spoken in line 79: "It's no use including all of the syllabus goals, in project-based work the reasoning is that the students just as much take part by setting goals". Teacher M is here directly criticising the reporting regime to be inadequate for them. In project work goals are supposed to be defined and generated within the project by the project participants. Pre-defined goals are therefore according to teacher M a symptomatic error that represents the typical academic subject division which is embedded in the reporting sheet. This paradoxical position between the reporting procedure and the teaching practice in vocational media studies seems to be very upsetting for teacher M in this writing process. This frustration is expressed in line 77, where teacher M is using capital letters to state her point; a frustration based mainly on the notion that subject reporting misses out on core features in their own project-based teaching.

Understanding the tensions displayed in this last extract calls for an analysis by addressing all the above excerpts. We will do this in order to reveal how the reporting process has uncovered a latent tension within the teachers' team and their teaching practice. Below we will illustrate this in a visualized form within the activity model. The essence here is to bring forward the tension between subject reporting as a procedure versus the project-based teaching practice in the teacher team:

---

[4] Op. cit 11, table 2: Column 1 in the grid-sheet.

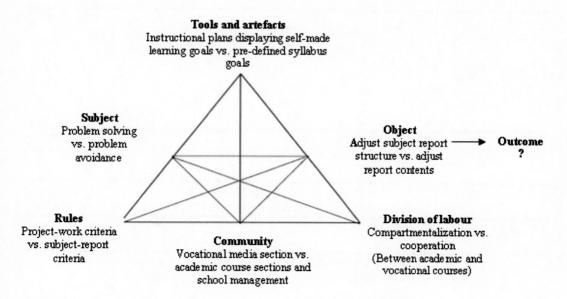

Tools and artefacts
Instructional plans displaying self-made
learning goals vs. pre-defined syllabus
goals

Subject
Problem solving
vs. problem
avoidance

Object
Adjust subject report
structure vs. adjust
report contents

**Outcome
?**

Rules
Project-work criteria
vs. subject-report
criteria

Community
Vocational media section vs.
academic course sections and
school management

Division of labour
Compartmentalization vs.
cooperation
(Between academic and
vocational courses)

Figure 5. Tensions expressed by the teachers during the writing process of the subject report.

What we see from the illustration above is that both practices (reporting and project-based teaching) are of a contradictory and paradoxical nature. In the teachers' conversations they seem to differ in the sense that it is impossible both to report on the basis of the reporting regime and at the same time to respect the ground rules in project-based teaching. This seemingly hopeless situation leads to frustration.

As we mentioned in the theory section, the concept of contradiction in CHAT is empirically exposed as tensions or conflicting incidents. Moreover, these tensions are not failures but a potential for growth and development (Foot, 2001). But the potential for development is not readily at hand but needs to be created. The teachers are here in a situation where they can either conform to or go beyond the given structures in their activity, which illustrates the conception of the proximal zone of development.

In essence, this means that the tension we see in the teachers' conversations is between the fixed structures of reporting on the one hand and strict rules in their project-based teaching practice. The zone of proximal development is somewhere in between and according to Engeström therein lies the opportunity for transition. In our next extract we are looking more closely at how the teachers approach this "space of opportunity" in the IM conversation:

Extract 4: Suggesting a Solution

133.	M: (22:13:57)	I actually feel that I learn a lot from this which is of value regarding next year.
134.	J: (22:14:54)	Concerning adjusting the plans in relation to filling in the subject reports??? :)
135.	M: (22:15:44)	Regarding thinking through actual learning goals before a project.- think that we have a lack of visibility on this towards the students

136.	M: (22:16:56)	For example, we have written following learning goals in the start-up of the web-project: - Know about basic differences in information pages, commercial pages and portfolio on the web. - Be able to present individual goals in a project - Be able to actively use the analytic chart (scheme) in the process of developing suggestions and ideas
137.	M: (22:17:41)	If the students would have seen these goals on print before kick-off (of the projects) we could have avoided this information disorder (confusion). What do you think?
138.	J: (22:17:51)	**Yes, agree, learning goals are more important than syllabus goals as they are drawn up in the existing syllabus. Prefer new syllabuses**
139.	M: (22:19:16)	Why haven't we been better at writing down these then?
140.	J: (22:19:42)	**Learning goals give direction to our projects. Those are the ones used to measure the students, not additive and subtractive colours…**
141.	M: (22:20:17)	I indeed have a lot to talk about in colleague-counselling. The factor of input is going to develop substantially next year.
142.	M: (22:22:27)	And I think that this dialogue we are having shows the importance of the team. Even in vain and mentally slightly aggressive state one finds oneself in an ecstatic stage of learning and development. Wouldn't have happened without this chat. At least not this effectively/quickly. I'm <:o) for that.
143.	M: (22:28:18)	I've just come up with something which I at the moment find rather clever. I'm putting the heading over the first column syllabus goals that follow the part-process in the project. The example in the same row as the learning goals I have sent with the heading: "Start-up in web project". This makes THE WHOLE THING SO DAMN MORE EASY-TO-FOLLOW. AUREKA
144.	J: (22:29:09)	Don't get it…
145.	M: (22:29:42)	I'll send it over. – But not quite finished yet. Do you prefer seeing it now or wait until I'm finished.
146.	J: (22:29:51)	Finished
147.	M: (22:31:07)	I get it. The ones I'm sending you are of course not completely finished, but sketches. Thought I'd write through it tomorrow. But I'm probably going to spend some time on the web project; going to try out this new thing.
148.	M: (22:39:47)	Suddenly, all of our strategic plans appear so scrappy. I'm a bit embarrassed.

In this extract the dialogue between the teachers is taking a different and rather unexpected turn. It starts with teacher M pointing out in line 133 that this process in fact is a substantial learning experience to her. Teacher J seems more sceptical, and asks if she finds it a great learning experience to fill out a pre-structured form (134). Teacher M rejects this and starts explaining that the learning experience in fact points towards constraints in their own teaching practice: "Regarding thinking through actual learning goals before a project - think that we have a lack of visibility on this towards the students". This utterance is a turning point in the sense that teacher M seizes an opportunity to improve their own periodic plans and eventually make the goals of their teaching clearer for their students. This utterance is followed by an actual revision of how to structure and model their instruction plans. In line 143 teacher M has employed her new idea and seems excited about it.

What seems to be the innovative idea in this extract is that teacher M is putting together "heading over the first column of syllabus goals" with the row of "learning goals". What she also is saying is that their own instructional plans have a weakness by not connecting learning goals with syllabus goals. Learning goals do here mean the practical aims set for the classroom activities, while the syllabus goals are the general aims set in the national curriculum. What the teachers have been struggling with is making this connection so that the students can see what the practical efforts in the classroom are supposed to realize in the subject syllabus. Although this situation seems to be a momentary uncovering of a contradiction and release of the tension, teacher M points out that realizing this innovative adjustment also demands a working period, thereby slowing down the process in the conversation. The utterance in line 147 clearly indicates that this process is going to take some time: "... I'm probably going to spend some time on the web project; going to try out this new thing". She is seizing the opportunity opened up by the tension created between reporting and their instructional practice. This last mentioned preparation decides whether the contradictions are innovatively resolved or end up in stranded opportunities.

Whether this opportunity is realized needs to be established based on the outcomes of either the report writing process or the teachers' adjusted periodic plans. In order to establish whether this has happened, we need to employ slightly different data describing the aftermath of the teachers' online discourse. In order to do so, we carried out a follow-up interview with the involved teachers. This follow-up interview displays the progression after the IM conversations and we are also given the opportunity to cross-check the tensions we claim appeared in the teachers' discussions.

OUTCOMES: ONE YEAR LATER

We carried out follow-up interviews almost one year after the IM conversations above. These follow-up interviews were generally oriented toward the teachers' classroom practice and assessment routines. We also asked them to point out things that were important regarding their own professional development during the last year but avoided to ask leading questions about the subject reporting incident.

During the interview, both teachers M and J explain that the subject syllabus is a demanding but important document for their instructional planning. Teacher J explains that the syllabus is an important guide for both students and teachers in the sense that it provides a set of premises and knowledge standards for what the students are supposed to learn. The problem is that the students have trouble understanding the syllabus; as teacher J explains:

"… over and over again the (students) said 'we don't get it, we don't get it…'". Teacher J goes on explaining how they experienced this problem in their teaching practice and in writing their periodic plans:

> *Teacher J:* We were very focused on the subject syllabus; that the students ought to understand the syllabus goals. But we did not "translate" the goals at all. We had to make it much clearer by connecting (the syllabus) goals to our own teaching and what we expected the students to learn.

Teacher J here describes the problem teachers were experiencing in carrying out their responsibility to make the students understand how syllabus goals are connected to the tasks and doings in the classroom. He also expresses a self-critique in this respect; that their working methods failed to connect classroom tasks and doings with syllabus goals. They found themselves struggling with the syllabus and as a result the students felt alienated from the curriculum. Hence, one of the most significant efforts for these teachers during the last year was to bridge this gap by "translating" syllabus goals into locally defined tasks and doings defined in the periodic plans. On basis of this information we asked the teachers to pinpoint where and when this idea of "translating goals" happened:

> *Teacher M:* It happened when we wrote the subject reports.
> *Teacher J:* Yes. We discovered that it was difficult to write the reports because we didn't really know what they had attained and learnt in each (project) period.
> *Researcher:* Was it here that you came up with the solution?
> *Teacher M:* Yes, it was. It was an early stage. I don't remember if it was him or me, but I remember that we came up with an idea which we formulated on MSN.

The teachers are here referring to the IM conversation we have analysed in this chapter. The specific idea they are referring to is in this IM conversation explicitly expressed in extract number 4, line 143:

143.	M: (22:28:18)	I've just come up with something which I at the moment find rather clever. I'm putting the heading over the first column syllabus goals that follow the part-process in the project. The example in the same row as the learning goals I have sent with the heading: "Start-up in web project". This makes THE WHOLE THING SO DAMN MORE EASY-TO-FOLLOW. EUREKA

This idea of connecting "syllabus goals" with "learning goals" was a first step in resolving a key contradiction between the local classroom and teaching practice and the course syllabus. It took the teacher team almost a year to materialize this idea into plans, reporting documents and actual classroom teaching. Extract 4, which we referred to as the turning point in the teachers' online conversations, is in the interview pinpointed as the starting point for reorganizing periodic plans to make the syllabus goals clearer to both students and teachers. The tension emerging in the online conversation is therefore confirmed in the follow-up interviews. The discrepancy between local instructional plans versus syllabus goals is emphasized in these interviews. If we yet again apply the activity model into this context, the effort in realizing the above idea has now materialized itself in a concrete outcome:

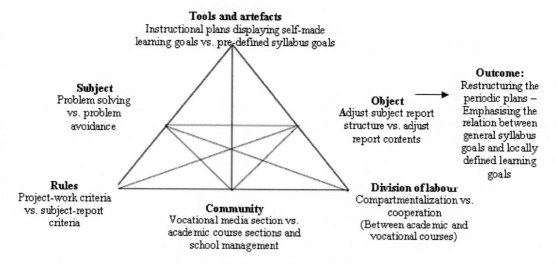

Figure 6. Outcomes following from the writing process of the subject report.

The above model illustrates how the tensions opened up a way to connect the contradicting features in an experimental outcome of new periodic plans, which in detail describe how tasks and doings are connected to syllabus goals. As we mentioned in the theory section, contradictions are viewed as conflicting incidents and the conflict which the teachers felt most pressing was the failure to put together their teaching with the subject syllabus. This tension was articulated in the IM conversation but the solution was not immediately realized. The conversation was a first step which created a zone of proximal development. Improving their plans was a stepwise process which gradually seems to release this tension. By implementing actual improvements in the periodic plans and creating overall competency plans the teachers are still constructing new premises for their teaching practice. One of the most important aspects in this process is, according to the teachers, the creation of a new planning tool guiding their teaching practice. The teachers go beyond the given structures in their activity. These improvements do not discard their practice. Rather, they involve adjustments which seem important to both teachers and students.

DISCUSSION AND CONCLUSIONS

Our analysis above displays an empirical slice of a professional teacher context. In this final section we wish to confront these empirical investigations in relation to the research questions presented in the introduction. In relation to the first research question, "What outcomes follow from the online discussions and co-writing process?", our analysis mainly reflects a gradual and chained process. This process stretches from identifying a felt discrepancy between reporting and teaching practice, the repair which involves the discovery of an idea during the online conversations and eventually the creation of new/adjusted tools. The creation of the new tool opens up a potential improvement of instructional planning and classroom practice. This process can be summarized in the following table:

Table 3. Chained process following the online conversations

Contradiction	New ideas	New tools	Potentials
Expectations in subject syllabus goals vs. daily working routines with locally defined tasks and learning goals	Directly connecting syllabus goals with locally defined tasks and learning goals	Merged chart columns with the periodic plans and subject reports; physically displaying connection with local tasks and syllabus	Give meaning to syllabus goals. More logical subject reports More coherent project periods Better connection between course levels

Potentials described to the far right in the table above refer to the teachers' own statements that the process of adjusting the periodic plans opens an awareness and new opportunities for the whole vocational section at "Longhill". In this sense we find it reasonable to claim that the outcome of the process is that the teachers have seized the opportunity given in a zone of proximal development. They have identified a problem and are introducing new tools to resolve this problem by adjusting their teaching practice.

Our second research question, "What part does instant messaging play in these outcomes?", focuses explicitly on how the teachers are using IM as a technical and communicative device during the first phase of this changing process. First of all, the MSN conversation in our case covers a specific work-mode in the report-writing process. For the teachers this reporting process is a matter of formality, initially without a deep value for their work in the classroom. What then happens is that the teachers, as a result of writing the report, pinpoint several problems in their teaching practice and periodic plans. In this process of pinpointing the IM conversation is essential. The informal jargon in IM allows the teachers to communicate these problems released from the rigid format of the subject report. Above all, the electronic exchange of report drafts provides a key source of information which gives the teachers the opportunity to pinpoint the problems in a very precise manner; not only concerning reporting as such, but also concerning their own instructional plans and syllabus goals. These issues are not superficial but substantial in the process of realizing a curriculum in practice.

We are careful about drawing a parallel between our empirical case and the theoretical notion of expansive learning as described by Engeström, who explains that expansion to him is: "… essentially a social and practical process, having to do with collectives of people reconstructing their material practice" (1987, p. 205 ff). So far our case resembles this relatively vague description. It is although doubtful that this process exemplifies a "… mastery of expansion from actions to a new activity" (ibid, p. 83 ff). We suggest that our findings display an important institutional development, but it is not a total transformation.

Going back to the research on IM lets us repeat the disorderly characteristics exposed in several studies. IM communications were described as short-lived, usually covering simple topics, distinguished by lack of communicative conventions which often led to tensions and dissolution of the conversation. The strong contrast between this research and our own findings is that the teachers in our case seem to have established coherent conventions and that this sort of consistency opens new possibilities in their professional practice. What we see from our case is a conversation that lasts for more than two hours and not only handles complex problems, but also is an arena for creative ideas. From these findings we conclude that our analysis reveals that it is possible to elucidate complex issues in IM conversations. Our study in this sense resembles Shin-Hung's assertions that IM might have a potential in doing both practical tasks as well as sophisticated problem solving. The main difference here is that Shin-Hung and colleagues have conducted on basis of an experimental study, while our case is based on a real life situation. Our example might be an exception in the sense that it presents a starting point for a more extensive readjustment of an institutional practice. Nevertheless, our case exemplifies that IM can facilitate and represent innovative collaborative processes. This reveals a potential that should be explored by further research.

Our analysis highlights yet another finding. This relates to teaching and planning on the one hand and official curriculum aims and standards on the other. The intention with curricular documents is to provide general criteria for teaching and learning in schools. Curricular aims serve as general guidelines to plan, manoeuvre, and assess classroom activities. In one way or another, these guidelines apply to all the people populating classrooms and schools. This also means that curriculum aims are truly *general* in nature. The challenge with general standards of this kind is that they need to be concretizes. Concretization of this sort is like adding "flesh and blood" to a modelled skeleton. This process of concretization calls for the teacher's active selection of methods, resources, handling of conflicts, etc., and is a crucial part of professional teaching. We believe that our analysis of the IM conversations reveals exactly this; an effort and contribution to make general aims understandable within a specific classroom context. To display such a process "in situ" is valuable on its own right. But what these data also display is how these teachers realize this gap between formal aims and classroom actions on basis of IM conversations. The IM conversation did serve as a connecting medium between different levels of abstraction, where the teachers turned curriculum aims and reporting schema into their own practical working tool. This connection was neither an explicit part of the subject reporting form nor a part of their planning practice before this conversation. In this sense, MSN as a medium contributed in accommodating for a more integrated teaching practice.

REFERENCES

Aasgaard, B. & Marksten, O. M. (2007). Kartlegging av bruk og behov for chat- og im-tjenester ved uio.[Mapping the use and needs of chat- and im- services at the University of Oslo] Report a: USIT, University of Oslo.

Barab, S., Schatz, S. & Scheckler, R. (2004). Using activity theory to conceptualize online community and using online community to conceptualize activity theory. Mind, Culture and Activity, 11(1), 25-47.

Cole, M. (1996). Cultural psychology. A once and future discipline. Cambridge, Massachusetts: Harvard University Press.

Cole, M. & Engeström, Y. (1993). A cultural-historical approach to distributed cognition. In G. Salomon (Ed.), Distributed cognitions. Psychological and educational considerations. Cambridge: Cambridge University Press.

Contreras-Castillo, J., Pérez-Fragoso, C., & Favela, J. (2006). Assessing the use of instant messaging in online learning environments. Interactive Learning Environments, 14(3), 205-218.

Directorate for Education and Training. (2005). Muntlig avgangsprøve i grunnskolen med bruk av ikt. Generell innledning til eksemeloppgavene. In Utdanningsdirektoratet (Ed.).

Ministry of Education. (2000). Subject syllabus for upper secondary education. The media and communication area of study. Specialized subjects in the media and communication foundation course: Ministry of Education, Research and Church Affairs.

Ministry of Education. (2001). Subject syllabus for upper secondary education - the media and communication area of study; specialized subjects - advanced course i. Media and communication p002: The Norwegian Board of Education.

Educause. (2005). Seven things you should know about instant messaging. Advanced Learning Through IT Innovation, November 2005, retrieved from http://educause.edu/ir/library/pdf/ELI7008pdf

Engeström, Y. (1987). Learning by expanding - an activity-theoretical approach to developmental research. Orienta-Konsultit Oy, Helsinki.

Engeström, Y. (1994). Teachers as collaborative thinkers: Activity-theoretical study of an innovative teacher team. In I. Carlgren, G. Handal & S. Vaage (Eds.), Teachers' minds and actions. Research on teachers thinking and practice. London: The Falmer Press.

Engeström, Y. (1999). Activity theory and individual and social transformation. In Y. Engeström, R. Miettinen & R. Punamäki (Eds.), Perspectives on activity theory (pp. 19-38). Cambridge: Cambridge University Press.

Engeström, Y. (1999). Innovative learning in work teams. In Y. Engeström, R. Miettinen & R. Punamäki (Eds.), Perspectives on activity theory. Cambridge, New York: Cambridge University Press.

Engeström, Y. & Miettinen, R. (Eds.). (1999). Introduction. Cambridge: Cambridge University Press.

Erstad, O., Gilje, Ø. & De Lange, T. (2007). Re-mixing multimodal resources: Multiliteracies and digital production in Norwegian media education. Learning, Media and Technology, 32(2), 183-198.

Erstad, O., Gilje, Ø. & De Lange, T. (2007b). Morgendagens medieprodusenter. Om mediafagselevers produksjonspraksiser i videregående skole. (media producers of tomorrow. Media production practices in Norwegian upper secondary education).Oslo: University of Oslo, Faculty of Education. Unipub.

Foot, K. (2001). Cultural-historical activity theory: Illuminating the development of a conflict monitoring network. Communication Theory, 11(1), 56-83.

Foot, K. (2002). Pursuing an evolving object: A case study in object formation and identification. Mind, Culture and Activity, 9(2), 132-149.

Isaacs, E., Walendowski, S., Whittaker, S., Schiano, D. J., & Kamm, C. (2002). The character, functions, and styles of instant messaging in the workplace. Paper presented at the Computer Supported Cooperative Work, Philadelphia.

Lovejoy, T. & Grudin, J. (2003). Messaging and formality: Will IM follow in the footsteps of email? Paper presented at the INTERACT 2003, Zürich, Switzerland.

Miettinen, R. (1999). The riddle of things: Activity theory and actor-network theory as approaches to studying innovations. Mind, Culture and Activity, 6 (3), 170-195.

Miettinen, R. (2005). Object of activity and individual motivation. Mind, Culture, and Activity, 12 (1), 52-69.

Nardi, B. & Bradner, E. (2000). Interaction and outeraction: Instant messaging in action. Paper presented at the Computer Supported Collaborative Work, Philadelphia.

Shin-Yuan, H., Albert, H. H., Yen, D., & Chang, C.-M. (2007). Comparing the task effectiveness of instant messaging and electronic mail for geographically dispersed teams in Taiwan. Computer Standards & Interfaces, 29(2007), 626-634.

Voida, A., Newstetter, W. C. & Mynatt, E. D. (2002). When conventions collide: The tensions of instant messaging attributed. Paper presented at the Human Factors in Computing Systems, Minneapolis, MN.

Vygotskij, L. S. (1978). Mind in society - the development of higher order psychological processes. Cambridge, Massachusetts, London, England: Harvard University Press.

Wertsch, J. V. (1998). Mind as action. New York, Oxford: Oxford University Press.

Yamagata-Lynch, L. C. (2003). Using activity theory as an analytic lens for examining technology professional development in schools. Mind, Culture and Activity, 10(2), 100-119.

In: Learning in the Network Society and the Digitized School   ISBN 978-1-60741-172-7
Editor: Rune Krumsvik   © 2009 Nova Science Publishers, Inc.

Chapter 5

RETHINKING THE PRINCIPLES OF PERSONALISATION AND THE ROLE OF DIGITAL TECHNOLOGIES

Tim Rudd

Futurelab,UK

ABSTRACT

Personalisation has been a key concept introduced into the UK educational arena this decade. Championed as a driver for systemic change to modernise education and to make it more flexible, dynamic and relevant for learners[1] in the twenty first century, it promised to offer greater choice and voice for learners. Following ministerial changes however, the concept appears to have stagnated somewhat and its theoretical and philosophical underpinnings have been under explored and changes in educational practice appear to be slow, confused and hampered by structural barriers. This paper argues it is time to reconsider the central tenets of choice and voice and consider how new technologies might be used as transformational tools to empower learners rather than as 'content delivery tools' for current system requirements. It is also argued that there is a need for policy makers and practitioners alike to engage more thoroughly with new ways of learning, teaching, participation and changes in practice that these new technologies can facilitate in order to deliver the systemic changes required by a truly personalised education system.

INTRODUCTION

The Origins of Personalisation in UK Education

The concept of personalisation has become a key concept in UK educational debates this decade. Initially, the term was brought into broader parlance in relation to developments in public sector services to summarise the types of changes required to modernise systems

---

[1] The term learner is employed in this paper to cover people in a whole range of people in the formal sector within the UK education system, although the main arguments presented are those within compulsory education.

(Campbell et al. 2007) and to harness the opportunities in the emerging 'electronic marketplace'. Its broader basis is partly derived from marketing theory (Hartley 2007) and the analysis of changes occurring in both patterns of production and consumption.

In the 1980's a range of theses which mapped the emergence and changes in the capitalist mode of production and organisation became prevalent. Whilst there are clear differences in their exact analyses, as well as criticisms of their interpretations (see for example Luarila & Preece 2003), terms like post Fordism, neo Fordism, Japanization and so forth, drew on a range of different perspectives, fields and conceptual and theoretical traditions, to chart the sorts of organisational changes in contemporary society. One such thesis, put forward by Piore and Sabel (1984), suggested that the era of mass production had been replaced by one of 'flexible specialisation', whereby consumers were increasingly being offered far greater choice in terms of products and services they could acquire to suit their personal needs and requirements. In turn, it was argued, this required the re-organisation of business and production models to ones which could offer greater flexibility and responsiveness. It was this thesis that underpinned the concept of personalisation which was introduced by some key researchers and the Government, whilst David Miliband, the then Minister of State for School Standards, was in office. In his speech at the North of England Education Conference (Miliband 2004a) he stated that we needed to draw on wider changes and developments in order to modernise education, improve standards, and ensure learning and teaching were more relevant. There was a clear emphasis on the need to focus not on what was taught but the way in which it was taught, delivered and organised, with an emphasis on providing greater *choice* and more *voice* for learners. Miliband was clear that the introduction and subsequent realisation of this concept would lead to systemic reform.

Personalisation then, had been introduced as a concept to guide educational transformation and a number of researchers and theorists began to develop the concept further, indicating what it might mean in practice. Hargreaves (2003; 2004), for example took the theoretical underpinnings and suggested there were nine gateways, or levers through which to introduce change. These are; the curriculum; advice and guidance; assessment for learning; learning to learn; school organisation and design; workforce development; new technologies (ICT); mentoring; and student voice. Leadbetter (2004) emphasised the need to engage learners in negotiation around the design of their own education through the development of individualised 'learning pathways', thereby creating greater responsiveness in the delivery of educational services. A number of other theorists, researchers and commentators also rose to the challenge and began help turn a somewhat abstract concept into something more tangible but it is debatable to what extent this translated into classroom practice and broader practitioner or public discourse.

The Stagnation of the Concept and the Resulting Confusion

Since its introduction, the concept appears to have lost some of its dynamism and transformational utility. Once Miliband moved from his position of Secretary of State for Standards, the theoretical basis of its development appeared to receive far less attention. Its increasing appropriation as a party political tool meant there was greater emphasis on its 'delivery'. Unfortunately political delivery of the concept required tangible measures but most of those that were operationalised resonated with existing system requirements and policy commitments, which to some degree mediated transformational possibilities. This also occurred at a time before wide and thorough debates and understandings about how the concept would translate into practice had materialised amongst the practitioner community. What has resulted seems to be a relatively incoherent and unclear utilisation in practice, with most personalised practice happening at best at the 'shallow' end of the personalisation spectrum, offering learners greater choice to navigate existing or pre defined content.

Others take this argument one step further and suggest that the concept should be viewed with significant cynicism because not only is it used so loosely that it represents little more than a 'duplicitous gimmick' (Beadle 2006) but also that its inherent 'political correctness' renders it redundant (Paludan 2006). The problem however may not lay with the concept itself; but through limited theoretical analysis and broader discussion of its underlying principles; the 'backward engineering' that has occurred to try and fit with other aspects of existing policy and practice; and the subsequent inability to effectively translate it into meaningful practice of a more 'deeply personalised' kind within the confines of existing systemic requirements.

To demonstrate the latter point more clearly, Leadbetter (ibid.) and others have suggested that personalisation can be viewed along a spectrum ranging from 'shallow' personalisation on the one hand, - which might be described as nearer to a form of mass customisation of education provided for learners, through to 'deep' personalisation - where individual learning 'pathways' are negotiated specifically catering for the needs of each learner and where approaches to the organisation, management, form and function of schools change in response. Yet 'deeply personalised' approaches remain largely absent to date and furthermore, the concept has been misappropriated as a 'buzz word' to legitimise decisions, or is regularly translated 'tokenistically', often by those supplying products and services who wish to be seen as in step with policy and the new related delivery requirements of schools.

REVISITING THE CONCEPT

So, there is a clear argument for revisiting the broader theoretical and philosophical principles underpinning the concept and to further add to debates around how it might, or perhaps should translate into practice. A need to re-examine what the implications are for teaching and learning, relationships between learners and educators, and what the broader competencies, dispositions and skills we should be looking to develop through the application of the concept, and also which tools - in particular new technologies, can offer new possibilities for delivering a truly personalised approach.

At the heart of the initial arguments for system reform that accompanied the introduction of personalisation was the need to offer greater 'choice' and 'voice' for students. In doing so there was also a call to move away from more pre-defined curriculum content, teaching methods and approaches, in order to account for learner's needs and interests and away from a 'one size fits all' approach. In so doing, it was argued, some of the institutionalised and systemic inequalities arising from a competitive system based around very similar approaches, requirements and methods of measurement for learners, might be alleviated. Miliband (2004b) identified five key components for developing personalised learning, which provided an early 'route map' for levering change. These focussed on the need to; understand the strengths and weaknesses of individual pupils; develop the confidence and competences of each learner based on individual needs; offer greater curriculum choice that engages and respects students; provide more radical approaches to school organisation; and engage the community, local institutions and social services supporting schools to drive progress forward in classrooms. However, whilst these provided a good starting point, there is still a need to challenge some of the theoretical bases on which the Government's introduction of personalisation were founded.

As noted above, Piore and Sabel's thesis informed initial theoretical developments of personalisation in UK education. The use of this thesis as a basis for educational change can be questioned on a number of levels. Firstly, the thesis was a generalised argument for changes in production and consumption patterns. How relevant or transferable this is or should be in terms of informing a model for education is questionable. There are also doubts cast because of the lack of clear empirical evidence identifying or justifying such changes in the education system. Furthermore, criticism may be levelled because such a potentially significant system wide transformation would require a concomitant set of policies and training that would help deliver the necessary changes in pedagogical approaches, methods of assessment, development of curriculum and bases for the 'measuring' educational standards and the performance of schools. However, perhaps a wider ranging criticism might be that the introduction of personalisation was premised on a thesis now two decades old. Whilst this does not necessarily make it a redundant argument, it does mean that some of the more recent changes may not have been adequately accounted for and that new developments, such as new digital technologies and the possibilities these may bring to support deep personalisation, may not have been adequately considered. Developments in the last twenty years have further transformed both the methods of production and the patterns and mechanisms for consumption. The increase in the number and type of tools that not only allow individuals more choice as consumers but also enable them to be both creators and consumers of others materials and resources has been significant. Understandably, this is an aspect that was not really considered or perceived in the 1980's theses and moreover, it gives a broader socio-cultural perspective to societal changes which may make it more relevant to the potential changes required to education systems. From a more specifically educational perspective, increasingly these tools potentially enable individuals more choice and greater control. The ability to create resources, share them with others, work on their development collaboratively or contribute, comment upon or edit others materials across 'traditional' geographical and demographic boundaries, offers a whole set of new possibilities to configure and design learning in ways previously unthinkable on a mass scale. Such changes and developments have been described as introducing an emerging 'network logic' (McCarthey *et al.* 2004) that is permeating society. It is argued that this demands new skills and dispositions, which are often at odds with the prevalent logic of a somewhat rigid and inflexible education system and in which institutions often operate in relative isolation from wider formal and informal learning communities.

Network Logic and the Network Society

Castells (2000a; 2000b), like Piore and Sabel has focussed on changes in society, the mode of production and patterns of consumption and argues there has been a change from the industrial to the information age. Communication technologies have been significant in helping to facilitate such changes by enabling the development of new social networks that structure society. For Castells, power rests in networks, which are often temporary, flexible and transient and are formed around particular needs that arise. Whilst Castell's thesis has received criticism for a number of reasons, ranging from being technologically determinist to over emphasising the changes this may bring to society, it does however demonstrate new possibilities for organising work and the collaboration and communication that can now happen between previously disparate groups and individuals. If we utilise Castell's arguments to rethink what is possible in developing communities or networks in education, we can begin to see how we might bring about some broader changes within education and a move toward a more personalised education approach. In moving from the macro analysis of the effects and developments of networks and their impacts and effects on how the world and business operates, to a position where we focus much more on the new forms of social and cultural networks that are now available to support a more dynamic, customised and learner focussed educational approach, we can perceive something very different than the system we currently have. This potentially offers much for terms of developing competencies and skills and new ways of actively designing individual learning pathways championed by early proponents of personalised education. However, as noted earlier, few structural or fundamental changes to the education have occurred which will enable greater innovation and risk taking to transform practice. Existing 'institutionalised logic' surrounding what a school is, how it will operate, and their purpose have been shaped by the existing system and have a limiting effect on perceptions about alternative approaches and practice. Government initiatives such as 'The Harnessing Technology Strategy' (DfES 2005), which has at its heart the delivery of a more personalised system, suggest the need for change but ultimately only promote 'shallow' approaches to personalisation that can happen within the constraints of the current system, at least in the short term. Again, this highlights the need to re-examine the underlying *principles of personalisation* so that we might better understand where and what type of changes in the logic of the existing system need to occur.

RE-EXAMINING NOTIONS OF CHOICE AND LEARNER VOICE

Whilst there is not space to thoroughly examine all of the aspects that make would comprise a more personalised approach to education, if we return to the initial suggestion that a personalised approach to learning and teaching would increase choice and empower learners to have greater voice within the system, we can begin re-examine what these both might mean in relation to required changes in the logic and operation of an education system. Moreover we can also consider how digital technologies might be used in a more transformational way that might help place learners as subject at the heart of the system by offering greater economies of scale, more diversity, placing learners in greater control over learning processes by offering new possibilities to create, share and edit content and communicate and collaborate in ways not previously possible.

Learner Voice: What Does it Really Mean?

The term 'learner voice' has received much wider attention in UK education since it was heralded as a key component of personalised learning. However, this concept too has suffered from lack of sufficient and wider philosophical and theoretical debate and a clear understanding of what this means in practice. Its embedding in wider political and educational discourse however, without greater scrutiny, meant that whilst it gained 'currency', it too also soon became a term often used unproblematically. It is not uncommon to see or hear of 'projects' or tools supposedly enabling learner voice, focussing on little more than gathering learners opinions on pre-defined and imposed questions or agendas. Even those highlighted as 'good' or 'best' practice seldom veer beyond the realms of consultation, and when they do they tend to occur sporadically, in isolation, or around issues that others, not the learners themselves, set and scope out the parameters of. Such approaches are waived as good practice merely because they are often an improvement on what has gone before in terms of engaging with pupils, and there is a real concern that these become the 'benchmark' for learner voice activities. Seldom however, are they scrutinised in terms of: the level of active involvement there is by the learners; whether learners are directly involved in setting the agendas and areas for debate; whether there are enough supporting mechanisms for them to introduce their own ideas and issues; whether they had real and genuine motives for involvement; whether the tools and mechanisms for debates and action are chosen by the learners or resonate with their own social and cultural activities, interests and practices; or whether there are sufficient mechanisms and routes for action and change on the basis of decisions made so that their involvement is empowering, real and important, rather than an activity that whilst it may have merits, doesn't capture the essence and the purpose of learner voice approaches.

At the heart of giving a voice to people is the degree to which they are participating within a given community and having opportunities to have their say and put forward their own views through appropriate mechanisms. Drawing on Arnstein's 'ladder of participation' (1969) and Hart's (1992) work on children's participation, involvement can be seen occur on a number of levels, ranging from 'non participatory' through to tokenism and then fully participatory, active and empowering involvement. These terms are useful for considering the degree to which learners voices are heard and acted upon in schools. It might be argued that currently, as children are generally legally and socially bound to attend school and schools are legally bound to deliver a set of learning content and deliver set targets that we seldom use the notion of a community to consider what goes on in our schools. As a result, most forms of engagement with pupils tend to focus around the 'non participatory' aspects of involvement which do little more than inform learners of decisions made, or at best ask their opinion a externally imposed sets of options or actions. But are such approaches failing to give learners full knowledge of their rights and denying them the opportunity to fully participate, which are actually the type of skills and information we would want them to be able to demonstrate in the future. In some cases we see degrees of consultation and partnership occurring. However, these again these may be viewed as tokenistic because whilst there is greater involvement and mechanisms for participation and to negotiate outcomes, there is often little learner input into setting the broader agendas and foci that surrounds these consultative activities. If we are to truly encourage and develop participatory and democratic dispositions amongst learners, then surely we have to move to more empowering involvement where learners are actively involved in shaping agendas and control aspects of the process of engagement and resolution.

There is a long history of research around learner voice (sometimes also referred to as pupil or student voice) and much theoretical work which captures the essence and purpose of more empowering activities (see for example Hargreaves 2004; Fielding 2004; Fielding and Bragg 2003). Davies et al (2007) note the a range of benefits arising from engaging learners in shaping, leading and defining their own education, including a greater sense of ownership of their learning, greater motivation, improved self esteem, improved relationships with adults, and increased self efficacy. Hargreaves (2004), identifies a range of other benefits that can arise from 'deeper' learner voice activities, such as deeper engagement, improved meta-cognitive skills, better relationships between teachers and learners and greater responsibility amongst pupils. In promoting learner voice we should be seeking to consider the perspectives of all learners, considering different methods of decision making and working in partnership so that an educational experience where learners are involved in decisions about how, when and what they learn and the environments and conditions under which it occurs. It is about a shift toward a broader cultural change for most institutions and this may mean utilising the most appropriate tools and techniques as part of an ongoing process to improve the quality of learners' engagement with learning and its broader processes. For such a cultural shift to occur means not merely focussing on existing issues and relationships but creating new ways in which learners can have a direct and tangible impact on their education. Such approaches are likely to engage learners in developing a whole range of other skills and abilities arising from debate, negotiation, organisation, agenda setting and planning activities that will arise from experiential activities with real outcomes and impacts, which engage learners as pro-active members of communities in which their input and influence can have a direct effect on the form, function, processes and practices of that community. Erickson and Schultz (1992) argue that learner or pupil voice projects should focus on enabling learners to develop critical awareness of their own abilities, methods and capacities for learning. However, it is also noted that the structure and organisation of schools negate the degree to which such activities occur. The prescriptive nature of what 'education' should be, what curricula are delivered, and the measures utilised will undoubtedly restrict such approaches. The political requirements of schools monitored in a 'competitive system' means that truly active participation in a learning community that sets and defines its own approaches and agendas is less likely. Clearly, there are differences across institutions and some examples of good practice, but is this sufficient to deliver the kind of cultural changes to practice demanded by 'deep' personalisation? This is not to say it cannot happen but merely there are structural forces that mediate against it. It may be argued however, that within the given system, there is space and opportunity to move toward such practices but often these are seen as 'risky' strategies to employ because they can be time consuming, at times 'messy', and do not automatically align themselves with the prevailing measures and standards that are used as a proxy to document school and pupil performance. So without clear changes in both policy and practice and clearer messages on what these approaches are trying to achieve, the likelihood of one of the supposed driving central tenets of personalisation being delivered is doubtful.

New Technologies: Giving Learners More Voice?

Increasingly we are seeing the development of a whole range of digital tools that can enable people to have greater involvement in a range of activities and communities. These tools allow individuals to access information, enable them to post and dissemination information into communities, create content, express their identities, create knowledge, share edit and develop new resources and content. Yet technology in schools has tended to be used largely as a delivery tool for existing content/ albeit sometimes in different and more engaging ways, but it is seldom used as a mechanism for empowering learners to take greater control over their learning or as a mechanism through which to have their voices heard. Many learners have a rich understanding of such tools and how they operate outside of the classroom, yet we are still to witness formal education drawing on this vast and untapped pool of knowledge and skill, possibly because it does not fit with existing approaches and perceptions of learning in the formal environment. So why should we consider these new developments in terms of empowering learners to have a greater voice? The United Nations Convention of the Rights of the Child (Article 13.1) states that:

> "The child shall have the right to freedom of expression; this right shall include freedom to seek, receive and impart information and ideas of all kinds, regardless of frontiers, either orally, in writing or in print, in the form of art, or through any other media of the child's choice."

Yet we still seem to see a resistance to such approaches and the use of many of these technologies to allow learners to have their say, to be proactive in their own learning development and learning community. New technologies are still largely regulated and controlled by schools and utilised for tasks and functions related to predefined curricula activities. Learners own technologies are largely excluded from use, with learners being asked to power down at the school gates (Rudd et al, 2006), and when access is allowed it tends to be restricted, mediated by 'walled gardens', and used for purposes set by others. Learners knowledge of the tools and processes is under-explored, perhaps arguably a form of 'dumbing down' at the school gates, and their use as tools for empowerment is overlooked, perhaps arguably undermining their rights as set out in the United Nations Convention cited above.

So, we must ask ourselves whether the traditional or existing mechanisms that are in place to enable some degree of learner voice are the only, or most useful ones, - whether they are relevant to today's learners or whether newer tools offer a whole new set of possibilities. Social software and social networking sites, mobile technologies, texts, podcasts, vodcasts, digital and video cameras, audio and video conferencing tools, wikis, blogs and so forth, potentially offer a whole set of rich resources that can support active participation and citizenship and enable learners to have more of a say, set their own agendas, collaborate and communicate around issues important to them and enable them to capture and display information in a range of ways that may be more appropriate to their preferred ways of communicating.

Re-Examining Choice

The second central tenet of personalisation is that of choice. Taken in its broadest sense, we have to recognise that children, for the most part, do not have a choice over whether they attend school. Their choices of school are limited to a large degree and choices tend to be made by them for others. Whilst this is not something many would challenge to a great degree, we must recognise the subtle signals this sends to learners about their power to choose and to begin to redress structural and hierarchical factors by encouraging learners to actively participate to help structure their own learning and the learning communities in which it takes place in order to avoid acculturation into a more passive form of education.

Learners have little choice about who they learn with, yet are aware of the far greater autonomy many of the new digital tools give them over such selection outside of schools. Many are also aware of the way these tools can be used and how they have permeated our society but this is often in stark contrast to their use, or indeed non use inside schools, which again perceptually sets up the school as operating under different 'rules'. Many are aware of the potential for them to be active creators of content and establish relationships, links, interact with others through a range of digital media, to become members of communities, to create identities and so forth, outside of the compulsory educational setting. Potentially these tools offer greater diversity for learning on a global scale, across traditional geographical and demographic boundaries, yet existing fixed and local and age-stage groupings dominate. They can offer a whole new range of potential learning pathways, more diverse and dynamic than any fixed curriculum but this requires changes in pedagogy, assessment and practices. In short, many learners have direct or indirect knowledge of creating their own 'pathways' outside of school but are restricted in their ability to use similar approaches in school. Luis Moll *et al.* (1992; 2005) promoted a much more culturally responsive, ethnographic approach to teaching and learning that accounted for learners existing skills, interests, abilities and home and community resources, yet we are failing to bring in many of the cultural tools and practices of young people into the classroom, even though they are often accepted mechanisms and tools beyond the school.

New digital tools also enable connections, communication and collaborations with people beyond the school walls and offer the sorts of flexibility in learning that cannot be provided by a single teacher in a classroom. The ability to find others interested in similar areas and get support from others with some degree of expertise in that area have been opened up by new technologies but not exploited to any significant degree by schools. Until these sorts of possibilities are further developed we cannot say with confidence that learners are being offered greater choice or that we are exploring the possibilities of personalisatrion.

Learners also have limited choices over what they learn. The National Curriculum and also the ways in which this is translated into practice in a system dominated by standardised tests and rigid achievement measures, mediates the potential choices that learners can make over both the content but also the form of learning they experience. Yet a personalised system requires greater choice, and moreover, choices that are informed by the needs and interests of learners themselves. It can be argued that there is still much flexibility in the system that can be exploited to enable more choice but there remains a need for stronger messages from policy makers and greater exploration of the broader, transferable competencies and skills we wish to develop in learners in the 21st century. Ultimately, if a truly personalised system is to be delivered, there will have to be significant changes in the current approaches to assessment, to curriculum development and the broader standards agenda.

New technologies now exist that can theoretically support new approaches to learning, teaching, assessment and offer ways of capturing, analysing and reflecting on learning processes. Software exists and/or is being developed that enables learners to take control of their own learning content. The fear is that these tools will be used a tools for control and monitoring in the hands of 'the guardians of the system' rather than for being adopted to empower learners.

The nature of new technologies also means we are presented with a whole set of new possibilities as to where learners learn. But again, how much choice do they really have in their formal and compulsory education? In offering a more personalised approach, theoretically learners would not have to proceed through fixed learning materials at the same pace as their age-stage peers but could engage with content when it is appropriate to their development. The ability to document, store, assess and retrieve learning experiences in new ways afforded by new technologies again offers potentially greater flexibility. New digital tools also mean that we can challenge the institutional notion that learners have to be grouped in the same space at the same time to learn, and potentially whether some pupils actually have to attend a school at all in person for their learning experiences. Whilst these statements sound like flights of fantasy, they attempt to illustrate the opportunities to rethink what we are used to, what we have come to expect, in order to start introducing greater choice for learners. The whole notion of choice around where learners learn is particularly interesting in light of large capital development initiatives, such as the £45 billion *Building Schools for the Future* programme in the UK[2] and possible new arrangements for learning that could develop, such as links and relationships with other institutions, learning spaces, workplaces, social services, local community resources, groups, individuals and so forth.

This paper merely scratches the surface in terms of the potential of new technologies to be utilised as transformative tools to offer greater choice and voice for learners, the two central tenets in moving to a more personalised education system. There is far more research to be done in this area, and there are some examples of good practice merging, yet until there is a more adequate re-examination of some of the broader underlying principles to inform the direction of policy and practice which will lever the type of systemic change that was heralded, it will remain unlikely that we will see a move toward a deeply personalised system in the near future.

CONCLUSION

The concept of personalisation appears to have stagnated somewhat since its introduction as a transformative concept earlier this decade. There is a clear need for both policy makers and practitioners to revisit the concept and re-examine and explore the central tents, the grounds on which the arguments for change were made, and also the key principles and benefits underpinning the concept. There is a need to challenge existing notions and operationalised versions of choice and learner voice if a truly personalised system is to

---

[2] More information on this initiative can be found at: Department for Children, Schools and Families. *Building Schools for the Future Programme*. http://www.bsf.gov.uk/

evolve. New technologies offer great potential to facilitate greater choice and voice for learners and can be utilised as tools to empower learners and encourage active participation and more involvement of the direction of their learning and form and function of learning experiences and institutions.

Existing research into empowering learners suggest that there are many benefits from such an approach, such as; developing a greater sense of ownership; improving motivation and self esteem, improved relationships with adults, increased self efficacy, deeper engagement, improved meta-cognitive skills, better relationships and so forth, yet examples of truly participatory practice remain rare, patchy, siloed or dubious in their nature.

In moving toward a more personalised approach we should be looking to give learners more voice and choice, and this means that pedagogical approaches will undoubtedly change. However, it is clear that this must be in order to develop a range of essential skills and competencies in learners, such as critical awareness of their own abilities, methods and capacities for learning, decision making, negotiation, collaboration and communication skills, research and information literacy skills, reflection, proactive dispositions to learning, creativity, problem solving skills, content creation and development abilities and so on.

New technologies offer great potential for empowering learners and as transformational tools to change the relationships and form of formal and compulsory learning as we know it. However, currently they tend to be predominately used to enhance learning within the confines of the 'logic' of the existing system. Their transformational qualities lay in the greater diversity, flexibility and scalability to support the delivery of multifarious individual learning pathways on an unprecedented scale and to empower learners to take control of their own learning. Policy makers and practitioners need to revisit the concept, tenets and principles underpinning personalisation and the systemic changes it requires and consider how best to utilise the dynamic learning tools to help bring about such changes.

REFERENCES

Arnstein, S. R. "A Ladder of Citizen Participation," Journal of the American Planning Association, Vol. 35, No. 4, July 1969, pp. 216-224.

Beadle, P. (2006). 'Just a slogan in search of a meaning'. The Guardian (03/10/06)

Campbell, R. J., Robinson, W., Neelands, J., Hewston, R. & Mazzoli, L. (2007). 'Personalised Learning: Ambiguities in Theory and Practice'. Journal of Educational Studies 55 (2), 135–154.

Castells, M. (2000a). 'Materials for an Exploratory Theory of the Network Society'. British Journal of Sociology Vol. No. 51 Issue No. 1 (January/March 2000) pp. 5-24.

Castells, M. (2000b). The Rise of the Network Society. U.S.: Blackwell Publishing.

Davies L., Williams C., Yamashita H. & Ko Man-Hing A., (2006), Inspiring Schools: a Literature Review. Carnegie Young People Initiative, Esmee Fairbairn Foundation. http://cypi.carnegieuktrust.org.uk/cypi/home

DfES (2005) 'Harnessing Technology: Transforming Learning and Children's Services'. http://www.dfes.gov.uk/publications/e-strategy (Accessed 03/01/08).

Erickson, F. & Schultz, J. (1992). 'Students' Experience of the Curriculum', in: P.

Jackson (Ed.), Handbook of Research on Curriculum. New York: Macmillan, pp.464–485.

Fielding M. & Bragg, S., (2003) *Students as Researchers: Making a Difference.* Cambridge: Pearson Publishing.

Fielding M., (2004), 'New Wave' Student Voice and the Renewal of Civic Society'. *London Review of Education*, Vol. 2, No. 3, November 2004. www.sussex.ac.uk/education/ documents/michael_**fielding**_new_wave_**student_voice**_the_renewal_of_c.pdf

Hart, R (1992). Children's Participation: From Tokenism to Citizenship. UNICEF.

Hartley, D. (2007). The Emerging Revised Code of Education. Taylor and Francis. PA.

Hargreaves, D. (2004). *Next Steps in Working Laterally.* Specialist Schools Trust. http://www.schoolsnetwork.org.uk/uploads/documents/4402.pdf (Accessed 01/03/08).

Hargreaves, D. (2003) *Education Epidemic: transforming secondary schools through innovation networks,* Demos, London.

Leadbeater, C. (2004) Personalisation through Participation, Demos, London.

Laurila, J. & Preece, D. (2004). Technological Change and Organizational Action. Routledge.

McCarthy, H., Miller, P. & Skidmore, P. (2004) *Network Logic.* Demos. London. (Accessed 03/01/08). http://www.demos.co.uk/publications/networks

Miliband, D. (2004a) *Personalised Learning: Building A New Relationship With Schools.* Speech by David Miliband to the North of England Education Conference (03/01/04). Belfast.

Miliband, D. (2004b) *Choice and Voice in Personalised Learning.* OECD. Accessed (03/01/08) http://www.oecd.org/dataoecd/58/36/39113236.doc

Moll, L.C., Armanti, C., Neff, D., & Gonzalez, N. (1992). 'Funds of Knowledge for Teaching: Using a Qualitative Approach to Connect Homes and Classrooms'. *Theory into Practice,* 31 (2), 132-141.

Moll, L., Gonzalez, N. & Amanti, C. (Eds.) (2005) *Funds of Knowledge: Theorizing Practices in Households and Classrooms.* Lawrence Erlbaum Associates Inc,US.

Paludan, J.P. (2006) 'Personalised Learning 2025 in Schooling for Tomorrow', *Personalising Education*, Paris, OECD Publishing.

Rudd, T., Colligan, F. & Naik, R. (2006), *Learner Voice*, Futurelab. http://www.futurelab. org.uk/resources/documents/handbooks/learner_voice.pdf (Accessed 01/03/08).

In: Learning in the Network Society and the Digitized School   ISBN 978-1-60741-172-7
Editor: Rune Krumsvik   © 2009 Nova Science Publishers, Inc.

Chapter 6

'LEARNING NETWORKS' – CAPACITY BUILDING FOR SCHOOL DEVELOPMENT AND ICT

Ola Erstad
University of Oslo, Norway

ABSTRACT

The focus of this chapter is on change processes in schools and the role of ICT. Based on former initiatives to promote Information and Communication Technologies (ICT) in Norwegian schools, the Ministry of Education decided in 2004 to establish a national program for school development and ICT called 'Learning Networks'. The program finishes in June 2009. By calling this program 'Learning Networks' it implies an interest in getting schools, principals, teachers and students to work together in networks, as a strategy for learning on different levels in and between school communities nationwide. Until now about 550 schools have been or are involved in this national program. My role in this program has been as head of the advisory board, to build on results from research to stimulate developmental activities, and to initiate evaluations of experiences and small scale research. In this article some preliminary results from this ongoing program will be presented as an example of a national strategy for creating capacities for school development and ICT in Norway.

INTRODUCTION

A major challenge for developments within technology and education today is to grasp the complexity of such developments. In general there has been a tendency to simplify the research approaches and understanding of how digital technologies might have an impact on schools and education systems (Cuban, 1986, 2001; Østerud, 2004; Erstad, 2004), and evidence of impact of ICT on educational practice has mainly been drawn from small-scale case studies (Condie & Munro, 2007). Both policymakers and researchers have created expectations towards the impact of information and communication technologies (ICT) on student learning, which has not gained strong support in the research literature (ibid.). Other researchers have been more interested in the new possibilities and limitations created by the implementation of digital technologies into educational settings (De Corte, Verschaffel, Entwistle & van Merrienboer, 2003). Again, other research and development initiatives have been more directed towards the institutional framework of school development and the use of ICT, as seen in such initiatives as the European Network of Innovative Schools (ENIS), the European Schoolnet (Balanskat, Blamire & Kefala, 2006), SITES M2 (Kozma, 2003) and PILOT (Erstad, 2004).

The challenge, and the complexity, rests on how these levels and perspectives relate to each other. This is a challenge of educational research in general, but especially when trying to understand the mechanisms involved in the educational use of ICT. In the research literature there is now a greater consciousness towards multi-level analysis and more holistic approaches towards learning and school development (Hakkarainen, Palonen, Paavola & Lehtinen, 2004; Arnseth & Ludvigsen, 2006). As David Olson has pointed out in his book 'Psychological theory and educational reform' (2003);

> The problem, I believe, is that the theories that gave us insight into children's understanding, motivation, learning, and thinking have never come to terms with schooling as an institutional practice with its duties and responsibilities for basic skills, disciplinary knowledges, grades, standards, and credentials... What is required, then, is an advance in our understanding of schools as bureaucratic institutions that corresponds to the advances in our understanding of the development of the mind (D. Olson, 2003:x-xi).

Of special relevance in discussions on school developments is the concept of networks, partly building on conceptualisations from Manuel Castells on the networked society (Castells, 1996). The argument goes that digital technologies have created a new situation for how organizations and people work together and relate to each other, as a globalising process. Education is also thought of in a more distributed way by using these technologies for educational purposes, such as in CSCL (Wasson, Ludvigsen & Hoppe, 2003) or collaboration between schools (Kozma, 2003). However, how this can be seen on a more practical level in schools beyond small scale activities and its implications is more unclear.

The focus of this article is on change processes in schools and the role of ICT. Based on former initiatives to promote Information and Communication Technologies (ICT) in Norwegian schools, the Ministry of Education decided in 2004 to establish a national program for school development and ICT called 'Learning Networks'. The program finishes in June 2009. By calling this program 'Learning Networks' it implies an interest in getting schools, principals, teachers and students to work together in networks, as a strategy for learning on different levels in and between school communities nationwide. Until now about 550 schools have been or are involved in this national program.

The overall research question for this article is; *How does network strategies support teachers' and schools' in approaching school development using ICT?* Within a Norwegian context network initiatives are defined as a way of moving beyond implementation and access issues of technology and also up-scaling of activities involving all Norwegian schools in their educational use of ICT.

BUILDING CAPACITIES THROUGH POLICY INITIATIVES

The year 2006 indicate ten years of strategic development on ICT in the Norwegian education system. These ten years can be divided into three main phases. The phases indicate the overall national agenda for scaling up activities using digital media in Norwegian schools. The three phases are also expressed in specific 'action plans' from the Ministry of Education.

The first phase, from 1996 until 1999, was mainly concerned with the implementation of computers into Norwegian schools. There was less interest in the educational context. In the next phase, from 2000 until 2003, the focus was more on whole school development with ICT and changing learning environments. The phase we are in now, from 2004 until 2008, puts more emphasis on digital literacy and knowledge building among students, and what learners do with technology, which opens future perspectives on technology and education. The presentation in this article is part of this last phase.

One immediate challenge in these developments has been the balance between 'top-down' and 'bottom-up' strategies. One element has been to commit the Ministry of Education in developing ICT in Norwegian schools, another has been to get schools to use ICT more actively. The latter has been more difficult, and there has in periods been too much pressure from 'the top' initiating projects, without too much happening at 'the bottom' (Erstad, Kløvstad, Kristiansen & Søby, 2005). During the last 3-4 years this has changed in the sense that more schools start activities themselves (Arnseth, Hatlevik, Kløvstad, Kristiansen & Ottestad, 2007).

As a consequence of such processes a discussion on knowledge creation on a national level has come to the surface in Norway. Some argue, based on PISA results, that knowledge in the basic skills of reading, writing and numeracy has a priority, while others argue that our conception of knowledge is under transition, creating a possible third way towards development (Østerud 2004).

An interesting compromise has been that digital literacy and the ability to use digital tools has been written into the new national curriculum, and defined as important as reading, writing and numeracy. The implication is that all students on all levels and in all subjects should use and relate to digital media in their learning processes in Norwegian schools. The emphasis is mainly on skills in using the technology, but imply also broader issues of competence such as evaluating sources critically when using the Internet and using ICT to collaborate (Erstad, 2005).

By defining 'the ability to use digital tools' as a basic skill throughout the new national curriculum, the Ministry of Education and Research has placed a strong emphasis on ICT as part of learning activities in schools. ICT should be an integrated part of learning activities among all students, at all levels of primary and secondary education and in all subjects. The way in which the use of ICT is implemented for the promotion of learning differs between the syllabuses. The major change from former plans on ICT in education is the demand for specific educational use of ICT in different subjects.

The framework for the new national curriculum is described in White Paper no. 30 (2003–2004) called 'Culture for learning'. In this document, digital literacy is highlighted and described as a new competence area of learning in schools. Digital literacy is defined as:

Digital literacy is the sum of simple ICT skills, like being able to read, write and calculate, and more advanced skills which make the creative and critical use of digital tools and media possible. ICT skills consist of being able to use software, to search, locate, transform and control information from different digital sources, while the critical and creative ability also needs an ability to evaluate, to use sources critically, to interpret and analyse digital genres and media forms. In total, digital literacy can be seen as a very complex competence' (Ministry of Education and Research, 2004a, p. 48, my translation).

The focus on ICT and digital literacy in the new national curriculum builds on former plans and documents. The important implications for the discussions in this article is the commitment this implies for teachers and students to use ICT much more broadly in the learning activities in schools. In this way a stronger push mechanism is created for school leaders and teachers to work towards capacity building on school development and the use of ICT in order to fulfil the challenges of the new curriculum. Important national objectives related to the new national curriculum can be summarized as follows:

- a focus on how ICT can contribute to an increased quality in teaching and learning;
- an increased use of new ICT-based means for cooperation and interchange of knowledge and experience at all levels of the educational system;
- a broad access to learning materials and the development of new and varied forms of learning in order to stimulate activity, independence, and cooperation;
- an increased focus on students' critical reflection with respect to the use of ICT in teaching and learning and in society in general;
- an increased focus on how to avoid creating digital divides.

The White paper 'Culture for learning' refers to the national ICT plan called 'Programme for digital literacy 2004–2008' (Ministry of Education and Research, 2004b). The overall vision in both documents is stated as 'digital literacy for all'. In elaborating on this vision, these documents refer to the role of education to implement the needed competence in using technology in the population at large in order for everybody to be fully active in working life and social participation. The programme mentions four main focus areas to accomplish 'digital competence for all'. These are: Infrastructure, Development of competence, Digital learning resources, curricula and learning practices, and Research and development. All these areas are thought to support school development in all parts of the country.

A NEW FRAMEWORK FOR SCHOOL DEVELOPMENT

For many years policy makers and researchers have been concerned with school development, even though the rationale for this has differed. A concern is often related towards how schools are part of broader developmental processes in our societies and cultures (Gray et al., 1999). At the same time several writers studying educational reforms argue that even though curricula are framed within arguments of school development and change, this is often not the case in educational practice in schools (Cuban, 1984; Goodlad & Anderson, 1984).

In his classic book 'the New Meaning of Educational Change' (1991), Michael Fullan presents a broad framework on different levels and involving different actors in understanding educational reform and school development. Also in his later book 'Change forces' (1993) he addresses the real complexity of dynamic and continuous change, showing the challenges this implies both on peoples' mind-sets and on mechanisms defining educational practices.

In recent years this has been taken up by other researchers trying to develop models to study and also to create interventions into educational practices in order to work towards school development. This represents a movement away from traditional models of change based on organizational theory like Senge or Nonaka and Takeuchi, towards models trying to grasp the complexity of change processes through the activities involved.

The most important perspective for studying change processes in schools in recent years has been activity theory, or more specifically cultural-historic activity theory (CHAT) (Engeström, 1987). This has grown out of the intellectual work done by the russian psychologist Vygotsky, in the 1920s and 1930s, and later on by Leontjev. The focus of this perspective is on activity as the unit of analysis and mediation between actors and certain cultural tools. Yrjö Engeström has then expanded this model beyond the person and the tools by introducing a larger framework of factors that are part of developmental processes on different levels, such as rules and norms, division of labour and communities of practice. The relation between these factors is defined as an activity system, and within an organisation and between organisations there might be several activity systems that relate to each other in different ways.

The focus on object orientation is of central importance because it implies the direction of the activity. It is the basis for how we understand development and change. An object might be material things like computers being introduced in school settings, or more abstract ideas and perspectives that are introduced, like a new working method, both influencing changes in the activity systems in such organisations. Engeström has used the concept of expansive learning to focus on the change processes going on, and especially the tensions and contradictions involved in different steps of the developments which have to be resolved. The following model (figure 1) shows expansive learning as a process where activity systems in an organisation like a school go through different tensions characteristic of each step, starting off from a commitment to change by some actors.

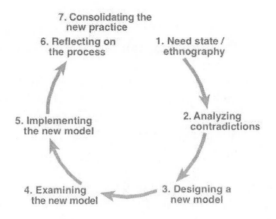

Figure 1. Steps of expansive learning.

Ethnographic Analysis of the Current Situation (Steps 1, 2)

Key challenge is to make tensions and contradictions explicit:

- teachers and school leaders questioning their present activity by jointly analyzing problematic situations in it;
- analyzing the systemic and historical causes of the problems identified;
- revealing and modeling inner contradictions of the systemic structure of the activity causing the problems

Transforming the Model (Steps 3, 4)

Key challenge is to create a new model to move beyond the tensions and contradictions:

- representing the systemic structure of the activity in order to find a new form for the activity that would resolve in an expansive way the inner incompatibilities between its components;
- finding a new interpretation of the purpose of the activity (object) and a new logic of organizing it,
- creating a new activity model

Implementing the New Model of Activity (Step 5)

Key challenge is to establish the new model in the organization:

- concretizing and testing the new model (e.g. what changes do we try next month ? putting first steps into practice, pushing the next steps)
- beginning to transform the practice by designing and implementing new tools and solutions.

Reflecting on the New Practice, Consolidating it, Spreading it (Steps 6, 7)

Key challenge is to move beyond implementation and create sustainable development, diffusion of innovation and reflection on future changes and new models:

- teaching others what we have learned,
- codifying the new rules etc.

This model is also a basic framework for the working methods of the Change Laboratory in Helsinki (Engeström, Virkkunen et al., 1996). In the Change Laboratory, the original 'task' of Vygotskian designs is represented by the *mirror* which contains challenging examples of problems and disturbances in the organization. Previous Vygotskian theorizing and research has mainly focused on a single individual or a dyad of two subjects using a single, well-defined mediating tool or artifact. Only language as mediator has demanded a more complex approach - but studies of semiotic mediation have commonly excluded material instruments and tools. In the Change Laboratory, the mediational setup is complex and multi-layered both semiotically and instrumentally.

In order to relate this activity theoretical framework more to the key issues of the school development project discussed in this article I will introduce two perspectives to elaborate the discussion, one related to knowledge creation and one related to networking. The way the model of expansive learning is used in this article is more as a way of systematically reflecting on school development and ICT than to analyse empirical data. The main point is to illustrate present initiatives in studying school development and educational change processes implying a broader set of issues and an acknowledgement of the complexity involved in studying such phenomena.

Knowledge Creation

Knowledge creation and knowledge building has been an issue within research communities dealing with computer supported collaborative learning (CSCL), studying how collaborative and distributed ways of working using different technological applications stimulate knowledge building among learners. This can be seen in the developmental work done by Marlene Scardamalia and Carl Bereiter in Canada (Scardamalia & Bereiter, 2006). Knowledge building, and the technological platform that has been developed (Knowledge Forum), aims for collective cognitive responsibility among learners. Collective responsibility refers to a condition in which responsibility for the success of the group is distributed across all members rather than being concentrated on the leader. Collective cognitive responsibility refers to taking responsibility to know what needs to be known on the cognitive level in addition to the more tangible practical aspects.

Central to the idea of knowledge building is that it differs from learning. Learning is internal unobservable processes that result in changes in belief, attitude or skill. Knowledge building, by contrast, results in the creation or modification of public knowledge, knowledge that lives in the world and is available to be worked on and used by other people. Creating public knowledge naturally results in personal learning but so does practically all human activity. In knowledge building, creating *new* knowledge, rather than just keeping abreast of advancing knowledge is the goal.

This perspective has been further developed by Hakkarainen, Palonen, Paavola & Lehtinen in their book on 'Communities of networked expertise' (2004), and what they describe as *trialogical learning*. Hakkarainen et al. contrast the trialogical framework with prevailing monological (cognitive) and dialogical (situated cognition) approaches. Five characteristics of trialogical approach to learning and cognition are distinguished: it is 1) an object-oriented process, 2) taking place across long timescales, 3) involving interaction between individual and collective processes, 4) relying on cross-fertilization of knowledge practices, and 5) relying on collaborative technologies designed to elicit object-oriented activities.

Networking

This brings me over to the second perspective mentioned above, dealing with networks and networking. Networking is a broad conceptualisation based on global perspectives on social development, but which also relates specifically to the role of education in moving towards knowledge societies and the role of networking in such processes. As an example, in the UNESCO report 'Towards Knowledge Societies' (2005) the concept of learning is closely tied to innovation and networking. Credé and Mansell (1998) have also shown how this thinking on knowledge societies and networking is fundamentally based on identifying new ICT opportunities.

Further, this focus on networking and networks can also be related to the concept of 'communities of practice' from Etienne Wenger (1998). Wenger frames this within different theoretical perspectives, partly reflecting the tension between theories that gives primacy to social structure (institutions, norms, rules) and those that give primacy to action (the dynamics of everyday interactions, agency and intentions). This perspective of 'communities of practice' gives meaning to how networks relates to both structural mechanisms of certain activities within situated contexts, and the activities and intentions creating the way for innovations and developments.

Networks can be divided between those that are formal, in the sense that they have defined objectives with members that are limited and easy to detect, and those that are informal. In this article it is the first kind of networks that are relevant to study. According to Marthinsen (2006) four aspects are preconditions for a well functioning formal network. These are:

- Incentives; that the participants see the advantages of participating,
- Demands; that participation demands active contributions from each actor,
- Attitudes; the participants need to be generous and positive towards sharing of knowledge,
- Openness; collaborations should be dominated by ethical standards and honesty without hidden agendas.

Organising by networks is an alternative to an hierarchical and rational goal oriented approach, where the main aim is to develop the collective competence in the group of members. Strategies for collaboration, developments of trust and support in addition to the advancement of knowledge and experiences are important. Of course the challenges for making such networks function optimal are huge and it might be difficult to find the right balance between a strong leadership for development and stimulate initiatives among participants where leadership is more invisible. Networks are by definition desentralized, which makes leadership and division of responsibility and labour a challenge. The question today is of course which role technology has in supporting and building networks for learning.

A National Program for School Development

Background

During the period 2000 until 2004 a few research projects were of special importance in a Norwegian setting in the way they studied up-scaling of activities using new digital technologies, from a few innovative teachers and schools towards whole school communities and including many schools. One important project was the PILOT project (Project Innovation in Learning, Organization and Technology) (Erstad, 2004). 120 schools took part in this four years research and development project based on interventions concerning the educational use of ICT and developing a framework within whole school settings. Results from this project showed that schools handled the challenges of change and the introduction of ICT as a new object in very different ways. Four typologies of schools were identified according to two dimensions, one going from working unsystematic versus systematic in the way school communities worked towards school development, and another going from being development oriented in the school culture towards being dominated by resistance towards change (Erstad, 2004).

One typology was termed *'the pendulum school'*, implying schools that were development oriented and wanted to change in order to work better using ICT, but which was doing this in a very unsystematic way. For example that they worked on portfolio assessment for half a year, and did not feel they managed that well, so they switched to focusing on using a special Learning Management System, but did not manage that well either, so they switched again, and so forth. The leadership at these schools did not manage to develop good and realistic strategies that they used for development work over time. Another typology of schools was termed *'the conflict school'*, which were dominated by internal problems and conflicts. They were unsystematic in the way they worked, with school leadership that did not manage to reorient the school community towards development. In addition they had a lot of resistance against change among the school staff, which was often due to overall conflicts at the school. At these schools, that were few in numbers, not much was happening. A third typology was termed *'the traditional oriented school'*, indicating a school that was dominated by being systematic in the way they worked and at the same time had a lot of resistance against change among teachers. This was often found among upper secondary schools, and these schools had less collaboration with other schools. The last typology was *'the school of affordances'*, typifying schools that were both development oriented, had realistic and widely accepted development strategies among staff, and were systematic in the way they worked. These were the kinds of schools that succeeded best in this material because both school leaders and teachers were all the time thinking how new digital tools, working together with other schools, and so forth could bring them new affordances and possibilities for development.

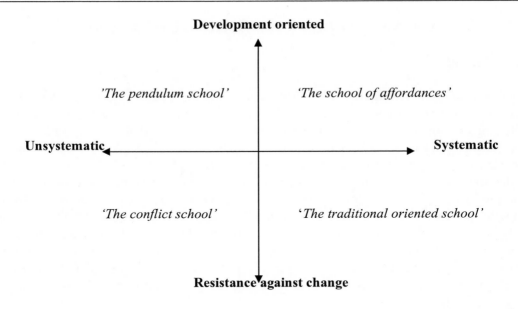

Figure 2: Typology of schools – developmentally oriented

Developments during the four years showed that many of the schools were building up experiences in using ICT as part of their efforts towards school development and capacities for handling new technologies in the organisation. However, this was not an easy task for most of the schools, and the developments always took a longer time than expected. One experience that turned out to be important for many of the small schools situated in remote areas of Norway was the collaborative efforts between these schools. A specific methodology was developed called 'dialogue conferences' (Lund, 2004). This was organised as meeting points where teachers from different schools met to present experiences of school development using ICT, reflect on these together by writing and talking, and making strategies for future developments that are brought up again at future meetings face-to-face. In between the meetings they collaborated online. Reports from the participants indicated very positive outcomes of such 'dialogue conferences' (ibid.).

Based on such initiatives and experiences to promote Information and Communication Technologies (ICT) in Norwegian schools, the Ministry of Education decided in 2004 to establish a national program for school development and ICT called 'Learning Networks'. It is structured with 10 schools in each network, from primary to upper secondary, and with one teacher training college leading each network. On the content side all networks are oriented towards the educational implications of working with ICT, and especially on the issue of digital literacy, which is now defined as a key component in our new National curriculum called 'Knowledge Promotion'. As a national initiative, involving all regions of Norway, a large number of schools and all teacher training colleges, this is an interesting development for school development and ICT. However, some critical questions needs to be posed, both concerning the strategy as such and the possible expansive learning involved and the knowledge building that takes place. Does the initial ideas from the Ministry of Education, building on former experiences with school development and ICT, really transcend to a practical level of networking?

Organizing the Program

From the start in 2004, about 550 schools and teacher training colleges, have taken part in this development program. Each network (10 schools and one teacher training college) consists of schools with different levels of experience in using ICT, covering different educational levels. After two years each network (about 25 each year) are supposed to change the 10 schools with 10 new schools. However, some networks have chosen to keep the same schools all through the four years period. All the 19 regions of Norway are participating with at least one network. In most regions schools applied to become part of networks based on a project description. However, in some regions the school agencies picked out schools, which made the school's motivation for participating unclear.

On a national level the Directorate of Education has been administrating the program, and distributing funds. Each school gets some funding by participating for travel expenses to meetings, and each teacher training college gets some more funds since they are defined as leaders of each network. In addition, on the national level there is an advisory board of experts, of which I am the leader.

The overall objective of the program has been; "Through sharing and development of knowledge in learning networks, schools, school owners (that is municipality and regional educational offices) and teacher training colleges should be made conscious and qualified so that ICT to a larger degree is used as part of the learning activities where it gives additional value in subjects and in pedagogy" (Ministry of Education, 2004b). This is also seen in relation to the new national curriculum of 2004 called 'Culture for Learning', where networking is defined as an important strategy for school development.

The discussion of results below is based on several studies of the impact of this program during the last couple of years. The advisory board for the program has taken several initiatives of different kinds of evaluation studies, both done by participants in the program and by external agencies. One evaluation is a survey done twice, in the beginning and towards the end of the program, with school leaders in participating schools. Some research is done within the teacher training colleges. In addition an external agency has been studying a few networks more in-depth (Skogerbø, Ottestad & Axelsen, 2007) and an external researcher has made an evaluation based on reports written by the schools and the network leaders at the teacher training colleges (Silseth, 2006).

Indications of Impact

My role in this program has been, as head of the advisory board, to build on results from research to stimulate developmental activities, and to initiate evaluations of experiences and small-scale research. In this article some preliminary results from this ongoing program will be presented as an example of a national strategy for creating capacities for school development and ICT in Norway. This will not be a presentation of the data themselves, done by using both quantitative and qualitative methods, but rather a presentation of the conclusions and reflections reported in the different evaluations and research projects done.

An important aim of the program has been diffusion of innovations to a large number of schools, through small funds and incentives. In the different reports during the last four years teachers and school leaders report that the economic funds have not been the most important incentives for participating. Rather it is the possibility of working with others in building capacities that make both each school but also the collective efforts in each network stronger.

Starting Up

The first year of the program was dominated by a lot of insecurity, unclear definitions of responsibility on different levels (locally, regionally and nationally) and technologies that did not work optimally between schools. During this first phase this was discussed and resolved for some networks, but not all, which had implications for developments within these networks. After the first year of piloting schools developed some experiences, and division of labour and responsibility was made clearer which created a platform to define a new phase of more strategic development. The intention of the program has been, as mentioned above, to stimulate activities and spread experiences by capacity building and learning together, which means that it is not defined as a project that should reach certain predefined objectives. It should rather build up capacities for learning and networking that can be further developed after the schools leave this time limited program implying a model for expansive learning and knowledge building.

By using a strategy of reflection on action, as mentioned in the description of dialogue conferences, that many networks have used, networks have been able to learn from the challenges and tensions during the first phase. For example in the way networks have become more focused in their work, concentrating on certain aspects of technology use and educational perspectives, instead of trying to be too broad in their approach.

Experiences by School Leaders

A recent report (Eliassen, Jøsendal & Erstad, 2008), based on a survey done among school leaders in the participating schools, shows that the overall impression is that there is a very positive attitude among both school leaders and school communities towards working together in networks in this way. A similar survey done in the beginning of the project shows that this positive attitude towards working together in networks has increased during the whole period.

The school leaders further report that (ibid. pp. 5-7);

- the experiences of working more closely with the teacher training colleges has been inspiring and created better conditions for school development because they get someone from outside their own community to follow them over time and give feedback on activities both online and offline.
- participation in this program has increased the amount of discussions about educational issues, on school development and the use of ICT.
- in general they have positive experiences of working with other schools, however mainly in smaller networks (mini-networks) between teachers from different schools or with one or two other school communities.
- it has made the schools more clearly move towards learning organizations according to the school leaders.
- the use of ICT at the participating schools has improved, but not as much as expected in the beginning of the program.
- the use of ICT for networking and collaborating online between schools is still a challenge that has not been substantially implemented.

- the biggest challenge for the participating schools is sustainability of the development work to be able to continue after the program finishes in 2009.

Diversity of Network Models

A research project was done by a national agency focusing on more qualitative issues of being in such neworks, doing interviews with different participants in a few number of networks. This study shows a broad diversity of experiences across different networks (Skogerbø, Ottestad & Axelsen, 2007), both related to the way networks work with different issues, and to the different ways networks are organized. The development process of the networks got more focused and became more meaningful for the participants when each network defined a specific issue or theme to concentrate on. For example, some schools focused specifically on multimodal texts and how teachers and students could use specific technology within different subject domains. Or how schools in a network could use a Learning Management System (LMS) to support collaboration. In this way the networks also got a clearer idea about the possible potential of using ICT for certain purposes which increased the reported time spent with using ICT at these schools.

An interesting outcome so far has been to see how networks organize themselves in different ways, often based on local interests and experiences. Some keep a hierarchical model where the teacher training college in the network is taking the lead. Others are organized in a much more horizontal way, with different schools contributing in different ways and taking responsibility, without any specific overall leaders. One success criteria for many networks has been the development of mini-networks within the larger network. In this way teachers within science education could develop their own network based on their interests and needs, or principals could have their own network. These mini-networks has shown interesting developments of knowledge building, focusing on how to build experiences and knowledge together over time. In some regions of Norway they also developed larger networks across established networks collaborating on specific goal directed activities.

The working method chosen in most networks was a combination of meetings where participants met face-to-face, and online collaborative efforts. The physical meetings turned out to be very important for the networks, because they got time to discuss and reflect together and to bring up tensions and problems in the developmental process at the schools, as part of expansive learning processes. The teachers and school leaders reported that these meetings had an important function to make the networks evolve as communities of learning.

Limitations and Challenges

Such a meta-evaluation of experiences and activities also show that there are important challenges with this kind of development work involving many actors on different levels of the education system. This also indicates that this program has limitations related to the initial objectives and ambitions of the program from policy level. Some important challenges have been:

- To get the teacher training colleges to get more development oriented. Many of these colleges have huge challenges in keeping up with developments within schools, especially on using ICT.

- Many teachers report lack of enough time to follow up development work as intended. The way schools are organized and the daily duties of teachers make development efforts come on top of everything else.
- Almost all networks have reported difficulties in keeping up activities between face-to-face meetings. Online activities to stimulate development work are difficult without special planning. In some mini-networks online collaboration has worked better because they have a more focused approach and a clearer understanding of why they use online resources for networking.
- Schools that already had experience with using ICT has reported that they felt that they gave more than they got in return. This is due to the way networks were organized, where schools with more experiences in using ICT should work with schools with less experiences in this area, but which might have experiences in other areas that they could bring into the collaboration. In many networks, especially during the two first years, this did not work as planned and schools with good experiences in using ICT felt they were stagnating.
- Commitment of school leaders and school owners to make sure of sustainability over time.

EXPANDING NETWORKS

The initiative for school development presented above has not yet been fully documented and researched. What has been presented here are some general impressions based on preliminary evaluation studies of different aspects of these networks.

Obviously, the number of schools, teachers, students and school leaders in this program has been a challenge to handle, and the structure of the program on a national, regional and local level has been complex. However, using the inspiration from 'dialogue conferences' has made certain 'meeting points' organized both on national, regional and local levels an important tool for stimulating and reflecting on development work using ICT. This has worked as capacity building by collecting experiences, not for sharing, but as a starting point for reflecting on how to move on, supporting each other across school communities.

Building on the model of expansive learning from activity theory, combined with theories on knowledge creation and networks, creates a framework for understanding development work on this scale and which is directed towards school development for the educational use of ICT. As highlighted by the theory of expansive learning, there are tensions that come to the surface during such development efforts and which have to be resolved in order to move ahead. Some of these tensions have been described above, between teachers training colleges and school communities, between school leaders and teachers, between ICT as a new object and the traditional structure of schools, and so forth.

Building on what has been described above, some key factors in networking as a strategy for school development seems to be;

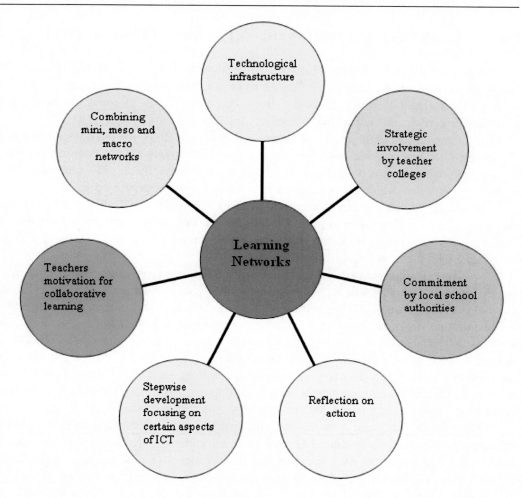

Figure 3: Elements influencing Learning Networks

The technological infrastructure is a precondition for networking in this way, and when it is not working it creates resistance and tensions. The strategic involvement by teacher colleges is important both for creating support for school development and doing interventions, and in the way such colleges themselves can learn from schools. To secure sustainability school owners in the regions have to be involved in development thinking and not as just administrative supporters. Specific steps for knowledge creation and reflection on action should be specified by the involved participants, so that they move beyond just sharing of experiences without nothing more happening. This also relates to stepwise development focusing on certain aspects of ICT in order to give the development efforts a direction and that participants can give input that support such developments. Teachers need to be motivated for collaborative learning. If they do not find it meaningful it will have the opposite effect of stimulating development. As shown in this program a combination of mini, meso and macro networks works best in the way development is thought on different levels related to different needs and interests.

LEARNING NETWORKS OR NETWORKS FOR LEARNING

An issue that has been discussed from the beginning of the program, has been to what extent the networks really are learning networks or just networks for sharing information. By calling this program 'learning networks' the intention has been to focus on the learning potential for participants in working collectively together.

Even though this program will not be finished until June 2009, the main impression from the different evaluations that have been done is that participants are positive and motivated for working in such networks. After a slow start most of the 55 networks have been able to focus their activities, which gives a clearer direction of the development work.

The teacher training colleges seems to be the ones that struggle the most to commit themselves in such development work. A few people from these colleges are involved in working with the schools. However, the broader commitment of the teacher training colleges in working with these schools is lacking.

The overall impression is that most networks function as networks for learning in the sense that participants experience that they are learning from each other of direct relevance for the educational use of ICT in their own practices. To what extent we might say that these are learning networks, as knowledge building communities where networking is the driving force, is still unclear. This is mainly due to the time factor involved, that these networks are new and needs time to create a solid foundation and a methodological approach where networks are sustainable. In the years to come it will be interesting to see how this will develop further as a strategy towards school development where the technology is both the supporting factor for networking and the focus of the content orientation.

This program has been seen as an important strategy for capacity building moving schools towards working on digital literacy as an educational objective in the new national curriculum. The important message from the developments in this program so far is that digital literacy should not only been seen as competencies in using the technology, but that digital literacy involves the whole school and influences development work on several levels at the same time.

REFERENCES

Arnseth, H.C., Hatlevik, O., Kløvstad, V., Kristiansen, T. & Ottestad, G. (2007). *ITU Monitor 2007*. Oslo: Universitetsforlaget (University Press)

Arnseth, H. C. & Ludvigsen, S. (2006). *Approaching Institutional Contexts: Systemic versus Dialogic Research in CSCL*. International Journal of Computer-Supported Collaborative Learning. 1(2).

Balanskat, A., Blamire, R. & Kefala, S. (2006). *The ICT Impact Report. A review of studies of ICT impact on schools in Europe*. European Schoolnet: EU Commission

Castells, M. (1996). *The Rise of the Network Society, The Information Age: Economy, Society and Culture, Vol. I*. Cambridge, MA; Blackwell

Condie, R. & Munroe, B. (2007). *The impact of ICT in schools – a landscape review*. London: Becta research

Credé, A. & Mansell, R. (1998). *Knowledge societies ... in a nutshell. Information technology for sustainable development.* Report for the UN Commission on Science and Technology for Development and the International Development Research Centre. Retrieved at www.idrc.ca/openbooks/858-9/, on 17. March 2008.

Cuban, L. (1984). *How Teachers Taught, 1890-1980.* Longman: New York.

Cuban, L. (1986). *Teachers and Machines: The Use of Classroom Technology Since 1920.* Teachers College Press: New York.

De Corte, E., Verschaffel, L., Entwistle, N. & van Merienboer, J. (eds.) (2003). *Powerful learning environments: Unravelling basic components and dimensions.* Amsterdam: Pergamon.

Eliassen, E., Jøsendal, J.S. & Erstad, O. (2008). Ledelse av Lærende nettverk. (Leadership of Networks for Learning) ITU. University of Oslo: Oslo.

Engeström, Y. (1987). *Learning by Expanding: An Activity - Theoretical Approach to Developmental Research.* Helsinki. Located online at http://lchc.ucsd.edu/MCA/Paper/Engestrom/expanding/toc.htm, 17. March 2008.

Engeström, Y., Virkkunen, J., Helle, M., Pihlaja, J. & Poikela, R. (1996). *The Change laboratory as a tool for transforming work.* Lifelong Learning in Europe, 1(2), 10-17.

Erstad, O. (2004). *'PILOTer for skoleutvikling.' (PILOTs for school development. Final and summary report of the PILOT project. 1999-2003).* Report no. 28, ITU, University of Oslo.

Erstad, O. (2005). *Digital kompetanse i skolen (Digital literacy in the school.)* Oslo: Universitetsforlaget (University Press)

Erstad, O., Kløvstad, V., Kristiansen, T. & Søby M. (2005). *ITU Monitor 2005 – På vei mot digital kompetanse i grunnopplæringen. (ITU Monitor 2005 – On the way towards digital literacy in basic education.)* Oslo: Universitetsforlaget (University Press)

Fullan, M.G. (1991). *The new meaning of educational change.* London: Cassell

Fullan, M.G. (1993). *Change forces. Probing the depths of educational reform.* The Falmer Press: London

Goodlad, J.I., Anderson, R.H. (1984). *A place called school.* Blacklick, OH.: McGraw-Hill

Gray, J., Hopkins, D., Reynolds, D., Wilcox, B., Farell, S. & Jesson, D. (1999). *Improving schools. Performance & potential.* Open University Press: Buckingham

Hakkarainen, K., Palonen, T., Paavola, S. & Lehtinen, E. (2004). *Communities of networked expertise.* Amsterdam: Elsevier

Kozma, R.B. (Ed.) (2003). *Technology, innovation and educational change. A global perspective.* Eugene, OR: ISTE Publ.

Lund, T. (2004). *PILOT spor mot fremtidens skole. ('PILOT tracks towards the school of the future').* Report no. 27, ITU, University of Oslo. Oslo.

Marthinsen, K. (2006). *Tenk nettverk. ('Think networks')* Oslo: Vidarforlaget.

Ministry of Education and Research (2004a). *Culture for Learning.* White Paper. Oslo.

Ministry of Education and Research (2004b). *Program for digital literacy. 2004 – 2008.* Oslo.

Olson, D. (2003). *Psychological theory and educational reform.* Cambridge: Cambridge University Press.

UNESCO (2005). *Towards Knowledge Societies.* UNESCO World Report. Paris

Scardamalia, M. & Bereiter, C. (2006). Knowledge building: Theory, pedagogy, and technology. In Sawyer, R.K. (ed.) *The Cambridge Handbook of the learning sciences.* Cambridge: Cambridge University Press

Silseth, K. (2006). *Om prosjektet Lærende netteverk – en sammenfatning av nettverkenes rapporter.* (On the project Networks for Learning – a summary of the reports from networks.) Directorate of Education. Oslo.

Skogerbø, M., Ottestad, G. & Axelsen, H.K. (2007). *Lærende nettverk – fra informasjonsutveksling til kunnskapsdannelse? (Learning networks – from information sharing to knowledge building?)* Report. ITU: Oslo

Wasson, B., Ludvigsen, S. & Hoppe, U. (eds.) (2003). *Designing for change in networked learning environments.* Dordrecht: Kluwer Academic Publishers

Wenger, E. (1998). *Communities of practice. Learning, meaning and identity.* Cambridge: Cambridge University Press

Østerud, S. (2004). *Utdanning for informasjonssamfunnet. (Education for the information society.)* Oslo: Universitetsforlaget (University Press)

In: Learning in the Network Society and the Digitized School   ISBN 978-1-60741-172-7
Editor: Rune Krumsvik   © 2009 Nova Science Publishers, Inc.

Chapter 7

THE DIGITAL DIDACTIC

Rune Krumsvik[1] and Aslaug G. Almås[2]

1) University of Bergen, Norway
2) Stord/Haugesund University College, Norway

ABSTRACT

This theoretical article focuses on how the digital society and the digitised school change the underlying premises for teaching and learning in today's schools. New policy documents, research and experiences from the practice field suggest there may be a need to develop a new educational theory of technology related to didactic, which embraces the new didactical streams teachers have to deal with in the new educational reform, the Knowledge Promotion. A new concept, digital didactic, and a new didactical model are developed to capture this time of upheaval and outline the elements which are most relevant for teachers in today's schools. One of the implications of the article is that both the concept and the model have to go through a construct- and ecological validation through research, in teacher education and in school to ensure their validation and to avoid previous negative connotations of the terms "technology", "educational technology" and "instructional technology."

INTRODUCTION

The main focus in this article is on how the digital school and the use of ICT make it necessary to revitalise[1] the didactic and develop a new instructional theory of technology related to a new didactical foundation, which capture the dilemmas and challenge both schools and the teacher education face in our Network society (Castells, 1996, 2001). This has become more pressing as a result of the new educational reform, *Knowledge Promotion* (KD, 2006) where digital skills is now the fifth basic competence in all subjects at all levels

---

1 Revitalise: To *rouse* from a state of *inactivity* or *quiescence* (http://en.wiktionary.org/wiki/revitalize). In this article this definition has a double meaning: firstly, it highlights the need to "awake" the concept didactic to be more used in instructional settings, and secondly, it highlights the need to incorporate the new, digital terrain in –and out of school.

(stage 1-13, 6-19 years). Consequently, Norwegian schools are infiltrated with new technology, and obligatory ICT in all subjects is in many ways making it a time of upheaval for both our general perception of "technology" as a term in education and for teachers' technology use in school. The introduction of this national curriculum creates a situation where the pedagogical and didactical conditions in Norwegian classrooms have changed considerably. This situation calls for a revitalisation of the term *didactic* (which means the art of teaching), where one has to elaborate how a new concept, *digital didactic*, and digital didactic model[2] can function as a new instructional theory of technology. Such didactic revitalisation will of course be influenced by teachers' prior perception of technology, their *practice theory* (Dale, 1997, 2001; Handal & Lauvås, 2000), their *folk pedagogy* (Bruner, 1996) and their *artistic connoisseurship* (Eisner, 1979), based on eclectic theories, curriculum (and hidden curriculum), school culture, methods and experience. The problems with these central concepts are that they do not embrace the technology sufficiently and thus lack a more in depth consideration in how ICT influence "how teacher teach and learners learn" in the digital era. This theoretical article therefore highlights the need to develop an instructional theory of technology in the light of policy documents, specially the *Knowledge Promotion* (LK-06, KD 2006), research studies (Krumsvik, 2006a,b, 2007a,b, 2008a,b; Almås & Krumsvik, 2007, 2008) and the general digitisation of schools (Utdanningsdirektoratet, 2008). A new concept, digital didactic, and its model will be presented and discussed in relation to the challenges teachers are facing in the digitised school. The question considered by the article is how a new digital didactic concept and a digital didactic model can contribute to a revitalisation of the general didactic and as a new instructional theory of technology in Norway.

PREVIOUS STUDIES ON PEDAGOGICAL USE OF ICT

In many ways we are in the middle of a pedagogical and didactical time of upheaval in Norwegian education, where new, societal streams challenge both schools and teacher education. There are several aspects to this time of upheaval, and ICT plays an important role for both pedagogy and didactics. However, the lack of a didactic based on an educational theory of technology are still missing in the digital era and this gives call for considering how research studies from pedagogical use of ICT can give "a new didactic" a starting point for a didactical development. Therefore in the following part we present relevant studies which reveal which success factors seem to be more important than others in educational changes in school in general and in pedagogical use of ICT. This is presented as a backdrop to the didactic framework described later in the article.

Michael Fullan's (1982) study about the challenges of change finds the following characteristic features (in general) of successful innovations in school: good relationship between teachers, support from the school management, a clear timeline, staff development and participation, good communications and an internal (or local) consultant to support teachers (Fullan, 1982, p. 6). In many ways, other studies (Schofield, 1995; Tyack & Cuban, 1998; Krumsvik, 2006a) of general ICT implementation in school have found the same

---

[2] The digital didactic model is the explicit part of the digital didactic concept and attempts to visualize the content of digital didactic.

tendencies as Fullan (1982), despite the differences of the focus in the studies. This shows that there are several similarities between implementations in general (new assessment forms, new curricula, etc.) and ICT implementations in school, but what do we know about the situation concerning the more specific pedagogical use of ICT among teachers?

The Norwegian study ITU Monitor 2007 (Arnseth et al., 2007) revealed that there is still no in-depth pedagogical reflection on ICT use among teachers in Norwegian schools and that the lack of sufficient digital competence is a significant obstacle to success.

A Norwegian study concerning ICT use in Norwegian teacher education (NIFU/STEP 2008) revealed the same tendency among teacher educators and also that tool competence still has the dominant focus concerning digital competence. The pedagogical use of ICT varies much from institution to institution, and this is partly because some teacher educators still think ICT does not fit with pedagogy's values, ethics and epistemology.

Mumtaz (2000) studied the factors which affected teachers' use of ICT over two decades. Her list of 'inhibitors' of teachers' pedagogical use of ICT is long, and a well-known, central factor (in Mumtaz's list) from a Norwegian perspective is 'lack' of experience with ICT. This lack of experience with ICT and digital competence, are common to many countries and very often seem to be a premise provider for other inhibitors of teachers' ICT use (scepticism, technophobia, etc.).

Webb & Cox (2004) conducted a review of pedagogy related to information and communication technology and found that new affordances provided by ICT-based learning environments require teachers to undertake more complex pedagogical reasoning than before in their planning and teaching. ICT-based learning environments incorporates knowledge of specific affordances and how these relate to subject-based teaching objectives as well as the knowledge teachers have always needed to plan for their students' learning (Webb & Cox, 2004, p. 235). Webb & Cox also highlight how teachers' existing practice theory can not only be strengthened by ICT, but also can be revitalised. Somekh (2007) gives an example of the first one, where ICT fit with existing practice, and highlights how interactive whiteboards (IWBs) have been adopted very quickly in primary schools in Britain.

Pelgrum & Law (2003) highlight an important part of the pedagogical ICT penetration in school: e-assessment. They state that: 'new pedagogies require assessment methods that are context-sensitive such that students' abilities to solve authentic problems can be evaluated' (Pelgrum & Law, 2003, p. 24). Krumsvik's (2006a) study supports this statement and that a new digital epistemology requires new assessment forms.

The national, Norwegian ICT project, PILOT (Almås, 2004; Krumsvik, 2006a) included 120 schools and had a special focus towards implementation of ICT in school. Research studies from PILOT showed that some schools have come quite a long way pedagogically and didactically in their development work during PILOT (Krumsvik, 2006a). What marked these leading-edge schools was that the innovative work was led by fiery souls who saw new technology as a tool for facilitating customised learning content, enabling access to a broader range of resources and more communication between teachers and experts outside school. The same study showed the importance of teachers having a genuine engagement in the pedagogical implementation of ICT, so as to avoid such implementation being merely cosmetic, as several other studies have shown throughout the last decades (Krumsvik, 2006a).

Almås & Krumsvik's (2007) study showed that there is a clear relation between the level of digital competence and the teacher's awareness of pedagogical and didactical dimensions.

Therefore, the study underlined the need to focus on increasing teachers' digital competence to achieve more in-depth pedagogical and didactical reflection on their ICT use in school.

Almås & Krumsvik (2008) found that teachers increase their tendency to reflect on ICT use if they participate in action research projects where several 'reflection loops' and authentic video recordings from their own classroom teaching are discussed in-depth in teacher-researcher communities.

From these studies we can infer a general tendency: the teacher must have a central voice when implementing ICT in schools. Teachers' digital competence is also very important and might be a catalyst for other implementation elements and to avoid well known inhibitors. In addition to this, we find from the Norwegian studies that didactical pillars like 'what', 'how', and 'why' have to be complemented by 'where', 'when' and 'who' because of the digitisation of school and schooling. As the Danish researcher Mie Buhl states: 'The teaching profession is gradually changing from an anchoring in physical space to also being able to take place in virtual space or in a mixture of both' (Buhl, 2008, p. 2). This increases the need for revitalising the didactics in school, where the physical classroom and the digital classroom merge together and become complementary[3].

DIGITAL DIDACTIC AND FOCUSING ON THE TEACHER

Until now there have principally been two main fields in Norway which deal with the implementation of ICT in learning and teaching: the didactic perspective and the theories of learning, the latter enjoying the dominant position. The theories of learning are inspired by a sociocultural approach, i.e. *activity theory* (Engestrøm, 1987) and *situated learning* (Lave & Wenger, 1991). Looking through these (among others) theoretical lenses we find that newer ICT paradigms such as CSCL (Computer Supported Collaborative Learning) (Koschmann 1996) have had a certain (intentional) impact on both teacher education and the practice field in Norway with regard to how to integrate ICT in education in general. The strong focus of the sociocultural approach and CSCL on ICT as a mediating artefact has made them into powerful frameworks for analysis because they clarify the relationships between ICT and other vital elements in teaching and learning. Still, these theoretical foundations has not been adopted widely neither in teacher education nor in school so far, partly because of scepticism towards technology in general but also the lack of necessary digital competence (at different levels) to utilize these theoretical frameworks.

At the same time we find that although didactics have been discussed broadly in the Norwegian educational system for decades, this concept is apparently less developed in the discussion about ICT and its impact on teaching and learning. Therefore, sociocultural learning theory as theoretical lenses and ICT as a 'mediating artefact' as a backdrop, we will examine didactic concepts in more depth since these have long traditions in Norwegian education. We will below give a brief introduction to the didactical area, which will be followed up in the next section presenting a didactical framework.

---

[3] The concepts "when, where, and who" has to a certain degree been attached to didactics earlier, but has become more highlighted and important in the digitized school because of the new "digital classroom" (LMS, VLE). This is one of the main reasons for the need to revitalize the didactic term to capture today's didactical terrain.

The Danish author Laursen defines didactics as the field of educational theory that provides guidelines and tools that are used to develop the practice of teaching (Laursen, 1994, p. 125). Didactics is therefore a way of concretising teachers' work. The two fields, didactics and theories of learning, complement each other because of their focus on understanding complexity and enlightening the social interaction and the environment in the learning process (Hokstad, 2002, p. 217). The term didactics is, however, nearly absent from the English language (Schnack, 2004), and there is a risk of confusion because the term may be used where others use pedagogy (Hamilton, 1999). Hopman & Riquarts state that *Didaktik* is the most important tool for planning, enacting, and thinking about teaching in most of northern and central Europe (Hopman & Riquarts, 2000, p. 3). In the English-speaking world *Didaktik* does not have a comparable importance, and the issues *Didaktik* addresses are presented in the different framework of 'curriculum and methods' or 'curriculum and instruction' (Hopman & Riquarts, 2000, p. 3). The didactical focus in our research is chosen because it places emphasis on the teacher and the way s/he performs her/his work. From the above studies we find that research on pedagogical use of ICT is very often conducted without didactics being mentioned at all and thus there is a need to develop an instructional theory of technology as underpinning for didactic in the digital era.

In the sections that follow, the article will first introduce a didactical framework before we try to elaborate different theoretical positions that have inspired us to develop our digital didactic model. Third, we discuss how the revitalisation of didactics can contribute to the development of a new concept, digital didactic, and a digital didactic model for teachers in the digitised school.

DIDACTICAL FRAMEWORK

Didactics as a concept has its roots in the ancient world and 2500 years ago the word (*didaskein = to teach*) was used in the Greek language as a concept for teaching and instruction; it was to have later impact on the Latin language as well. In more recent times the concept appears again in the works of Wolfgang Ratke (1571-1635) and Johan Amos Comenius (1592-1670). Comenius wrote the well-known *Didactica Magna* (1628/1638) which today is considered to be the main codex of didactic. During the seventeenth century didactics were developed both as a theory and a practise in Germany and the German influence have had strong influence in Nordic countries: "Most of the Danish/Norwegian educational system at around 1814 was copied from Germany" (Nordkvelle, 2004, p. 431). And this German influence has continued throughout the centuries.

In Norwegian, Nordic and German contexts it is usual to divide the didactical concept into *general didactic* (or just didactics) and *subject didactic*. General didactic has its starting-point in Comenius' thoughts and it was in the 1950s that the concept got its concomitant adjective 'general'. Although the use of this adjective has not yet been subject to theoretical clarification, general didactic has made its way into pedagogical language, and pedagogy has always had general didactic beneath its wings. The symbiotic relationship between general didactic and the more specific subject didactic occurs when general didactic is concrete; then the general didactic will exemplify from the subject didactic. In *Didactical Models*, Jank & Meyer define general didactic as: "...a science, which explores and structures, conditions, possibilities, consequences and boundaries for learning and teaching in a way which is theoretical based and useful in practise" (Jank & Meyer, 2006, p. 34). When it comes to subject didactic, they observe that this is: '....special science, which explores and structures conditions, possibilities, consequences and boundaries for learning and teaching within a subject field in or outside the school's context' (Jank & Meyer, 2006, p. 34). In this article it is general didactic which has a central focus.

During the 60—70's the didactic concept became associated with the term "educational technology" from US, which had underpinnings from behaviourism and goal taxonomies. The Tyler-rationale from Ralph Tyler (1949) which highlighted goal-steering, efficiency and scientific management got impact in the Nordic educational systems and technology as a term became closely associated with this educational wave. The critics of this educational wave meant that it was a close relationship between educational technology and instructional technology, and based much of their critique on the work by Jürgen Harbermas (Nordkvelle, 2004). This critique towards technology as a concept was raised by several Norwegian authors, e.g. the Norwegian philosopher Hans Skjervheim in his *Objectivity and the study of Man* (1959) and through his ground-breaking article *The Instrumental Mistake* (1972). In these texts Skjervheim is criticising the emergent 'technocratisation' of the Norwegian educational system, where he finds some positivistic foundations as premise provider for policymaking, pedagogy and didactic. Both Hans Skjervheim, Erling Lars Dale, Lars Løvlie and Jon Hellesnes identified educational technology and didactics as means to promote such technocratisation of our educational system. "These critics of educational technology and, more or less indirectly of didactic, rejected any positive interpretation of "technology (....) Distinction between "technique, "technology", and "technocracy" were not clear, and any notions with "positivism" were effectively ruled out. Nevertheless, the critique was devastating and significant for the further development of the pedagogical arena in the Nordic countries" (Nordkvelle, 2004, p. 434). In this way both didactic and technology got very negative connotations for decades in Norway and the heritage from this politicized period of Norwegian education we find that even today teacher educators who states that technology does not fit with their pedagogical basic view (NIFU/STEP, 2008). In the same study only 19% of the teacher educators support the following statement: "Digital competence is a large part of the teacher didactical foundation" (NIFU/STEP, 2008, p. 50). Myths, stereotypes and scepticism concerning technology seem to have prevailed throughout the decades because of the politicizing of the concept during the 60-70's in Norwegian education.

However, the didactic concept, despite critique, continued to develop throughout the 1970's. In general, we can say (from this era) that the most common use of the (general) didactic term was to divide questions: *what* (is the content), *how* (should this be performed) and *why* (should this be done)? The difference between didactical foundations is how they emphasise each of these questions (Bachmann, 2005). During the 1970's Bjarne Bjørndal developed a new didactical model which had great influence in the Nordic countries. Bjørndal & Lieberg (1975, 1978) widen *what, how* and *why* to the term Didactic Relational Design [didaktisk relasjonstenkning in Norwegian], where especially the "why" (with its political underpinning) were highlighted. The model was meant to help practising teachers to plan, process and evaluate teaching (Bjørndal & Lieberg, 1978) and has been a central part of the teacher education syllabus and in school in Norway for decades. The model emphasises the internal relationship between variables such as evaluation/assessment, content, goals, participants and external conditions. This particular model has been criticised for underestimating the importance of organisational aspects (Imsen, 2006, p. 336). The model is, however, well-known and well-reputed among in-service teachers because it is concrete and easily understood, and shows at the same time how the factors mutually interact with each other. The model has survived through several decades because it is (allegedly) not connected to a special theoretical position or ideology, and can be used by different learning theories and paradigms. Imsen (2006) states that the model Didactic Relational Design can be perceived as a combination of the traditional normative didactics (which underlines how teaching should be) and the frame factor theory [Rammefaktorteorien in Norwegian]. Lundgren's (1972, 1979) frame factor theory has been strongly influenced by the French structuralism, states that the normative didactic is not sufficient and that the teacher has several frames he/she has to consider and adapt to.

Nordkvelle (2004) states that: "With the rejection of positivist psychology as its knowledge base didactics sought a new foundation" (2004, p. 437). Some of this seeking for a new foundation can be summed up by Laursen (1994), who argues that from a historical perspective that we are facing three different basic didactic approaches: *prescriptive*, *rationalistic* and *reflective*. The *prescriptive theories* are the classical theories of teaching and they give concrete and precise guidelines on how to teach and how to plan lessons. *Rationalistic theories* suggest abstract and procedural guidelines on how to teach and how to plan lessons. They are not based on an analysis of actual teaching practices, but instead they focus on rationalistic principles and theories of learning. *Reflective theories* can be traced back to John Dewey and have been dominant during the last decade. They provide very abstract guidelines for teaching and are the only ones based on an analysis of teaching practices (Laursen, 1994, p. 126). The most common connection with the reflective didactic approach is that theoretical models can help teachers reflect in and on their own practice. The theory of Donald Schön (1983) has inspired most authors in this field and Michael Polanyi's (1968) focus on tacit knowledge has also been an important contribution. Schön says that planning of teaching and teaching practices is open to different kinds of pedagogical approaches. The various components interact with each other. The reflective didactic approach leads to active and reflective teachers and thereby prevents some of the criticism of didactic being normative.

Another educational researcher, who for decades has contributed to the fields of didactic, is the German pedagogue, Wolfgang Klafki. He engages in questions about purpose, content and methods of teaching, and suggests that preparation of instruction must start with questions about the content to be taught. A keyword in this reflection is *Bildung*[4]. Klafki speaks of Bildung as an important part of the discussion of teachers' behaviour and content in teaching (Künzli, 1994). Bildung is understood as a qualification for reasonable self-determination, for autonomy, for freedom for individual thought and for individual moral decisions (Klafki, 2000a, p. 87). Development of these terms leads to further knowledge, abilities and attitudes (Klafki, 2001, p. 165). Klafki claims that Bildung nowadays has to include reflections about key societal problems. As examples of contemporary key problems Klafki mentions problems related to war and peace, manmade diversity in society, environmental questions, new information and communication technology and human subjectivity in the gap between individual claims, humanity and acknowledgment of the other

---

[4] Bildung is a German word which does not have any synonyms in the English language. It highlights the ethical and moral issues of *being* and in school often attached to the moral development of pupils over time.

(Klafki, 2001, p. 73). This means that didactics is always connected to some context in society.

The introduction of ICT in teaching and learning and the discussion about what young learners need to know about digital media have revitalised Klafki's term Bildung in the Norwegian educational debate. Youth deals with technology in leisure-time and it is a tool for learning in school. 'Digital competence' and 'Digital Bildung' are terms often used in the discussion, in order to emphasise that the knowledge youths need is not restricted to practical skills in using ICT. The Norwegian Lars Løvlie (2003) started a discussion about Bildung in the information society, and used the term 'Technocultural Bildung' to describe changes in our understanding of *Bildung*. Technocultural Bildung points towards an integrated overall approach which enables us to reflect on the influence of ICT on different qualifications such as communicative competence, social competence, students' critical attitudes, etc. He describes Bildung today as an interface between the boundaries where the self and the culture meet (Løvlie, 2003). The ITU (2003) in Norway has also contributed to a further development of the Digital Bildung concept in general and Krumsvik & Støbakk (2007) relate Digital Bildung more to education, teachers and pupils.

The Bildung discussion is central to Klafki's work about teaching and learning, and it is a result of the introductory question: What is the content to be taught? Curriculum designers must comprehend content selection in a particular human, historical situation and with specific groups of children in mind (according to environment, school types, grade level) (Klafki, 2000b, p.150). The content of education is conveyed by examples that represent a larger set of cultural contents. ''A content of education must always make fundamental problems, fundamental relations, fundamental opportunities, general principles, laws, values, and methods understandable (…) Any specific content thus contains general substance' (Klafki, 2000b, p. 150). Only after fundamental reflections on the content of education and substance can the task of didactic analysis be more precisely defined. Klafki (2000b) has five questions for a didactic analysis and after this analysis the planning of the methodical arrangement of teaching and learning starts. The five questions are:

(1) Contemporary meaning – what does the planned topic exemplify, represent, or typify?
(2) Future meaning – where can the topic be picked up and used at a later date, either as a whole or as individual elements – insights, conceptions, work methods, techniques?
(3) Content structure – how is the content structured?
(4) Exemplary value – what wider or general sense or reality is exemplified and revealed to the learner by the contents?
(5) Pedagogical representations – what are the special cases, phenomena, situations, experiments, persons, elements of aesthetic experience, and so forth, in terms of which the structure of the content in question can become interesting, stimulating, approachable, conceivable or vivid for children of the stage of development of this class?

Klafki (2000b) states that after these questions have been worked through, the next step is the planning of teaching or the outline of the lesson. That work is concerned with the 'how?' question. The search for teaching methods started with subject content and it is in the last and practical phase that teachers interplay between experiences and reflection finds its expression in practical work. Methodological principles, assessment, and organisation will be considered by the teacher. Klafki divides didactic into: didactic in a wide sense (general didactic) and didactic in a narrow sense (subject didactic) (Jank & Meyer, 2006), which is the understanding on which this article is based.

As a summary of this section one can claim that didactic is not primarily planning or seeing the world through a particular narrow subject, but a social practice in which knowledge construction can be made visible. While general didactic has a general content in Norway (and a broader knowledge focus), however, we find that subject didactic has a narrower focus towards specific subjects and their knowledge. And didactics can hardly be separated from our conception of knowledge. Such a separation will reduce didactics to a series of techniques applied to *any* assumption of what knowledge is and the epistemological implications (Lund, 2003, p. 80). And as we have seen technology as a concept has had negative connotations within didactic and even today we find very few didactical approaches which deals with the impact of technology in teaching and learning. Therefore, we will in the following section explore how certain approaches can give contribution to the didactics of today's schooling.

TECHNOLOGICAL PEDAGOGICAL CONTENT KNOWLEDGE

Klafki's ideas have had great impact on Scandinavian teacher education as a guide for lesson planning by student teachers. There are some links between the Scandinavian work and that of the American educational psychologist Lee Shulman (1987), who has widely studied the interrelation between pedagogy and content knowledge. He said that teachers have to build their own knowledge for teaching, and this theory building, which is distinctive to teachers, results in pedagogical content knowledge. Teachers develop pedagogical content knowledge through being reflective practitioners, inter alia. In Shulman's view, pedagogical content knowledge is a form of practical knowledge that is used by teachers to guide their actions in highly contextualised classroom settings. Shulman (1987) emphasised the importance of teachers in innovative work with school reforms, asserting that teachers know things not understood by others and can transform understanding, performance skills, or desired attitudes or values into pedagogical representations and actions. Teaching begins with each teacher's understanding of what is to be learned and how it is to be taught (Shulman, 1987, p. 227). To characterise the complex ways in which teachers think about how particular content should be taught, Shulman (1986) argued that 'pedagogical content knowledge' (p. 9) is the content knowledge that deals with the teaching process, including 'the ways of representing and formulating the subject that make it comprehensible to others' (p. 9). If teachers are to be successful they need alternative ways of representing their subjects. They need to confront both issues of content and pedagogy simultaneously by embodying 'the aspects of content most germane to its teachability' (Shulman, 1986, p. 9). This knowledge also includes an understanding of what makes the learning of specific topics easy or difficult. The kind of conceptions and preconceptions that students of different ages and backgrounds bring to learning are important to grasp.

Mishra & Koehler (2006) extended Shulman's definition to technological pedagogical content knowledge (TPCK), and describe how ICT expands and challenges teachers' pedagogical content knowledge. The transformation of content, pedagogy and technology is difficult, or messy, as Mishra & Koehler (2008) would say. They have introduced concept TPACK, which both stands for 'Total PACKage' and in addition describes how teachers are responsible through their total Technological, Pedagogical and Content Knowledge (Figure 1). It is a complicated work which needs creative solutions. The solutions are not right or wrong, but are unique and context-dependent, and often generate new problems (Mishra & Koehler, 2008), as Krumsvik (2006a) found in his study of teachers attempting to implement ICT.

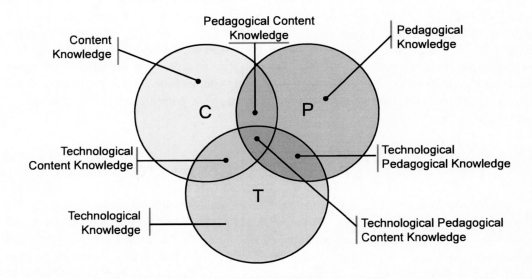

Figure 1. Technological, pedagogical, content knowledge (Mishra & Koehler, 2006, p.1025).

In many ways it is this seamless integration of pedagogy, content knowledge and technology that teachers in Norway are striving for, because of the clear command in the national curriculum that teachers should use ICT in all subjects at all stages. We can observe a clear relation between Mishra & Koehler's use of concepts and the concepts from didactics: a. when they use pedagogy, this can be related to general didactics; b. when they use content knowledge, this can be related to the subject didactics; and c. when they use the technology concept this is of course similar to the technology concept used in school. In this way we find these concepts complementary and useful to use as underpinnings for our own concepts and model. This is important because it is quite obvious that the lack of revitalised didactical approaches is evident in today's teacher education and among in-service teachers, and therefore we will present a new approach concerning this issue in the next section of the article.

THE REVITALISATION OF DIDACTIC AND AN EMERGING DIGITAL DIDACTIC-MODEL

When we attempt to revitalise general didactic within the Norwegian context, there are two important frame factors that must be considered: the digitalisation of society and school in the last ten years and the new national curriculum content and goal-steering. These frame factors have altered so many of the underlying conditions for teaching, learning and knowledge that even if many of the former conceptions of general didactic are still valid, we find it necessary to revitalise general didactic to take into account the new didactical streams we are facing today. To incorporate this situation in conceptual terms, we find it appropriate to present a new concept, digital didactic, which takes into account the didactical terrain teachers, pupils, teacher students and teacher educators are facing in the digitised school. In the same way as general didactic has the adjective *general*, which focuses on general didactics elements in teaching, our concept has the adjective *digital*, which puts a special focus on digital didactic elements in teaching. A definition of this concept is: 'Digital didactic is an instructional theory of technology which puts a special focus towards the art of teaching in technology dense learning environments'. Such a new concept, however, can always be criticised for being vague, too narrow and with limited ecological validity in the practice field and in teacher education. It can also be criticised for not dealing with the fact that the new national curriculum strong goal steering, has fragment of both the Tyler-rationale (Tyler, 1949), criterion-referenced assessment (Glaser 1962) and Blooms Taxonomi (Blooms, 1956) as underpinning. Even if this critique is relevant, our preliminary findings from a pilot study (survey) among teachers in upper secondary school (n= 83) and an action research study among teacher educators (n=3), show that the majority (92%) of these informants answered that there is a need for new concepts of digital didactics as well as a new digital didactic model in this new didactical terrain. Nevertheless, the construct validity of the concept of digital didactic is of course still low, so further studies, use of the concept and validity communities is necessary to increase this construct validity.

It comes clear that teachers' didactical or pedagogical reasoning must be understood in a broad framework of educational practice. Illuminating teachers' practice in teaching and learning with ICT requires examination of teachers' ideas, values, beliefs and the thinking that leads to observable elements in practice (Alexander, 1992). A didactic model can be seen as a combination of Alexander's statements, traditional normative didactics and a tool for capturing the complexity in praxis. The notorious gap between normative thinking and experiences from practice and context (descriptive aspects) is a common discussion topic for teachers. The norms, national guidelines and ideals combined with the descriptive and analytical information constitute teachers' use of ICT in their teaching practice. Our creation of a new digital didactic model is also a combination of normative and descriptive because we try to illustrate the 'digital practices' in school with questions of what the contents and work methods for teaching should be and why teaching turns out the way it does. The didactic model does not remove from the teacher a personal responsibility for making educational decisions. That is an important role of the professional teacher and his pedagogical content knowledge.

When the didactic for the digitised school is revitalised, however, it is quite clear that one have to give particular consideration to the structures which have strongest impact on teachers' professional development today. Several of the studies mentioned earlier as well as Krumsvik (2006a, 2008a) found that ICT only has an impact on teachers' practice and willingness to achieve better digital competence, if it is clearly attached to the vital structures of school: assessment and exams, curriculum and syllabus. How then are these structures reflected in the new national curriculum? Below we will illustrate and describe the five structures which are an important backdrop for our revitalised general didactic (which will be presented later as Figure 3) and constitute the different elements in our first digital didactic model (Figure 2, with focus on a macro level).

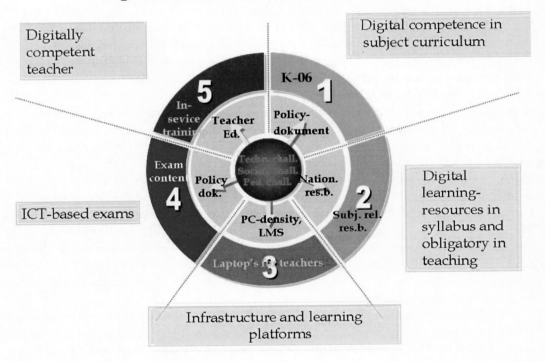

Figure 2. The digital didactic model 1 (focuses on a macro level).

First, (up, right in the model) digital competence is the fifth core competence in the new national curriculum and is strongly anchored in every subject and subject theme throughout compulsory and secondary school (6-19 years, stage 1–13). This makes the use of ICT obligatory in every subject and for the first time in history teachers are now saying that 'there is no way back – ICT is here to stay'. Both nationally and internationally this is a historical event, because Norway is the first country in the world highlighting digital competence so clearly. A prerequisite for handling this digital competence is that pupils have both the necessary *tool competence* and *interpretation competence*, which give the digital competence term a wider content than the more instrumentalistic underpinnings in former curricula. In this way, the pupils must learn to put focus on *subject use of ICT* in school, and not only the *ritualistic ICT use* from their digital life world outside school (this will be described later in the article).

Second, (down, right in the model) the implementation of digital learning resources and digital textbooks as part of the syllabus has given ICT a higher status as a learning resource and requires teachers to use them in their teaching and in their preparation for exams (together with textbooks). This is also a historic event in Norwegian educational terms, because such digital textbooks and learning resources have never had such a high status as they do today.

Third, (down, middle in the model) learning platforms (LMS) have been implemented in all secondary schools in Norway in the last five years. They form a new 'digital classroom' for teachers and pupils which are complementary to the traditional, physical classroom. Learning platforms have thus become a very important structure in secondary school which require teachers to inform, communicate and collaborate with pupils and through which formative assessment of pupils must be conducted. These learning platforms have implemented obligatory elements for teachers to carry out, such as noting pupils' absence from teaching, registering term grades (School Arena) and registering that compulsory assignments are delivered by the pupils. The more subject-related activities are increasingly used by teachers and it is expected by the school owner that learning platforms will become an even more important digital classroom with increasing focus on subject matter. In addition, the majority of teachers in secondary school have now their own laptop provided by the school and together with very good PC density among pupils (almost 1:1 in upper secondary school) and infrastructure, this is a catalyst for teachers' ICT use. This is a leap from only five years ago when the situation was quite different and it gives good opportunities for teachers to focus more on didactical elements than lack of technology and technical obstacles (which were quite common before).

Fourth, (down, left in the model), the most important steering instrument for advancing the use of ICT by teachers is that Norway has now implemented ICT-based exams. This means that pupils e.g. can use their own laptops in exams in upper secondary schools. This is a milestone in the Norwegian school system and it is clear that it has increased the status of ICT considerably. The content of the assessment forms for these ICT-based exams is still in its infancy, however, and needs to be developed to reflect a broader view of the knowledge-building occurring in pupils' everyday practice.

Fifth, (up, left in the model), the teachers' digital competence is a vital structure in this model to realise the other structures in the model. Today we can register that digital competence among teachers is not sufficient and there is an urgent need to support teachers to develop their digital competence (this issue will be discussed in more depth later in the article). Therefore, both teacher education and in-service training are important providers to produce better digital competence among teachers.

It is evident that these five structures create a different didactical terrain from before and is a leap from the earlier didactic models (Bjørndal & Lieberg, 1975, 1978), even if there are similarities as well. Today's classroom practice under the new educational reform is a combination of virtual rooms (net) and the physical classroom, and a continuation of the practice on net takes place when students leave school in the afternoon. Teaching is thus nowadays taking place outside schools and didactics is not limited to schools. A continuation of the school day at home may have existed in the predigital period, but we observe to a great extent that the teacher is available and an active user on LMS in the afternoon and the evening together with the collaborating pupils. The complex interplay between these different levels is essential in our issuant digital didactic model. Since the traditional classroom is expanded we may describe them as (a) physical classroom and (b) a digital classroom. The digital didactic model II (Figure 3) is presented below and divided into five elements that will be further explained and attached to both these classroom arenas.

The first digital didactic model (Figure 2) that we presented above highlighted five important structures in school today and can be considered as a model which captures the premise providers for the more concrete digital didactics (Figure 3 below). As an addition to the five structures, the centre of the model (Figure 2) focuses on three challenges attached to ICT-based learning environments and will be highlighted in the next part. These are inspired by Mishra & Koehler's (2006) Technological, Pedagogical, Content Knowledge (A & C) and Klafki's (2001) Bildung concept (B).

A. Technological Challenges

This aspect was not a big issue in the traditional, computer-free classrooms of the past. Today the situation is completely different and even if the technology is easier to use, we find new technical challenges which teachers must always reflect upon, both fundamentally and practically. How can I manage to weave the technology seamlessly together with the general didactics and subject didactics? Does the ICT function? Do I need to check some equipment beforehand? How should I arrange the use of laptops for pupils? Do the pupils get access to the subject links that I have prepared on the Net? Teachers have to deal with a greater complexity of ICT than ever before and therefore must consider this as an important part of planning teaching lessons (even if the technology itself is easier to use than before).

B. Sociocultural Challenges (Bildung Aspects)

The sociocultural challenge is attached to the fact that teachers of today have another reference frame and have never had the experience of growing up in a digitised society. The pupils of today have therefore been through childhood and a digital Bildung journey that neither society nor school have experienced before. They are in many ways the New Millennium Learners (Pedro, 2006) and their reference frame is a society where Internet and mobile telephones have existed throughout their whole life span and Bildung journey. Many of these digital youngsters live an online existence and their ontological development is strongly influenced by a digital culture (i.e. Second Life, YouTube, Facebook, MSN Messenger, mobile phones, etc.). Teachers need to reflect about how 'teachers teach and learners learn' in this 'newborn' digitised society and school, and thus this sociocultural aspect is different today from that in the school in the past. That is, the digital classroom is in many regards an extension of the physical classroom and needs to be considered as a new 'room' for learning that goes hand in hand with pupils' sociocultural development and online existence. The complementary possibilities of this are interesting, but challenging.

C. The Pedagogical Challenges

How can one as a teacher weave the pedagogy seamlessly together with the technology and didactics? A reflection around the pedagogical issues of teaching has always been a part of teachers' practice theory. But the digitised school creates both possibilities and challenges that teachers did not face earlier (e.g. one laptop for each pupil, etc.), as the research studies presented in the first part of the article showed us. This has to be considered when teaching is planned, and also the kind of strategies teachers need to have when different pupil actions occur in the teaching lessons. The pedagogical challenges relate largely to part two of the national curriculum and the importance of well-founded class management in an ICT-dense learning environment.

Figure 3 (below) shows a concretisation of the digital didactic model 1 (Figure 2 above) and puts focus on a meso level. This model is partly a further development of Jank & Meyer's (2006) pentagon – a hermeneutic structure model for teaching. It is called hermeneutic because it is based on hermeneutic methods and a close relationship with practice. Especially the PILOT-project (Almås, 2004; Krumsvik, 2006a), our later research studies (Almås & Krumsvik 2007, 2008) and the project "Teach as we preach" (Krumsvik, 2008c) has been important in relation to this issue.

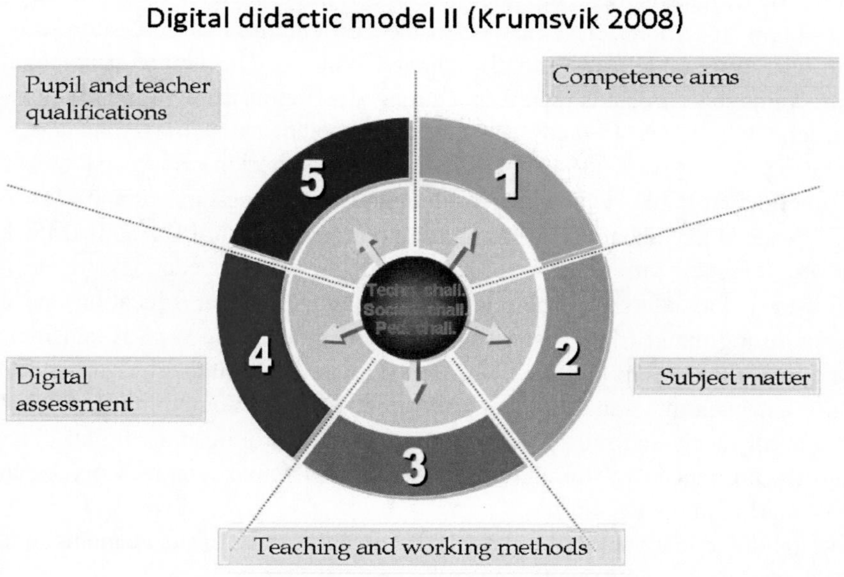

Digital didactic model II (Krumsvik 2008)

Figure 3. Digital didactic model II (focuses at a meso level).

The digital didactic model is also a partial extension of Bjørndal & Lieberg's (1975, 1978) Didactic Relational Design model. Their model has an underlying normative perspective, but is also influenced by the frame factor theory (Lundgren, 1972, 1979). Bjørndal & Lieberg's model was meant to help practising teachers to plan, process and evaluate teaching and emphasise the internal relationship between variables (Bjørndal & Lieberg, 1975, 1978). Bjørndal & Lieberg's model has six parts in contrast with Jank &

Meyer's pentagon (our model is also a pentagon). Our model is also inspired by Laursen's *reflective didactic approach* (Laursen, 1994), and Klafki's (2000a, b, 2001), Shulman's (1987) and Mishra & Koehler's (2006) foundations. At the same time our digital model is a leap from traditional didactic models, because of the new directives and demand teachers are facing in a digitised society and school and which are important steering instruments and frame factors, even if this is a kind of goal steering which has similarity to the Tyler rationale. In the following part we will explore this model in more depth and make clear the different parts.

THE ELEMENTS IN THE DIGITAL DIDACTIC MODEL II

Like the didactic models of Jank & Meyer (2006) and Bjørndal & Lieberg (1975, 1978), this digital didactic model focuses on the most relevant elements teachers' need to consider in the digitised school. It is therefore based on the new regulations in policy documents such as the new national curriculum (LK-06, KD, 2006), White Paper nr. 31 (KD, 2008), and our own research (Krumsvik, 2006a, b, 2007a, 2008a,b,c; Almås & Krumsvik, 2008) within this area is used to embed this new didactical terrain in the model.

From our own analysis of LK-06 and the Directory of Education's preliminary guidelines to the curriculum, it is quite clear that when the curriculum is as goal-steered as it is, it is difficult to base this model on normative didactics alone. The new concept in the subject curriculum, competence aims, is therefore a strong steering instrument for teachers' everyday practice in schools of today. In many ways these competence aims have traits and roots going back to the Tyler rationale (1949), Glaser's (1962) criterion-referenced assessment and Blooms Taxonomy (1956), which many thought was a long-gone era of the Norwegian educational system. The debate centring on the poor results from PISA, TIMMS, PIRLS and national tests, together with a massive critique of the reform pedagogy in the Norwegian context, however, has altered the conditions for schools, teacher education and curriculum development during the last few years. Even if the methodical freedom is considerable in the LK-06, one can still observe that the competence aims are stronger steering instruments and that ICT use has been integrated in these competence aims as something that is to be used in all subjects at all levels and during ICT-based exams. Therefore, this digital didactic model will be mostly influenced by Lundgren's (1972, 1979) frame factor theory because of the strong goal steering in the LK-06.

The digital didactic model probes how ICT influences each of the elements in the didactic model and below we will examine these one by one.

1. Competence Aims

Each subject in the new curriculum is structured into main subject areas for which competence aims have been formulated. Use of digital tools is part of these competence aims and the teacher is responsible for organising a learning environment where students can achieve these goals in both the physical and digital classrooms. This means that teachers need to integrate both digital textbooks and digital learning resources in the syllabus and in teaching lessons to fulfil the requirements of the national authorities. The grade scales for the final assessment in school reflect high and low achievement of these competence aims, which have therefore had great impact[5] as a new structure of teachers' digital didactic. On this basis the competence aims establish the goal structure (Jank & Meyer, 2006) as one of the five elements in the model.

2. Subject Matter

In the former curricula we find less goal-steering, for example in Mønsterplanen 1987 (M87, KUF 1987) than in LK-06 (KD, 2006), where the teacher had a higher degree of autonomy. Although LK-06 has considerable methodical freedom for the teacher, one can observe that the competence aims are steering the subject content in the teachers' everyday practice. Therefore, the subject matter of teachers' digital didactics is more than ever attached to the competence aims in the new national curriculum. Only five years ago teachers could choose if they wanted to use ICT or not in their teaching lessons. Today this is obligatory and calls for their didactic for subject matter in the digitised school to be revitalised. The didactical pillars, *why*, *what* and *how*, are not sufficient in today's digital terrain in and out of school, and need to be complemented by *when*, *where* and *who*. This gives reason to consider how teachers teach subject matter in the *physical classroom* and how this should be carried out in the *digital classroom* (e.g. using learning platforms (LMS) in study time, during homework, in leisure time, etc). A consequence of this is that teaching in the physical classroom hands over to the digital classroom after the ordinary lesson is over. Nevertheless, in both classrooms it is required that both teachers and pupils use ordinary textbooks attached to the actual subject matter but also digital textbooks and learning resources with equal status. A consequence of this is that teachers must prepare themselves for teaching the actual subject matter in textbooks, digital textbooks and digital learning resources. In particular, the complementary aspects of multimodality gives new didactical possibilities for teachers to teach in general but also visualise subject matter in new ways.

Below, a model (Figure 4) illustrates the complexity of teaching subject matter in the digitised school. The didactical reflections around subject matter have to consider both how to teach subject matter related to competence aims with quality assured digital learning resources (*subject use of ICT*) and also how one as a teacher can utilise the *ritualistic ICT use* to let the pupils learn the subject matter. The didactical reflections must also consider what teaching activities should occur in the physical classroom versus the digital classroom.

As a consequence of the digital revolution and new, digital learning resources, some subjects in school have been strongly influenced by this development and changed the subject content considerably. E.g. the subject Geographic has got quite new conditions through Google Earth, and Adobe Photoshop and Google Sketch Up has "transformed" the Art & Handcraft-subject. This show how *subject use of ICT* has potential to develop and transform subjects and give the pupils new possibilities for knowledge construction.

---

[5] These competence aims have been criticised by researchers, pedagogues and teachers because of a narrow focus on taxonomies and clear relation to Blooms Taxonomy, the Tyler rationale and Glaser's criterion-referenced assessment.

The complementary aspects of ritual and subject use of ICT

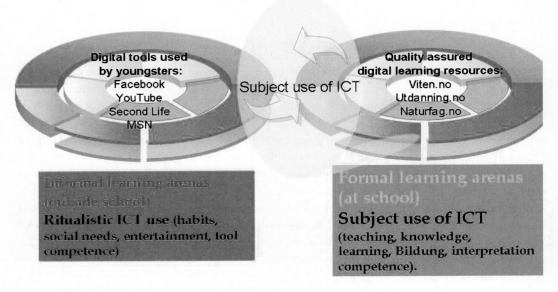

Figure 4. Ritualistic ICT use versus subject use of ICT.

However, the problem in Norwegian schools today is that the *ritualistic ICT use* (with the tool competence in the front seat) is dominating the classrooms. This happens because teachers have not yet developed their didactic framing of a *subject use of ICT* (which has the interpretation competence in the front seat) and a sufficient digital competence, and of course this creates a lot of frustration among teachers today. This calls for a stronger focus on the digital didactic of *subject use of ICT* in the first place and over time incorporation of the *ritualistic ICT use* from the youngsters' online existence outside school. However, the situation in Norway of today is that a lot of well meant digital learning resources are being developed by publishers, directorate of education, commercial firms, teachers and others. Even if much of these initiatives are positive, one has to ask how many of these digital learning resources are based on research findings within the area of multimedia learning. This seems to be special important in relation to create a valid content to the concept *subject-use of ICT* and to carry out research based teaching for both teacher educators and teachers. Below I will mention some of Richard Mayer's (2001) main findings within the area of multimedia learning, as an example of how this *subject-use if ICT* can be more research based in the design of such digital learning resources:

- *Multimedia principle*: Students learn better from words and pictures than from words alone.
- *Spatial Contiguity Principle*: Students learn better when corresponding words and pictures are presented near rather than far from each other on page or screen.

- *Temporal Contiguity Principle*: Students learn better when corresponding words and pictures are presented simultaneously rather than successively.
- *Coherence Principle*: Students learn better when extraneous words, pictures, and sounds are excluded rather than included.
- *Modality principle*: Students learn better from animation and narration than from animation and on-screen text.
- *Redunancy principle*: Students learn better from animation and narration than from animation and on-screen text.
- *Individual Differences Principle*: Design effects are stronger for low-knowledge learners than for high-knowledge learners and for high-spatial learners rather than for low-spatial learners (Mayer 2001: 184).

In many ways such research findings can give both adapted education and differentiation new conditions if it is considered as part of the *subject-use of ICT* where teaching, knowledge and learning has the main focus. At the same time this may prevent a Matthew effect (Merton 1973) and digital gaps between the pupils based on social background, which has been a big problem in the educational system in Norway for decades.

On this basis the subject matter establishes the content structure (Jank & Meyer, 2006) as one of the five elements in the model.

3. Teaching and Working Methods

In the new national curriculum there is great local and methodical freedom for teachers and this opens the possibilities for teachers to use a broad spectrum of methodical entry points in teaching and in pupils' working methods. ICT opens this free space up even more and gives teachers the possibility to meet the Millennium Learners (Pedro, 2006) on their 'home ground' and online existence. In the physical classroom this is possible, but it can be complemented by the digital classroom as well, where learning platforms have become an important structure in today's schools. These widespread learning platforms have been widely implemented, especially in upper secondary schools in Norway but also at lower levels. Primarily, a learning platform is a 'digital classroom' on the internet, accessible from home and school round the clock, with lecture material disseminations, evaluation mechanisms, discussion forums, chat and tools for collaboration and response writing. Learning platforms merge the physical classrooms and the digital classrooms in school today and it is quite clear that such complexity needs a more expanded view on didactics than in traditional schooling. This situation establishes new challenges and triggers new questions that teachers have never dealt with before. When do we as teachers read the pupils' emails and SMS? How can we utilise pupils' digital self-confidence in classrooms without losing the subject focus? How can we make the different classrooms complementary and meaningful? Several dilemmas are present and it is quite clear that it is more time-consuming to check the homework at the learning platforms (digital classroom) and give written feedback to students on their text through learning platforms than it is to do a quick check on homework in the physical classroom. We can also ask if teachers should have to strive for communication with students on students' own communication channels (MSN Messenger, Skype, SMS, Facebook, etc.) or if pupils should keep their communication channels to themselves? At the same time we find that class management in such technology-dense learning environments is quite tricky and didactical dilemmas and challenges occur because of the digitised school.

One of the reasons that the digital didactic model builds on the frame factor theory of Lundgren (1972, 1979) is that 'newborn' frame factors are quite new for teachers and need certain didactic consideration for keeping the necessary class management in today's Norwegian classrooms. These frame factors have to be considered by the teacher in the light of didactical planning in Norwegian schools of today. We might say that some of these factors are obvious (mobile telephone and Ipod turned off when the teacher is teaching), but they create a lot of difficulty in Norwegian secondary schools. Therefore, the didactical reflection of today must embed such frame factors, to avoid difficult conditions in class management.

How can support structures help teachers in handling these 'newborn' frame factors which have such a strong influence on class management in today's schools? Ten years ago it would have been a futuristic Orwellian scenario to speak about the need for surveillance of pupils' computers. Today the situation in our digitised schools in Norway means that teachers, researchers and policymakers are discussing this issue seriously. This is grounded on the fact that the high PC density (almost 1:1, pupils' laptops) combined with wireless broadband in school and mobile phones creates a lot of challenges attached to classroom management (mentioned above). It seems therefore consensual that those schools which need to implement such support structures for teachers should be allowed to do so. This is underlined in the new White Paper nr. 31 (2007-2008), *Quality in School* from the Government in Norway:

> 'Many pupils are used to having laptops and access to net societies and computer games from home, and net access in classrooms can give the pupils the possibility to access PC activities that are not related to the teaching. Access to the net and other ICT activities must be steered as part of the classroom management and the awareness of digital Bildung. We find technological solutions today that make it possible to regulate net access in classrooms attached to the kind of activity that is being carried out. The teachers must create clear boundaries about which teaching situations laptops are forbidden. The Ministry of Knowledge will strengthen the work with tutoring on technical solutions and digital bildung to avoid misuse of ICT in classrooms' (KD, 2008) (our translation).

It is interesting that a White Paper is so clear about this issue and Norway have never before considered such issues in educational contexts. The most common support structures discussed in Norwegian schools in 2008 are: PC screen surveillance (teachers have full overview of what pupils have on their PC screens in the physical classrooms), 'digital trace dog' (plagiarism tool which helps teachers to see pupils' cut & paste actions), firewalls (restrict the network to hinder use of e.g. Facebook, Youtube, etc. by pupils), network switch (teacher can turn off the wireless network when he/she finds it appropriate) and 'mobile stall' (hinders mobile use in the physical classroom). Such technological support structures have to be considered as part of the digital didactic for the digitised school, but the necessity will vary from teacher to teacher (based on digital competence and the ability of class management in general). Over time this need will hopefully fade away, as the teachers become increasingly digitally competent and the pupils recognise that they also need a knowledge navigator in digital classrooms.

On this basis the teaching and working methods establishes the social structure (Jank & Meyer, 2006) as one of the five elements in the model.

4. Digital Assessment

The element digital assessment has to be considered in relation to the other elements in the model and is maybe the most important issue in today's ICT use in Norwegian schools. During the 1990s ICT was operating on a side track in Norwegian schools, where assessment-issues were not considered properly as part of the ICT implementation. In the last five years this situation has been considerably altered and ICT-based exams show us that assessment and ICT are woven increasingly together in the Norwegian educational system.

This has changed the frame factors for summative assessment (like ICT exams), because these have to reflect a broader content of the syllabus where digital textbooks and digital learning resources are valued equally with the textbook. This increased status of ICT in summative assessment is positive, but from a didactic perspective the content of such exams has to be revitalised in the light of a 'digital epistemology' in today's schooling.

In the new national curriculum (LK-06) the formative assessment and *assessment for learning* have been especially highlighted. There are several reasons for this, but one of them is because this curriculum is quite goal-steering. In relation to the formative assessment this implies that pupils should be given *feed forward* in how they can achieve better goal achievement in relation to the competence aims. This constitutes a situation where formative assessment, assessment for learning and feed forward have been given a lot of attention in the curriculum and in next turn, can produce a summative assessment better than before.

As a consequence of this, the digital assessment element in the digital didactic model highlights three concepts that have to be considered didactically in the light of the new demand in the curriculum which is inspired by Hattie & Timperley (2007). These are *feed up, feed back* and *feed forward*. Below we will describe them in more depth:

1. *Feed up.* This concept is based on the question 'Where am I going?' (Hattie & Timperley, 2007) and in this context it means that it is attached to the new national curriculum's (LK-06) competence aims. The former curricula (R94 and R97) were criticised for vagueness about what the pupils should actually learn in different subjects and we might say that the competence aims are a remedy for the former 'pitfalls' in curricula. The example in the right column in Table 1 shows the most important steering instruments for 'Where am I going?' (feed up) in Norwegian schools today, competence aims.

2. *Feed back.* This concept is based on the phrase 'How am I going?' (Hattie & Timperley, 2007) and has very long traditions in all kinds of schooling. This important issue has, however, been given new conditions in today's digitised society and schools. While one originally had to be at school physically to receive feedback from the teacher, we know that today this is complemented by the digital classroom (learning platforms, e-mail, etc), which expands the possibilities of receiving feedback considerably. This constitutes a situation whereby pupils of today can

receive feedback on subject matter any time, anywhere and from anyone, which of course fuels the possibility of succeeding with, for example, adapted education (if this is utilised). Valerie Shute (2008) challenge our traditional perception of the best way of giving feedback when she states:

> Give unbiased, objective feedback, written or via computer. Feedback from a trustworthy source will be considered more seriously than other feedback, which may be disregarded. This may explain why computer-based feedback is often better than human-delivered in some experiments in that perceived biases are eliminated (Shute, 2008)

In other words; computer based feedback can be complementary to traditional face-to-face feedback, and our massive implementation of learning platforms (LMS/VLE) in Norwegian schools give quite new possibilities of handling this issue.

3. *Feed Forward.* This concept is based on the phrase 'Where to next?' (Hattie & Timperley, 2007) and underlines how assessment for learning (formative assessment) is very important for the *assessment of learning* (summative assessment). The Pupils' Survey of 2007 (Elevundersøkelsen, Oxford Research 2007) revealed that Norwegian pupils claim that they receive too little feed forward too seldom in their schooling in general. The survey reveals that this area might have been undercommunicated, because of the strong position feedback has had in the Norwegian educational system. This gives call for in-service training of formative assessment, because many teachers say that they feel incompetent in giving this *assessment for learning* properly and systematically. Table 1 shows how this can be carried out in regard to Hattie & Timperley's (2007) model.

Table 1 underlines the need for a local, systematic planning of the relationship between *feed up, feed back, feed forward* and *assessment for learning* (formative assessment) in general. This has to be attached to the competence aims and *the assessment of learning* (the summative assessment). We find today a swarm of new ICT-based possibilities to carry out the formative assessment in the digitised school. This has to be attached to the local curriculum work and reflected upon in relation to the teacher digital didactic. The key point in the formative assessment in ICT-dense learning environments is to make clear to the pupils what the competence aims are, what they will be assessed in relation to and that *content* must have a stronger focus than *form* (i.e. fancy PowerPoint presentations is not enough). How to carry out the formative assessment more concrete is highlighted e.g. in an extensive literature review by Valerie Shute (2008). As Shute (2008) finds, there is a reason to claim from these studies that computer based feedback often are better than other types of feedback (e.g. oral, grades, etc.) in formative assessment. This form of digital assessment (with clear focus on formative assessment) will constitute a focus towards *subject use of ICT* and an interpretation competence, rather than a focus towards the *ritualistic ICT use* and a tool competence.

Table 1. Formative assessment - Feed up, Feed back and Feed forward in the digitised school

Level	Feed Up	Feed Back	Feed Forward	Example
	Where am I going?	How am I going?	Where to next	Competence aims (LK-06)
Task level How well tasks are understood/ performed				
Process Level The main process needed to under-stand/perf. tasks				
Self-regulation level Self-monitoring, directing, and regulating of actions				
Self level Personal evalu-ations and affect (usually positive) about the learner				

When it comes to individual differences between pupils Shute mentions that:

> (...)Provide early support and structure for low-achieving students (or those with low self-efficacy) to improve learning and performance (...) Novices or struggling students need support and explicit guidance during the learning process (...) thus, hints may not be as helpful as more explicit, directive feedback (...) high-achieving or more motivated students benefit from feedback that challenges them, such as hints, cues, and prompts (...). (Shute 2008 p. 180).

In relation to the strong focus on adapted education and differentiation in the new national curriculum in Norway, it is quite clear that both feedback – and feed forward has to be tailored each pupils abilities and qualification – specially in ICT-dense learning environments.

The *assessment of* - issue (summative assessment) also has a strong impact on teachers and pupils, because of ICT-based exams being implemented in every secondary school (where pupils can use their own laptops). It goes without saying that the relation between the formative and summative assessments must be clear for both teachers and pupils to fulfil the goal of a holistic assessment system.

On this basis the digital assessment establishes the action structure (Jank & Meyer, 2006) and assessment structure (Bjørndal & Lieberg, 1978), as one of the five elements in the model.

5. Pupil and Teacher Qualifications

5a. Pupil Qualifications

The digital native pupils in schools of today have been exposed early to the technology but have less experience with the combination of learning and technology. Drotner (2001) emphasises that innovators in the technology arena, the youth, can give us new perspectives on how to utilise the technology in knowledge building. Drotner (2001) also warns, however, against the possible hazards if we overestimate the value of youngsters' digital competence in pedagogical settings. Sørensen (2006) found that many teachers thought it was stressful to have to deal with technology which had 'gone down' or with which they were not sufficiently familiar. The teachers often allied themselves with pupils who could be regarded as power users, or digital front-runners, autodidacts who used their self-acquired knowledge to solve, or attempt to solve, the problems which arose. The pupils were able to use their wide knowledge reflexively, were extremely familiar with the technical aspects of the digital media and went through a learning process because of the opportunity to make their knowledge explicit and consider how their knowledge could best be communicated to others (Sørensen, 2006, p. 17).

As a consequence of this, adapted education has been given new conditions. The pupil's digital competence gives new opportunities for the teacher to utilise these ICT skills as a gateway to knowledge building and learning. It also implies, however, that the teacher has the necessary digital competence actually to utilise this potential. At the same time the pupils must be aware that in teaching the *subject use of ICT* is in front, not the *ritualistic ICT use*. Here, we can observe that a premise for developing such *subject use of ICT* is that the pupil develops an *interpretation competence* (and not only a tool competence, which is quite good), as part of their digital competence. At its best, this can give new forms of differentiation in teaching which capture different pupils' needs and abilities in a better way than in the former curriculum (which also underlines the adapted education perspective).

5b. Teacher Qualifications – Digital Competence as a Premise for Teachers' Digital Didactic

The National Curriculum for Knowledge Promotion emphasises the teacher as a competent and responsible professional, and s/he is given opportunities to practice his/her teaching the way he/she wants, within given boundaries. This is based on the considerable, local methodical freedom teachers have in this new educational reform. Their professional knowledge consists of content competence, didactic competence, social competence, professional ethics competence and adaptive and developmental competence (UFD, 2003).

The introduction of ICT brings new opportunities, but at the same time presents many challenges for the teachers, who will have to cope with greater complexity in their everyday practice. Teachers' practice builds on their own learning and teaching experiences, but when it comes to ICT and teaching they have to create conditions for learning that they themselves may never have encountered before. Teachers who were born before 1980 do not know what it is to grow up in a digital world where cell phones and a minimum of one computer in each home are the norm. Neither did they receive training where they were introduced to the digital era. Another problem is that even today ICT is not incorporated properly in teacher education (NIFU/STEP, 2008) or in the national curriculum regulations for teacher education in Norway

(UFD, 2003), and there is a danger of a gap between teachers' education and the practices they encounter afterwards.

It is evident that the digital didactics examined so far carry one very important assumption: that the teacher has the necessary digital competence. When we approach the narrower content of digital competence and what this means for learning in both physical and digital classrooms, the need for digitally competent teachers becomes even more apparent. Internationally a number of important contributions have been made towards the definition of *digital literacy* in recent years. Lanham (1995), Gilster (1997), Tyner (1998), Knobel (1999) Lankshear & Knobel (2003) and Buckingham (2003, 2006) have particularly contributed towards the concepts of *computer literacy, media literacy* and *digital literacy*. Despite the importance of these international contributions in providing a conceptual understanding of the terms, it is clear that not all of them can be easily transferred to the context of Norwegian schools and digital competence among Norwegian teachers under the new national curriculum. It is therefore important that attempts have been made to create a Norwegian understanding of complex digital competence in the light of the didactical circumstances in Norway. In an attempt to incorporate its implications for the individual teacher's digital didactic, Krumsvik has developed a definition aimed at describing the digital competence of the teacher which is attached to the digital didactic: 'Digital competence is the teacher's proficiency in using ICT in a professional context with good didactic judgement and his or her awareness of its implications for learning strategies and the digital Bildung of pupils'(Krumsvik, 2007b, p. 74). This definition is attached to a model (Figure 5) which visualises this definition of teachers' digital competence (see Almås & Krumsvik (2008) for more detailed descriptions).

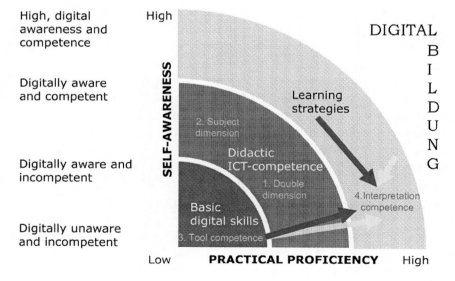

Figure 5. Teachers' digital competence (Krumsvik, 2007a).

This definition implies that teachers distinguish themselves from other technology users by their focus on the *subject use of ICT* for education and instruction – not entertainment, social communication and habits (*ritualistic ICT use*). In relation to the digital didactic model and teacher qualifications it is first and foremost the *didactic ICT competence* (related to subject use of ICT, in the middle of the model) which stands in the centre. The crux of this is that the teacher has to possess a *double dimension* as an important part of their didactic ICT competence. This means that teachers will in some way or another be *role models* in teaching (1) pupils' *subject use of ICT*. To 'teach as they preach' will be an important guiding star in digitised learning environments for teachers and presumes a digitally confident teacher. At the same time teachers must continually make didactic judgements which focus on a *subject dimension* (2) which implies how ICT can expand the learning possibilities for pupils in subjects (e.g. based on research findings like the previous mentioned from Mayer (2001)). This *double dimension* constitutes a didactic ICT competence for teachers with a greater complexity than citizens' everyday digital literacy, which often only entails using ICT for personal purposes (internet banking, e-mail, SMS, etc.).

The next part of the teacher digital competence is the focus on digital learning *strategies* required for handling the *subject use of ICT*. The point here is that the teacher has the necessary qualifications (digital competence) to teach and guide the pupils in relation to this issue. This implies that the teacher must utilise the pupils' good *tool-competence* (3) (basic digital skills) as a starting-point, but has to keep a strong focus on the *interpretation competence* (4) which makes them able to delve deeper into the subject use of ICT in teaching and guiding, and also let pupils do this on their own (e.g. homework). This gives a situation where digitally confident pupils have to use their good tool competence (learning for using) as a springboard actually to 'learn' how to develop their own interpretation competence (using for learning) and that there is a symbiotic relationship between these aspects.

From this we can register that teachers' digital competence is much more complex than digital literacy in other occupations and among average citizens. This requires an awareness of such complexity and how the digital didactic will be carried out for teachers will very often depend on their digital competence. Therefore it is necessary to establish a pedagogical framework and didactic content related to teachers' practices in school if one wishes to incorporate this complex digital competence requirement in the digitised school. The problem with such frameworks, definitions and descriptions is that they lack functionality in practice unless they are operationalised in a teaching context, to secure ecological validity and construct validity. It is therefore necessary that teachers' digital competence is clearly linked to the digital didactic and thus the different elements of the digital didactic model (and the digital competence model), are created to prompt teachers to reflect on their own digital competence which takes on board the various key elements contained in this concept.

On this basis the pupil and teacher qualifications establish the pupil and teacher qualifications-structure (Bjørndal & Lieberg, 1978) as one of the five elements in the model.

The five structures mentioned in digital didactic model I (Figure 2), the three core challenges and the five elements in the digital didactic model II (Figure 3) have to be considered in relation to each other. This underlines the complexity of such digital didactic and that a revitalisation of didactic in general is necessary in today's digitised schools.

IMPLICATIONS

This theoretical article has highlighted that the extensive use of ICT in our digitised society gives a situation where school, spare time and home activities melt together, and new policy documents give new regulations for both teachers and pupils. A new concept, digital didactic, and a new digital didactic model have therefore been presented and discussed in relation to the challenges teachers are facing in the digitised school. The problem examined by the article is how a new digital didactic concept and a digital didactic model can contribute to a revitalisation of the general didactic and as a new instructional theory of technology in Norway.

The introduction of the Knowledge Promotion (KD, 2006) attached ICT to pupils' learning more than ever and the pedagogical and didactic conditions in Norwegian classrooms have changed considerably. Consequently it may have changed large parts of the educational system because, for example, teacher education has to reflect what is going on in the practice field. One of the reasons for this is that our education system has been built upon the premise that access to teaching and information is limited to school and physical classrooms. The distribution of information has been through teachers' lectures and written papers. The article has highlighted that the situation of today is that 'information is not ordered into disciplines or differentiated according to the capabilities of the user (age or level of education), and hence the power differentials embedded in formal knowledge structures are removed' (Somekh, 2007, p. 114). The Internet with possibilities for information and knowledge sharing, participation in online courses, wikis and communities is knitting different sociocultural circles together. The fusion of school and home, and the physical and virtual/digital classroom, includes also a discussion about formal and informal learning. This calls for revitalising didactical concepts and didactical models to incorporate this new pedagogical terrain, and this article has attempted to present such a digital didactic model which incorporates these new pedagogical streams. But it is also necessary to update and revitalize our perception of the concepts "technology", "educational technology" and "instructional technology" to avoid pitfalls from the past. The revitalization of these concepts have to bear in mind that the technology of today are completely different than for 30 years ago and that the technology itself gives a lot of new educational opportunities which has to be incorporated in a new instructional theory of technology, which this article have tried to communicate.

As a consequence, the article has launched a new concept, digital didactic, which gives possibilities but is also problematic since it still has low ecological validity and construct validity in teacher education and in school. The word 'digital' can be perceived as ambiguous and instrumentalistic, because of its roots within the technology area. At the same time this word and the concept in general attempts to capture the didactic terrain today's teachers are facing in a digitised school, and even if the concepts and model are still tentative, we can observe that the majority of the teachers in a pilot study (n=83) and the action research study (n=3) for teacher educators indicate there is a need to develop such new didactic concepts and models (Krumsvik, 2008c). In any case, the concept and the models presented in this article have to be developed further and go through a further validation concerning ecological validation and construct validity.

The revitalisation of the technology concept, the general didactic concept and the didactic pentagon in this article is attached to former ideas, concepts and theories within didactic. More specifically, our digital didactic model is inspired by Laursen's *reflective didactic approach* (Laursen 1994) and the foundations laid by Bjørndal & Lieberg (1975, 1978), Jank & Meyer (2006), Klafki (2000a,b, 2001), Shulman (1987) and Mishra & Koehler (2006), and these are an important backdrop to this digital didactic model. The model is also based, however, on the need to be aware of the 'newborn', ICT-based frame factors which influence teachers' didactic strongly and therefore Lundgren's (1972, 1979) frame factor theory has been important in the light of this issue as well as the new, goal-steering national curriculum (LK-06, KD 2006), research studies (Krumsvik, 2006a,b, 2008a,b,c; Almås & Krumsvik, 2007, 2008) and the general digitisation of schools (Utdanningsdirektoratet, 2008). Therefore, the digital didactic model has to be considered as a follow-up from previous attempts as well as a leap from these to incorporate the complexity of teachers' digitised practice in a didactical model.

In revitalisation of the didactic concept in this article it is quite clear that there has to be a seamless relationship between teachers' digital competence and the digital didactic. The higher teachers' digital competence is, the better the reflection around the digital didactic will be. Larson & Marsh (2005, p.74) touch on this when they define teachers as 'design consultants' in relation to new digital competence, but they are not trying to provide a definitive set of roles which characterise literacy teaching in a new media age. In a Scandinavian setting digital 'design consultants' will be holders of a kind of 'digital didactic', which in many ways is a kind of tacit knowledge which needs to be made explicit and incorporated through reflection and staff discussion. It is, however, often difficult for teachers (and teacher educators) themselves to articulate their didactical considerations in their teaching since they themselves are a part of it during the teaching lessons. The entire 'digital didactic circle' is therefore seldom thought through in busy everyday practice, but our previous studies (Krumsvik, 2006a; 2008a,b,c; Almås & Krumsvik, 2007, 2008) revealed that action research function very well as a methodological gateway to let teachers reflect on their digital didactic and make their tacit knowledge explicit. In these studies we found that teachers actually were 'design consultants' with a common goal to develop a digital didactic model for digitised schools in the Norway of today. Therefore, the digital didactic model presented in this article is in many ways a result of a researching partnership with teachers (e.g through PILOT and post-PILOT) which highlights the complexity teachers cope with in different 'classrooms', and how different factors influence each other. We therefore find at this early stage in revitalisation of the didactic concept that digitally competent teachers are one of the most important factors in orchestrating the learning environment in and out of school and contribute to our digital didactic model. This might give an important contribution to teacher education as well and bridge the notorious gap between teacher education and the practice field.

ACKNOWLEDGEMENT

This article is supported by a PEK grant from the University of Bergen.

REFERENCES

Alexander, R. (1992). *Policy and Practice in Primary Education*. London: Routledge.

Almås, A. G. (2004). *Innovasjon, IKT og læringssyn. PILOT. Delrapport Rogaland og Hordaland* [Innovation, ICT, and learning perspectives. PILOT. Partial report from Rogaland and Hordaland county; in Norwegian]. ITU series nr. 26. Oslo: Unipub.

Almås, A. G. & Krumsvik, R. (2007). Digital literate teachers in Leading Edge schools in Norway. *Journal of In-Service Education*, 33(4), 479-497.

Almås, A. G. & Krumsvik, R. (2008). Teaching in Technology-Rich Classrooms: is there a gap between teachers' intentions and ICT practices? *Research in Comparative and International Education*, 3(2), 103-121

Arnseth, H. C, Hatlevik, O., Kløvstad, V., Kristiansen, T. & Ottestad, G.(2007). *ITU Monitor 2007 Skolens digitale tilstand 2007* [ITU Monitor The Digital Conditions in School 2007; in Norwegian]. Oslo: Forsknings- og kompetansenettverk for IT i utdanning.

Bachmann, K.E. (2005). *Læreplanens differens. Formidling av læreplanen til skolepraksis*. Doctoral dissertation, NTNU.

Bjørndal, B. & Lieberg, S. (1975). *Innføring i økopedagogikk: en studiebok for lærere* [Introduction in ecopedagogy: a studybook for teachers; in Norwegian]. Oslo: Aschehoug.

Bjørndal, B. & Lieberg, S. (1978). *Nye veier i didaktikken* [New ways in didactic; in Norwegian]. Oslo: Aschehoug.

Bloom, B. S. (1956). *Taxonomy of Educational Objectives, Handbook I: The Cognitive Domain*. New York: David McKay Co Inc.

Bruner, J. (1996). *The Culture of Education*. Cambridge, Mass.:Harvard University Press.

Buckingham, D. (2003). *Media education: Literacy, learning and contemporary culture*. Cambridge: Polity Press.

Buckingham, D. (2006). Defining digital literacy – what do young people need to know about digital media? *Digital kompetanse* [Nordic Journal of Digital Literacy], 1(4), 263–276.

Buhl, M. (2008). New teacher functions in cyberspace – on technology, mass media and education. *Seminar.net – International journal of media, technology and lifelong learning*, 4 (1), 1-16.

Castells, M. (1996). *The Rise of the Network society*. New York: Oxford University Press.

Castells, M. (2001). *The Internet Galaxy*. New York: Oxford University Press.

Dale, E. L. (Ed.) (1997). *Etikk for pedagogisk profesjonalitet* [Ethics for pedagogical professionality; in Norwegian]. Olso: Gyldendal.

Dale, E. L. (2001). Den profesjonelle læreren [The professional teacher; in Norwegian]. In T. Bergem (Ed.), *Slipp elevene løs!* [Let the students be free!; in Norwegian]. Oslo: Gyldendal.

Drotner, K. (2001). *Medier for Fremtiden. Børn, unge og det nye medielandskap.* [Media for the Future. Children, Youngsters and the New Media Landscape; in Norwegian]. Copenhagen: Høst & Søn.

Eisner, E. W. (1979). *The educational imagination: on the design and evaluation of school programs*. New York: Macmillan.

Engeström, Y. (1987). *Learning by expanding*. Helsinki: Orienta-Konsultit.

Forsknings og kompetansenettverk for IT i utdanning (ITU) (Network for IT Research and Competence in Education). (2003*). Digital Kompetanse. Fra 4. basisferdighet til digital dannelse. Problemnotat* (Digital competence. From the fourth basic skill to digital education. Problem memo, in Norwegian) (Electronic version). Universitetet i Oslo. Oslo: ITU.

Fullan, M. (1982). *The meaning of educational change*. Toronto: Ontario Institute for Studies in Education .

Gilster, P. (1997). *Digital literacy*. New York: Wiley Computer.

Glaser, R. (1962): Instructional technology and the measurement of learning outcomes – Some questions. In W.J. Popham (ed.), *Criterion-Referenced Measurement,* (pp. 5-14). NJ: Educational Technology Publications, Englewood Cliffs.

Hamilton, D. (1999). The Pedagogic Paradox (or why no didactics in England?) *Curriculum studies*, 7(2), 135-152.

Handal, G. & Lauvås, P. (2000). *Veiledning og praktisk yrkesteori* [Supervision and practical occupational theory; in Norwegian]. Oslo: Cappelen.

Hattie, J. & Timperley, H. (2007). The Power of Feedback. *Review of Educational Research,* 1 (77), 81-112.

Hokstad, L.M. (2002). IKT og læring- et didaktisk perspektiv [ICT and learning – a didactic perspective; in Norwegian]. In S. Ludvigsen & T. L. Hoel (Eds.) *Et utdanningssystem i endring: IKT og læring* [A changing educational system: ICT and learning; in Norwegian] (pp.208-225). Oslo: Gyldendal Akademisk.

Hopmann, S. & Riquarts, K. (2000). Starting a Dialogue: A Beginning Conversation Between Didaktik and the Curriculum Traditions. In Westbury, I. , Hopmann, S., Riquarts, K. (Eds.) *Teaching as a Reflective Practice: The German Didaktikk Tradition* (pp. 3-11). London: Lawrence Erlbaum Associates.

Imsen, G. (2006). *Lærerens verden* [The Teacher's world; in Norwegian].Oslo: Tano Aschehoug.

Jank, W. & Meyer, H. (2006). *Didaktiske modeller. Grundbok i didaktikk* [Didactical models. Basic book in didactics; in Danish]. København: Gyldendal Forlag.

Klafki, W. (2000a). The Significance of Classical Theories of Bildung for a Contemporary Concept of Allgemeinbildung. In Westbury, I. , Hopmann, S., Riquarts, K. (Eds.) *Teaching as a Reflective Practice: The German Didaktik Tradition* (pp. 85-109). London: Lawrence Erlbaum Associates.

Klafki, W. (2000b). Didaktik Analysis as the Core of Preparation of Instruction. In I. Westbury, S. Hopmann, K. Riquarts (Eds.) *Teaching as a Reflective Practice: The German Didaktik Tradition* (pp. 139-160). London: Lawrence Erlbaum Associates.

Klafki, W. (2001). *Dannelsesteori og didaktikk – nye studier* [Theory of growth and didactic – new studies; in Norwegian]. Århus, Denmark: Forlaget KLIM.

Knobel, M. (1999). *Everyday literacies - Students, Discourses and Social Practice*. New York: Peter Lang.

Koschman, T. (1996). Paradigm shifts and Instructional technology. An Introduction. In T. Koschman (Ed.) *CSCL: Theory and practice of an emerging paradigm* (pp.1-23). New Jersey: Lawrence Erlbaum Associates.

Krumsvik, R. (2006a). *ICT-initiated school development in lower secondary school*. Ph.D. thesis. The University of Bergen. Bergen: Allkopi.

Krumsvik, R. (2006b). The digital challenges of school and teacher education in Norway: Some urgent questions and the search for answers. *Education and Information Technologies*, 3-4 (11), 239-256.

Krumsvik, R. (2007a). *Ein modell for digital kompetanse for lærarar* [A model of digital competence for teachers] Unpublished paper. Bergen: UoB.

Krumsvik, R. (Ed.). (2007b). *Skulen og den digitale læringsrevolusjon* [The school and the digital learning revolution; in Norwegian]. Oslo: Universitetsforlaget.

Krumsvik, R. (2008a). The emerging digital literacy among teachers in Norway (The story of one digital literate teacher). In R. Kobayashi (Ed.), *New educational technology* (pp. 105–125). New York: Nova Science.

Krumsvik, R. (2008b). Educational technology, epistemology and discourses in curricula in Norway. *US-China Education Review*, 5(5), 1-15.

Krumsvik, R. (2008c). *"Teach as we Preach". Teacher educators professional development in relation to digital competence*. Unpublished paper. PEK-project. University of Bergen

Krumsvik, R. & Støbakk, Å. (2007). Digital danning [Digital Bildung]. In R. Krumsvik (Ed), *Skulen og den digitale læringsrevolusjon* [The school and the digital learning revolution; in Norwegian]. Oslo: Universitetsforlaget.

Kunnskapsdepartementet (KD)[Ministry of Knowledge] (2006). Læreplanverket for Kunnskapsløftet (LK 06) [National Curriculum for Knowledge Promotion in Primary and Secondary Education and Training (LK 06)] Available online at: http://www.regjeringen.no/en/dep/kd/Selected-topics/andre/Knowledge-Promotion.html?id=1411 (accessed 08 October 2008).

Kunnskapsdepartementet (KD)[Ministry of Knowledge] (2008). *Stortingsmelding nr. 31 (2007-2008), Kvalitet i skolen.* [White paper nr. 31 (2007-2008), Quality in school; in Norwegian]. Oslo: Statens Forvaltningsteneste.

Künzli, R. (1994). *Didaktik: Modelle der Darstellung, des Umgangs und der Erfahrung.* Aarau: Didaktikum.

Lanham, R. (1995). Digital literacy. *Scientific American*, 273(3), 160–161.

Larson, J. & Marsh, J. (2005). *Making Literacy Real. Theories and Practices for Learning and Teaching.* London: SAGE Publications.

Laursen, P. F. (1994). Teacher Thinking and Didactics: A Prescriptive, Rationalistic and Reflective Approach. In I. Carlgren, G. Handal, S. Vaage (Eds.) *Teachers' minds and actions: Research on teachers' thinking and practice.*(pp.125-136). London: Falmer Press.

Lankshear, C. & Knobel, M. (2003). Digital Literacy and Digital Literacies: Policy, Pedagogy and Research Considerations for Education? *Digital kompetanse* [Nordic Journal of Digital Literacy], 1(1), 12-24.

Lave, J. & Wenger, E. (1991). *Situated learning. Legitimate peripheral participation.* Cambridge: Cambridge University Press.

Løvlie, L. (2003). Teknokulturell danning [Techno-cultural growth; in Norwegian]. In R. Slagstad, O. Korsgaard, & L. Løvlie (Eds.) *Dannelsens forvandlinger* [The transformation of growth; in Norwegian] (pp. 347-371). Oslo: Pax Forlag.

Lund, A. (2003). *The Teacher as Interface. Teachers of EFL in ICT-Rich Environments: Beliefs, Practices, Appropriation.* Doctoral dissertation. Oslo: University of Oslo.

Lundgren, U. P. (1972). Frame factors and the teaching process. A contribution to curriculum theory and theory of teaching. *Göteborgs studies in educational sciences 8.* Stockholm: Almquist og Wiksell.

Lundgren, U. P. (1979). *Att organisera omvärlden: en introduktion till läroplansteori* [To organize the world around: an introduction to curriculum theory; in Swedish]. Stockholm: Liber.

Mayer, R. (2001). *Multimedia Learning.* New York: Cambridge University Press.

Merton, R. K. (1973). *The Sociology of Science: Theoretical and Empirical Investigations.* Chicago, IL: University of Chicago Press.

Mishra, P. & Koehler, M. J. (2006). Technological Pedagogical Content Knowledge: A new framework for teacher knowledge. *Teachers College Record*, 108(6), 1017-1054.

Mishra, P. & Koehler, M. J. (2008). Introducing technological pedagogical content knowledge. Paper presented at the Annual Meeting of the American Educational Research Association. New York. Available online at: http://punya.educ.msu.edu/presentations/AERA2008/MishraKoehler_AERA2008.pdf (accessed 02 October 2008).

Mumtaz, S. (2000). Factors affecting teachers' use of information and communications technology: a review of the literature. *Journal of Information Technology for Teacher Education*, 9(3), 319-342.

Kirke-, undervisings- og forskingsdepartementet (KUF) (1987). *Mønsterplanen for grunnskolen* [The Curriculum for the primary and secondary school]. Oslo: Ministry of Education, Research and Church affairs.

NIFU/STEP (2008). *Digital kompetanse lærerutdanningen* [Digital competence in teacher education; in Norwegian]. Oslo: NIFU/STEP.

Nordkvelle, Y. (2004). Technology and didactics: historical mediations of a relation. *Curriculum Studies*, 4 (36), 427-444.

Oxford Research (2007). *De viktige få. Analyse av Elevundersøkelsen 2007* [The important few. Analysis of the Pupils Survey of 2007; in Norwegian]. Kristiansand: Oxford Research.

Pedro, F. (2006). *The new millennium learners: challenging our Views on ICT and Learning.* OECD-CERI.

Pelgrum, W. J. & Law, N. (2003). *ICT In Education Around The World: Trends, Problems And Prospects.* Paris: UNESCO, International Institute for Educational Planning.

Polanyi, M. (1968). *The Tacit Dimension.* New York: Anchor Books.

Schnack, K. (Ed.) (2004). *Didaktik på kryds og tværs.* Copenhagen: Danmarks Pædagogiske Universitets Forlag.

Schofield, J. (1995). *Computers and classroom culture.* New York: Cambridge University Press.

Schön, D. A. (1983). *The Reflective Practitioner.* San Francisco: Jossey-Bass.

Shulman, L. (1986). Those Who Understand: knowledge growth in teaching. *Educational Researcher*, 15(2), 4-14.

Shulman, L. (1987). Knowledge and teaching: Foundations of the new reform. *Harvard Educational Review*, 57, 1-22.

Shute, V. J. (2008). *Focus on Formative Feedback. Review of Educational Research*, 1(78), 153-189.

Skjervheim, H. (1959). Objectivism and the Study of Man. *Filosofiske problemer*, No. 23

Oslo: Universitetsforlaget.

Skjervheim, H. (1972). Det instrumentalistiske mistaket [The Instrumental Mistake; in Norwegian]. In N. Mediaas, J. Houge-Thiis, S. Haga & J.B. Ellingjord (Eds.) *Etablert pedagogikk - makt eller avmakt* [Established pedagogy – power or powerlessness; in Norwegian](pp.45-52). Oslo: Gyldedal.

Somekh, B. (2007) *Pedagogy and Learning with ICT: Researching the art of innovation.* London and NewYork: Routledge.

Sørensen, B. H. (2006). Digital Media and New Organisational Forms: Educational Knowledge Leadership. In: Buhl, M., Sørensen, B. H. & Meyer, B. (Eds.) *Media and ICT – learning potentials* (pp. 11-30). Copenhagen: Danish University of Education Press. Retrieved 12.05.2008 from: http://www.dpu.dk/site.asp?p=8803

Tyack, D. & Cuban, L. (1998). *Tinkering Toward Utopia.* Cambridge (Mass.): Harvard University Press).

Tyner, K. (1998). *Literacy in a digital world: Teaching and learning in the age of information.* New Jersey: Lawrence Erlbaum.

Tyler, R.W. (1949). *Basic principles of curriculum and instruction.* Chicago: The University of Chicago Press.

Undervisnings- og Forskningsdepartementet (UFD) [Ministry of Education and Research (MER)] (2003). *Rammeplan for lærerutdanning* [National curriculum regulations. General Teacher Education; in Norwegian] Available online at: http://www.regjeringen.no/Upload/KD/Vedlegg/UH/Rammeplaner/Lærer/Rammeplan_la erer_eng.pdf (accessed 10 February 2008).

Utdanningsdirektoratet (2007) [The Norwegian Directorate for Education and Training](2008). *Utdanningsspeilet 2007. Analyse av grunnskole og videregående opplæring i Norge* [The Education Mirror 2007. An Analysis of primary and secondary schools in Norway; in Norwegian] Oslo: The Norwegian Directorate for Education and Training. Available online at: http://www.utdanningsdirektoratet.no/upload/Rapporter/Utdanningsspeilet_2007/US_200 7.pdf (accessed 10 July 2008).

Webb, M. & Cox, M. (2004). A review of pedagogy related to information and communications technology. *Technology, Pedagogy and Education*, 13(3), 235-286.

In: Learning in the Network Society and the Digitized School   ISBN 978-1-60741-172-7
Editor: Rune Krumsvik   © 2009 Nova Science Publishers, Inc.

Chapter 8

USE OF TECHNOLOGY IN EDUCATION: DIDACTIC CHALLENGES

Astrid M. Sølvberg[1] and Marit Rismark[2]
NTNU, Norway

ABSTRACT

Studies show that school leaders, teachers and students are insecure about how to use an LMS to enhance learning. The main purpose of this article is to develop insights into some didactic considerations that need to be addressed. Use of technology in education involves deciding priorities within the areas of technology, learning theories and issues of educational practice. We suggest that the interrelatedness of these areas may represent a main framework for developing didactic practices. One didactic approach may be to reduce complexity in teaching through sequencing of the learning process.

Keywords: LMS in education, didactic sequencing, enhancing student learning, teaching complexity.

INTRODUCTION

Due to the considerable role technology plays in young people's lives, the younger generation is often referred to as the internet generation, screenagers, homo zappiens or millenials. They connect, download, search, navigate, communicate, construct and collaborate by means of technology. In terms of time spent on activities, a 21-year old will have used 15 000 hours on formal education, 20 000 hours in front of the TV and 50 000 in front of his or her PC (Krumsvik, 2007). Naturally, this results in a situation where young people often are very skilful users of technology. Researchers suggest that there is only a minimum of compatibility between the work methods in schools and the internet generation's approach to problem solving outside school (Erstad, 2006; Krumsvik, 2007). It seems reasonable to expect that students weigh the use of technology in school against their use of technology outside school. Thus, the skilled technology users may experience a gap between education and life, where students and teachers may have differing expectations and perspectives on technology per se, as well as the subsequent pedagogical possibilities (Erstad, 2006).

One common perception of schools is that they make little use of technology (Krumsvik, 2007), with several reasons being suggested for this. On the primary-school level, many teachers are insecure as to the ways in which technology can be used to enhance learning (Arnseth, Hatlevik, Kløvstad, Kristiansen & Ottestad, 2007). Moreover, schools may lack an updated technological infrastructure and it seems realistic to assume that teachers may not even be comfortable with the idea that technology can function as a positive learning asset. One consequence of this is that pupils may be compelled to apply other frames of reference and make use of other lines of action and work procedures within schools than they do outside schools. This situation may thus exacerbate the problems caused by the persistent gap between school and life (Jackson, 1968).

During the last decade LMS's have been used to a broad degree in organizations as well as in compulsory and higher education. The systems appear to be quite popular in Nordic higher, further and continuing education. In fact, one would be hard pressed to find a Nordic institution that does not have experience of learning management systems (Paulsen, 2003). The compulsory Norwegian educational system also uses LMS's extensively. A national study (Arnseth et al., 2007) has shown that nearly all Norwegian upper secondary schools use such systems and six of 10 primary and lower secondary schools use LMS's. However, these investments have not led to any considerable pedagogical gains (Erstad, 2006). There is no clear evidence that teachers and schools have a broad repertoire of how to use LMS's as a tool for learning. Studies show that school leaders, teachers and students in primary education are insecure about how to use an LMS to enhance learning (Erstad, 2004). Teachers state that they are not sure how they should integrate it into their teaching practice. They also claim that LMS's are designed from the teacher's perspective, and that students become passive receivers of the teachers' provision of information. The use of these systems seems to serve administrative rather than learning purposes (Morgan, 2003; Erstad, 2004). If an LMS is to serve learning purposes, the didactic competence of teachers is a key issue. Teachers are facing new didactic challenges: how should teaching be planned, carried out and evaluated? Currently, Norwegian teachers by and large lack such competence (Erstad, 2004). The main purpose of this article is to develop insights into some didactic considerations that need to be addressed when an LMS is utilized as a learning asset.

RESEARCH CONTEXT

The Norwegian University of Science and Technology (www.ntnu.no), located in Trondheim, has a long tradition of being on the cutting edge of technological development, and continuing this tradition the university launched an interdisciplinary research and development project in 2005. The overall objective of this ongoing study is to develop knowledge on how to design virtual learning environments that promote effective learning. The project is developing multimedia content, technology and educational designs for various university courses, where the technology implemented in the various courses aims to provide examples of how technology in general can complement and add value to the current learning practices.

The findings in this text stem from three sub-studies. The first was a study of students enrolled in a sociology course (Rismark & Sølvberg, 2007). Arrangements were made so that students could both sit in on lectures and access them as multimedia presentations from wireless networked PDAs, mobile phones and laptops. The second sub-study was of students enrolled in a biology course (Rismark, Sølvberg, Strømme & Hokstad, 2007; Sølvberg, Rismark, Strømme & Hokstad, 2007; Sølvberg, Rismark & Strømme, 2008) who used PCs and mobile phones to access course material that was made available through the university's LMS. The third study is an ongoing sub-project examining students enrolled in a biology teacher education programme. We study these students both during university lectures and when they have teacher training in primary and lower secondary schools. In all three sub-projects we have used observation and interviews to collect data material. The projects have different focuses and priorities. However, they all touch upon which didactic considerations are necessary when LMS is utilized as a learning asset.

A CONCEPTUAL FRAMEWORK FOR TEACHING AND LEARNING WITH THE USE OF TECHNOLOGY

Schools and teachers are key players when integrating technology into educational practice. Several areas of knowledge must be taken into consideration. The Cognition and Technology Group at Vanderbilt (1996) maintains that the challenge of discussing the use of technology in education is based on the interrelationship between at least three key areas: technology, theories of human potential and human learning, and educational issues. In addition to these three areas, the context, characteristics of the learner and the relevance of the learning material to the learner must be considered. Thus, when teachers are to use technology in education they are dealing with issues related to the technology used, educational issues, the underlying learning theories and the context where the learning takes place. These interrelated areas and where they intersect, are illustrated schematically in Figure 1.

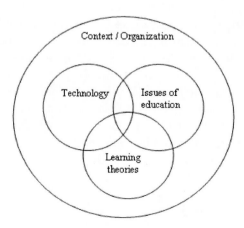

Figure 1. Intersecting areas requiring consideration when technology is to be integrated into education.

A change in one area introduces changes in the intersecting areas. Thus, schools and teachers are faced with the challenge of simultaneously relating to changes within each area as well as the interrelatedness of the areas.

Complexity in the Field of Technology

Technology that is available today was hardly imaginable just ten years ago. The tempo of change is increasing and this makes it almost impossible to foresee what will be possible within even a short time span. This presents educational administrations with quite a challenge when it comes to choosing which technology to implement in schools. For example, investing in commercial LMS's is a costly endeavour (Paulsen, 2003), and the hardware and software to run them is also a large but necessary expense. Furthermore, one must expect considerable expenditures for the staffing and maintenance of the systems, hardware and software. Due to the rapid pace of technological development, new technology is continuously available in the market, which means the threat that your technological devices and systems will rapidly become outdated is very real. In Norway, large investments have been made in implementing LMS's. However, these investments have not led to any considerable pedagogical gains. Erstad (2006) points to the lack of pedagogical planning and strategic work that has pedagogical needs rather than technological possibilities as the point of departure. When pedagogical needs are put first, learning theories and education issues need to be seen in conjunction with the technology at hand.

Complexity in Learning Theories

Visions of technology in education look very different depending on the tacit or explicit theories of learning that guide their design and implementation (Cognition and Technology Group at Vanderbilt, 1996). There is a myriad of learning theories, each providing different focus and priorities. Accordingly, some theories focus on the importance of cognitive factors for learning, while others put more emphasis on interaction as a learning asset. Over the years different theories of learning have played key roles for researchers, policy-makers and practitioners within education. There have been shifts of focus between behaviouristically based approaches and constructivist perspectives encompassing both cognitivism and social-cultural perspectives (e.g. Greeno, Collins & Resnick, 1996). Depending on the learning theory that is in focus, this has implications for how technology-based applications are used and assessed. For example, if interaction is seen as a key for learning, schools and teachers will likely put emphasis on implementing technology that enhances collaboration. Also, changes in technology open for new learning opportunities, which in turn may introduce new elements into theories on learning.

Complexity in Issues of Education

The primary goals of education have also shifted over recent decades. Perhaps the most important shift involves the assumption that all students must be prepared to be lifelong learners and hence must learn to think, learn and reason on their own (Resnick, 1987). The Cognition and Technology Group at Vanderbilt (1996) claims that this requires a shift from an exclusive focus on basic skills to one that emphasizes the use of relevant skills and knowledge in the context of pursuing meaningful learning and problem-solving goals. The Norwegian school curriculum also reflects these shifts. However, the current Norwegian school situation is described as putting less emphasis on learning and knowledge than desired (Bergesen, 2006). Technology then has to find its form as a learning asset within a school that has inconclusive attitudes and views on learning and work methods.

Didactic Practices

When teachers use technology in education they must decide priorities within the areas of technology, learning theories and issues of educational practice. We suggest that the interrelatedness of these areas may represent a main framework for developing didactic practices. Figure 2 illustrates the complexity of establishing such practice, where each area undergoes continuous shifts and developments. As each area is constantly shifting, developing and interrelate with the other areas, changes in one area lead to changes in the intersecting areas. Thus, establishing teaching practices is about *making priorities* within these fields of complexity.

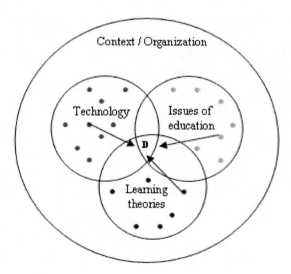

Figure 2. Didactics (D) finds its form by relating priorities within the intersecting areas to one another.

On a fundamental level didactics is about issues related to teaching and learning (Klafki, 1997). The classical didactic triangle features the learner, the teacher and some subject matter content. There are three main relations in the didactic situation: the relationship between the teacher and student, between teacher and content, and between student and content. Teachers may understand and emphasize these relations differently and plan learning situations accordingly.

A broad understanding of didactics includes "form" and methods, in addition to learning aims and subject matter (Fibæk Laursen, 1999). When teachers plan for upcoming lessons and manage the teaching and learning sequences, they likely have different considerations. Besides considering *what, why* and *how* in teaching and learning, didactics needs to reflect on such issues as *who* should learn, *where* they should learn and *when* they should learn (Jank & Meyer, 1997:17). All in all, these priorities encompass both theoretical and practical issues of didactics. Within the field of didactics we find a steadily growing tendency to include both the theory and action levels being reflected on (Gundem, 2003).

An understanding of didactics that takes into account both theory and practical aspects involves "practical-theoretical planning, implementation, assessment and critical analysis of education and learning" (Hiim & Hippe, 1999:9). When technology enters the lives of the younger generation and also becomes a main tool in schools this naturally influences ways of understanding culture, values and thinking. Thus, ideas about which learning activities (how), which subject matter content (what) and above all, which work methods agree with the ideals for education (why) may need reconsideration. If not, schools may risk using work methods and learning activities that do not prepare pupils for life in society.

LMS AND DIDACTIC CHALLENGES

Complexity is about a manifold of things and applies to human cognition as well as to communication in social systems. There is always more to think about than what is possible to consider and there is always more to communicate than what is possible (Rasmussen, 2005). The amount of knowledge and information in our society is constantly increasing at the same time that knowledge is developing and changing. As we have seen, when teachers use technology in education they have to deal with this complexity.

Teaching is characterized by complex challenges. Problems cannot be dealt with in isolation but within and in relation to the social system of the school in which they occur. Rasmussen (ibid.) illustrates this complexity by using billiards as a metaphor. It is possible to analyse the game if one ball is used, it is also possible, although more challenging to analyse the game when two or three balls are involved. With a larger number of balls in play, it becomes almost impossible to analyse the game. The same phenomenon also applies to teaching. It seems almost impossible to simultaneously relate to all aspects involved when teachers plan, carry out and evaluate teaching and learning. The well of options forces the teacher to make choices, and for every decision that is made another is just as obvious. Teachers need to make justified choices within each of the intersecting areas in Figure 2 by continually addressing core concepts, such as the "what's", "why's" and "how's" in didactics.

Didactic Sequencing

In our studies we find that *didactic sequencing* (to focus on selected parts of the learning process) may be an overall initial step towards reducing teaching complexity. It provides the teacher with some centre of attention when making justified choices within the intersecting areas.

Didactic sequencing was the main teaching approach in two of our projects about how to use LMS for learning purposes. Considerations within one of the three areas, learning theories, made a departing point for designing the learning environments. Some researchers claim that prior knowledge may affect comprehension and learning outcomes. Students who have prior knowledge learn more effectively than students who lack such knowledge (Alexander et. al., 1997; Alexander & Jetton, 2000). For example, studies show that when students have prior knowledge about the topic of a text, this contributes positively to their text comprehension (Samuelstuen & Bråten, 2005). Thus, the aim in our pedagogical design was to encourage students to start learning activities prior to their lectures. The LMS was used to support preparation activities. The idea was that students may prolong their learning process. To support students ahead of lectures, the teacher provided preparation assistance in videos that were displayed on the LMS.

Short video-recorded highlights (four to six minutes) of upcoming lectures were available on the university's LMS, usually a couple of days prior to the lecture (an example of addressing the "how" in didactics). In the video the professor presented main themes and pointed at some key elements the students should look into prior to the next lecture. The videos provided a short summary of the upcoming topic, where the professor emphasized what was considered important prior knowledge in the topic. Key elements in the upcoming lecture were also presented (an example of addressing the "what" in didactics). In some videos the professor introduced main figures, pictures and concepts for the students to look into by reading their textbooks and using other learning material. In other videos the students were introduced to current problem areas and encouraged to elaborate on these. The professor also raised questions for the students to look into before they came to the lectures. The intention was to encourage the students to use the textbook or other learning sources in advance of their lectures. The videos were digitally processed and posted on the LMS in three versions, one for PCs and two for mobile phones adapted to different bandwidths [1].

Learning Benefits with Didactic Sequencing

Findings from the projects suggest that teaching approaches that involves didactic sequencing may enhance student learning. Students who were assisted during the preparation phase were positive about the learning arrangements ahead of lectures:

---

[1] In one of the courses the professor prepared the introduction videos together with the university multimedia centre. In the videos the professor talked about selected topics using slides, while text and graphics were gradually introduced in a Power-Point presentation. The video productions were recorded in a studio with the professor seated in front of a lighted green screen, and using a technique called keying, the finished video appeared to show the professor in front of the various Power-Point slides (http://en.wikipedia.org/wiki/Greenscreen). The result was a composite picture that showed the professor in the foreground and the Power-Point slides in the background. This was an appropriate approach as the content (biology, mammal tissue knowledge) was descriptive and thus required visual studies of pictures at a detailed level. In the other course (biology, teacher education program) the lecturer developed the videos without any assistance from the multimedia centre. This course did not require the same detailing level in the videos. Recordings were made by means of mobile phone, web camera or an ordinary video recorder. In this way the composition of the video content and the choices of production methods are closely connected to the course content the videos are preparing students for.

"The videos make it easier to prepare, and when you are prepared it is a lot easier to remember things, to follow (arguments) and to comprehend during lectures… […] … When I have heard about the matters, seen it in beforehand, I learn faster, it makes it easier to remember.".

The learning benefits during lectures may be described through the theoretical concept of *intersubjectivity*. The concept has proven useful to understand human interaction within schooling (Rogoff, 1990). A basic educational challenge that teachers commonly face is how to create a shared focus of learning activities in the classroom (Matusov, 2001). A shared focus of attention requires some common ground. In educational literature this is referred to as 'intersubjectivity'. According to Wertsch (1984) intersubjectivity exists between participants who act in the same setting when they share the same definition of the situation and know that they share it. In the biology course common ground was found when students accessed and used the videos that were displayed in the LMS.

Students used the videos in different ways to prepare for lectures. The videos drew attention to some concepts and provided brief outlines of the coming lecture. Watching the video without other preparation activities provided the students with 'surface subject knowledge', the first step towards intersubjectivity. Looking into a few concepts and the purpose of the lesson, and a brief outline of main curriculum priorities, provided some common ground for lecturer and students. In addition to communicating subject expectations, the lecturer also managed to get communication expectations across to the students. The students had to be prepared to explain concepts and answer simple curriculum questions when attending lectures.

'Detailed subject knowledge' came about when students attended lectures with a higher level of intersubjectivity. This came about when they watched the videos, read the material proposed by the professor and worked on the assigned tasks. When the students did preparation activities, they spent time on this work, using a plethora of learning aids and information sources. The textbook, other books, the internet, dictionaries and other reference works were used to prepare for the lectures. This was precisely the type of student activity the professor wanted the video to encourage. These types of preparation activity prior to the lectures paved the way for a higher level of intersubjectivity. In this way the video provided students with a *preparation focus* about how to undertake the preparations and what subject knowledge to look into. This higher level of intersubjectivity reaches beyond a shared focus of attention.

SUMMARY AND IMPLICATIONS FOR TEACHER EDUCATION

The main purpose of this article was to develop insights into some didactic considerations that need to be addressed when technology is used in education. This involves deciding priorities within the areas of technology, learning theories and issues of educational practice. We have suggested that the interrelatedness of these areas may represent a main framework for developing didactic practices, and that complexity in teaching can be reduced through sequencing of the learning process.

The discussions presented here have implications for a broader discussion about how student teachers may develop didactic competences about the use of technology in education.

It is insufficient for student teachers to be introduced to a well of functions in learning technologies and to train in basic ICT skills in teacher education programs. By the time they enter working life, new technologies with new possibilities will more than likely be available. What they need is more general insights into how to design learning environments based on didactic considerations of the three intersecting areas. This involves that student teachers need to establish some centre of attention before making justified choices within the intersecting areas. We have suggested that didactic sequencing is one teaching approach that provides such centre of attention.

One way to go about is to present student teachers with practical cases about the use of technology in education. When approaching the cases students should be introduced to how didactic sequencing may reduce teaching complexity. After establishing this centre of attention, students may elaborate further by addressing the core concepts of didactics (i.e. what, how and why). This needs to be done in conjunction with priorities that are set according to insight into the intersecting areas. In our example, justified priorities within the field of learning theories made the centre of attention (preparation phase) and guided further choices within the three areas (technology, learning theories and issues of education).

Didactic sequencing is one teaching approach that may reduce complexity in teaching. Future research should search to identify additional teaching approaches and explore how they can be implemented into teacher education. Such knowledge may contribute to an effective teacher education that actually influences the way technology is used in schools.

ACKNOWLEDGEMENTS

The writing of this article was supported by a grant from the Network for IT Research and Competence in Education, ITU (Forsknings- og kompetansenettverk for IT i utdanning).

REFERENCES

Alexander, P. A. & Jetton, T. L. (2000). Learning from text: A multidimensional and developmental perspective. In M. L. Kamil; P. B. Mosenthal; P. D. Pearson & R. Barr (Eds.) *Handbook of reading research* (Vol. 3, 285-310). Mahwah, NJ: Erlbaum.

Alexander, P. A.; Murphy, P. K.; Woods, B. S.; Duhon, K. E. & Parker, D. (1997). College instruction and concomitant changes in students' knowledge, interest, and strategy use: A study of domain learning. *Contemporary Educational Psychology, 22*(2), 125-146.

Arnseth, H.C, Hatlevik, O., Kløvstad, V., Kristiansen, T. & Ottestad, G. (2007). *ITU Monitor 2007. Skolens digitale tilstand 2007* [ITU Monitor 2007. The digital situation in schools 2007]. Olso: Universitetsforlaget.

Bergesen, H. O. (2006). *Kampen om kunnskapsskolen* [Struggle over the "knowledge constructing" school]. Oslo: Universitetsforlaget.

Cognition and Technology Group at Vanderbilt (1996). Looking at technology in context: A framework for understanding technology and education research. In C.C. Berliner & R.C. Calfee (Eds.), *Handbook of Educational Psychology* (807 – 840). New York: Macmillan.

Erstad, O. (2004). *PILOTer for skoleutvikling. Samlerapport fra forskningen 2000-2003* [PILOTs for school development. A report with summary of research 2000-2003]. Oslo: ITU, skriftserie, nr.28.

Erstad, O. (2006). *Digital kompetanse i skolen. En innføring* [Digital competence in school. An introduction]. Oslo: Universitetsforlaget.

Fibæk Laursen, P. (1999). *Didaktikk og kognition* [Didactics and cognition]. København: Gyldendal.

Greeno, J., Collins, A. M. & Resnick, L. (1996). Cognition and Learning. In Berliner D.C. & Calfee, R. C (Eds.), *Handbook of Educational Psychology*. New York: Macmillan.

Gundem, B.B. (2003). Innledende refleksjoner over begrepet didaktikk [Preliminary reflections about didactics]. In P. Arneberg & B. Overland (Eds.), *Pedagogikk. Mangfold og muligheter* [Pedagogy. Diversity and possibilities]. Oslo: Damm.

Hiim, H. & Hippe, E. (1999). Hva er yrkesdidaktikk? Om sammenhengen mellom yrkes- og profesjonsdidaktikk, yrkeskunnskap og yrkesrelevant forskning [What is vocational didacticts? About connections between didactics of trades and didactics of professions, trade related knowledge and trade relevant research]. *Norsk Pedagogisk Tidsskrift, 83*, 177-183.

Jackson, P.W. (1968). *Life in Classrooms*. New York: Holt, Rhinehart and Winston.

Jank, W. & Meyer, H. (1997). Didaktikens centrala frågor [The main didactic questions]. In M. Uljens (Ed.), *Didaktik – teori, reflektion och praktikk* [Didactis – theory, reflection and practice]. Lund: Studentlitteratur.

Klafki, W. (1997). Kritisk-konstruktiv didaktikk [Critical-constructive didactics]. In M. Uljens (Ed.), *Didaktik – teori, reflektion och praktikk* [Didactics – theory, reflection and practice]. Lund: Studentlitteratur.

Krumsvik, R. J. (2007). Situert læring i nettverkssamfunnet [Situated learning in the network society]. In R. J. Krumsvik (Ed.), *Skulen og den digitale læringsrevolusjonen* (194-254) [Schools and the digital revolution]. Oslo: Universitetsforlaget.

Matusov, E. (2001). Intersubjectivity as a way of informing teaching design for a community of learners classroom. *Teaching and Teacher Education*, 17, 383-402.

Morgan, G. (2003). *Faculty use of course management systems*. University of Wisconsin System: Educause center for applied research (ECAR).

Paulsen, M. F. (2003). Experiences with learning management systems in 113 European institutions. *Educational Technology & Society, 6*(4), 134-148. Available at http://ifets.ieee.org/periodical/6_4/13.pdf

Rasmussen, J. (2005). *Undervisning i det refleksivt moderne* [Education in the reflexive modern]. København: Hans Reitzels Forlag.

Resnick, L.B.(1987). *Education and learning to think*. Washington DC: National Academy Press.

Rismark, M. & Sølvberg A. M. (2007). Implementation of mobile technology in higher education: Student experiences. *Proceedings of International Conference on Information Technology and Management*, CITM2007/ICAIT2007. Hong Kong, China, 3-5 January 2007. ISBN 9889731150.

Rismark, M., Sølvberg, A. M., Strømme, A. & Hokstad, L. M. (2007). Using mobile phones to prepare for university lectures: Student's experiences. *The Turkish Online Journal of Educational Technology, 6*(4), 85-90.

Rogoff, B. (1990). *Apprenticeship in thinking: Cognitive development in social context.* New York: Oxford University Press.

Samuelstuen, M. & Bråten, I. (2005). Decoding, knowledge, and strategies in comprehension of expository text. *Scandinavian Journal of Psychology*, 46, 107 – 117.

Sølvberg A. M , Rismark, M. & Strømme, A. (2008). Fra skippertak til jevn studieinnsats; mobiltelefon som støttespiller i læringsarbeidet [From all-out effort to continuous work efforts; the mobile phone as support in learning]. *Uniped 31*(1), 25-38.

Sølvberg, A. M.; Rismark, M; Strømme, A. & Hokstad, L. M. (2007). How mobile technology promotes effective learning. *Computers and advanced technology in education (IASTED / CATE2007)* (475-480). Beijing: ACTA Press.

Wertsch, J.V. (1984) The zone of proximal development: Some conceptual issues. In B. Rogoff & J.V. Wertsch (Eds.), *Children's learning in the "Zone of Proximal Development". New Directions for Child Development* (7-18). San Francisco: Jossey-Bass.

In: Learning in the Network Society and the Digitized School
Editor: Rune Krumsvik
ISBN 978-1-60741-172-7
© 2009 Nova Science Publishers, Inc.

Chapter 9

USING VIDEOPAPERS TO COMMUNICATE AND REPRESENT PRACTICE IN POSTGRADUATE EDUCATION PROGRAMMES

Federica Olivero[1] and Elisabeth Lazarus[2]
University of Bristol, UK

ABSTRACT

The chapter explores Videopaper as a multimodal tool that mediates the representation and communication of practice across a range of postgraduate courses. Videopapers integrate and synchronise different forms of representation including text, video and images in one single non linear cohesive document. Research is currently investigating their potential and use in a variety of contexts ranging from teacher education to professional development as well as research collaborative practices. This paper discusses practical and theoretical issues about the processes for the creation of, and interaction with, videopapers, and argues that videopapers can be considered a new form of discourse; as such they require a process of appropriation before their more extensive integration in postgraduate courses.

1. INTRODUCTION

The Education department at the University of Bristol attracts a range of practitioners (mainly teachers) coming to study for postgraduate programmes aimed at the development of their skills or the learning of new skills to be applied to their practice. The development and learning of practitioner skills require a process of observing, reflecting, analysing, representing, communicating and/or practising, with the aim to become an effective practitioner. Even though videorecordings of practice are sometimes used in this process, the way in which, traditionally, practitioners are asked to represent and communicate this process is through written essays. The transformation of the complexity of the practice field into a linear text that has to fit predetermined academic criteria, may lose some of the key elements defining the world of the practitioner, which is in itself multimodal.

This chapter explores the use of an innovative tool like Videopaper to communicate and represent practice in a range of postgraduate courses. The chapter will argue that this tool enables the coexistence of elements belonging to practice and elements belonging to the academic world and therefore may transform the way in which practice can be analysed, represented and communicated.

After outlining the theoretical ideas and rationale behind the use of videopapers and the range of projects exploring their use at the University of Bristol, the chapter will focus on a case study in the context of initial teacher education to illustrate the main issues in relation to the potential of this new tool. The chapter will conclude with a discussion of more general implications for practice.

2. THEORETICAL BACKGROUND

2.1. The Idea of Discourses

Using the definition of Discourses given by Gee (1999) as "ways of behaving, interacting, valuing, thinking, believing, speaking, and often reading and writing that are accepted as instantiations of particular roles (or types of people) by specific groups of people" (p.13), research studies within education show that teachers and academics work within different Discourses, embedding different criteria for establishing validity and different ways of integrating and using knowledge (Bartels, 2003). If we try to characterise these different Discourses (Olivero, John, & Sutherland, 2004), the academic Discourse seems to be aimed at providing scholarly and theoretical foundations for effective pedagogy, expressed through specialised terminology, propositions and prescriptions, stream of words. The teacher Discourse on the other hand aims to support practitioners to value their classroom experiences and use those experiences as a 'text' to study and analyse in order to better understand their crafts; as such it calls for means of representation that capture the language of the practice, i.e. the sights, sounds and interactive features of the classroom together with visual, oral and physical cues.

The concept of Discourse and the differences there might be between academic and teacher/practitioner Discourses is particularly important in contexts where educational practitioners access postgraduate programmes with the aim to develop their skills or learn new skills as part of their professional development. These practitioners need to work within the academic Discourse and incorporate theoretical ideas in the analysis of their practice, and at the same time they need to be able to integrate the teacher/practitioner Discourse in a way that resonates with their practice. However, traditional genres of publication have remained monomodal or strictly hierarchical in including a secondary mode (Olivero et al., 2004) and the means offered to practitioners to represent and analyse their practice do not often address and represent the different Discourses. The development and use of more multi-modal representations of educational knowledge and practice that integrate visual, aural, oral and physical cues that are part of the natural world of communication of teachers is called for, as argued in the next section.

2.2. Multimodality

Visual and multimodal representations have increasingly gained importance in the education research literature (see e.g. Cope & Kalantzis, 2000; Kress & van Leeuwen, 2001; Matthewman, Blight, & Davies, 2004). Moreover, the recent rapid development of technology has enabled the potential of multimodal communication to be realised to a larger extent (Snyder, 2002). In the move from page to screen a range of representational modes (including image, movement, gesture, and voice) are available as meaning-making resources and these modes, compared to text alone, have caused a move towards the reconfiguration of image and writing on screen, in both writing and reading practices (Jewitt, 2005). Research also shows that the affordability of a text is closely related with the ways in which it is constructed (Kress, 2003). When thinking about the different academic and teacher Discourses, these concepts point towards the need to provide practitioners who enter postgraduate courses with tools that integrate different modes of communication beyond language and therefore enable them to represent and communicate analysis and reflection grounded in their practice. A written description of a lesson may not convey the same meaning as a video-recorded lesson. Even though both modes aim to capture and describe the same content, they may not be able communicate in the same way for example the kind of interactions happening in the classroom.

One of the tools that has been extensively used as a powerful engagement and portrayal tool to help teachers connect with and improve their understandings and interpretation of their practice is digital video (Carraher, Schliemann, & Brizuela, 2000; Pea, 2003; Sherin, 2004). The development of new technologies has recently made possible the integration of digital video into multimedia environments, as for example videopapers (Nemirovsky, DiMattia, Ribeiro, & Lara-Meloy, 2005), that integrate and synchronise multiple modes in one cohesive document (Beardsley, Cogan-Drew, & Olivero, 2007). This chapter explores how videopapers, by integrating multiple modes, may afford the author an innovative way of communicating and representing practice that integrates the different Discourses.

3. THE CONCEPT OF VIDEOPAPER

The Videopaper technology was developed as part of the Bridging Research and Practice project at TERC (Boston, MA) to create an alternative genre for the production, use, and dissemination of educational research. The project conjectured that teachers, researchers and other communities interested in education could use videopapers to make their conversations more grounded in actual events, more insightful, and more resistant to oversimplifications (Nemirovsky, Lara-Meloy, Earnest, & Ribeiro, 2001).

A videopaper integrates and synchronises different forms of representation such as text, video and images in one single non-linear cohesive document, as shown in Figure 1. Text and video are linked through 'Play' buttons that activate the part of the video that is relevant to a particular part of the text or viceversa bring up a page that talks about what is happening in the clip at that particular moment. A videopaper can be read in different ways: readers can decide which page(s) to read, play and pause the video as they choose, activate the Play buttons, follow internal hyperlinks and external hyperlinks to outside sources of information.

"Combining the video with the text creates a fluid document that is more explicit than the text or video alone, while remaining contained and controlled by the author" (Olivero et al., 2004, p.183), as will become evident in the analysis presented later in the chapter.

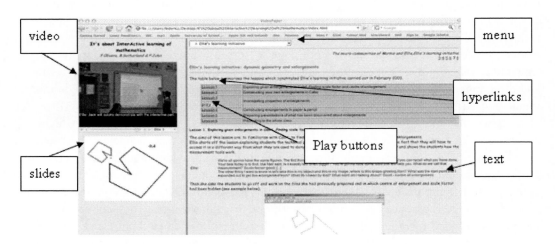

Figure 1. A videopaper

Videopapers are created with the free software VideoPaper Builder 3[1]. The creation process involves three stages: editing a video into a short (5-10 minutes) clip, writing the text, creating the links between text and video through the Play buttons, synchronising the images with the video. All these stages can be seen as a 'whole' process, because although the continued role of writing in these multimodal texts is not in question (Lanham, 2001), decisions about what each of the elements and the links between them represent have to be taken throughout the creation process, as the analysis will show. The final stage is the publishing process, through which the VideoPaper Builder 3 software brings together all the different elements and creates a document that can be opened in any web browser, without needing an Internet connection or the VPB3 software.

Videopapers are intrinsically different from other currently available tools, as for example weblogs, in terms of structure and purpose. Videopapers integrate different modes in one document rather than opening different windows and the video is always there as the pages change while reading the text. The links in the text point to particular parts of the video but the reader can also choose to play the video as they are reading the text. Amongst the many definitions of weblogs, Winer (2002) (cited in Martindale & Wiley, 2004) defines them as "often-updated sites that point to articles elsewhere on the web, often with comments, and to on-site articles" while one element that distinguishes videopapers is the fact that the process of creation is aimed at a final product, despite possibly going through more than one iteration. As concerns blogs though research shows "less evidence than expected of blogs as interlinked, interactive, and oriented towards external events; rather, most of the blogs in our corpus are individualistic, even intimate, forms of self-expression, and a surprising number of them contain few or no links" (Herring, Scheidt, Wright, & Bonus, 2005, p.163). With this respect we could say that videopapers may serve a similar purpose when used to reflect and

---

[1] Free download of VideoPaper Builder 3 at http://vpb.concord.org/.

represent practice, despite their not continuous process of writing. Despite the differences from tools like weblogs, we could say that videopapers in the same way as blogs, "rather than deriving from a single source, are in fact a hybrid of existing genres, rendered unique by the combination of features of the source genres they adapt, and by their distinctive technical affordances" (Herring et al., 2005, p.160). This will be clearly shown in the analysis of the reading and creation of videopapers in the next section, where we will see how the student teachers are working towards combining all the available modes and show a transformation or adaptation from the known genres.

3.1. Research on Videopapers

Although Videopaper as a tool is being used quite widely in a range of settings around the world, the research literature on the use of videopapers is still limited. Two main broad areas predominate so far: the investigation of videopapers as a tool for bridging research and practice (looking at videopaper as a 'product') and as a tool to support reflection mainly in teacher education (focusing on the 'process' of creating a videopaper). Besides, videopaper has also been trialled as an alternative way to publish academic research papers (Nemirovsky et al., 2004), although no research has been carried out yet as to how these videopapers are taken on within the research community.

3.1.1. Using Videopapers for Bridging the Gap between Research and Practice – Videopaper as a Product

Olivero et al (2004) explore the way videopapers may contribute to bridging the gap between research and teaching practice, due to the fact that they are more authentic than traditional papers and they can model innovative teaching practice grounded in research through the co-existence of the visual and textual element. Beardsley et al (2007), reporting on the case of a teacher creating his own videopaper to represent the work he carried out within a research project, show how videopapers may enable the representation of both research ideas and evidence from practice in the same environment. The teacher Dan reported that his videopaper contains "Not just lesson plans, it's got a lesson plan that teachers can follow, if they want to follow mine but it's also got the theory behind it so they can change it themselves without ruining it, that's the idea" (Dan, interview extract). Therefore his videopaper gives access to both the reality of the classroom and the specific lesson plan, and the ideas underpinning that lesson. This provides the reader with the tools to adapt that to their own context without losing its essence.

Along the same lines, the project carried out by Armstrong et al (2005) looks at the creation of videopapers to represent a collaborative research process in which both researchers and teachers interpreted classroom episodes within a series of mathematics and science lessons. Similarly to what McGraw et al (2007) found in relation to the discussion of multimedia case studies, having people with different knowledge and expertise looking at the same data provides the possibility for different understandings of a lesson to be put forward and productively interact to create new knowledge (Barnes & Sutherland, 2007). The subsequently created videopaper embodies this process, enabling the multiple perspectives to coexist and to be grounded in the reality of the classroom (Galvis & Nemirovsky, 2003).

Another study (Smith & Krumsvik, 2007a, 2007b) presents an analysis of the effects of the reading and discussion around a videopaper integrating key educational theories that prospective teachers are normally exposed to. Video illustrations of these theories, taken from the authors' own teaching practice, are incorporated in the videopaper. This videopaper was read by prospective teachers, teacher educators, and researchers in conferences. Smith and Krumsvik argue that this way of using videopapers contributes to bringing together communities that would not normally exchange ideas around teaching; they also found that the prospective teachers appreciated the fact that the practice field was brought to the university and the fact that they could "see" the reality of the profession rather than just "hear" about it.

This connects to what Nemirovsky et al (2005) found, with respect to high school teachers discussing a videopaper presenting the analysis of classroom conversations which occurred in a high school mathematics class. They argue that by moving beyond typical textual narratives, videopapers allow the reader to feel closer to the interaction shown in the video and move beyond their own previous experience to a higher level of discourse. These videopapers have also the potential of providing teachers with realistic models of "what is possible", constituting a ground on which they can build their confidence, in cases in which they have no real class situations to watch and learn from (Olivero et al., 2004).

3.1.2. Using Videopapers for Reflection in Teacher Education – Videopaper as a Process

Even though limited, research in this area indicates that videopapers could be fruitfully used as a support for teacher reflection (Beardsley et al., 2007; Nemirovsky et al., 2005). According to DiMattia & Cogan-Drew (2003), videopapers facilitate the integration of video for reflection on classroom experiences and the exchange of ideas. Working with professional teachers they argue that by creating a videopaper, teachers are forced to explain in detail their teaching practice due to the fact that their practice can be 'seen' in the video and this requires them to have profound knowledge of their own practice. Galvis & Nemirovsky (2003) add that the incorporation of video, text, images and surrounding material, enhances a teacher's understanding of his/her lesson. Nemirovsky et al. (2005), investigating the type of talk that teachers engage with while reading videopapers, also argue that the inclusion of the video affords the opportunity for teachers to have a closer view of teaching moments that would not be possible by using only textual descriptions. They also indicate that when viewing a videopaper, the video "allows the speakers to richly grasp the overall 'climate' of an interaction, and notice when things diverge from what participants (teachers) tended to project on the basis of their own previous experiences" (p.390). Furthermore, the analysis of the text offers a perspective, ideas and questions with which to watch the episode, while at the same time it demonstrates how the classroom episode relates to broader issues that matter to the speakers.

Following similar lines, the Department of Education at Tufts University has been integrating videopapers in the Master of Arts in Teaching, as a tool for reflection in teacher preparation since 2001 (Beardsley et al., 2007). The aims of the project are for teachers to reflect on their practice through the use of videopapers, present their work and experience to other teachers and build a 'VideoPaper library' of best teaching practices. Their work is based on the idea that as a vehicle for presenting useful strategies to his/her colleagues, the videopaper provides its author with an equally significant opportunity to reflect on his/her own teaching.

Although, as discussed above, there are a number of initiatives implementing the use of videopapers in various settings, research on their impact and effectiveness in terms of the processes they involve – reading and creating – is still limited. The next sections will discuss some exploratory research findings in relation to these issues, which show that, although generally beneficial, the introduction of videopapers does not come without tensions, due to the different forms of representation that it incorporates, embodying both academic and practitioner Discourses. As one of the students involved in the project said: "It's like writing the first essay; it's a completely new way of doing things", *a new form of Discourse* perhaps.

4. EXPLORATORY VIDEOPAPER PROJECTS IN POSTGRADUATE EDUCATION PROGRAMMES

The Education department at the University of Bristol attracts a range of practitioners who come to study for postgraduate programmes with the aim of developing their skills in a chosen field or learning new skills as part of their professional development. A series of 'videopaper projects' started in 2005[2] to explore the use and integration of videopapers as an alternative form to traditional essays or videotapes for the analysis, representation and communication of practice required by some courses. These projects have worked with four groups of practitioners:

- student teachers[3] learning to teach within the initial teacher education programme;
- educational practitioners learning the skills of counselling to support their students (see Trahar, 2008);
- postgraduate students and new university staff developing teaching skills;
- teachers and educational practitioners learning research skills within Master's courses and integrating them in their practice[4].

In each of these different contexts, the practitioner goes through a process of observing, developing and/or practising a set of skills that are necessary to become an effective practitioner. The process requires the practitioner to integrate evidence from their practice and theoretical underpinnings. Drawing on the discussion around different Discourses carried out at the beginning of the chapter, it can be argued that it is important to provide these educational practitioners with opportunities to express themselves in a way that can incorporate features of their own Discourse, which may differ from the traditional academic Discourse they are working in. Giving ways to practitioners to represent research informed

---

[2] These projects were carried out in collaboration with the colleagues Kate Hawkey, Sheila Trahar, Marina Gall and the research student Maria Daniil.

[3] We are working with Modern Foreign Language, History, English and Music student teachers.

[4] These studies are generating examples of videopapers of several types: (i) Practitioners reflecting critically on the development of their counselling skills; (ii) Student teachers reflecting on their lesson planning, teaching and evaluation skills; (iii) Postgraduate students and new staff reflecting on their teaching skills; (iv) a University supervisor reflecting on her post lesson feedback skills; (v) Master's students writing up their small scale research projects and analysing empirical data, showing their research skills.

practice and to communicate their use of theoretical instruments to interpret their practice becomes crucial. Taking into account its affordances and multimodal character, as outlined in the previous section, we identified Videopaper as a possible tool to enable this to happen. Overall the aims of these ongoing projects are:

- to investigate the possible applications of videopapers as a tool for communication and representation of professional learning, in particular to support reflection on practice, and for assessment of the development of (new) skills;
- to compare and contrast the use of videopapers with the more conventional use of videos, observation tasks and assignments;
- to investigate the assessment process and criteria about the produced videopapers;
- to compare and contrast the participants' experience of producing a videopaper across programmes.

The process the participating students are asked to go through is similar for all groups and includes a number of workshops focusing on principles and potentiality of the software, reading existing videopapers, learning how to edit a clip and create a videopaper, creating own clip and videopaper. The videopapers are then assessed by the course tutor. The whole process lasts about two months.

5. COMMUNICATING AND REPRESENTING PRACTICE THROUGH VIDEOPAPERS: MAIN FINDINGS IN THE CONTEXT OF INITIAL TEACHER EDUCATION

This section will discuss some of the main findings related to the Modern Foreign Language student teacher groups, with particular reference to the role of the multimodal aspect of the tool in the communication and representation of professional learning and practice, in relation to the different Discourses. Three groups of volunteer student teachers were involved in the project over the course of three different academic years (Group 1, Summer Term 2005; Group 2, Autumn Term 2006; Group 3, Summer Term 2007[5]), for a total of 17 students[6]. The volunteer student teachers were asked to create a videopaper instead of a written essay for one of the units in their teacher training programme that required them to reflect on two or three issues related to their practice. A series of workshops was organised to support the students in this process and various data were collected, as outlined in Table 1.

---

[5] This paper draws on the analysis of Groups 1 and 2. The findings related to Group 3 are in Daniil (2007) and Daniil & Olivero (2008).

[6] All students volunteered to take part in the videopaper projects. Making the videopapers optional with respect to the traditional essays was considered an important aspect of the projects at this stage because of the features of the tool that require quite different skills from writing an essay – as discussed in this section. Given that the videopapers are formally assessed, the tutors want to leave students free to choose the tool they prefer to best express their ideas.

Table 1. The process of creating the videopapers: workshops and data collection

Workshops	*Data collected*
Workshop 1 - reading videopapers previously created by other student teachers reflecting on their practice	• Observations of pairs reading vp • Initial Group Interview
Filming one lesson in which the student teacher was teaching and collecting relevant materials from the classroom	
Workshop 2 - watching and editing the video of the lesson down to a 5-10 minutes clip	• Observations • Editing process Group Interview
Workshop 3 - writing the text and finally creating the videopaper to be submitted on a CD	• Final Individual or Group Interviews • Collected videopapers
Workshop 4 - reading each other's videopapers	• Observations of pairs reading vp • Final reading Group Interview

We considered the whole process as important and put an emphasis on the concept of 'videopaper as a *process*', in which all steps contributed to the communication and representation of practice. The analysis of the processes of reading and creating the videopapers highlighted how the multimodal features of videopapers mediate the way the student teachers communicate and represent their practice. The tension between the different (academic and practitioner) Discourses that can be represented in the videopaper also became explicit.

5.1. The Process of Reading a Videopaper

The process of reading a videopaper can be described as a dialogue between the reader and the author through the text, the video clips and the Play buttons that refer the reader to particular clips while reading the text. This dialogue, in which the reader becomes a writer, is potentially a qualitatively different process from watching a video without text or reading a text without video, as emerged from the analysis. We might need to re-think whether we 'read' or 'watch' a videopaper, or better maybe 'interact with' a videopaper. A range of issues were highlighted in the interviews and observations, ranging from practical issues, related to the non linear structure of a videopaper, to theoretical issues pointing at the representation of and tension between the two Discourses as expressed in the videopapers that were given to the students to read[7].

5.1.1. Reader as Writer

The discussion of the reading of the videopapers shows elements towards the definition of 'reader as writer' during the process of interaction with the videopaper itself. The co-existence of video and text in a videopaper enables the reader to enter into a dialogue with the author. The fact that video is almost endlessly rich as data type (Lemke, 2007) points to the

---

[7] The students were given videopapers created by previous student teachers in response to a similar assignment.

critical role of the viewer/reader. The transcripts show how, differently from a traditional paper, through the video the reader can 'enter' the space of the portrayed event and can bring in their own perspective/analysis, before starting to interact with the author's perspective represented in the text, as expressed in Extract 1 by Clare when asked about the difference between reading a videopaper and a traditional article:

> I think with a normal article you are more interested in what the text is saying, maybe with one of these you are more interested in watching the video and *make up our own mind about what's happening.*
>
> Extract 1. Clare [Gr1, initial group interview]

This is also reflected in the observed reading processes in which the video was generally the first element attended to. A consequence of this was the feeling of being *more involved* in the reading process of a videopaper (as Christine points out in Extract 2 when asked about what inspires her in a videopaper) because of the possibility of seeing a lesson rather than depending on the author's description of the event.

> We want to discover how the kids react to this and then watch the video and then that's how I would analyse the situation. That would be *far more like you are involved* ... because you also can decide or give your opinion or you feel the reader wants your opinion.
>
> Extract 2. Christine [Gr1, initial group interview]

Extract 2 also seems to suggest that the reading of a videopaper is a more active process than that of a traditional paper because it is felt that the author wants the reader's opinion. Generally the videopapers enabled the student teachers to be more critical and reflective than they usually are when reading papers, on the event the videopaper was focused on because of the fact that the video provided them with more details about the setting, which would normally not be available in a paper. Therefore the videopaper allowed the students to 'be part' of the event and look at it 'from the inside', as the video seemed to be considered a true representation of what happened.

5.1.2. This is Real

The realism brought in by the video in a videopaper is one of the key issues highlighted in the interviews. "Video is a seductive medium. [...] It makes us believe that we are simply seeing what is there, rather than interacting with and interpreting in very specific ways a very partial record of an activity" (Lemke, 2007, p.46). Being able to *see* what the videopaper is about is considered very important by all student teachers, as typically expressed by Dave when asked about the potentialities of videopapers:

> You can actually *see* it, you don't have to try to imagine.
>
> Extract 3. Dave [Gr2, initial group interview]

This enables a discussion around what actually happened rather than around the author's interpretation of what might have happened and through what the reader can imagine. It is interesting to notice how the video was immediately taken as a real representation of the event when reading the sample videopapers, even if the discussion around the editing process clearly showed how the clip that went into the videopaper was *constructed* by the author in a particular way and how the positioning of the camera was recognised as having a role in what the reader could see, as discussed in the next section.

Another aspect of the realism attributed to the videopapers, resides in the fact that videopapers, when compared to traditional essays, were thought to be less abstract and allowing a better interweaving of theory and practice, as Clare argues when asked about the potential of videopapers, after reading a couple of examples.

> If you compare it to a normal essay it gives you a *realistic dimension* because *it is not abstract* any more; you're not talking about behaviour management, big theories, here you have the reality, practice, it's not just writing but *connecting theories to the practice and the other way*.
>
> Extract 4. Clare [Gr1, initial group interview]

If we refer back to the idea of Discourses, this may be seen as a realisation that academic and practitioner Discourses may co-exist through the different available modes. The possibility of 'showing' the event, the reality, the practice rather than 'talking about' it also makes the videopaper more real and as Lemke (2007) suggested, the reader can be drawn 'inside the box'. And the Play buttons enable a constant move back and forth from analysis/theory to practice and viceversa.

5.1.3. A Way In

Due to the characteristics mentioned above, videopapers can be considered a way to 'hook' practitioners or student teachers into theoretical analysis grounded in the practice, which is represented in the video, as Liz states in Extract 5, when asked about her first impressions of the videopapers she read.

> I was very interested and I thought oh yes, I want to have a look at this and see what it's all about. *I wasn't as intimidated* as I would be if I'd approached a huge thick tome.
>
> Extract 5. Liz [Gr2, initial group interview]

The video element, which better connects to the practitioners' world, can be a less intimidating starting point than text. Being able to see also seems to provoke an affective response (Lemke, 2007) to the event presented in the videopaper, through which one can very quickly get the idea of what a person wants you to know and can feel how the person is, as shown in Extract 6.

> I think that's one of the best things that you get ... even if you're just picking out one little snapshot *you do get a feel* for the type of school perhaps or the kids or where they're 'Oh those are a bit more like my kids'.
>
> Extract 6. Catherine [Gr2, final group interview]

The initial affective response stimulated by the video may be a 'way in' through which the student teachers may connect to the context first, relating it to their own context, and are then able to engage with the issues discussed by the author (Nemirovsky et al., 2005).

5.2 The Process of Creating a VideoPaper

The studies this chapter draws on showed that what is most important in terms of the analysis, representation and communication of practice, and consequently the development of practitioners' skills is the 'process' of actively creating a videopaper. Creating a videopaper involves watching and editing a video, writing the text and inserting the Play buttons. This process is qualitatively different from simply watching a video of a whole lesson to reflect on one's practice as clearly shown in the data.

5.2.1. Editing Process

It is the editing process, i.e. the process of having to select relevant clips that represent an aspect of practice to be discussed in the videopaper, that initiates an analytical process that might not necessarily happen if the students just watched a whole lesson without needing to either produce a written text or select parts of it to include in the final product (Daniil, 2007; Lazarus & Olivero, 2007). A process of 'stepping outside the box' (Lemke, 2007) seems to be happening during the move from simply watching the video-recording of the lesson to editing the clips to insert in the videopaper. Laura in Extract 7 describes a shift from an emotional response to the video (paying attention to the *awful sounding language*) to a more detached view.

> It was nowhere as painful as I perhaps thought it would be. I was so absorbed with trying to work out how to actually edit, the mechanics of doing that, I think *I started to forget that the person moving around was actually me*, and became immune to the sort of awful sounding language.
>
> Extract 7. Laura [Gr2, final group interview]

In the same way as when reading videopapers, there seems to be a transition from an emotional response to their own video to an analysis of it. The editing process is the starting point of the interpretation process, which produces a representation of the lesson, as Catherine puts it in Extract 8.

> But the video or the footage we used, the raw footage, is a representation of the lesson anyway, it's a representation of what went on. *Now that we've edited it we've got a representation of a representation.* You know we've chosen either consciously or subconsciously the bits that we wanted to include.
>
> Extract 8. Catherine [Gr2, final group interview]

From Extract 8 it seems to be clear to the students that the video does not show an objective reality or may not portray a real picture of the classroom, given that for example you could select any 5 minutes to make the class look great. Answering back to this comment Patricia brings in the other element of the videopaper, i.e. text, highlighting how the fact that a videopaper includes both elements makes the product *more true*, as we can see in Extract 9.

> *But then you've got the words to go with it as well* and you've got what you say, and you've got both. So think of the people who only wrote about the lesson, they can even more omit things. And you can even lie, you can say ... you invent things if it didn't go well.

Whereas with the videopaper you can't invent things that didn't go well, you've got to find them. And *they're even more true because you've got to look for them.*

Extract 9. Patricia [Gr2, final group interview]

Extract 9 also points to the importance of the co-existence of text and video in the meaning making process, which will be discussed in the next section. The fact that you have video and text in a videopaper means that you 'can't lie', and this is one of the key issues that the student teachers highlighted when thinking about the differences between creating a videopaper and writing an essay.

5.2.2. Creating a Videopaper vs. Writing an Essay

When talking about the creation of their videopaper in the interviews, the students highlighted that there needs to be more thinking behind the text, and the whole videopaper, because you can't 'hide' what really happened (DiMattia & Cogan-Drew, 2003), while you can write an essay about anything that you like, because you don't need to include the evidence for your point in it, as Christine argues:

> *It makes it even harder that you know they can see what you want to tell them.* It would be easier to write an essay about whatever. While now even if the text is smaller it is much more thinking behind.

Extract 10. Christine [Gr1, editing group interview]

This relates to the fact that in a videopaper you offer the reader 'raw' data (through the video) and therefore as an author you are more exposed, you can't 'hide behind words', as mentioned by Dave in Extract 11.

> You've got the raw evidence, the video footage rather than in a sense being able to hide behind your own transcript of what goes on.

Extract 11. Dave [Gr2, initial group interview]

This is a rather important point that changes the relationship between author, reader and data, due to the co-existence of the different modes. The videopaper becomes more personal than an essay in that in the videopaper you can see/show yourself, you have to describe and analyse your practice while in an essay there seems to be a certain distance from the text, which could *even lie* as Patricia points out in Extract 9.

5.3. Multimodality of Videopaper

Looking across the processes of reading and creating videopapers, some common themes related to the multimodal aspects of the tool emerged. According to Jewitt (2005) "different modes offer specific resources for meaning making, and the ways in which modes contribute to people's meaning making vary" (p.316). In the case of a videopaper, all of its elements may contribute to the meaning making process; however the reader can freely interpret each one from their own perspective. The text integrated in the videopaper could be self-contained as concerns the meaning the author wants to communicate, however, as Jewitt (2005) indicates, "the writing needs to be understood in relation to the other modes it is nestled alongside" (p.316). During both the interviews and the individual work, there was a lot of discussion about the roles that video and text should have in a videopaper and what relationship should link them. This clearly shows that the student teachers were aware that having at their disposal different modes would affect the way they constructed their 'essay' and the way a reader would make meaning out of their videopaper. Eager to know what a 'good' videopaper was, they realised that for them it was like going back to the first time they wrote an essay as the processes involved were completely different and new.

5.3.1. Relationship Video/Text

A videopaper gives the reader a choice of where to start from, i.e. it gives different entry points that will affect the meaning making around the event represented in the videopaper. No agreement between whether they should start from the video or from the text when reading a videopaper was achieved amongst the student teachers, but they all agreed with the fact that it is through all the elements of the videopaper that you can make sense of the event and analysis. More research is called for about the reading process in order to have evidence for how the reading process of a videopaper affects meaning making. As expressed in Extract 1, starting from the video enables the reader to *make up their own mind* before reading the author's perspective. However, at times the video itself does not provide enough elements to understand what is portrayed. The video in a videopaper is a selection of clips, made with a purpose and if that purpose is not made explicit, it may be hard to understand it. This highlights the difference between having a video by itself and having a video within a videopaper, as commented by Patricia in Extract 9.

5.3.2. What Roles for Video and Text?

Looking closer at the multimodal aspects of the videopaper leads to trying to define what roles video and text have within the videopaper. As Kress (2003) points out, 'the world narrated' is a different world to 'the world depicted and displayed', meaning that even if different modes may seem to encode the same content, they are nevertheless conveyors of qualitatively different kinds of messages. Questions that arise in our context are: What should the text say and what should the video show? This issue was discussed at length in the two groups both during the creation of their videopapers and during the reading of the sample videopapers. Different possibilities for the roles of video and text were highlighted in the various videopapers: the text just repeated information that could be seen in the video without adding new information; the clips didn't show as strong evidence as the text was saying; no interpretation of the video from the author in the text; the text interprets what can be seen in the clips without describing it. Extract 12 and Extract 13 represent two different points of view that were expressed by the group of student teachers when interviewed about creating their own videopaper.

> I didn't explain what was going on in the clip because I think it keeps the surprise. So I just would say 'I did this and this' and then the play is somehow just an invitation if you want to have a look how I do it just look at the clip, but I never really describe everything that is happening in the clip. [...] With this [videopaper] I felt more freedom in just putting something there and then *up to the reader to*, don't know, to *analyse* or up to the reader to actually interpret what I'm writing.
>
> Extract 12. Christine [Gr1, final individual interview]

Christine leaves the interpretation of the video with the reader (cf Extract 2, reader as writer), assuming that the reader will see different things from her anyway and therefore there is no point in providing her own interpretation of the clip as it may not match what the reader thinks. This is only possible because of the existence of the video element.

> Writing is what I think but other people may see different things in the video so to understand my videopaper they *need to watch and read.*
>
> Extract 13. Clare [Gr1, final individual interview]

Clare is aware of the possibility that the same video may be interpreted in different ways and therefore might not constitute evidence by itself for the points she wants to make. Therefore she highlights the fact that the meaning of her videopaper is conveyed by watching and reading at the same time. An important distinction is made between what the teacher sees, in her/his role as 'insider', and what a reader might see as 'outsider'. Even though the video might be a 'way in' the event portrayed, it is still important that the author's perspective is expressed in the text so that a dialogue can take place between reader and writer. This is an affordance of videopapers that does not have a correspondence in other media like video or text. In fact, in a video the author's perspective only comes in implicitly through how the clips have been cut together, and in a text, there is only the author's perspective without access to the event as it took place.

5.3.3. Text - A Different 'Genre?'

Following on from the previous discussion, if we look at the textual element only, questions arise around whether the text should be different from the text that would be written in a traditional paper essay or not., i.e. whether what is new about videopapers is simply the fact that different modes co-exist or whether this implies a re-thinking of what kind of text is appropriate for a videopaper. Going back to the discussion around the different Discourses, does the text embody the academic Discourse or does the videopaper format allow the interweaving of the two Discourses also within the textual element? As this format was new for the tutors as well, initially we did not give any criteria to the student teachers about what they should write in the videopaper or what structure they should follow or how many words the text should be. One element that was appreciated by some students was the freedom that using a new tool allowed them, for example in terms of word limit.

More practical issues around how much text there was in each page brought the students to reflect on how different the text in the videopaper was/should be from an 'academic' text. The very fact that they started talking about the difference between a videopaper and an academic text shows how they thought that videopaper could not be an academic text in itself. What seems to come up here is how they have a clear idea of what an academic Discourse is, and that that is what is 'taken seriously', and how they think videopaper is 'something else'. However, one student put forward the idea that the text in the videopaper could be like a traditional essay in order to give the videopaper a certain academic status.

> Could you not get away from that problem by keeping it quite academic and not worrying so much about breaking it up all the time. *So you're keeping more to the traditional essay.* I don't see why you should make it less academic just because it's a video paper.
>
> Extract 14. Catherine [Gr2, initial group interview]

Overall, it seems that the students consider the text as the academic part (theory) and the video as the practice part that can be brought together in a videopaper but not without difficulties in some cases. Having the video meant having to constantly refer to their own practice and made it more difficult to write what could normally be written in an essay i.e. more references to the literature and less personal reflection. This opens up a whole new area around the issue of whether we need to become 'videopaper writers', and therefore change our 'writing' practices, or we can simply transfer the existing *genres* to the new tool.

6. VIDEOPAPER AS A NEW TOOL TO COMMUNICATE AND REPRESENT PRACTICE

The main conclusions we can draw around Videopaper as a new tool for the communication and representation of practice from these exploratory studies are outlined below. It is important to highlight that what emerges strongly from our research projects and the literature is the power of the 'videopaper concept', i.e. an environment integrating textual and video elements in a cohesive way. The Videopaper technology is currently the easiest tool that enables the creation of this type of representation but as technology is bound to evolve, it seems important not to focus too strongly on the particular tool as such but rather on the concept.

6.1. Realism

One of the main conclusions is the realism brought by videopapers for both writer and reader. In the creating process the students appreciate the possibility of being able to 'see' their own practice rather than having to 'visualise'. In the reading process the video enables readers to be more critical and reflective than they are when reading traditional papers due to the fact that they can 'enter' the event that is being analysed. This resonates with other projects (Olivero et al., 2004) in which teachers reading videopapers that represented research findings have highlighted the realism of them comparing it with traditional papers in which they believe things can be "made up" by the researchers. It is interesting to notice how a priori the video is taken as a true representation of practice as opposed to, for example, a transcript of classroom dialogue, despite the fact that a video is also constructed in some way thorugh the editing process.

6.2. Multimodality

The co-existence of video and text in a videopaper potentially offers the possibility of representing both the academic and practitioner Discourse in an interactive process through the different available modes. The video may embody the sights, sounds and interactive features of the classroom and of the teaching, while the text may 'crystallise' the reflection and analysis. However, video and text interact through the Play buttons and therefore theory and practice are interwoven. Questions we need to ask when creating a videopaper therefore are: What video? What text? What interactions between the two? Research shows the power of video in terms of enabling teachers to go beyond developing procedural knowledge of "what to do next", and rather develop "knowledge of how to interpret and reflect on classroom practices" (Sherin, 2004, p.17). In particular "the intellectual work the videopaper demands arises from the fact that video, text, and slides must be connected in order for the narrative to emerge. This interconnectedness pushes the author to closely examine the relationship between the images and their text, to think carefully about exactly how to generate meaning from their media" (Beardsley et al., 2007, p.489). This implies a re-definition of what is the 'text' in a videopaper and suggests that we might need to learn to become 'videopaper writers'. Different expectations from reading and creating a videopaper were observed in terms of the amount and structure of the text in relation to the video, in particular as concerns the non-linearity of the videopaper; the possibility of creating a narrative structure (Laurillard, Stratfold, Luckin, Plowman, & Taylor, 2000) through the use of menus and Play buttons seems to be a key issue that needs further research.

6.3. A Dialogical Process

As discussed in the chapter, the reading of a videopaper can be seen as a 'dialogical process' between reader and writer through the video and text. Videopapers allow for multiple perspectives to be elicited around a shared context, represented by the video element; these perspectives can co-exist and be represented in the textual element and offer potential for collaboration, as other projects have also explored (Barnes & Sutherland, 2007). Videopapers *crystallise* the representation of practice of the teacher creating them, through video and text, and this 'resonates' (Goldman, 2008) with the teachers reading them, through the dialogue and interaction with the video and the text created by the author.

6.4. Videopaper as a Process

Videopapers are artefacts that are created by the student teachers with the purpose of representing and analysing practice and eventually communicating and sharing it. Therefore, what emerges as important is the process of creating videopapers, first as *private tools* embodying personal reflections and representing what is 'seen' and 'noticed' and then as *public tools* communicating and sharing these reflections with others. The tutors marking the videopapers highlighted how the quality of the final product did not always reflect the amount of work and learning about practice that had taken place in the process of creation, showing how the creation process is the stage where the learning predominantly takes place.

7. IMPLICATIONS FOR PRACTICE AND FUTURE RESEARCH

On the basis of what discussed above we can argue that videopapers may be a *new form of Discourse* and as such they need to be gradually appropriated by both writers and readers before they can really become an integral part of teaching and learning processes.

One main issue to consider is the assessment process for the videopapers. Can we begin to define the characteristics of a 'good' videopaper in the same way as we have criteria for 'good' written essays? These criteria would have to address both the separate elements (videoclip, text, slides) and their interrelationship and in the same way as videopapers may be considered a new form of discourse we might need new assessment criteria that address this. However we would argue that we are still at an early stage and more research needs to be done to better understand the contribution of the processes of reading and creating videopapers to learning.

Future research will focus on exploring more in depth the processes involved in the reading and creation of videopapers through comparing and contrasting the experiences of practitioners across the different programmes and disciplines. In particular it will investigate how the Videopaper tool is transformed and taken on board in different ways according to the background the practitioners bring to the activity of reading and creating. The instrumentation framework (Rabardel, 2003) will be used to interpret this process together with the multimodality literature, in order to shed light on these processes, in comparison also with other multimodal texts as for example webpages, weblogs etc. The integration of other tools currently available that could support the process of creating videopapers will also be investigated. In particular analytical tools, like Studiocode[8], and collaborative tools, like Diver[9] (Pea & Hoffert, 2007), might be a useful way of analysing practice and selecting the clip(s) that will then form the video for the videopaper.

ACKNOWLEDGEMENTS

The project investigating the context of Modern Foreign Language initial teacher education was funded by an ESCalate grant and the project looking at the other contexts is funded by a University of Bristol Teaching and Learning Award.

REFERENCES

Armstrong, V., Barnes, S., Sutherland, R., Curran, S., Mills, S., & Thompson, I. (2005). Collaborative research methodology for investigating teaching and learning: the use of interactive whiteboard technology. *Educational Review, 57*(4), 457-469.

Barnes, S., & Sutherland, R. (2007). *Using Videopapers for multi-purpose: disseminating research practice and research results.* Paper presented at the 12th Biennial Conference on Learning and Instruction, Budapest.

Bartels, N. (2003). How teachers and researchers read academic articles. *Teaching and teacher education, 19*(7), 737-753.

Beardsley, L., Cogan-Drew, D., & Olivero, F. (2007). Videopaper: bridging research and practice for pre-service and experienced teachers. In R. Goldman, R. D. Pea, B. Barron & S. J. Derry (Eds.), *Video Research in the Learning Sciences* (pp. 479-493). Mahwah, New Jersey: Lawrence Erlbaum Associates.

[8] http://www.studiocodegroup.com/Studiocode%20Education.htm
[9] http://diver.stanford.edu/

Carraher, D., Schliemann, A. D., & Brizuela, B. (2000). *Bringing out the algebraic character of Arithmetic.* Paper presented at the Videopapers in Mathematics Education conference, Dedham, MA.

Cope, & Kalantzis, M. (Eds.). (2000). *Multiliteracies: literacy learning and the design of social features.* London: Routledge.

Daniil, M. (2007). *The use of videopapers from Modern Foreign Language student teachers as a tool to support reflection on practice.* University of Bristol, Unpublished Master's thesis.

Daniil, M., & Olivero, F. (2008). The use of VideoPapers from Modern Foreign Language student teachers as a tool to support reflection on practice. In *Proceedings of the 6th Panhellenic conference with international participation Information Communication Technologies in education* (pp. 429-436). Limassol, Cyprus.

DiMattia, C., & Cogan-Drew, D. (2003). Monday's lesson: using VideoPaper Builder 2. *@Concord, 7*(1), 6-7.

Galvis, A., & Nemirovsky, R. (2003). *Sharing and Reflecting on Teaching Practices by using VideoPaper Builder 2.* Paper presented at the World Conference on E-Learning in Corporate, Government, Healthcare, and Higher Education 2003, Phoenix, Arizona, USA.

Gee, J. (1999). *An introduction to discourse analysis.* London: Routledge.

Goldman, R. (2008). Video representations adn the perspectivity framework: epistemology, ethnography, evaluation, ethics. In R. Goldman, R. D. Pea, B. Barron & S. J. Derry (Eds.), *Video research in the learning sciences* (pp. 3-38). Mahwah, New Jersey: Lawrence Erlbaum Associates.

Herring, S. C., Scheidt, L. A., Wright, E., & Bonus, S. (2005). Weblogs as a bridging genre. *Information Technology & People, 18*(2), 142-171.

Jewitt, C. (2005). *Technology, literacy, learning. A multimodal approach.* London: Routledge.

Kress, G. (2003). *Literacy in the new media age.* London: Routledge.

Kress, G., & van Leeuwen, T. (2001). *Multimodal discourse: the modes and media of contemporary communication.* London: Arnold.

Lanham, R. (2001). What's Next for Text. *Education, Communication, and Information, 1*(1), 15-36.

Laurillard, D., Stratfold, M., Luckin, R., Plowman, L., & Taylor, J. (2000). Affordances for learning in a non-linear narrative medium. *Journal of Interactive Media in Education, 2,* 1-19.

Lazarus, E., & Olivero, F. (2007). *Using videopapers for professional learning and assessment in initial teacher education.* Paper presented at the 12th Biennial Conference on Learning and Instruction, Budapest.

Lemke, J. (2007). Video epistemology in-and-outside the box: traversing attentional spaces. In R. Goldman, R. D. Pea, B. Barron & S. J. Derry (Eds.), *Video Research in the Learning Sciences* (pp. 39-52). Mahwah, New Jersey: Lawrence Erlbaum Associates.

Martindale, T., & Wiley, D. (2004). Using weblogs in scholarship and teaching. *TechTrends, 49*(2), 55-61.

Matthewman, S., Blight, A., & Davies, C. (2004). What does multimodality mean for English? Creative tensions in teaching new texts and new literacies. *Education, Communication & Information, 4*(1), 153-176.

McGraw, R., Lynch, K., Koc, Y., Budak, A., & Brown, C. (2007). The multimedia case as a tool for professional development: an analysis of online and face-to-face interaction among mathematics pre-service teachers, in-service teachers, mathematicians, and mathematics teacher educators. *Journal of Mathematics Teacher Education, 10*(2), 95-121.

Nemirovsky, R., Borba, M., Dimattia, C., Arzarello, F., Robutti, O., Schnepp, M., et al. (2004). PME Special Issue: Bodily Activity and Imagination in Mathematics Learning. *Educational Studies in Mathematics, 57*(3), 303-321.

Nemirovsky, R., DiMattia, C., Ribeiro, B., & Lara-Meloy, T. (2005). Talking About Teaching Episodes. *Journal of Mathematics Teacher Education, 8*(5), 363-392.

Nemirovsky, R., Lara-Meloy, T., Earnest, D., & Ribeiro, B. (2001). Videopapers: Investigating new multimedia genres to foster the interweaving of research and teaching. In M. v. d. Heuvel-Panhuizen (Ed.), *Proceedings of the 25th Conference of the International Group for the Psychology of Mathematics Education* (Vol. 3, pp. 423-430). Amersfoort, The Netherlands: Drukkerij Wilco.

Olivero, F., John, P., & Sutherland, R. (2004). Seeing is believing: using videopapers to transform teachers' professional knowledge and practice. *Cambridge Journal of Education, 34*(2), 179-191.

Pea, R. D. (2003). *Point-of-View authoring of video for learning, education and other purposes.* Paper presented at the PARC Forum, Palo Alto, CA, 13 March 2003.

Pea, R. D., & Hoffert, E. (2007). Video workflow in the learning sciences: prospects of emerging technologies for augmenting work practices. In R. Goldman, R. D. Pea, B. Barron & S. J. Derry (Eds.), *Video research in the learning sciences* (pp. 427-460). Mahwah, New Jersey: Lawrence Erlbaum Associates.

Rabardel, P. (2003). From artefact to instrument. *Interacting with Computers, 15*(5), 641-645.

Sherin, M. G. (2004). New perspectives on the role of video in teacher education. In J. Brophy (Ed.), *Using video in teacher education* (pp. 1-27). NY: Elsevier Science.

Smith, K., & Krumsvik, R. (2007a). Video Papers – a Means for Documenting Practitioners' Reflections on Practical Experiences: the story of two teacher educators. *Research in Comparative and International Education, 2*(4), 272-282.

Smith, K., & Krumsvik, R. (2007b). *Video-papers: an attempt to closing the notorius gap in teacher education.* Paper presented at the 12th Biennial Conference on Learning and Instruction, Budapest.

Snyder, L. (2002). Hybrid vigour: reconciling the verbal and the visual in electronic communication. In A. Loveless & V. Ellis (Eds.), *ICT pedagogy and the curriculum.* London: Routledge.

Trahar, S. (2008). VideoPaper and assessment. *Therapy Today, 19*(2), 41-43.

Winer, D. (2002). The history of weblogs.   Retrieved March 18, 2004, from http://newhome.weblogs.com/historyOfWeblogs

In: Learning in the Network Society and the Digitized School   ISBN 978-1-60741-172-7
Editor: Rune Krumsvik   © 2009 Nova Science Publishers, Inc.

Chapter 10

COPYING WITH COMPUTERS: INFORMATION MANAGEMENT OR CHEATING AND PLAGIARISM?

Ingvill Rasmussen
InterMedia, University of Oslo, Sweden

ABSTRACT

A pressing question for teachers today is how to deal with copying. Teachers have experienced and research has demonstrated that if pupils or students use networked computers they copy. It is generally argued that copying does not require genuine effort and that pupils use it to complete school tasks rather than to create new understanding. Copying is therefore seen as unproductive – as a sign of laziness. The purpose of this chapter is to study how pupils use copied texts when working with networked computers on projects, and to investigate whether the practices are as educationally unproductive as is often claimed. I will propose that the normative conclusion that characterises previous studies on copying and the use of computers is the result of a too narrow scope. I suggest that, by analysing peer-group interaction over time, new aspects of the activities emerge. By focusing on a specific theme like 'copying' I hope to contribute to the understanding of learning and the use of computers as a more general theme. I will analyse how new practices result from the emergence of new means and their connection to the social practice of the institution.

INTRODUCTION

It is often argued that if learners use networked computers in school tasks they will copy in order to complete the task without having to make much effort. Copying is therefore seen as unproductive and a sign of laziness. Learners who are caught having copied content are accused of cheating and plagiarism. At the same time, it is considered important that learners become competent in using computers and other electronic aids and applications including the Internet. A central characteristic of computers is their capacity to store information and that this information can be easily attained, reused, transformed and transported. However, it is not easy to manage information, and knowing how to locate, select and integrate different types of information can be a difficult task. This social and cognitive challenge is historically new, and studies have found that such skills and competences are central to taking advantage of computers in school tasks (Rasmussen, 2005). As important as such skills may be, many learners receive surprisingly little instruction in how to manage information (Arnseth, Hatlevik, Kløvstad, Kristiansen & Ottesen, 2007). Furthermore, there are still few studies that have investigated the process of how learners search for information on the Internet and how they use the texts that they copy. The purpose of this chapter is to study how learners use copied texts when working with networked computers and to investigate whether or not the practices attached to this work are as educationally unproductive as is often claimed. The question raised is therefore not whether pupils copy texts, but rather: *how copied texts are used.*

The aim is to generate insight into how pupils manage information and how they use the texts that they have copied in a setting where they are expected to construct knowledge together. I am, in other words, interested in collaborative knowledge construction and the resources that learners appropriate for this purpose. Collaborative knowledge construction refers to efforts to share, understand, scrutinize, criticize and/or elaborate upon contributions from others in order to create a common object (Stahl, 2006).

To frame copying in relation to school activities and collaborative knowledge construction I will start by referring to reading and writing as historical school practices in order to show the shifts in what has been meant by these terms. Then, I will move into research about how pupils summarize texts and how they use the Internet. This will be followed by an empirical study of learners' searches for information and their use of copied text during project work. In particular, I will recreate the trajectory of one group of primary school pupils through the various stages of their group work. Finally, I will discuss my findings in relation to the normative conclusions that have dominated previous studies on copying and the use of computers. I will argue that, by analysing peer-group interaction over time, new aspects of the activities emerge.

RELEVANT RESEARCH

In education, reading and writing are among the most central activities with regard to learning. Still, what it means to master reading and writing should not be taken as a given. Historically, the meaning of these terms has changed significantly (Säljö, 2004). For example, in schools around 1600-1700, reading usually meant to read familiar texts and writing with the intent of reproducing a copy of a text (Resnick, 1983). Egil Johansson's studies of literacy in Sweden found that pupils in this period were expected to read The Ten Commandments and the most commonly used prayers. It was not expected that they could read unfamiliar texts (Johansson, 1985). It makes sense then that the lexical explanation of the word copy according to Webster's Dictionary is tied to writing activities such as composing and drafting texts, and to the reproduction of content (1996: 323). Gradually, following the invention of the printing press, types of texts other than simply religious materials were used in schools. With the introduction of these new texts came also the expectation that pupils should learn subject content from reading unfamiliar texts and be able to follow written instructions (Scribner, 1984; Säljö, 2004). Put differently, this shift introduced learners in schools to new types of challenges – challenges that nowadays are taken as given. One central question in terms of knowledge construction then arises: what kinds of strategies do learners employ when they are given texts from which they are expected to learn, and how do they write summaries of such texts?

Brown and her colleagues have studied the strategies that learners employ when summarising expository texts (Brown & Day, 1983; Brown, Day, & Jones, 1983). Based on empirical studies of different age groups, from fifth-graders to college students, Brown and her colleagues suggest that the ability to separate importance from trivia is a late-developing skill. They report that younger pupils usually rely on a simple *copy/delete* strategy. This is described as reading text elements sequentially and then either deleting unnecessary material or eliminating anything redundant (Brown & Day, 1983: 2). However, Brown et al. also describe writing strategies that relate to more advanced knowledge construction (Stahl, 2006; Vygotsky, 1986). One of these relates to pupils' use of generalisations. In this case, a generalisation is defined as constructing "a superordinate term that represents some content", or it could mean "to split a superordinate term into sub-components" (Brown & Day, 1983: 3). Other more advanced strategies were identified in relation to either the selection of the central components from a text or to the effort in capturing the meaning of a text in one's own words (Brown & Day, 1983). What Brown and her colleagues describe as strategies for learning are also identified and discussed in, curiously enough, a study of how Italian University students write cheating slips (Engeström, 2005; Engeström, 2007). The questions that are posed in the exams at this university are of such a detailed character that it is considered impossible to answer them by memory alone. Creating good cheating slips is therefore essential in order to master these exams. Engeström finds that in creating a slip, the students are very careful in selecting the most essential parts of the topic and at the same time representing these parts in the most condensed, but still understandable way. Hence, in creating cheating slips the students separate importance from trivia and extract the essential parts of the topic – that is, activities essential for knowledge construction.

However, in terms of computer use the story changes. In contrast to copying by hand or by typing, the copy function inscribed in the computer saves the source code, allowing the user to paste the copied content easily in a single operation. This function of computer technology creates, in other words, changes in how information is reproduced, but also in how it is stored and organised. As mentioned, copying is usually talked about today in connection with cheating in schools and not in terms of reproduction of content to be learned. This movement in use has followed the common use of computer technology. Studies that have discussed copying and computers use have generally argued that copying is done without a focus on understanding. As the following quotation illustrates, researchers are passionate in their characterisation: "The copy/delete strategy is particularly perverse, because it can be carried out with practically no thought by simply copying text and deleting elements that do not seem necessary for the purpose at hand" (Collins, 2001: 43).

Today pupils are expected to search, by reading, through texts and select relevant content from sources ranging from text books to the Internet. Therefore, understanding how pupils manage information from the Internet is important. Land & Green (2000) show the limitations of the strategies used by students. One of the main strategies is termed *data driven*. Data driven strategies means that learners proceed through the material in a bottom up fashion, "acquiring information in absence of an overarching application" (ibid, 2000: 61). The limitation of this strategy is that the students' understanding ends up being fragmentary. So, simply put, if learners just gather a whole range of information they will not be able to create an understanding of the phenomenon that they are studying. However, this study also shows that participants that worked in peer groups performed better than those working alone. This was because pupils that worked with others were corrected when their strategies were unsuccessful. Hence, they were quicker to adjust their strategies (Land & Greene, 2000).

In terms of the use of information from the Internet, studies have described learners' strategies with metaphors such as "transport and transform", "scrapbook" or "sampling" (Limberg and Alexandersson, 2004; Nilsson, 2008; Lund and Rasmussen, 2008). The "transport and transform" metaphor emphasises learners' tendency to transport "facts" from the Internet into their own product and the teacher's tendency to ask whether the texts are written "in their own words", which again leads learners to become focused on transforming words only slightly (Limberg and Alexandersson, 2004). Also, studies (Nilsson, 2008) have pointed to the role of the teacher in helping learners to analyse content in order to extract the essential meaning and to be able to use it productively when writing. "Sampling" and "scrapbook" are terms that learners themselves use to describe how they first copy and paste to get an overview of their specified topic while at the same time being protective in terms of their own contributions. This protective behavior seems to link up with another common cheating accusation in schools, namely that of being a free-rider in a group project (Lund and Rasmussen, 2008).

This brief review demonstrates that copying is part of both intended and unintended learning practices in schools and universities, and that we can discriminate between strategies connected to copying that are more productive or less productive in terms of learning. To gain new insight on how learners search for and use information when working with networked computers, I argue that we need to follow pupils' activities over time. No study has, to this point, followed pupils' activities over time with this particular analytical focus. However, before the empirical section, it is necessary to lay out the theoretical and methodological tools that will be used to perform the analytical work.

FOLLOWING PARTICIPATION TRAJECTORIES TO STUDY LEARNING

Relatively few classroom studies have followed specific learning activities over long periods of time. One explanation for this might lie in the theoretical as well as methodological challenge that an investigation of learning activities over time poses for the analyst (Littleton, 1999: 182). One theoretical solution to this methodological challenge can be found in the concept of *trajectory* expounded by Lave & Wenger (1991) and Nielsen & Kvale (1999). These authors have used the concept of trajectory to understand how learning develops over time. One limitation is that these studies are not conducted in classrooms. The concept of trajectory in relation to classrooms has only been used in a limited number of studies (but see: Boaler & Greeno, 2000; Engle & Conant, 2002; Krange, 2007). This study follows up on how we can study the development of learning over time when conceptualised by the use of a trajectory metaphor and also explores the contributions that such an analytical approach provides.

The trajectory as a unit of analysis creates possibilities for the researcher to trace the way in which participants construct knowledge and understanding in interaction. However, these paths are not easy to identify, analyse and present. In social interactions, topics are introduced, discussed, left, and reintroduced. By following a path of talk and activities over a period of time, certain patterns emerge. In contrast to a linguistically-oriented analysis of talk, my concern is not simply to identify patterns, but to specifically identify patterns in terms of their significance with regard to learning. These motifs are identified and discussed so as to investigate how participants construct knowledge and understanding from participating in school activities.

The analysis is based on a sociocultural approach to thinking, reasoning and learning. The sociocultural position has reframed human learning and development as the ability to participate in different social practices, rather than as embedded in individual mental processes and structures (Lave & Wenger, 1991; Säljö, 2004). This implies that an investigation of school learning should include an analysis of the social practices of the institution in which the process originates. Pupils learn through recurrent participation in school activities. They appropriate ways of doing schoolwork that make sense within the particular social setting. To analyse learning within this perspective, one should focus on interdependency across situations and over time. This includes focusing on how learners construct knowledge and understanding through the use of tools. From this point of view, the research task becomes not to establish the effects of computers, but to explore their use in relation to social interaction within a specific context (Säljö, 2004). Thus, the idea that learning can be seen as participation trajectories is the perspective that I shall adopt in order to address how pupils learn within a school context. Finally, to account for the paths that participation trajectories take, I suggest the use of the two concepts: *positionality* and *improvising* (Bakhtin, 1986; Holland, Lachiotte, Skinner, & Cain, 1998). These concepts enable me to analyse teaching and learning as mutually constitutive processes, including how teachers and pupils take a stance in relation to activities and knowing, their positionality or how they as individuals take part in social interactions, and the improvisations that are part of the responses that teachers and pupils as participants create in response to particular situations. Furthermore, analysing the pupils' improvisations during *in situ* responses to tasks can provide valuable evidence for how the activities unfold unpredictably. In other words, improvisations draw attention to the unexpected or unplanned. In effect, the focus of the analysis is on *interdependency* across situations and between different participation structures and resources.

DATA AND METHOD

The empirical study was undertaken at a Norwegian primary school that used project work and networked computers on a regular basis. The school will be referred to as Stony Lake Primary School. It is located on the outskirts of Oslo and has about 150 pupils, with one class for each grade from the first to the seventh grade. The pupils in this study are 11 to 12 years of age and are accustomed to working on projects with the aid of networked computers.

The analysis presented in this chapter is from my PhD thesis (Rasmussen, 2005). While analysing data from two field studies, I found that copying texts represented the main strategy employed by pupils to retrieve content while working with networked computers. I followed up on this initial finding in the main study where I focused on how pupils used what they copied in their joint creation of a multimedia presentation. The data excerpts that were selected and that will be presented in the following section exemplify a type of practice that was used extensively at Stony Lake Primary School, and that I have since observed at several other primary and secondary schools (Lund and Rasmussen, 2008). The project work analysed in the main study lasted five weeks, taking two or three half days each week. I collected data from one focus group and two contrast groups – that is, a total of 15 pupils out of a class of 25. Most of the data has been used as a background against which the video analysis is carried out. In the following section I will combine detailed examinations of excerpts from moment-to-moment interactions with ethnographic descriptions of the local school culture and practices. The combination of the different levels of description makes it possible to see social interactions as part of longer periods of activity.

ANALYSIS

As an educational practice and method, project work is often described in relation to pupil activity, group work and the creation of a specific product (Berthelsen, Illeris, & Clod Poulsen, 1987; Voogt & Pelgrum, 2003). In the present project work the product to be made was specified in the task which read: *'Make a multimedia presentation about an immigrant from Asia. In the presentation of this person, you should include the following: about the country, clothes, food, religion, the high festivals, childhood and family'*. This task was introduced together with an Internet site that contained presentations of personal experiences by people from all over the world who had migrated to Norway. The task was introduced in a whole class session while the teacher talked and explored the content of this site as it was projected to the front of the classroom. After this the pupils were divided in groups to start their work. The initial phase of the group work was described by the teachers as formulating problem statements, hypothesis or initial ideas in a plan. This plan had to be approved by the teacher.

The focus group whose work will be analysed consisted of two girls (Ann and Mary) and three boys (Sebastian, Simon and Michael). The group decided to make their presentation about an immigrant from Vietnam. This person's story, as presented on the Internet site, contained personal experiences from the Vietnam War. The pupils, especially the boys, wanted to find out more about the Vietnam War and they wanted to make a small film about the war. The pupils were allowed to do this. With permission from the teachers and with the school's camera the group went to a nearby forest to shoot their film. Having done this, they divided the task. The boys both edited the film and searched the Internet for facts about the Vietnam War. The girls searched the Internet to find out about food, clothes and religion in Vietnam. In the following analysis I have selected excerpts to provide an overview of the pupils' encounters and discussions as they generated content from the Internet.

Searching for School Content

While the boys were searching the Internet, one of the things that they kept searching for was the dates of the Vietnam War. Even though this might appear to be an easy task, it was not the case. This first excerpt (1) took place at the end of a twenty-minute period of searching for the dates of the war. Having struggled with hits on many English sites that they tried to comprehend jointly, Michael asked Simon to search again for sites with Norwegian texts.

Excerpt 1[1]

1. Michael	Can't you look for pages in Norwegian – it is easier to read.
2. Sebastian	Can't find any – forget it!
3. Michael	Search the World then [there is a choice between searching: 'Norway' or 'the World' in the search engine they are using. That is: 'Kvasir' at http://www.startsiden.no/].
4. Simon	[Types: 'Vietnam-krigen']
5. Sebastian	The Vietnam War, history, facts about USA, facts about Vietnam [reads aloud from the resulting search page].
6. Simon	[Clicks on one of the search results and a web-page is downloaded. When the page is loaded a component plays back a sound file of a sampled fanfare]
7. Sebastian	WOW! OK!
8. Simon	[Leans happily back in the chair]
9. Michael	[Nods eagerly]
10. Simon	[Leans towards the computer] There you go!
11. Sebastian	[Reads aloud from the text] From 1939 till 1975. Yes!
12. Simon	There you go [clicks fast through several links on the page]!
13. Sebastian	[What did I say – what I can find
14. Michael	Read that then [Points at the link where it says: 'The History'].
15. Simon	OK [Clicks the 'The History' link and reads aloud]. The Vietnam War is the name of a military battle in Vietnam from 1959 till 1975. It started as a specific … [reads aloud a bit further].

First, we see that they are quite pessimistic about finding "pages in Norwegian" (1: 1). Having searched the Internet for twenty minutes, Sebastian appears to have come to the conclusion that finding texts in Norwegian is almost impossible. When they finally hit a relevant link, a sound file of a sampled fanfare was played back as the web page loaded. The

---

[1] The following conventions are used in the transcripts:

[ ]   Resources in use are described in square brackets: [clicking on the mouse].
     Indications of what the teachers or the pupils are doing and also other comments/interpretations of what is going on are given in square brackets.

( )   Short pauses and overlaps are indicated in the text. Pauses are shown between brackets (…) and the length of measurable pauses is shown in seconds (0.3)

:   Stretched sounds are represented by sets of colons: c:::::ity

!   Exclamation point indicated addend emphasis, but not necessary a loader volume: It is here!
     Words in capitals are uttered louder than the surrounding talk: It is not RIGHT!

| [ ]   Turns taken out. This is used when talk less relevant to the issue being discussed is taken out

-    A single dash indicates a cut-off in one persons talk

[Left hand brackets indicates overlapping utterances

boys were all impressed! Sebastian immediately started to read aloud and was pleased when he found out when the Vietnam War took place. Thereafter, Simon read parts of the text aloud. I should point out here that the text that Simon read (1: 15) was identical with the text that was used in their multimedia presentation.

The web-page that they encountered resulted from a school project in an upper secondary school.[2] The site contained brief texts in Norwegian, pictures and audio-files. The texts went under the following headings: The History, Facts about the USA, and Facts about Vietnam. It is interesting that the three boys' responded in the same way. There was no doubt that they agreed that this was what they had been searching for, and after only a brief scanning of the content, they concluded that this site contained sufficient information for them to complete their task.

While the boys found content about the Vietnam War, the two girls found content about the country. They too had searched the Internet. In the following excerpt, Mary and Ann met up with the boys to deliver their part of the task. They entered the group room with a printed text about the country. Just as the conversation started, Mary handed the print-out to Sebastian (see Excerpt 2).

Excerpt 2

1. Sebastian	OK, so what have you found out?
2. Mary	Yes. Not that much.
3. Sebastian	Let's see [Mary gives Sebastian a print-out].
4. Sebastian	[reads aloud from the print] Population, capital, language. Those who can read and write are 94 per cent. Expected lifespan 68 years (0.2).

This excerpt represents a typical illustration of how the pupils shared knowledge. Mary handed Sebastian a printed text containing factual information about Vietnam, which he read aloud to the group, commenting on the information as he read. The pupils often shared, approved or rejected texts by reading aloud and commenting on them. It was also typical that there were no objections to the content when this was factual information. Furthermore, at this stage of the project the pupils worked in small units or individually, but would meet their peer groups regularly to share knowledge in the manner just described.

The first two excerpts demonstrate how the pupils went about exploring information on the Internet. Looking at the process as a whole, exploring the Internet to find out about some topic involved the use of several strategies in terms of both search techniques and of knowledge construction. First, it was usual for two or three pupils to sit together around a computer. They would often use search techniques in conjunction with each other, trying out combinations of words and different search engines to find new sites. It is important to stress that they conducted a number of searches before finally finding the information they were after, and that their selection of sites was not random. Rather, they were searching for content that was typically of a factual nature (Nilsson, 2008; Alexanderson & Lindberg 2004).

Secondly, the practice of reading texts aloud was characteristic of how they supported each other in understanding what they encountered. However, it was rare for long texts to be read aloud. More often they would read parts of texts and *then* comment on them. Thus, this

[2] http://home.online.no/~heaarsta/Vietnamkrigen/index.html. (access date 11. 12. 2004)

practice appears to be a collective scanning of information that could possibly be both relevant and irrelevant. In the case of English texts, reading aloud was used to facilitate comprehension. Despite this effort, several texts were too difficult to comprehend – they were, so to speak, beyond their developmental zone (Vygotsky, 1986).

Thirdly, the pupils evaluated the information they encountered on the Internet and commented positively when they found anything relevant. Sebastian's comment may illustrate my point: "From 1939 till 1975. Yes!" (1: 11). As mentioned, by looking at the whole process it becomes clear that the group was seeking a specific type of content. The text that the girls contributed represents a typical example and it was immediately approved as relevant. By comparing content that was approved with that which was rejected it appears that the pupils had a shared understanding of the type of content that a school task requires: factual information similar to the type of information contained in textbooks. Overall, an analysis of the excerpts shows that the pupils classified content as either relevant or irrelevant according to this interpretation of schooling.

Finally, the texts that the pupils classified as relevant were copied. Simon's reading of the text fragment in Excerpt 1 confirms this assertion as the text read in the first excerpt was identical with a text that appeared in their end product. Hence, the process of generating texts can be briefly summarised as follows: first, divide the task; second, explore and interpret in order to find a specific type of content; *then* copy; and finally, meet up and share the information through *jigsawing* (Brown & Campione, 1994).

In the next two sections I will continue to focus on the sharing of copied texts. I will focus on three types of practices concerning how copied texts were used in the making of the multimedia presentation, and I will start with the way in which the pupils managed to construct a coherent story from the disjointed texts. Then, I will look at the types of changes that the pupils made to the texts. Thirdly, I will describe what is meant by the term *technology-driven recaps*. These three practices have also been observed during the first two field trials and therefore represent patterns observed in the larger data corpus of the present study.

Integration

By the time of the following excerpt, the pupils had generated texts about the country, religion, clothes and food. The texts that were not copied from the Internet were copied from textbooks. However, before analysing how the pupils made use of these texts, it is necessary to note that Excerpts 3 and 4 are somewhat difficult to follow. To understand these excerpts we have to draw on activities done earlier in the trajectory. As we will see, the pupils are using a plan document that was made earlier. The pupils always had to make a plan that had to be approved by the teachers as part of any project. It is just such a plan that the pupils are using in the following two excerpts (Figure 1). Here the pupils were drawing on and switching between two documents on the computer: one was the plan document (see Figure 1), and the other a diagram that was made to illustrate the relationship between the texts, including the film (Figure 2). Before the recorded episode, the pupils had made the diagram using the texts as resources. Simon was the one conducting the computer work and the pupils were talking about how the texts, as represented in the diagram, related to each other.

1.

Om· Vietnam :

- Maten   = "Ris, pasta, supper (kjøtt m.m.)"
- Krigen   = "Massemord, masakre, tortuering,
                                       Sør-Vietnam m/USA, Nord-Vietnam
                                       m/Russland, Tyskland"
- Religionen   = "Buddhisme, Hinduisme, litt kristendom"
- Klær   = "Stråhatt, T-skjorter,
                                       orange kapper"

Whyn Lam :

- Barndommen = Torsdag 18. April 02
- Minner = Torsdag 18. April 02
- Overgangen til Norge = Torsdag 18. April 02

2. Skuespill om Vietnam-krigen = Fredag 19. April 02
3. Konklusjon = Onsdag 24. April 02
4. Multimedia(Slime) = Onsdag 24. April 02
5. Frist = Tirsdag 30. April
6. Presentasjon = Torsdag 2. Mai eller Fredag 3. Mai 02

Figure 1. The Plan from the Vietnam Group.

Below the heading "Vietnam", the plan has four sub-headings: "Food", "War", "Religion" and "Clothes". Against these headings are listed the following words: "food – rice, pasta, soups (meat, etc.)"; "war – mass murder, massacre, torturing, South Vietnam with USA, North Vietnam with Russia and Germany"; "religion – Buddhism, Hinduism, a little Christianity"; "clothes: straw hat, T-shirts, orange robes". Below the heading "Whyn Lam" is a list of a set of tasks and dates. The tasks listed are: "childhood, memories, the transition to Norway, a play about the Vietnam War, conclusion, deadline, and presentation" (Figure 1).

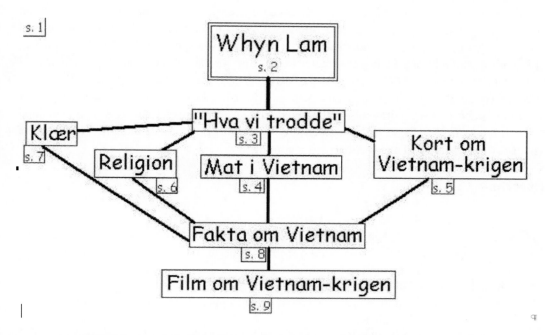

Figure 2. Diagram Illustrating the Connection between the Copied Texts.

The upper box reads "Whyn Lam" and represents a copy of the picture in Figure 7.3. The box below "Whyn Lam" reads "What we thought", and the text in the boxes from the left reads "Clothes", "Religion", "Food in Vietnam", "Briefly on the Vietnam War". The two boxes at the bottom of the diagram read "Facts about Vietnam" and "Film about the Vietnam War" (Figure 2).

Excerpt 3

1. Michael	Briefly on the Vietnam War. I sort of don't know what you mean by that.
2. Simon:	It's like, how many killed – when it happened, how many dead.
3. Michael	But, they'll get that in [pointing at the box: "Film about Vietnam War"].
4. Simon	I know, but –
	| [15]
20. Simon	So, we need to have it there because we say here briefly [points to the box: "Briefly on the Vietnam War"]. That is in what we thought (…). And then we'll say something about the war [shifts between the diagram that is on the screen and the plan document by using Alt+Tab].
21. Michael	Yes, I know what you mean, but like this, right? We will say what we mean. Aren't we going to have any answers to this [points at the text in the plan document]?
22. Simon	Yes, these are the answers [shifts back to the diagram].

Here, Michael asked what a box in the diagram represented. In explaining this, Simon briefly summarised the text (3: 2) and Michael appears to understand. However, he argued that it was not necessary to include the text "Briefly about the Vietnam War" at the beginning of the presentation because it appeared later in the film. Simon acknowledged this, but argued that the information should be given twice. As they disagreed, other members of the group commented on the matter. Simon and Michael (3: 20, 21) elaborated the basis for their diverging views and were drawing on the two documents in figures 1 and 2. Simon explained that the boxes in the diagram represented the answers to their initial thoughts. Meanwhile, Michael was not satisfied and the discussion continued.

Excerpt 4

		[11]
34. Simon	That page shall contain what we have found out about clothes, and what we have found out about religion [points at the text boxes in the following order].
35. Michael	Food in Vietnam –
36. Simon	Food in Vietnam, what we have found out BRIEFLY about the Vietnam War?
37. Michael	NO BECAUSE THAT SHOULD GO UNDER FILM so there's no point in –
38. Mary	BUT THEN THEY CAN READ IT instead of watching the film.
39. Sebastian	Yes, but it says on the screen.
		[14]
54. Simon	That page right there contains this [switches back to the plan document], which is what we have found out about religion.
55. Michael	Yeah, yeah.
56. Sebastian	All that is correct.
57. Simon	No, it isn't.
58. Sebastian	It's not?
59. Simon	No. The North Vietnamese did not get support from Germany (…). They got support from Russia and China.
60. Sebastian	Yes, Germany is what is wrong. Germany.

Simon continued to explain the connection between the boxes in the diagram – the texts. In so doing, he switched between the two documents. Michael confirmed that he understood. Still, he argued for a different ordering of the line of argument. Simon repeated that the text about the Vietnam War should be presented twice (4: 36). At this point, having argued for a while, Michael raised his voice (4: 37). Mary supported Simon's argument and Sebastian supported Michael's (4: 38, 39). Meanwhile, in line 55, Michael conceded with a resigned "Yeah, yeah". Sebastian, on the other hand, argued that there was no reason to emphasise the relationship between their initial ideas and their findings because "[a]ll that is correct" (4: 56). Simon replied that this was not the case. He explained that "[t]he North Vietnamese did not get support from Germany (…). They got support from Russia and China" (4: 59).

The two excerpts demonstrate pupils' efforts and their joint correction of a mistake: they had initially thought that Germany was part of the Vietnam War, but this was corrected. The texts, copied from one context, were integrated into a new context created by the pupils. This act of copying from one context to another requires social and cognitive effort. The pupils created a diagram to illustrate the connection between the disjointed texts they had copied. As such, the creation of the diagram represented an act of integration. This integration activity has much in common with the creation of a superordinate term (Brown & Day, 1983). The connection between disjointed texts is not represented by a superordinate term, but by a diagram that represents a graphical superordination.

The pupils' perception of what was relevant, as well as their understanding of the copied texts, was central to this effort. Simon briefly summarised the texts to which the boxes in the diagram referred, and Michael confirmed that he understood (4: 32-6). In so doing, they were recapping their trajectory: first, what they thought, and then what they had found out. Sebastian thought that all their initial thoughts were correct, but as they argued this misunderstanding was resolved. As a result of Simon's challenges, Sebastian was able to reformulate his initial knowledge (Mercer, 2000). The analysis of the closure of the project demonstrated that Sebastian told the class about this 'discovery' (Rasmussen, 2005).

Looking at the development during the course of the excerpt, we can see that the pupils started by giving reasons for their positions (Mercer, 1995). However, as the conversation unfolded, they came to understand that they disagreed, and as a result, the character of the conversation shifted from one of exploration to one of dispute (Mercer, 2000). Michael and Sebastian both argued that it was sufficient that the facts about the Vietnam War were integrated into the film as text posters. Contrary to this, Simon and Mary both argued that they should repeat the facts in order to emphasise their work process and their discovery. Mary insisted that the audience should not have to wait for the film to read the facts, saying, "BUT THEN THEY CAN READ IT instead of watching the film" (3: 38). Her statement illustrates that the pupils changed their orientation to that of "the other", or in other words the audience and the teacher (Bakhtin, 1986). By the same token, this demonstrates a conflict of framing: the pupils are torn between entertaining the audience with the film or emphasising factual information and the work process.

Across the groups, similar integration and organisation efforts were found. However, integration by the means of a diagram was not observed in the contrast groups. They made similar integration efforts by using organising tools in the software. Some pupils used an organising tool included in software that was used during this project (Figure 3). Other groups that used Power Point also applied the organising functionality in this software.

Put differently, my findings demonstrate that when texts that had been copied were integrated into the context of a group presentation, the pupils would present and rewrite their content in order to construct a coherent line of argument. As the dialogue in Excerpt 4 displays, constructing coherence in a group presentation required engagement and effort. Moreover, this way of using copied content has been found in several other studies both at the primary and secondary levels, and students themselves often refer to this method as sampling or patchwork compositions (Nilsson, 2008; Lund and Rasmussen, 2008).

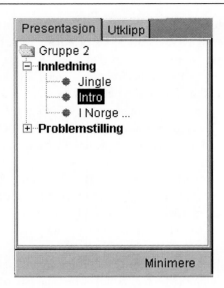

Figure 3. Organising Tool in Software.

Copying

In order to further investigate the use of copied texts, I will now turn to an excerpt in which the pupils were checking the status of their work. At the time of the following conversation, the pupils had already been working on the presentation for some time. At this point they were looking through their work and discussing what was left to do. Simon was clicking on the organising tool (Figure 3) and the rest of the group was seated around him.

Excerpt 5

1. Simon	The food is ready. Briefly about Vietnam – not ready. Religion – not ready. Clothes nearly ready [clicking on the scenes in the scene-graph].
2. Sebastian	Facts are ready.
3. Simon	Facts are ready. The film is not yet included in the presentation because it's so large that it takes forever.
		[4]
8. Simon	We have facts about religion.
9. Sebastian	Yes, that's true.
10. Mary	Put it into the presentation.
11. Simon	[finds the file in the explorer. He opens the word document and then uses select all, copy and paste into SLIME]
12. Michael	But that's just plain copying!
13. Sebastian	Oh what a shame [said in a sarcastic voice]!
14. Simon	Does it matter [laughs]?
15. Michael	We don't need all of it.
16. Simon	I'll read through it [Simon reads the text and changes it].

While Simon was clicking on the headings in the scene-graph, the rest of the group were checking out what was ready and what was not. Food and facts were ready. The film was ready, but was not integrated into the presentation because of the size of the file. In line 8, Simon remembered, "We have facts about religion" (5: 8). While he opened the text and inserted it into the presentation, Michael cried out, "But that's just plain copying!" (5: 15). However, this argument against the use of copy/paste was ridiculed (5: 13–14). Nevertheless, Michael was insistent, arguing that they did not need all the content of that particular text (5: 15). In turn, Simon read through the text and removed redundant material. The strategy he employed can be characterised as copy/delete (Brown & Day, 1983).

The negotiation that accompanied the creation of the diagram (Figure 2) showed that the pupils made an effort in terms of constructing an overall argument. In contrast, Excerpt 5 is an example of how the pupils negotiated the use of copied text by choosing whether to go for the easy option or to make an effort. The tension between whether to work further on a text or simply to copy/paste shows that the pupils were aware of the institutional quest for reflection and effort. Their verbal exchanges reflected their awareness that "plain copying" (5: 15) was not what they were asked to do in this context. They knew very well that it was not 'the institutionally appropriate' thing to do. However, knowing what is appropriate does not necessarily mean that one always does the right thing (lines 13–14). In this case, the group negotiated the problem of how to relate to the requirements set by the school, and this negotiation reflects the individuals' position in the group (Holland, Lachiotte, Skinner, & Cain, 1998). Michael's argument was heard and Simon deleted parts of the text that were redundant, although he did not discuss with the others which parts they regarded as redundant; rather, he simply deleted part of the texts. As such, the pupils' joint investment in working on this text was rather poor (Collins, 2001; Land & Greene, 2000). However, new aspects will emerge as we follow the trajectory of this group further in order to investigate the effort they made with regard to this particular text about religions in Vietnam.

Technology-Driven Recaps

In answering the question raised above I will analyse a way of working with texts that was employed by nearly all the groups: they read texts aloud and recorded their own readings. The school was well-equipped with multimedia computers, and some even had microphones and recording facilities. When the pupils recorded their own readings, standard recording software was used (Figure 4). After the pupils recorded their readings, the sound files were integrated as part of the multimedia presentations. Even though most pupils were quite skilful at using different kinds of computer-based resources, they needed help from the school's technical support staff to synchronise the texts and the sound files. This recording practice spread quickly throughout the class and represents one of the ways in which copied texts were used. I will now analyse how this was done in the focus group.

Figure 4. Example of Recording Tool.

The group split up when texts and pictures were integrated in the multimedia presentation. Simon, Mary and Ann formed one group and Michael and Sebastian formed another. Both groups were to record texts, and because this could be done on several computers, they divided the texts between them. I followed Simon, Mary and Ann with an audio recorder while my camera recorded Michael and Sebastian. The following brief excerpt of Ann's recording illustrates the reading aloud and recording practice that became so popular during this project work. In Excerpt 6, Ann was reading aloud a part of the text about religions in Vietnam. This is the same text that Simon edited (cf. analysis of Excerpt 5). The part that Ann was reading was about the historical Buddha. She was seated in front of a computer reading into a microphone.

Excerpt 6

1. Ann	Being part of a highly developed culture, he was surrounded by gifted people. After having achieved enlightenment he shared his methods for discovering enlightenment for forty-five years. This is the reason why his teachings, called Dharma, are so enormous
2. Simon and Mary	YOHOOO! THAT WAS GOOD!!!
3. Simon	One, two, three and then you can read this.

Ann had practised her reading quite a few times before this recording. When it was finally approved, Mary continued. They carried on taking turns and reading the rest of the text aloud, always making several attempts before they were satisfied with the result. After finishing the recording, they integrated the sound files into the multimedia presentation. The sound files were activated as the text appeared on the screen. The Vietnam group recorded and integrated sound files of all their copied texts. The school's technical support staff helped with the technicalities.

The whole process can be described as follows: First, the pupils would read, practise and record the texts aloud several times before they were pleased with the result. Then, when the sound files were integrated as part of the multimedia presentation they would again listen to their recordings. They would play parts, or the whole presentation, over and over, becoming quite excited by the sound of their own voices. Finally, they played through the whole multimedia presentation in order to make final adjustments before the in-class presentation.

By recapitulating the process, the copied texts appeared in different modes:

- as a word document
- as represented by a text-box in the diagram
- as texts that were printed before they were read aloud for the recording
- as an audio file listened to by the class

Even though tools do not determine the use, they make certain forms of use more relevant than others (Säljö, 2004). In this case, the practice of recording texts appeared to result from possibilities inscribed in the software and the pupils' improvisations with regard to this technology. Likewise, the reoccurring recaps appear to result from the pupils' improvisations with the software (Holland, Lachiotte, Skinner, & Cain, 1998). Initially these improvisations had little to do with working on understanding. However, it is reasonable to argue that the outcome of the improvisations afforded the pupils the opportunity to engage actively with the texts. The recording meant that they read aloud texts that they had not necessarily copied themselves. When the files were integrated into the multimedia presentation, the pupils listened to *all* the texts several times. Thus, it can be argued that these improvisations played a significant role in the pupils' appropriation of the texts they copied. With regard to more conventional learning practices, teachers' repetitions are described as a way to elicit common knowledge. That is, teachers recap earlier events in order to construct knowledge among members of the class (Mercer, 2000). The recaps described here were tied to the software and were hardly done with the same intention. Nevertheless, these technology-driven recaps afforded engagement with the copied texts in terms of reading, listening and integration efforts.

COPYING WITH COMPUTERS: A PEER GROUP PARTICIPATION TRAJECTORY

I will now summarise what characterised the pupils' participation trajectory and discuss how this relates to the social practices of the school. Overall, the strategies that the pupils employed were quite similar to those identified in other studies (Brown, Day, & Jones, 1983, Alexandersson and Limberg 2004). Most commonly used was the copy/delete strategy, and my findings do not contradict previous research (Collins, 2001; Hewitt, 2002; Scardamalia & Bereiter, 1996). However, by following the activities as a trajectory, new elements appear that are connected to the manner in which copied texts are utilised. What first appeared to be only a technique that the pupils used for rapid task completion (Hewitt, 2002) seems, in my study, to contain aspects of engagement and effort. To say that pupils copy because they are 'lazy' appears to be a somewhat superficial and hasty conclusion.

While exploring information on the Internet, the pupils supported each other's understanding of the texts by reading aloud and commenting on the information rendered. The analysis revealed that they were looking for a specific type of content and that they copied the content they encountered, but only content resembling textbooks was approved. Although the pupils commonly employed the copy/delete strategy (Brown & Day, 1983), their efforts to integrate the disjointed texts can be compared to a more advanced strategy that is mainly used by older students: superordination (Brown, Day, & Jones, 1983). The tendency to split the task and then to meet and share information created a situation in which some kind of artefact was required in order to organise the composition of the multimedia presentation. A diagram was created to serve this purpose. They created a superordinate representation of the connection between the disjointed texts (Figure 2). Other groups used software organising tools. Thus, the more advanced efforts were identified as the pupils made their multimedia presentations. As such, these efforts were attached to the pupils' efforts in constructing an overall story or line of argument.

Similar efforts were not observed in relation to pupils' attempts at summarising texts (Brown, Day, & Jones, 1983). However, as Nilsson et al. (2002) points out in their study of the difficulties encountered in learning to write original texts: "the distinction between reproductive and creative techniques is centred on whether the students are trying to say something in 'their own words' or are merely transmitting in the voice of someone else" (ibid, 2002: 6). In my case, when the pupils engaged more deeply with the content this was often done during their joint attempt to create a coherent line of argument in their presentation where they refomulated and contrubuted with their own words. The focus group engaged in a dispute about the ordering of the line of argument. This type of engagement, which was not uncommon, accompanied cognitive effort and can be characterised as productive from an educational standpoint.

In response to the claim that the pupils do not exert much effort in understanding, it appears that this is not the case in this instance. Although it should be emphasised that the pupils were copying text to cut corners, the analysis shows that they were aware that this practice was controversial (excerpt 5). The negotiations that accompanied the use of directly copied texts confirm an awareness of the demands of the institution. Of course, the outcomes of the pupils' negotiations varied: some chose to ignore the quest for reflection and cognitive effort, whereas others followed it. Still, even though the technology allows corners to be cut, the important point regarding new technologies in terms of learning is not that the learning process becomes better or more efficient. Rather, the important point is to understand how technology changes the manner in which information is organised, stored, communicated and interpreted.

Moreover, as a result of the pupils' improvisations with different possibilities in the learning environment, new practices emerged. The pupils' improvisations with the available software resulted in the very popular practice of making recordings of themselves reading the texts aloud. Moreover, improvisations with the software afforded the pupils the opportunity to play their recordings *and* to play the whole presentation over and over. I have called these activities technology-driven recaps to stress the many repetitions that characterised the process. With regards to both core and supplementary data, the following list summarises key elements that characterised the peer group work and the pupils' participation trajectory:

- The pupils divided tasks, working in groups of two or three
- They explored the Internet, read aloud, and scanned content in order to increase comprehension
- They copied and pasted, and then deleted redundant material using the copy/delete strategy

- They contributed to the group by approving texts and integrating disjointed text elements. The pupils also used jigsaw and superordination processes
- They negotiated what was relevant and necessary with regard to their schoolwork
- They used technology-driven recaps

The concept of trajectory demonstrated here gives a new perspective on the phenomena investigated. My basic argument is that even a micro-phenomenon such as the use of copy/paste should be analysed as a trajectory if the focus is learning. Circumstances, if analysed as a trajectory, might have a different significance in terms of learning. The aim has been to recreate a group's trajectory with the intention of analysing exactly what it is that characterises participants' engagements. Detailed analyses, such as those presented here, can contribute to knowledge about how new practices are created in relation to new tools, and under what conditions these practices may be characterised as productive from an educational perspective. The empirical analysis shows that the pupils were quite apt at creating new artefacts by copying and pasting existing artefacts and integrating them in fanciful ways, even when the sources came from different media types such as text, sound, and video.

Copying is made particularly relevant when using computers, and it appears to be a worthwhile information management strategy in an environment that contains a massive amount of information. However, computer technology does not in itself encourage pupils to reflect upon the information they copy, and learners often need the teachers' assistance to reason within a subject domain (Lund & Rasmussen, 2008). Before a student is accused of cheating and plagiarism, it is important to consider at what level it is reasonable for that student to perform. The learner who takes a text and alters some of the words may be taking the first step of a long trajectory leading toward the construction of knowledge and the understanding of a subject area. "Seen from this perspective it is not so easy to speak about cheating and plagiarism. The process of developing a language of one's own (if even possible) on a subject area holds strategies where it is a necessity to use the thoughts and thereby the words of those before us" (Nilsson, Eklöf & Otteson, 2002: 8). By the same token, I propose that the normative conclusion that characterises previous studies on copying and the use of computers is the result of a scope that is too narrow. This study has demonstrated that by analysing peer-group interaction over time, new aspects of the activities emerge. These aspects are important to recognize in order to understand and be able to support learning in contemporary school contexts where networked computers are a part of the learning environment.

REFERENCES

Alexanderson, M. & Lindberg , L (2004). *Textflyt och sökslump: Informastionssökning via skolebibliotek. (Textflow and seaching: Informationsearching via school libraries)* Stockholm: Liber.

Arnseth, H. C., Hatlevik, O., Kløvstad, V., Kristiansen, T. & Ottesen, G. (2007) *ITU Monitor 2007.* Oslo: Universitetsforlaget

Bakhtin, M. M. (1986). *Speech genres and other late essays* (V. W. McGee, Trans.). Austin: University of Texas Press.

Berthelsen, J., Illeris, K. & Clod Poulsen, S. (1987). *Innføring i prosjektarbeid. (Introduction to project work)* (E. Kokkersvold., Trans.). Oslo: Tiden.

Boaler, J. & Greeno, J. G. (2000). Identity, agency and knowing in mathematics world. In J. Boaler (Ed.), *Multiple perspectives on mathematics teaching and learning.* Stanford CT: Elsevier Science.

Brown, A. L. & Campione, J. C. (1994). Guided discovery in a community of learners. In K. McGilly (Ed.), *Classroom lessons: Integrating cognitive theory and classroom practice.* (pp. 229-270). Cambridge, MA: MIT Press.

Brown, A. L. & Day, J. D. (1983). Macrorules for summarizing texts: The development of expertise. *Journal of verbal learning and verbal behaviour* (22), 1-14.

Brown, A. L., Day, J. D. & Jones, R. S. (1983). The development of plans for summarizing texts. *Child development* (54), 968-979.

Collins, A. (2001). The Balance between task focus and understanding focus: Education as apprenticeship versus education as research. In T. Koschmann, R. Hall & N. Miyake (Eds.), *CSCL 2. Carrying forward the conversation.* Mahwah, NJ: Lawrence Erlbaum.

Engeström, Y. (2005). Studying learning and development of expansive phenomena. Lecture at the faculty of education, University of Oslo.

Engeström, Y. (2007). Putting Vygotsky to work: The change laboratory as an application of double stimulation. In H. Daniels, M. Cole & J. Wertsch (Eds.), *The Cambridge companion to Vygotsky* (pp. pp. 363-382). New York, Melbourne, Madrid, Cape Town, Singapore, São Paulo: Cambridge University Press.

Engle, R. A. & Conant, F. R. (2002). Four principles for fostering productive disciplinary engagement: explaining an emergent argument in a community of learners classroom. *Cognition and instruction, 20*(4), 399-483.

Hewitt, J. (2002). From a focus on task to a focus on understanding: The cultural transformation of a Toronto classroom. In T. Koschmann, R. Hall & N. Miyake (Eds.), *CSCL 2. Carrying forward the conversation.*

Holland, D., Lachiotte, W. J., Skinner, D., & Cain, C. (1998). *Identity and agency in cultural worlds.* Cambridge: Harvard University Press.

Johansson, E. (1985). Popular literacy in Scandinavia about 1600-1900. *Historical social research* (34), 60-64.

Kintsch, W. & van Dijk, T. A. (1978). Towards a model of text comprehension and production. *Psychological review, 85*, 363-394.

Krange, I. (2007) *Students conceptual practices in science education-productive disciplinary interactions in a participation trajectory.* Cultural Studies in Science Education 2 (1): 171-203.

Land, S. M. & Greene, B. A. (2000). Project-Based learning with the world wide web: A qualitative study of resource integration. *ETR&D, 48*(1), 45-68.

Lave, J. & Wenger, E. (1991). *Situated learning. legitimate peripheral participation.* (Reprinted 1999 ed.). Cambridge: Cambridge University Press.

Littleton, K. (1999). Productivity through interaction. An overview. In K. Littleton & P. Light (Eds.), *Learning with computers. Analysing productive interactions* (pp. 179-194). London: Routledge.

Mercer, N. (2000). *Words and minds. How we use language to think together.* London: Routledge.

Nielsen, K., & Kvale, S. (Eds.). (1999). *Mesterlære. Læring som Social Praksis. (Apprentiship. Learning as Social Practice)*. København: Hans Reitzels Forlag.

Nilsson, L.E., Eklof, A. & Ottosson, T. (2002). *Cheating as a preparation for reality.* Paper presented at the 32st congress of the Nordic Education Research Association (NERA) in Reykajavik, Iceland.

Nilsson, L.E. (2008). *"But can't you see they are lying". Students moral positions and ethical practices in the wake of technological change"* Unpublished PhD thesis, Kristiansand University Colleague.

Rasmussen, I. (2005). *Project work and ICT: Studying learning as participation trajectories.* Unpublished PhD thesis, University of Oslo, Oslo.

Resnick, D. P. (1983). Spreading the word: An introduction. In D. P. Resnick (Ed.), *Literacy in historical perspective*. Washington, D.C.: Washington Library of Congress.

Scardamalia, M. & Bereiter, C. (1996). Adaptation and understanding: A case for new cultures of schooling. In S. Vosniadou, E. De Corte, R. Glaser & H. Mandl (Eds.), *International perspectives on the design of technology-supported learning environments* (pp. 149-163). Mahwah, New Jersey: LEA.

Scribner, S. (1984). The development of literacy in American schools. *American journal of education, 93*(1), 6-21.

Säljö, R. (2004). *Lärande & kulturella redskap. Om lärprocesser och det kollektive minnet.* Falun: Norstedts Akademiske Förlag.

Stahl, G. (2006). *Group cognition: Computer support for building collaborative knowledge*: MIT Press.

Voogt, J. & Pelgrum, W. J. (2003). ICT and the curriculum. In R. B. Kozma (Ed.), *Technology, innovation, and educational change. A global perspective* (pp. 81-124). Eugene, OR: International Society for Technology in Education.

Vygotsky, L. S. (1986). *Thought and language*. Cambridge: Massachusetts Institute of Technology. The MIT Press.

Webster, Noah (1986). *Webster's encyclopedic unabridged dictionary of the English*. New rev. ed.] New York : Gramercy Books.

In: Learning in the Network Society and the Digitized School   ISBN 978-1-60741-172-7
Editor: Rune Krumsvik   © 2009 Nova Science Publishers, Inc.

Chapter 11

LEARNING IN THE NETWORK SOCIETY AS AN IDEAL FOR LEARNING IN SCHOOL

Peder Haug
Volda University College, Norway

ABSTRACT

A closer look at classroom research from Norwegian schools shows that some of the characteristics of learning in the network society have already become established practice in teaching and learning in school. The article discusses what might be the consequences of introducing such ideals into school. In the article this is seen in relation to a certain definition of adapted teaching, that teaching in school should fit every pupil's interests, background, ability and qualifications. Research indicates that this approach to teaching and learning will give advantage to some groups of students, but not to others, a contribution towards maintaining social reproduction in Norwegian schools.

INTRODUCTION

According to some researchers, a world crisis in education has now lasted for more than 50 years, and involves many issues (Coombs, 1968, 1985; Husén, Tuijnman, & Halls, 1992). Among these, the low level of students' achievements has recently been given much attention in many countries. International studies like PISA and TIMSS, but also national evaluations have contributed to the notion that one of the main challenges for school in many nations is to increase students' competence.

One of the measures introduced to make students more able is adapted education, i.e. that each individual in school should receive an education especially suited to him or her. This implies that teaching and learning content should be adapted in accordance with their experiences, interests, background, ability and qualifications. This issue is not new. Individualisation and differentiation are fundamental aspects of teaching, and have been formulated as central principles in education for decades, and in many countries. According to Alexander, celebrating each child's unique individuality has for a long time been fundamental to the philosophy of education in many countries (Alexander, 2001).

There is a distinction between a broad and a narrow understanding of the concept adapted education (Bachmann & Haug, 2006). The broad approach gives priority to the teaching of the whole class as a community, and to making this teaching of as high quality as possible. The narrow version is to construct the teaching especially for each individual student. They should receive their own teaching plans, have their own adapted content, tasks and exercises etc. The crucial question then is what constitutes high-quality teaching, a point I will shortly return to later in the article.

Our students grow up in what has been called the network society (Castells, 2000). Organising relationships in media networks is gradually replacing or complementing the social networks of face-to-face communication. A network society is defined by new technology, but it also represents ideologies and values that will have cultural, economic and political consequences far beyond the technology, as for instance in school. Learning by media and informal networks has become increasingly important. Children and youngsters in many countries live an online-existence when not in school, with a high consumption of digital technology. By the age of 21 they could well have been busy in informal media network arenas for three or four times as many hours as they have spent in school (Krumsvik, 2007). To introduce elements from the network society into school could therefore make interesting and important contributions to students' learning and development, as among others Krumsvik (2006) has documented. There is no doubt that new media and ICT could be a great help to make education more individually adapted both in the broad and the narrow sense. To develop digital competence by integrating media and ICT in teaching and learning in school has therefore become a priority in the recent Norwegian Reform – 06 in school. An important question is how to do it.

Krumsvik & Jones (2007) argue that in order to develop the students' digital competence, school should build on the students' needs and on their digital experiences from outside school. To have the individual student's characteristics as a main point of reference when teaching is also what adapted education is all about. Therefore, there are many points of connection between these two issues. There are, however, some questions related to basing education on the students' needs and experiences from outside school that I will look into here. My interest is not to discuss whether the use of media and ICT in school could contribute to adapted education, and to increasing students' results, which is almost self-evident. I am not concerned with the technological aspects of networking, even though they are important. I will not argue against the importance of education taking students' own experiences and interests from outside school into consideration when deciding on curriculum and teaching. Instead I want to discuss some aspects of learning in the network society as a model or metaphor for teaching and learning. I look into some basic educational ideas and values in the network society and see them in relation to how teaching and learning in school actually works. More precisely I study whether and how research on certain aspects of adapted education could provide information on how to proceed in developing digital competence in school. This is an issue which should be of interest for educators, but which has not been given much attention, as opposed to the direct use and knowledge of ICT in teaching and learning in school and how to succeed (Cuban, 2001; Krumsvik, 2007), which is quite another matter. The empirical data presented refer mostly to Norwegian schools.

THE NETWORK SOCIETY AND THE DIDACTIC TRIANGLE

I introduce the didactic triangle, and discuss the relevant developments in the network society and school in the light of this didactical theory that represents basic ideas about education. The didactic triangle is a schematic representation of different didactical models (Künzli, 2000). It represents three basic variants of didactics (culture-theory didactics, communicative didactics and didactics oriented to theory of learning and experience), thus covering the main elements in teaching, presenting the teacher, the teaching and learning content, the student and the relationships between each of them. (Künzli, 2000).

The triangle also illustrates possible tensions between the different elements in education, by studying the contrasts between the extremes in each of the three axes in the triangle (Klafki, 2001; Westbury, 1998). That is what I do here, cf. Figure 1.

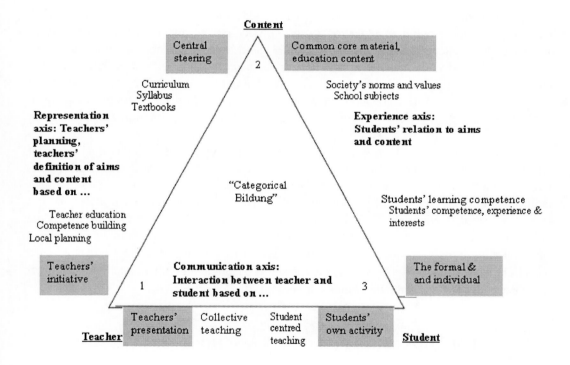

Figure 1. The didactic triangle (cf. Haug & Bachmann, 2007).

The representation axis makes visible a possible tension between teacher interests and learning content. In one corner we find the teacher's subject and didactical competence and his knowledge of the local communities and the students. At the other end we find the learning content as described in curriculum, syllabus and textbooks. The tension is here between the teachers' professional freedom and the state regulation of the education. The experience axis represents a possible tension between the material aspects of education defined by the learning content as selected by national and local authorities and the formal aspects defined by work methods and the individual students' experiences, interests and competence. The communication axis defines the relations between teacher and student. The possible tension here is between a teacher-oriented and a student-oriented teaching. A balanced education according to the didactic triangle should take account of all these aspects, as is indicated by Klafki's concept "categorical bildung" (Klafki, 2001).

THE NETWORK SOCIETY IN THE TRIANGLE

I will argue that the centre in the network society as an arena for learning will be close to the third corner in the triangle, oriented around the students' own interests. They are free to choose both the material and formal aspects they want to go into, and with whom. The activities are self-directed and self-regulated, the students are free to withdraw or respond whenever they wish.

The "content" and "teacher" dimensions are hidden in several respects, and therefore being deprofessionalised in an educational sense. Firstly, content matter, what in the network substance the students go into and experience is of their own choice, and cannot be monitored. Secondly, the teacher as a metaphor for a professional education interest in the network society is difficult to identify, if there is anything at all similar. The nearest we come could be the editors, the network owners etc. Thirdly, there is no common educational ideology behind the network interests, and therefore there is no common subject core or approach.

The conclusion is much in line with Wellman, in his emphasis on individualisation or "networked individualism". This contributes to an increasing individualisation in a postmodern society, where each individual can plan and act according to his or her own interests and needs more than ever before (Wellman, 2001). This also means that each individual has gained increased freedom to act. This is, of course, enhanced by the fact that the use of net and media is mostly done in leisure time, with no or very few controllers. In an educational sense, learning in the network society is close to the narrow definition of the concept adapted education: the learning is tightly constructed to suit each single individual, and the constructor of the learning situation is the individual learner himself.

THE DIDACTIC TRIANGLE IN A SCHOOL CONTEXT

To be able to make comparisons, I next present some research about teaching in school in relation to the didactic triangle. There are noteworthy differences in how teaching is done and what results the students achieve in different classrooms in Norwegian schools. Differences between schools are small, while within school variation is large (Kjærnsli et al., 2007). This can partly be explained by differences in teacher competence. The individual teacher plays a decisive role in what kind of teaching each student is offered.

There is, however, no doubt that a dominant pattern in the teaching as it is practised in school is also concentrated around the third corner in the didactic triangle, around the students' own interests, their free choice and around the formal aspects of education, the work or learning methods. The teachers seem to be distant, and the subject content seems to be of less importance than the formal and self-regulated aspects.

The documentation of this conclusion can be found in recent Norwegian classroom research that has studied among others issues adapted education. It shows that there is a high level of activity in many classrooms. Much happens, the students are working and moving, but the purpose of all this activity is often unclear (Klette, 2004, 2007). To be working and active seems to be of more importance than what kind of learning is taking place. The activities change often both in content and form, the students can move from one form of tasks to another at a high speed. This reduces the possibilities to concentrate and dwell on a task or an issue, making content and substantial systematic less clear; and reducing meaning and understanding.

Very often the students are given work plans for a week or more at a time. Then it is up to them when and how to fulfil them. In some classes students are occupied with individual tasks for most lessons during a week. They sit by themselves working individually. Their fellow students do the same, but the chances are small that they are working with the same subject and the same tasks at the same time. For this reason it becomes difficult for them to help each other, and therefore it is not possible for the teachers to give support collectively. They must teach each student individually, and very often time is not adequate for that (Haug, 2006; Klette, 2007).

The teacher offers the students little direct support in the learning process. Teachers' motivational initiatives, control, repetition, questioning, summing up, sanctioning etc. are sparse (Haug, 2006). Norwegian students in compulsory school are among those who are least followed up and controlled by teachers in the OECD-area, according to TIMSS (Grønmo et al., 2004). Other persons must therefore be accessible for the students when and if they need assistance (Opheim, 2004).

Showing initiatives for learning is very much up to the students themselves, their choices of subjects and tasks and their understanding of what is best for them (Haug, 2006; Klette, 2007). With self-directed learning and plans for whole weeks, each student does as he or she wants, and independently of the teacher and fellow students, as long as the point of reference is the work plan for the week.

To conclude, a widespread way of teaching and learning in Norwegian schools gives the students freedom to choose both the material and formal aspects they want to look into, and even with whom. Many of the activities are self-directed and self-regulated; the students are free to withdraw or respond whenever they want to.

In a comparative empirical study Alexander (2001) identifies two major dimensions of difference between the Central European and Anglo-American pedagogic traditions as they appear in the classrooms, the latter being closest to the Norwegian research:

> The centre of gravity in the first tradition is the class as a whole; in the second it is the group and the individual. In the first tradition the most prominent activity is structured and public talk; in the second it is seatwork, reading, writing, and relatively unstructured, informal and semi-private conversation (Alexander, 2001), p 536.).

These two traditions have their central points in respectively the first and third corner of the didactic triangle.

THE NETWORK SOCIETY AND SCHOOL DIDACTICS

What we then see, when comparing the ideas that come forward when analysing the informal "network education" and teaching in many schools, is that they have several similarities when seen in relation to the didactical triangle. They represent some kind of antiauthoritarian ideas, giving the student a lot of influence over education. Prioritization of time that is devoted to many other measures than concentration on systematic subject learning, diffuse objectives for learning, high levels of activity without any proper direction, an increasing degree of self-regulated learning, weak fellowship between individuals, distant and indulgent grown-ups not mastering student heterogeneity are all characteristic of school practices and could be close to practices in many young people's informal use of media and ICT in the network society. Further adopting these ideals and values from the network society in school does not immediately seem to be a good idea. There are, of course, differences between these two sites for learning. School is a formal and compulsory arena for learning, even though there is widespread informal and hidden teaching and learning. Learning in the network society is informal and voluntary.

What I argue here then, is that school has already adopted some of the ideals and values from the network society. There are two questions to be discussed about this situation. The first is the consequences of this development; secondly I look into the reasons behind these developments and how to react to them.

THE RESULTS

In the evaluation of Reform 97 it is concluded that:

> School seems to function best for those pupils who belong to those groups that traditionally have been successful in school. During the years school has constructed standards for what is needed to profit from being there, and is best suited for those who fit into that pattern. School is most insensible to those who are different. School does not master heterogeneity, diversity, deviation, the colourful, those who are otherwise and strange. Students that cannot meet school on school's established premises are in danger of getting into trouble one way or another (Haug, 2003).

At the same time, most Norwegian students report a high level of well-being in school, and a good relationship with the teachers and with each other. The results achieved are referred to as the Norwegian education paradox. Norway spends more money on compulsory education than most other countries, but the student achievements do not fully reflect this investment. There are still large differences in the students' learning outcome. Especially the students with less potential for learning are not benefiting sufficiently from being in school (Opheim, 2004). It cannot be expected that all groups of students should experience and achieve the same. Both research and experience from education contradicts that alternative. Education cannot erase variations and differences between individuals, but education most probably can reduce them; the problem is that the differences in Norwegian education are greater than before. An interesting issue is that Norwegian education policy for more than 60 years has had a declared intention to reduce these differences, and then we can conclude that they most probably have been increasing.

I will offer three distinct explanations for these results. The first is that school teaches as if students were alike. There is too little variation in teaching and learning methods within classes. The notion of "the normal student" has become widespread and effective in use. This is the student that teachers have as their mental reference when planning and implementing classroom activities and tasks. Those who do not fit into this notion will evidently not be taught according to their own needs and characteristics, and this will affect their learning. From this follows the political wish to develop adapted education as a key target in Reform 06 in Norway.

Secondly, students benefit differently from self-regulation and free choice. One extreme is that classroom observations show that some students choose not to do any tasks at all, and they manage to get away with that. While one of the main arguments for this kind of organisation of the teaching and learning was "learning by doing", the result for some of the students has become "doing without learning". They have developed advanced instrumental strategies for finding the right answers to the tasks, without working on them substantially (Bäckman, 2008; Klette, 2007). The students that benefit most from this kind of teaching and learning are those with the most cultural capital at home. They who have the most support from home, and whose parents give the most prestige to education are the ones who cope best. This explains the relatively high social reproduction in Norwegian schools (Opheim, 2004). From this follows a growing interest in teacher education and qualification, and in how teachers actually teach.

Thirdly, individualisation has increased. Fellowship in a school-class as the context for teaching and learning has become less important than before. Research indicates that the broad version of adapted education would benefit many of the students, reducing the numbers of those who will need individual measures (Bachmann & Haug, 2006). From this follows a growing interest in learning as a community-oriented activity. Classes and groups are not only ways to organise teaching. They also are communities of importance for the students' social and substantial learning. Being together and sharing a subject, an issue, a question or a problem in a community often increases learning benefit and the sense of well-being. When students are allowed to share experiences, talk together about a matter, help each other they also learn a lot, at least when this is done well (Dysthe, 1995). Research into the effects of social capital in a group of students shows that when positive, it has great impact on each individual (Engen, 2007; Norges forskningsråd, 2005).

With reference to the research presented, poor learning results for certain groups of students could be explained by not having taken all the different elements in the didactic triangle into consideration when planning and implementing teaching. Weak achievements could be explained by among other things unsystematic studying, weak progression in learning, lack of fellowship in studying, lack of teacher inspiration and assistance, lack of assessment and control, marked instrumentalism in doing exercises etc. For these reasons the recent mediocre level of student achievements is not surprising. In the next section I will discuss what might be explanations and possible new initiatives.

REFORM-ORIENTED CONTEXT

This situation must be understood as a consequence of changes in Norwegian school and society accelerating in the late 1960's, as in several other western countries (Hargreaves, 1994). School reforms, developments in educational science and developments in society at large can explain it all. The length of compulsory school in Norway increased from 7 to 9 years. The relations between students and teachers were at the time not so good. Teaching was dominated by teacher monologue and rote learning, inspired by the Central European teaching tradition. Many students were unhappy in school, and became underachievers (Hovedkomiteen for norsk forsking, 1976).

The alternative that gradually developed was the radical antiauthoritarian reform-oriented education, associated with the Anglo-American tradition in education. This orientation can historically be traced back to early 1900, but started to escalate in Norway after the Second World War. Here I present four characteristic issues that as early as 1939 were formulated in The National Curriculum as fundamental ideas for teaching and learning in school (Kyrkje- og utdanningsdepartementet, 1964/1939). These were accepted politically and within education; they became also the left-wing's educational alternative, developed in a companionship between radical teachers, researchers and politicians (Rovde, 2004).

The first issue is giving the students more room to take part, to let them influence what goes on in school and to give them responsibility for their own learning. This gradually changed the teachers' and the students' roles. The students were to learn to learn, and were to become the most active party in the learning process in school, not the teachers. The practical consequences for the teacher were widespread and most dominant with the older students. The teacher became withdrawn, kept his or her distance to the students and left the arena for learning more for them to control (Dale & Wærness, 2003). Second, the teacher were not only to be concerned with subject matter or knowledge, but also be aware of the social aspects of the teaching. Much time is today spent on non-curricular activities (Haug, 2006). Third, to teach the whole class from the front fell into disrepute, but to engage students in group work, project work or doing individual tasks were examples of high-quality teaching. The National Curriculum from 1939 acknowledged that whole-class teaching was a waste of time and effort: "Doing individual tasks will […] motivate and save time." (Kyrkje- og utdanningsdepartementet, 1964/1939, p. 12). Teaching has become more individualised over time (Klette, 2007). Fourth, education should be individually adapted, taking each student's experiences and interests into consideration. The main strategy for adapted teaching has been to give each student more freedom for self-regulation and to emphasise that they themselves are responsible for their own learning.

After more than 30 years of experience with this mode of teaching, we are in a position to draw some conclusions. On the one hand the results have turned out as intended. That goes especially for the social aspects of schooling and the sense of well-being. The shift has not produced what was promised and expected in several academic subjects such as reading, mother tongue, mathematics and science. And still school is best for the elite, for those students who have the highest abilities and best-educated parents.

THE TIME CONTEXT

Another interesting discussion to emerge from this presentation of educational quality and adapted teaching in Norwegian compulsory school is this: how can it be explained that changes in ideals for teaching and learning introduced in the late 1930s, escalating during the 1960s and 70s, first take effect now and can this experience have any relevance to the involvement in network society-based learning in school?

I here present three different perspectives on the questions that partly can provide information about how to proceed when introducing new elements to teaching and learning. The first explanation is related to the Second World War. Because of the war, all reforming in school was postponed for many years. When reforms re-started during the 1950s and 60s, the orientation was no longer inspired by the Central European tradition, but by the Anglo-American pedagogy.

Second, a most obvious explanation is that relevant information about developments in school was not accessible before the late 1990s. One of the main conclusions in the OECD evaluation of Norwegian education policy in the 1980s was a systematic lack of information about school in all its aspects (OECD, 1989). Only recently has the school received information about how teaching is done and about the students' achievements. Still there is very little information about how media and ICT are actually used in teaching and learning in school. There is an undisputable need to gather systematic evidence about the matter.

Third, it is difficult to introduce intentional changes in complex and complicated organisations like schools, which is one of Krumsvik's conclusions when studying the implementation of digital competence in schools: "[…] even if one designs and establishes new structures […] it is a long way to go to get a meaningful content that both teachers and students find natural, and actually use for learning purposes." (Krumsvik, 2006, p 160.) Very often results differ from what have been the intentions; they are defined as reform hybrids (Cuban, 1993), combinations of old and new aspects from the institutions. Most successful in Reform 97, for instance, were the arrangements introduced long before the reform was initiated (Haug, 2003). Findings like these have been presented in many cases and reforms (Cuban, 2001; Fullan, 2001). As a rule school will need a great deal of time to implement changes, and it is not to be expected that the changes that appear are identical with those which are intended. The different elements in school must function together. They must adapt and become a part of the larger entirety. In addition students, parents and teachers must get to know the new initiatives, they must accept them, become accustomed to them and they must master the practical consequences of them. They also must accept getting rid of established ways of working, understanding, behaving etc. that should be replaced. Teaching and learning are also close tied up to personality and personal competence. For all these reasons it will take time to fully implement extensive changes in school. Therefore we see that structural changes are easier to make than changes concerning teaching and learning methods and approaches. It has, for instance, been possible for schools to provide students with computers, but to integrate them into the ordinary, everyday teaching and learning processes represents a much higher threshold (Cuban, 2001).

CONCLUSION

This chapter has discussed what might be the consequences of introducing certain ideals from learning in the network society into school. The concept of adapted education has been a common frame of reference, and the educational approaches in the network society and school have been related to the didactic triangle. A closer look at classroom research from Norwegian schools shows that some of the characteristics of learning in the network society have already become established practice in teaching and learning in school. It has been argued that a common element is extensive individualisation, self-regulation and freedom of choice and activity. To a certain extent at least, adaptation has been up to each individual's own initiative and choice. Research in school indicates that this approach to teaching and learning will give an advantage to some groups of students, and not to others, a contribution towards maintaining the social reproduction in Norwegian schools.

To be able to increase the quality of teaching and learning in Norwegian schools, a change of ideology seems to be of paramount importance. This goes both for adapted education in general and for developing digital competence by using media and ICT in teaching and learning as well.

The quality of teaching and learning is embedded in many different issues both historically, politically and ideologically. Educational change as in adapted education and the use of media and ICT therefore cannot be understood as an instrumental or a technical method, easy to handle and control, which seems to be one of the most widespread misunderstandings today. In order to realise adapted education as a means to meet the defined challenges, school has to change its orientation, and to replace existing educational ideology and practice with alternative approaches. To implement adapted education without taking this into account and preparing the ground would probably have little effect.

Against this background it would be easy and even natural to recommend replacing one method of teaching and learning as an ideal with another. The individualised and self-regulated Anglo-American educational ideal could, for instance, be replaced by reintroducing the Central-European way of collective teaching. From a research point of view, the most problematic point is the notion that some ways of teaching a priori are seen as better than others. There is no research evidence for that argument. Research cannot document that one way of teaching and learning is always better than all others for all students. On the contrary, all methods of teaching and learning can give both high results and low results (Rasmussen, 2004). As Dewey stated "Everything depends upon the *quality* of the experience which is had." (Dewey, 1938/1988, p. 13). It is not the methods of teaching and learning that are the main challenge, but how they are practised in class and by individual students. For instance, for self-regulated learning to function for all students probably requires a very active and controlling teacher who knows what tasks and problems each student is engaged in at any given time, and how well they manage. Only then will they be able to give assistance and support when needed. Nothing will be gained if we, for instance, reinstate whole class teaching from the front as the best and right way to do it, or if we declare self-regulated learning as unwanted. Instead, we must develop perspectives on each approach's strengths and weaknesses, possibilities and pitfalls within the context of school, teachers and students.

This also means that the different methods of teaching and learning in the anti-authoritarian approach could function well, given the right circumstances, but also they might not. Therefore we have to conclude so far that in principle all approaches to teaching and learning have a potential to function very well at least for some students, given the right conditions (Bachmann & Haug, 2006). That is the reason why teachers now are recommended to master a whole range of teaching and learning approaches, and over time to act according to all the elements in the didactic triangle. Through variation it is possible to make more students succeed.

The second insight I wish to emphasise is the importance of the teacher for the students' learning. Dewey's view on this is very clear: "It is absurd to exclude the teacher from the membership in the group [class]." (Dewey, 1938/1988, p 36.)The importance of the teacher has been rediscovered, teachers matter for students' learning (Day, Sammons, Stobart, Kington, & Gu, 2007). Research indicates that an active and engaged teacher will assist more students to learn, than will the distant passive teacher. It is then the teacher's competence will come into play (Markussen, Brandt, & Hatlevik, 2003).

A report from the Danish Clearinghouse for Educational Research has analysed more than 6000 studies about the relation between teacher competence and student benefit from the teaching and learning (Nordenbo, Søgaard Larsen, Tiftikçi, Wendt, & Østergaard, 2008). The number of studies reaching the defined quality-measures was about 70. From these studies it is concluded that four aspects of teacher competence positively affect student achievements. The students' achievements increased with higher teacher competences in these areas. They were: teachers' social competence, teachers' classroom leadership competence, teachers' school subject knowledge and teachers' didactical knowledge and abilities. Other summaries of educational research have produced roughly the same conclusions, for instance (Pianta, La Paro, & Hamre, 2006).

From this it seems probable that school will not be successful for all students if the basic learning ideologies from the network society are adopted. On a normative basis, there is only one way in which school can meet this challenge, and that is to represent an alternative. A crucial point seems to be that to develop digital competence, school has to adopt other approaches than those which the students are accustomed to when they engage in media and ICT in their leisure time. The individual freedom and self-regulation as ideology and practice for learning in the network society has so far not produced satisfactory results in school for all students. As always, school has to prepare the students for life in the society in which they live, and to make them understand how it functions and why. This is not done by making school as similar to society as possible, but by making school an arena for discussions about and an analysis of society as a whole. The didactic triangle represents the challenges that have to be met.

REFERENCES

Alexander, R. (2001). Culture & Pedagogy. International comparisons in primary education. Oxford: Blackwell Publishing.

Bachmann, K. E., & Haug, P. (2006). Forskning om tilpasset opplæring. (Resarch on Adapted Education) Volda: Volda University College..

Bäckman, A. (2008). "Vi leitar i boka, litt her og litt der ..." (We search in the textbook, a bit here, a bit there.) Unpublished Master's Degree thesis, Volda University College.

Castells, M. (2000). The Rise of the Network Society, sec. ed. Oxford: Blackwell Publishers ltd.

Coombs, P. H. (1968). The World Educational Crisis: A Systems Analysis. New York: Oxford University Press.

Coombs, P. H. (1985). The world crisis in education. The View from the Eighties. New York: Oxford University Press.

Cuban, L. (1993). How Teachers Taught. Constancy and Change in American Classrooms 1880 - 1990. Sec. Ed. New York: Teacher College Press.

Cuban, L. (2001). Oversold and Underused. Computers in the Classroom. Cambridge: Harvard University Press.

Dale, E. L., & Wærness, J. I. (2003). Differensiering og tilpasning i grunnopplæringen. Rom for alle - blikk for den enkelte. (Differenciation and Adaptation in Basic Education. A place for all – an eye for all) Oslo: Cappelen Akademisk Forlag.

Day, C., Sammons, P., Stobart, G., Kington, A., & Gu, Q. (2007). Teachers Matter. Maidenhead: Open University Press.

Dewey, J. (1938/1988). Experience and Education. In J. A. Boydston (Ed.), John Dewey. The Later Works 1925 - 1953, Volume 13: 1938 - 1939. Carbondale: Southern Illinois University Press.

Dysthe, O. (1995). Det flerstemmige klasserommet. Skriving og samtale for å lære. (The Polyphonic Classroom. Writing and talking to learn). Oslo: ad Notam Gyldendal.

Engen, T. O. (2007). Tilpasset læring i et sosiokulturelt perspektiv. (Adapted Education in a Socio-cultural Perspective) In G. D. Berg & K. Nes (Eds.), Kompetanse for tilpasset opplæring. (Competence for Adapted Education) Oslo: Utdanningsdirektoratet (Norwegian Directorate for Education and Training).

Fullan, M. G. (2001). The New Meaning of Educational Change, 3rd. ed. New York: Teachers College Press.

Grønmo, L. S., Bergem, O. K., Kjærnsli, M., Lie, S., & Turmo, A. (2004). Hva i all verden har skjedd i realfagene? (What on Earth has happened in the Scientific Subjects?) Oslo: Institutt for lærerutdanning og skoleutvikling, (Department of Teacher Education and School Development Universitetet i Oslo (University of Oslo).

Hargreaves, A. (1994). Changing Teachers, Changing Times. Teachers Work and Culture in the Postmodern Age. London: Cassel.

Haug, P. (2003). Evaluering av Reform 97. (The Evaluation of Reform 97). Oslo: Noregs forskingsråd (The Research Council of Norway).

Haug, P. (Ed.). (2006). Begynnaropplæring og tilpassa undervisning. (Initial Education and Adpated Education.) Bergen: Caspar Forlag.

Haug, P. & Bachmann, K.m (2007). Grunnleggjande element for forståping av tilpassa opplæring. (Basic Elements for Understanding Adpated Education.) In G.D. Berg, & K. Nes (Eds.). (Competence for Adapted Education). Oslo: Utdanningsdirektoratet (Norwegian Directorate for Education and Training).

Hovedkomiteen for norsk forsking (The Main Committee for Research in Norway) (1976). Opplærings- og utdanningsproblematikk. Rapport fra kjernegruppe 4. (Problems connected to Education and Training). Oslo: Hovedkomiteen for norsk forskning (The Main Committee for Research).

Husén, T., Tuijnman, A., & Halls, W. D. (1992). Schooling in Modern European Society. Oxford: Pergamon Press.

Kjærnsli, M., Lie, S., Olsen, S. V., & Roe, A. (2007). Tid for tunge løft. Norske elevers kompetanse i naturfag, lesing og matematikk i PISA 2006. (Time for Heavy Lifting. Norwegian students' competence in natural science, reading and mathematics.) Oslo: Universitetsforlaget.

Klafki, W. (2001). Dannelsesteori og didaktikk - nye studier (Theories about Bildung and Didactics – New Studies.) Århus: Klim.

Klette, K. (1998). Klasseromsforskning - på norsk. (Classroom Research – in Norwegian) Oslo: Ad Notam Gyldendal.

Klette, K. (2004). Lærerstyrt kateterundervisning fremdeles dominerende? Aktivitets- og arbeidsformer i norske klasserom etter Reform 97. (Teachers' Collective Teaching still dominating? Activities and working methods in Norwegian classrooms after Reform 97) In K. Klette (Ed.), Fag og arbeidsmåter i endring? Tidsbilder fra norsk grunnskole. (Subjects and Working Methods in Change. Scences from Norwegian Compulsory School.) Oslo: Universitetsforlaget.

Klette, K. (2007). Bruk av arbeidsplaner i skolen - et hovedverktøy for å realisere tilpasset opplæring? (Use of Working Plans in School – a main Tool to Implement Adpated Teaching?) Norsk pedagogisk tidsskrift (Norwegian Journal of Education) (4).

Krumsvik, R.J. (2006). ICT in the school. ICT-initiated school development in lower secondary school.PhD degree thesis. Bergen: Universitetet i Bergen.

Krumsvik, R.J. (Ed. 2007). Skulen og den digitale læringsrevolusjonen. (Schoool and the Digital Revolution in Learning) Oslo: Universitetsforlaget.

Krumsvik, R.J. & Jones, L. Ø. (2007). Digital kompetanse og tilpassa opplæring. (Digital Competence and Adapted Education.) In R.J. Krumsvik (Ed. 2007). Skulen og den digitale læringsrevolusjonen. (Schoool and the Digital Revolution in Learning) Oslo: Universitetsforlaget.

Künzli, R. (2000). German Didaktik: Models of Re-presentation, of Intercourse, and of Experience. In I. Westbury, S. Hopmann & K. Riquarts (Eds.), Teaching as a Reflective Practice. The German Didaktik Tradition. Mahwah New Jersey: Lawrence Erlbaum Associates.

Kyrkje- og utdanningsdepartementet. (Ministry of Church and Education) (1964/1939). Normalplan (Mønsterplan) for landsfolkeskulen. (National Curriculum for Compulsory School) 4. opplag. Oslo: H. Aschehough & Co.

Markussen, E., Brandt, S. S., & Hatlevik, I. K. R. (2003). Høy pedagogisk bevissthet og tett oppfølging. Om sammenheng mellom pedagogikk og faglig og sosialt utbytte av videregående opplæring for elever med spesialundervisning. (High Consciousness and Close Continous Observation. About the connections between teaching and substantial and social benefit in high school for students in need of special education.) Oslo: NIFUSTEP rapport nr. 5/2003.

Nordenbo, S. E., Søgaard Larsen, M., Tiftikçi, N., Wendt, R. E., & Østergaard, S. (2008). Lærerkompetanser og elevers læring i førskole og skole (Teachers' Competences and Students' Learning in Kindergarten and School). København: Dansk Clearinghouse for Uddannelsesforskning. Danmarks Pædagogiske Universitetsskole, Århus Universitet. (Danish Clearinghouse for Research in Education, The Danish School of Education, University of Århus.)

Norges forskningsråd. (Research Council of Norway): (2005). Sosial kapital. Innstilling fra et utredningsutvalg oppnevnt av Norges forskningsråd. (Social Capital. Report from a

Committee appointed by the Research Council of Norway.) Oslo: Norges forskningsråd. (The Research Council of Norway)

OECD. (1989). OECD-vurdering av Norsk utdanningspolitikk. Norsk rapport til OECD: Ekspertvurdering fra OECD. (Reviews of National Policies for Education. Norway. Report to OECD. Reviews of National Policies for Education.) Oslo: Aschehoug.

Opheim, V. (2004). Equity in Education. Oslo: NIFUSTEP, rapport nr. 7.

Pianta, R. C., La Paro, K. M. & Hamre, B. K. (2006). Class. Classroom Assessment Scoring System. Manual.

Rasmussen, J. (2004). Undervisning i det refleksivt moderne. Politik, profesjon, pædagogik. (Education in the Reflexive Mordern. Policy, Profession, Education.) København: Hans Reitzels Forlag.

Rovde, O. (2004). Vegar til samling. Norsk lærarlags historie 1966 -2001. (Roads to Unification. The History of Teachers' Union in Norway 1966 – 2001). Oslo: Det Norske Samlaget.

Wellman, B. (2001). Physical Place and Cyber Place. International Journal of Urban and Regional Research.

Westbury, I. (1998). Didaktik and Curriculum Strudies. In B. B. Gundem & S. Hopmann (Eds.), Didaktik and/or Curriculum. New York: Peter Lang.

In: Learning in the Network Society and the Digitized School   ISBN 978-1-60741-172-7
Editor: Rune Krumsvik   © 2009 Nova Science Publishers, Inc.

Chapter 12

CHALLENGES AND OPPORTUNITIES IN DIGITAL ASSESSMENT

Kari Smith
University of Bergen, Norway

ABSTRACT

The position taken in the current paper is that Information Communication Technology (ICT) is to be viewed as a pedagogical and didactical means which enhances the instructional encounter, the meeting point where teaching, learning and assessment interact. With this in mind, the focus of the paper is digital assessment in relation to students' learning, in alignment with the current discourse of "assessment for learning", however, without disregarding" assessment of learning" administered in a class room context. The paper does not deal with electronic large-scale high-stakes testing. Some of the challenges with digital assessment are highlighted before the multiple opportunities ICT offers educational assessment, are discussed.

INTRODUCTION

A few months ago, at a conference on Information Communication Technology (ICT) in education, I had the opportunity to learn about, which was to me, an educational practitioner lacking expertise knowledge of digital technology, a remarkable new dance and competition form. Two young men performed, as part of the opening ceremony of the conference, a dance on a large computer pad. Based on my ignorant understanding, the two competed with each other, and the scores of each dancer were presented on a big screen as points, accompanied by flashes with comments such as terrific, excellent, and good. Apparently the two dancers did not perform worse than that.

I was intrigued to learn more about the impressive performance I had witnessed, and the first place I searched for information was, not surprisingly, Wikipedia, where I found the following:

Dance Dance Revolution, commonly abbreviated to **DDR**, is a music video game series produced by Konami. The game is typically played on a dance pad with four arrow panels: left, right, up, and down. Additional gameplay modes may utilize two four-panel pads side-by-side (doubles mode), or a single six-panel pad with additional arrows corresponding to the upper diagonals (solo mode). These panels are pressed using the player's feet, in response to arrows that appear on the screen in front of the player. The arrows are synchronized to the general rhythm or beat of a chosen song, and success is dependent on the player's ability to time and position his or her steps accordingly (http://en.wikipedia.org/wiki/Dance_Dance_Revolution, 01.03.08).

The reason why I have chosen to tell the above story is mainly to illustrate how ignorant many of us are of the speedy technological development in general, and for the purpose of this paper, the use of technology in assessment practices.

The position taken is that ICT is to be viewed as a means to enhance the instructional encounter (Smith, 2001), the interaction between teaching, learning and assessment, and not to be viewed as a separate subject to be taught in school in isolation. The paper focuses on *Assessing Learning* with ICT. The understanding is that ICT is used as a tool for assessment practice instead of, or in addition to, more traditional pen and paper based assessment. The focus of the paper is therefore not to discuss Assessing *Learning with ICT* which would deal with the value of ICT based instruction (Crook, 2001, p.331). However, it is difficult to use ICT based assessment if ICT is not integrated into the learning and teaching process, so in a way we can say that integrating ICT in classroom instruction is a prerequisite for using digital assessment.

Furthermore, the paper deals with digital assessment in relation to students' learning, much in line with the current discourse of *assessment for learning*, however, without disregarding *assessment of learning* administered by the teacher (Black & Wiliam, 1998). The paper does not deal with ICT related large-scale high-stakes testing.

In light of the above, the paper briefly discusses basic beliefs about teaching and learning, before more attention is given to the issue of assessment. It then proceeds to dealing with ways in which ICT can be integrated in all three processes. There are several challenges that need to be handled if the multiple opportunities ICT offers education, are to be fully exploited.

THE INSTRUCTIONAL ENCOUNTER

Teaching, learning, and assessment processes are optimized when they integrate without any clear distinction of each process separately. The physical meeting point for the three processes is usually the classroom, however, independently of location, the conceptual meeting point is the instructional encounter, in which teaching, learning and assessment processes blend. An example of this is when students are working on an assignment, and the teacher gives feedback, not in form of assigning a grade, but by pointing out problems and suggesting alternatives for improving the assignment. The feedback can be in written form or on-spot oral feedback to the individual student. In this situation, teaching is providing information, based on assessment, which is fed into the student's learning process. Feedback can be given by peers, and thereby students take on the role of teachers. Teachers become learners of students' learning positions as well as of his or her own teaching, all of which feeds into future teaching. Processes going on in the classroom integrate and can, to a large extent, not be distinguished as separate processes. There is a meeting point where teaching, learning and assessment mix, and an instructional encounter is created (Smith, 2001).

The character of the instructional encounter depends on the philosophy of education held by the teacher, the context, and by the system in which he or she works, all of which serve as meta-perspectives dictating classroom practice. If the teacher favors a teacher focused approach, the instructional encounter will be characterized by clear roles of who the teacher is and who the learners are, assessment will follow teaching and learning. If a behaviorist view on learning is preferred, knowledge is considered to be objective, measurable and can be transferred from the one who knows (the teacher) to the ignorant ones (the students), and successful learning means that the learner can reproduce what was taught (output = input). Assessment practice is measuring the extent to which learners reproduce input, and is often characterized by objective items, to which the right answer is easily definable.

Going back to the dancing competition described in the opening of the paper, the young men's skilled performance is the product of a learning process mainly rooted in a behaviorist theory. The skill they exercise is response to musical stimulations, rhythm and visual clues (arrows), supported by a high level of coordination and nearly automatic decision making about the next move, a kind of gestalt reaction. The teacher is a trainer whose job is mainly to help the performer develop the required skills and see to that sufficient practice takes place so the actions become automatic at the highest level. The winner is the dancer who best times and positions his steps according to the musical stimulations. There is a clear "correct" response. The e-assessment employed in the game suits the approach to learning, success can be measured by counting scores, and the flashing encouraging comments are programmed to translate a certain number of scores within a specific time into comments such as excellent, very good, etc.. The learning product is measurable, and assessment becomes rather straightforward. The scores do not provide any information about the performers' learning processes and the coaching and feedback they probably had been receiving from the trainer during the process prior to the impressive performance. There is a summative objective score at the end of the game.

This type of learning is frequently criticized within educational systems which favor educational approaches built on constructivist learning theories stemming from Vygotsky's (1978, 1986), Bakhtin's (1981), and Wegerif & Mercer's (1997) work. Learning is enhanced when the learner engages in processes in which he or she personally constructs knowledge with the support of teachers. Socio-constructivists claim that learning is more effective when taking place in a social context, in dialogue with others, teacher as well as peers. Deep learning processes are essential to and precede high quality learning outcome. Recent criticism of constructivist views on learning is that too much emphasis is put on the processes, and the product of learning has been forgotten. It is especially policy makers who express these views in light of disappointment with scores of their respective countries on international comparative tests.

Teachers who prioritize a socio-cultural approach to learning are likely to create instructional encounters with space for dialogues between the teacher and the students, and among the students themselves. There is a natural integration of teaching learning and assessment activities.

Teachers' integration of ICT in the instructional encounter is independent of the specific teacher's educational philosophy. It can be used just as much in a teacher focused classroom where the teacher mainly lectures, as in a learner focused classroom where interpersonal dialogues play an important role. Beliefs about teaching and learning are independent of the extent to which ICT is used in the classroom. Thus, teachers' philosophies of education can be viewed as meta-perspectives, and new technology developments do not change these, but have the opportunities to facilitate or hinder effective practices in the classroom.

ASSESSMENT

Due to the intimate relationship between teaching, learning and assessment, currently common approaches to learning as briefly described above, have initiated developments of alternative forms to assessment , alternatives to traditional measurement methods. In the assessment literature clear dichotomies have been noticed, mainly between formative and summative assessment, as illustrated in the below table:

Table 1.

Formative Assessment	Summative Assessment
Assessment	Measurement
Contextual/ ipsative paradigms	Psychometric paradigm
Low stakes	High stakes
Internally administered	Externally administered
Including learners in assessment processes	Excluding learners from assessment processes
Supporting learning	Judging learning
Small groups	Large groups
Perceived to be for learning	Perceived to be of learning

The role of assessment within the instructional encounter is more related to formative assessment than to summative assessment. The latter usually comes at the end of the learning process and is often judgmental and reported by a grade. Formative assessment takes place in the classroom, embedded in the daily encounters between teachers and students. It is often unplanned and takes the form of spontaneous feedback to the learners. Whereas assessment of learning is frequently associated with summative assessment, it is important to understand that assessment *for* learning cannot take place before the learner's current status of learning has been mapped, before assessment *of* learning has been carried out. Teachers who practice assessment for learning, make use of the information received from assessment of learning, in planning future teaching, learning and assessment. The quality of the instructional encounter is therefore very much in hands of the teacher, who is expected to hold what can be called *pedagogical assessment competence.*

DIGITAL ASSESSMENT (E-ASSESSMENT)

Digital assessment, or as often called, e-assessment, is defined by the Joint Information Systems Committee and the Qualifications and Curriculum Authority in UK as *..the end- to end electronic assessment processes where ICT is used for the presentation of assessment activity and recording of responses* (JISC/QCA, 2007, p.6). In this paper e-assessment (interchangeable with digital assessment) simply means assessment which is carried out by the use of digital devices.

ICT has the potential to play a major role in enhancing the instructional encounter independently of teaching approaches. There is, however, a basic pre-requisite which needs to be met, digital assessment can only be applied if the same type of technology has been used during the teaching/learning processes. An early lesson of mine in classroom assessment was that "You assess what you teach the way you teach it". Students need to be familiar with the assessment instruments and techniques, and the assessment context is not the place and time to introduce new techniques or item formats.

Regarding the use of digital assessment, the main problem is that when introducing e-assessment, an equity problem is likely to occur. A commonly perceived problem is that not all students have access to ICT, and it is not sufficiently integrated into the instructional encounter to be used for summative assessment. International comparative tests (PISA, TIMMS, PIRLS) are still mainly in paper and pencil form, and the same goes for national tests in many countries. Lie, Hopfenbeck, Ibsen & Turmo (2005) argue that the validity of the National tests in Norway from 2005, is likely to be related to the pupils' in- and out-of-school experience with ICT. However, a recent problem encountered in Norway, for example, is that today there is a high level of computers at home (85%). 17 % of 15 year olds report that they use computers daily in schools (Kjærnsli, Lie, Olsen & Roe, 2007). In some regions in Norway (Bergen) all secondary schools students have been given lap tops, but external testing, often high stakes, is still traditionally carried out, and a new kind of equity issue has, per today, developed. McCormick (2004) claims that assessment has not kept up with recent developments in education and technology, a fact that has a serious impact on the validity of externally administered tests. It needs to be said, however, that several projects introducing e-assessment are currently being piloted in Norway.

Digital assessment has, surprisingly a long history from 1926 , when Pressey reported on using a simple machine which *gives tests and scores.* E-assessment started off by delivering traditional tests in an electronic mode, also called computer adaptive tests (CAT). These tests contain mainly objective test items, and the learner receives immediate feedback when making mistakes and is guided, by programmed responses, to the correct answer. The main affects of the CAT approach has been in reducing students' anxiety and increasing their feeling of self-efficacy, and it has also been valued as a diagnostic tool. There seems, however, to be little effect on learning outcomes (Lilley and Baker, 2004)

Today, a more common use of ICT in relation to assessment is the use of e-portfolios, a tool which combines the many benefits of portfolio assessment (personal, documents process as well as product, involves learners in the selection of the content, enhances reflection on learning, develops meta-cognition (Smith, 2001)) with the advantages of accessibility, revision, storing etc. ICT offers.

The implementation of e-assessment in today's classrooms is, however, not as straightforward as could be expected.

In the following I will discuss some of the challenges related to digital assessment before I proceed to discussing the many advantages of implementing ICT in the instructional encounter, with a special focus on assessment for learning.

CHALLENGES FACED WHEN INTRODUCING ICT NTO THE INSTRUCTIONAL ENCOUNTER

I. Changes Related to Teachers

A major obstacle in introducing changes in education is to make teachers change their classroom practice, and the characterisitc of the instructional encounter. Almås & Krumsvik (2008) claim that the way ICT is implemented by teachers in their in teaching is related to teachers' knowledge of the subjects they teach as well as of their ICT competence. Timperley et al. (2007) who carried out a large meta-study examining professional development activities for teachers with a positive impact on students' learning, found that several conditions have to be in place, some of which are:

- Teacher learning requries time (6 months to 2 years, even up till 5 years)
- Teachers need to become engaged in the activity
- Teachers need to be challenged on current positions, especially in relation to students and learning
- Teachers need to feel they are surrounded by a safe "learning community"
- The activity has to be in line with recent developments and research

The above conditions require resources and patience over a longer period of time, and there is no quick fix, whatsoever, for changing teachers' practice in ways which at the end lead to a positive impact on students' learning.

Moreover, regarding teachers' management of instructional encounters integrating ICT, the situation is that we seem to be in a transmission period in which students are more computer literate than teachers (Arnseth et al., 2007). This presents an additional challenge to implementing ICT in the classroom, empowering teachers in ICT competence so they have a feeling of mastering ICT, and can integrate ICT in correspondence with their pedagogical vision. Thus the tension between compulsion and choice (Gray et al., 2007) is likely to be reduced. Roberts (1998) claim that *teachers will only try out what they are confident they can cope with* (p.305), and in a situation in which students are more competent than teachers, it is likely that these teachers opt out of an ICT rich educational encounter. Gray (2007) reports on research on effective teacher learning in relation to ICT, and she summarises some essential conditions for this to take place:

- The individual perceives a personal need to learn.
- He/she foresees a positive outcome from a cost/benefit calculation.
- There is sufficient and appropriate time and space to learn.

- The individual is personally and professionally stable enough to tolerate ambiguity and uncertainty without undermining their feelings of self-efficacy.
- The teacher can determine for themselves the direction and pace of learning.
- The environment is supportive for learning.
- The individual has access to a range of useful resources which suggest new ideas and challenge their teaching.

The personal need to change is often directly related to governmental directives, and teachers decide if they want to get deeply involved with new learning processes, or if they decide it is not sufficiently beneficial. Reasons for this might be that they are close to retirement, might want to change profession or decide to pay lip service to the new directive as they have experienced so many in their careers (Day et al., 2007). In such cases the change will only be cosmetic (Day, 1999). Learning is a process, also for teachers, so in agreement with Timperley et al.'s (2007) findings, sustained changes of practice runs over a longer period in tact with the teacher's professional development within a supportive environment exercising a culture of learning. The feeling of confidence to learn by error and mistake without fear of criticism and, if taking it to the extreme, losing the job, is essential in any learning process, and perhaps, even more so for teachers. Teachers are, to a certain extent, expected to be unfaultable. Teachers' tolerance of ambiguity is being increasingly tested when the focus of change is ICT, and even more so, concerning assessment applying digital technology, both of which are causes of insecurity among a number of teachers (Gray, 2007).

II. Programmed Assessment

As previously mentioned, in early days of digital assessment it was mainly pre-programmed and the quality of the assessment depended on the quality of the soft-ware. Assessment meant testing which was programmed independently of classroom teaching, and the assessment approach suited a teacher focused style of teaching. The problem was that the introduction of computerised testing used objective tests items, yes/no questions, multiple choice questions, and other test items which have been criticised for tapping mainly lower order cognitive levels and measurable knowledge. Research and literature on assessment had, in the meantime, developed in different directions, especially by people like Birenbaum and Dochy (1996), Black and Wiliam (1998), Sadler (1989) Boud (1995), and Crooks (1988), among others.

Even though today there is more awareness of the limitations of computerized adaptive tests (CAT) as a means to support learning, it is still common. If used intelligently, it is a quick way for students to get a picture of how they master basic facts of a given topic. The tests can be taken anywhere and at any time, and it lends itself to testing large numbers of candidates in a quick and cost-effective way. It is the pedagogical aspect of this type of assessment which is problematic. If going back to the dance on the digital pad, the pre-programmed measurement of the performances gave information of the number of points the competitors scored, but did not give any information about the extent to which the two performers held a deeper understanding beyond the automatic performance of the impressive skill they exercised. Pre-programmed e-assessment cannot possible inform about how the learner constructs learning and develops knowledge. Nor does it tell about misconceptions and difficulties, the awareness of which are essential to future learning. If we want to explore the why and not only the how of the performance, other assessment approaches are to be used, including digital assessment, but in different ways.

Learning is a personal process, also when it takes place within a community of learners. Each member of the learning community constructs their personal knowledge, even in situations in which they are provided with the same input. They process the input differently, and the processes have individualised starting points. This means that the outcome of learning, if looking at higher order cognitive levels, will be unique to each learner, and programmed assessment cannot tap this. One can say that knowledge, as product of learning, has a measurable component (facts, dates, names) which creates the foundation for cognitive activities at a high level such as understanding, analysis, synthesis and evaluation (Bloom's taxonomy, 1956). Output of learning taking place at the higher cognitive levels does not easily lend itself to pre-programmed objective assessment, and the human judgment still plays a major role (Jordan, 2008). ICT offers enormous opportunities how to support the student developing such learning, but this kind of assessment cannot easily be pre-programmed and standardised. Assessment of learning can, in many ways, be compared to assessment of ski-jumping, there is a measurable component that is digitally measured (the length), and there is an impressionistic component which is assessed by human referees according to clear criteria (the style). A jumper has to jump long and stylish if he or she shall have any chance to win competitions.

III. Increased Opportunities for Plagiarism

Plagiarism has become an increasing challenge in the digital era. ICT has made it easy for learners not only to access information and knowledge produced by others, but the copy and paste function has also made it quite simple to present other people's work as one's own. The figures related to plagiarism internationally are frightening. Dordoy (2002) report that 74 % of students believed that plagiarism in one form or another was common among their peers, whereas De Lambert et al. (2006) report on studies showing that already in the 90ties, around 80% of students in USA admitted to having been involved with dishonest activity, and there is no reason to believe that the number has decreased as the technology has become more advanced. Moreover, in New Zealand, the same authors (De Lambert et al., 2006) found in their own study in New Zealand that 88.3% of students admit they have been involved with dishonest academic practice whereas 98.7% of teachers say they have encountered such practices in their own teaching contexts. In light of these numbers, one might question the validity of qualifications given to graduates of tertiary education as well as of secondary school.

Ridgway, McCusker & Nicholson (2008) state that an integrated part of teachers' professional knowledge today is to hold a critical view on the exploding wealth of information and misinformation (IaM) which is publicly accessible. It is the teacher's responsibility to help learners develop a critical use of IaM, including proper citation rules. Much of the plagiarism we find today is done without students intentionally planning to be dishonest, but lack of competence in handling IaM makes them guilty of plagiarism.

However, at the same time as ICT has caused an increase in academic dishonesty (MacDonalds & Caroll, 2006; Pickard, 2006; Leask, 2006; McKeever, 2006) and reduces the validity of assessment and the credibility of qualifications, most of the solutions to fight the problem are also offered within ICT. Various types of detective software are available on the market, and some of them are planned for implementation jointly with human judgment (Culvin & Lancaster, 2006). ICT has increased the problem of plagiarism, but it is also one of several other means to fight it.

IV. Form Over Content

ICT has enabled students to present information and knowledge in a variety of forms whereas previously a written text was the main means. Creative and impressive graphics, down-loaded pictures and cartoons, are only some of the effects that easily impress the audience, including teachers in assessment situations. The content, the quality of personally developed knowledge, is in danger of receiving less attention as long as the "wrapping" is attractive. It is not said that one should avoid using ICT in presenting personal knowledge, however, teachers need to be aware that the presentation does not become the focus instead of the content. A possible solution is to provide students with clear rules of the format in which they are to submit written assignments. In other situations (e.g. oral presentations) where the accompanied use of graphics is part of getting a message across to the audience in the best possible way, students can be informed, when the assignment is given, about the part of the grade allotted to the form of presentation, the content, time-keeping etc. Developing criteria for assessment jointly with the students allows for a deeper understanding of the purpose of the assignment, as well as it provides them with tools for self- and peer assessment.

OPPORTUNITIES OFFERED BY DIGITAL ASSESSMENT

Bearing the above challenges in mind and engaging in an ongoing process of meeting the challenges, it is time to open up to the many opportunities offered by using digital assessment to improve the instructional encounter where teaching, learning and assessment meet. The thoughts presented below are not meant to be a scientific representation of what is currently known about digital assessment. It is more meant to be suggestions for how ICT can be more profoundly integrated into the assessment part of the daily classroom work of teachers and students.

I. Feedback becomes Feed Forward

Digital technology has given the concept of formative feedback a new meaning which can better be called formative feed-forward to enhance assessment for learning. Teachers have the opportunity to engage in learning dialogues with students without having to make appointments of time and place. The personal tutoring which means working within the personal optimal learning zone of the individual learner, The Zone of Proximal Development

(Vygotsky, 1986), becomes practically feasible as the learners' assignment drafts can be read and commented on by teacher and peers, a process which forms and strengthens learning. By support of ICT, the enriched learning dialogue, an essential part of the instructional encounter, becomes independent of place. ICT enables learners and teachers to conduct multiple virtual meetings and share ongoing comments, all of which enhances learning. It is the information that is given by significant others which takes the process forward, and not the grades (Black & Wiliam, 1998).

II. Simplifies Revisions

ICT does not, however, only simplify the communication between the learner and the teacher(s) in an informal way, so the learning process is taken forward, it also enables the learner to undertake necessary revisions without having to start afresh every time a revision is required. The possibility of inserting comments into the document (whatever type it is) and to make changes in the existing document is not only a didactic advantage, but is likely to help sustain motivation for keeping on working on the assignment, as even major revisions do not require the learner to start afresh every time. It enables the learner to make better use of the learning time, as it is spent on thinking how to improve the assignment instead of on copying from previous versions. Moreover, documentation of the learning process is available and can easily be stored. Thus, assessment of process and not only of product is simplified through digital assessment.

III. Multiple Ways of Presenting Knowledge

Any assessment is based on learners' presentation of knowledge and skills. It is the presentation that serves as documentation on which assessment is based. In light of the presentation assessors draw conclusions about learners' current competence within the current subject or field. What is not presented or performed cannot be assessed, even though the learner might have the requested knowledge and hold the desired competence. The learner can choose not to present competence, or the assessment form does not sufficiently allow for the learner to exhibit personal competence. The latter is an equity question which questions the extent of bias in currently applied assessment forms. The most common way in which learners are asked to present knowledge and to a certain extent also skills, is in paper and pencil form or any other form decided by others than the learner her/himself. This is not only an equity and bias issue, it can be considered to be an ethical and, perhaps, even a legal issue. Gardner (1983) and others have reminded us of the fact that people learn in different ways and have individual strengths and preferable modes and ways of expressing themselves. The notion of diversity has been protected by the UN convention, the rights of the child (1989), paragraph 13.

> "The child shall have the right to freedom of expression; this right shall include freedom to seek, receive and impart information and ideas of all kinds, regardless of frontiers, either orally, in writing or in print, in the form of art, or through any other media of the child's choice."

One might question to which extent the above paragraph is given attention in relation to assessment procedures found in classrooms and in national and international test procedures (Smith, 2001; 2006, Leach, et al. 2007). The most common assessment instrument is still uniform paper and pencil tests.

However, current technology provides teachers and assessors with multiple opportunities to allow for diverse assessment forms and individual suited presentation and performances. The written text is not the only possible mode of presentation any more; arts, graphics, models, movements, music, films are other means by which the learner can express knowledge, ideas and skills. The varied documentation allows for a more valid assessment as the learner has, by use of digital technology, the opportunity to choose multiple ways of presentations, thus documenting competence. It requires an open mind on the assessors' part, and much work has to be put into developing criteria for different modes of performances. The main challenge lies in using multiple modes of presentations in high stakes testing. However, when looking at classroom assessment with the main purpose of strengthening learning for the individual learner, the opportunities go beyond the challenges for open-minded teachers with an ipsative and constructivist pedagogical philosophy. We have the technology, but do we have the courage and open-mindedness to exploit it for assessment purposes which are so deeply rooted in traditions and beliefs?

IV. Quick Self-Checks

An important function of assessment emphasised in current literature, is that classroom assessment practice should support the learner in developing assessment competence, an essential competence for life-long learning (Boud, 1995; Black & Wiliam, 1998; Boud & Falchikov, 2006). Students can only achieve a learning goal if they understand that goal and can assess what they need to achieve it (Sadler, 1989; Black and Wiliam, 2006).

Digital assessment offers the opportunity to put these visions into practice by allowing for quick self-checks of factual knowledge, correct uses of skills and techniques. The feedback is immediate, often attractive and encouraging, as with the game on the dance pad, all of which helps maintaining motivation also when success is still to come. The goals in programmed assessment are clear and concrete, and there is little room for misunderstanding if the goal has been achieved or not. Digital assessment of this kind allows the learner to take an active role in planning, following and documenting the learning process of essential basic information without the need to be assessed by teachers. Programmed digital self-checks are also economical and leaves time for the learner and the teacher to spend on more advanced levels of learning. Moreover, the learner can easily document and monitor the process of learning, an important step on the way to developing independent learning competence. However, as previously stated in this paper, it is important that teachers know the limitations of computerized adaptive tests (CAT).

V. Simulations, Increased Authenticity

An additional criterion for quality assessment discussed in recent assessment literature is ecological validity, the degree to which the assessment and the results from the assessment reflect real life uses of the knowledge or competence tested (Backman and Palmer, 1996; McNamara, 2000). In traditional forms for assessment, such as paper and pencil tests, authenticity is a serious issue in many subjects. Most assessment tasks would be classified as what McNamara (2000) calls a *weak sense* implying that the task is artificial and lacks ecological validity.

Ridgway et al. (2008) found that students aged 12-14 were capable of handling unsimplified data when asked to analyse and evaluate information from research reports published in the media. They were also given assignments looking at the causal effects of different data by enabling them to play around with the data on the computer. This was done in a variety of subjects, mathematics, physics, geography and social sciences.

Through multiple opportunities for simulation offered by digital technology, knowledge, skills and techniques can be elicited and performed in the *strong sense* (McNamara, 2000), representing reality outside the classroom. The learners can simulate reality in numerous subjects both in terms of presenting situations, collecting information and presenting solutions. Limitations to applying ecological valid assessment are not found in the existing technology, but more in tradition, mindsets, beliefs, and perhaps knowledge of decision makers and practitioners within the educational system.

VI. Group-Learning, Group Assessment

Another aspect of ecological validity of assessment lies in the opportunities ICT offers assessment within communities of learning (Wenger, 1998). Team work and team learning are implemented in many workplaces (Brodie & Irving, 2007). Educational systems and teachers have shown openness to introducing team learning activities, however, there has been much more reluctance to extend this to assessment procedures. Group assessment ought to be naturally integrated into group learning, group assessment of learning processes and of learning products. The gap between learning/teaching and assessment form is probably mainly rooted in strong traditional views on how assessment should be, but it is also a question of logistics, monitoring processes and presentation of products. This part can easily be solved by using ICT, especially concerning documentation of group learning processes, keeping record of facilitated intra-group communication and individual input into the group process and product. Digital technology enables the teacher to monitor group processes as well as individual learning processes, making it possible to carry out individual as well as group assessment.

VII. Assessment of Complex Learning Processes (Problem Solving)

ICT offers opportunities to enhance all processes integrated into the instructional encounter, learning, teaching and assessment, in ways that are yet to be fully explored. A good example of such an encounter was given by Professor Gabriel Salomon from the University of Haifa in a public debate a few years ago. When discussing new ways of assessing learners at the end of high school by means of separate matriculation exams for each subject, he suggested having one group exam covering several subjects consisting of only one test item:

A previous USSR nuclear submarine has disappeared in one of the Norwegian fjords. Solve the problem for the Norwegian government. Present your solution digitally.

Salomon did not go into details of how to implement his suggestion, however some alternatives are proposed below.

The learners are fully equipped with digital technology and internet connection and they have sufficient time to carry out the task which involves integration of a variety of disciplines: Geography of Norway and the Norwegian fjords, political history and diplomacy, physics, mathematics, English, international law, just to mention a few.

In addition to presenting subject matter knowledge, the learners need to exhibit the ability to apply a variety of learning strategies; finding information, selecting critically what information to use, much of which would be in English, integrating information from various sources and disciplines, calculations, creative thinking and problem solving, social strategies for communicating with other group members, recognising personal weaknesses and strengths, and those of others, in order to optimise the learning processes as well as the learning product.

Moreover, the learners are required to present the product, their solution, in ways which represent the complexity of the problem as well as the proposed solutions. ICT makes it possible to use multiple presentation forms such as pictures, graphs, simulations, voice, and texts.

What prevents us from putting Salomon's progressive idea into practice is not the technology, but a common reluctance to revisit current teaching, learning and assessment practices.

CONCLUSION

In the modern world ICT literacy is a basic competence every citizen is expected to have, and its importance will only increase in the future. More and more students come to school with a solid ICT competence. Schools, to be relevant to the needs of these students, cannot meet the students at where they are in terms of ICT competence. Students must be invited to a school which is not only more advanced in its use of ICT, but also critical in the ways ICT is being integrated as a built-in part of classroom work. Governments are aware of this, and more and more ICT based instruction is being introduced in our schools through reforms, pre and in-service education of teachers, and by ensuring that up-dated technical equipment is installed and available.

The application of new technologies in itself does not necessarily guarantee a high quality of the learning, teaching and assessment processes which blend in the instructional encounter. There are meta-perspectives such as beliefs and attitudes about teaching, learning, and assessment, what students can do and cannot do, all of which are translated into practices which determine the character of any instructional encounter.

Today we are still at the very beginning stages of integrating digital technology into education, and we are not yet able to envisage where new technologies will take us. Limitations to new developments do probably not lie with the technology, but in the mindset of decision makers and educators who are in danger of being caught in nets of tradition, attitudes and perhaps a kind of anxiety for the unknown and insecurity of keeping up with rapid developments. Assessment seems to be an area within education which has not fully aligned with developments in integrating ICT into teaching and learning processes. Challenges faced when implementing digital assessment are many, especially the current danger of moving away from an assessment culture (Birenbaum, 1996) and returning to a psychometric testing culture which easily lends itself to pre-programmed digital assessment focusing on reproduction of information. The weight given to international and national tests by policy makers is worrying. However, if the rapidly developing knowledge field of assessment which sees assessment competence as essential to independent life-long learning, joins forces with digital developments, the opportunities for enhancing the instructional encounter for all learners are huge. Today we have only started to scratch the very surface of the possibilities.

Perhaps at the next conference on Information Communication Technology I will not be impressed by how digital assessment is used out of the classroom, but how it has successfully been fully integrated into the teaching, learning and assessment processes and how digital technology is used to improve the instructional encounter in the classroom.

REFERENCES

Almås, G. A. & Krumsvik, R. (2008). Teaching in technology-rich classrooms: is there a gap between teachers' intentions and Ict practices? *Research in Comparative and International Education, 3* (2): 103-121.

Arnseth, H.C., Hatlevik, O., Kløvstad, V., Kristiansen, T. & Ottestad, G. (2007). *ITU Monitor, The digital status of the school 2007* (Oslo, Universitetsforlaget). Norwegian.

Bachman, L. F. & Palmer, A. S. (1996). *Language Testing in Practice* (Oxford, Oxford University Press).

Bakthtin, M. (1981). *The dialogic imagination* (Austin, TX, University of Texas Press).

Black, P& Wiliam, D. (1998). Inside the black box. *Phi Delta Kappan, 80:* 139-148.

Black, P. & Wiliam, D. (2006). Developing a theory of formative assessment. In J. Gardner (Ed.) *Assessment and Learning* (London, Thousand Oaks, New Delhi, Sage Publications) (pp.81-100).

Birenbaum & F.J.R.C. Dochy (Eds) (1996). *Alternatives in Assessment of Achievements, learning Processes and Prior Knowledge* (Boston, Dordrecht and London, Kluwer Academic Publishers).

Bloom B. S. (1956). *Taxonomy of Educational Objectives, handbook 1: The Cognitive Domain* (New York, David McKay Co Inc.).

Brodie, P. & Irving, K. (2007).Assessment in work-based learning: investigating a pedagogical approach to enhance student learning, *Assessment & Evaluation in Higher Education, 32*(1), 11-19.

Boud, D. (1995). *Enhancing Learning Through Self-Assessment* (London, Kogan Page).

Boud, D. & Falchikov N. (2006). Aligning assessment with long-term learning. *Assessment & Evaluation in Higher Education, 31*(4): 399-413.

Crooks, C. (2001).Current research (editorial), *Journal of Computer Assisted Learning*, 17 (4): 331.

Crooks, T. J. (1988). The impact of classroom evaluation practices on students. *Review of Educational Research, 58:* 438-81.

Culwin F. & Lancaster, T. (2001). Plagiarism issues for higher education. *Vines, 123:* 36-41. accessed September 2006 from http://www.heacademy.ac.uk

Day, C. (1999). Developing teachers: The Challenges of Lifelong Learning (London: Falmer Press).

Day, C., Assunção, F., & Viana, I. (2007). Effects of national policies on teachers' sense of professionalism: findings from an empirical study in Portugal and in England, European Journal of Teacher Education, 30(3), 249-266.

de Lambert, K., Ellen, N. & Taylor, L. (2006). Chalkface challenges: a study of academic dishonesty amongst students in New Zealand tertiary institutions. *Assessment & Evaluation in Higher Education, 31* (5): 485-503.

Dordoy, A. (2002). Cheating and plagiarism: student and staff perceptions at Northumbria. In A. Dordoy & C. Robson, (Eds.) Proceedings of Northumbria Conference- educating for the future, Newcastle upon Thyne, Northumbria University. http://www/jiscpas.ac.uk/apppage.cgi?userpage=7509 (accessed September, 2005).

Gardner, H. E. (1983). *Frames of Mind. The theory of multiple intelligences* (New York, Basic Books).

Gray,C., Pilkington, R., Hagger-Vaughan, L., & Tomkins, (2007). Integrating ICT into classroom practice in modern foreign language teaching in England: making room for teachers' voices. *European Journal of Teacher Education, 30* (4): 407-429.

Kjærnsli, M., Lie, S., Vegar Olsen, R., & Roe. A. (2007). *Time for heavy changes* (Oslo, Universitetsforlaget) Norwegian.

Jordan, S. (2008). *Online interactive assessment with short free-text questions and tailored feedback.* Paper presented at the EARLI/Northumbria Assessment Conference, Potsdam, August, 2008.

JISC/QCA (2007). *Effective practices with e-assessment.* Joint Information Systems Committee and Qualifications and Curriculum Authority http://www.jisc.ac.uk/media/documents/themes/elarning/effpraceassess.pdf

Leask, B. (2006). *Assessment & Evaluation in Higher Education, 31* (2): 183-199.

Leitch, R. Gardner, J., Mitchell, S. Lundy, L. Odena, O. Galanouli, D. & Clough, P. (2007). *Consulting pupils on the assessment of their learning (CPAL)* Research Report, CPAL ESRC TLRP.

Lie, S., Hopfenbeck, T. N., Ibsen, E., & Turmo, A. (2005). *Testing National Tests. Report from a sample study analysing and evaluationg the quality of tasks and results of national tests, spring 2005.* Oslo, Institute for Teacher Education, University of Oslo.

Lilley, M. & Barker, T. (2004). The development and evaluation of a software prototype for computer-adaptive testing, *Computers & Education*, 43 (1-2): 129-123.

Macdonald, R. & Carroll, J. (2006). Plagiarism- a complex issue requiring a holistic institutional approach. *Assessment & Evaluation in Higher Education, 31* (2): 233-245.

McCormick, R. (2004). ICT and pupil assessment, *The Curriculum Journal, 15*(2): 115-137.

McKeever, L. (2006). Online plagiarism detection services- saviour or scourge? *Assessment & Evaluation in Higher Education, 31* (2): 155-165.

McNamara, T.F. (2000). *Language Testing* (Oxford, Oxford University Press).

Pickard, J. (2006). Staff and student attitudes to plagiarism at University College Northampton. *Assessment & Evaluation in Higher Education, 31* (2): 215-232.

Pressey, S.L. (1926). A simple apparatus which gives tests and scores- and teaches. *School and Society, 23* (586): 373-376.

Ridgway, J., McCusker, S., & Nicholson, J. (2008). *Alcohol and aMmash-up: Understanding Student Understanding*. Paper presented at the EARLI/Northumbria Assessment Conference, Potsdam, August, 2008.

Roberts, J. (1998). *Language Teacher Education* (New York, Arnold).

Sadler, R. (1989). Formative assessment and the design of instructional systems, *Instructional Science, 18*: 119-144.

Smith, K. (2001). Children's rights, assessment and the digital portfolio: Is there a common denominator? In A. Pulverness (Ed.) *IATEFL 2001, Brighton Conference Proceedings*. Whitstable Kent, UK, IATEFL, pp. 55-68.

Smith, K. (2006). *Assessment in Light of the UN Convention on the Rights of the Child*. Paper presented at the NERA 34th Congress, Orebro, 2006. htpp://www.ibl.liu.se/content/1/c6/07/77/58/Smith20061.pdf

Timperley, H., Wilson, A., Barrar, H., & Fung, I. (2007). *Teacher Professional Learning and Development* (Wellington, New Zealand Ministry of Education).

United Nations (1989). *Convention of the Rights of the Child* (Geneva, Switzerland, Office of the United Nations High Commissioner for Human Rights).

Vygotsky, L. (1978). *Mind in Society. The development of higher psychological processes* (Cambridge, MA, Harward University Press).

Vygotsky, L. (1986). *Thought and Language* (Cambridge, Mass., MIT Press).

Wegerif, R. & Mercer, N. (1997). A digital fra,,ework for researching peer talk, in R. Wegerif & P. Scrimshaw (Eds) *Computers and talk in primary classroom* (Clevedon, Multilingual Matters), 49-61.

Wenger, E. (1998). *Communities of Practice: learning, meaning and identity* (Cambridge, Cambridge University Press).

In: Learning in the Network Society and the Digitized School   ISBN 978-1-60741-172-7
Editor: Rune Krumsvik   © 2009 Nova Science Publishers, Inc.

Chapter 13

MULTIVOICED E-FEEDBACK IN THE STUDY OF LAW: ENHANCING LEARNING OPPORTUNITIES?

Arne Vines
University of Bergen, Norway

Another potentially transformative force in legal education consists of the new computer technology and information highways. This new technology has the potential to open up the discipline and to make possible more and different kinds of research, more writing and more individualized feedback to students than is provided by the case method/final examination system. Yet this technology may reinforce important disciplinary routines.
— Philip C. Kissam, *The discipline of law schools. The making of modern lawyers*.

... understanding and response are dialectically merged and mutually condition each other, one is impossible without the other.
— Mikhail M. Bakhtin, *Discourse in the novel*.

ABSTRACT

In this article I attempt to contribute to our understanding of the dialogical dynamics and learning potential involved in group-based electronic peer feedback. Electronic feedback (e-feedback) is increasingly incorporated as an intrinsic part of important discursive and assessment practices in many academic disciplines with longstanding interests in student learning, to the extent that it has developed into a new pedagogical genre or literacy practice in higher education. Through an interpretative content analysis of a large sample of peer and teacher assistant feedback, conducted at a Norwegian law study programme, I have identified three main categories, or metafunctions, of e-feedback; affirmatory, evaluative, and challenging. In order to discuss the productive aspects of e-feedback in general, and the learning potential in each of the three categories in particular, I have drawn on Bakhtin's ideas of multivoicedness and dialogicality. The findings of this study suggest that exchanges of genuine disagreements, multiple and conflicting perspectives on each other's texts are productive for the student's development as an independent critical thinker and writer in the discipline.

INTRODUCTION

Higher education has traditionally been heavily dependent on lectures and individual study, and legal education in Norway is no exception. The law faculty at the University of Bergen (Norway) has undergone a range of changes in order to ensure better student learning. This faculty has been recognised as exemplary within Norwegian higher education because it has taken seriously the challenges posed by high student failure and drop-out rates, as well as its radical adjustment to the recent Quality Reform.[1] In this article I will focus on one important component of this teaching-learning environment, namely feedback practices as facilitated by the virtual learning environment.[2] This is particularly important because recent research literature has shown that feedback is one of the most powerful influences on student learning and achievement (e.g. Hattie & Timperley 2007; Hounsell 2003; Nicol & Milligan 2006; Topping 2003). Ramsden (2003) contends that effective commenting on students' work constitutes one of the key characteristics of quality teaching. What is considered as 'effective' feedback will differ, however, in light of the goals the feedback is meant to accomplish, the theoretical underpinnings, and the pedagogical context. Bangert-Drowns et al. (1991) state that: 'An understanding of the conditions of effective feedback […] should help refine both theoretical development as well as instructional practice' (p. 230; cf. Askew & Lodge 2000). I should mention at this point that I prefer to use the term 'productive' to 'effective', as the former indicates that learning, in this case mediated by e-feedback, should be analysed in relation to both processes and learning outcomes. According to Lillejord and Dysthe (2008), learning is primarily a sociocultural knowledge-producing activity, and the concept 'productive' simultaneously embraces the learning process and the outcome of the process (p. 75). This point is particularly pertinent in light of previous research on electronic peer response and peer response in general, because of its unilateral focus on social construction processes. Thus important meaning aspects related to products or reifications of these processes have been downplayed (Tannacito 2001).

My aim in this article is to contribute to both theory and practice. Remarkably few research studies have so far tried to develop new theoretical frameworks and conceptions that could further our understanding of productive feedback practices in higher education. While most studies and models of feedback have been based on behaviouristic or cognitive perspectives, my approach is underpinned by sociocultural and in particular dialogic theory (Bakhtin 1981, 1986; Linell 1998; Morson & Emerson 1990; Wegerif 2007; Wertsch 1991, 1998). This approach was chosen due to the complex nature of communicative interaction involved in e-feedback. Moreover, if we are to attempt to understand feedback as a joint activity, revealing and expanding strengths (and weaknesses) in others' texts is a very important dialogic component. I shall return to this point in a later section.

Networked technologies per se do not guarantee any forms of educationally productive dialogues. In fact, recent research shows a growing concern about the opposite tendency, that

---

[1] The Law Faculty received the Norwegian Educational Award in 2004, which is given in recognition of outstanding work for educational quality in higher education. The Quality Reform of Norwegian higher education, fully implemented from January 2004, is a close follow-up of the Bologna Declaration (http://ec.europa.eu/education/policies/educ/bologna/bologna.pdf). The Quality Reform emphasises the need for teaching methods involving a high level of student activity, in combination with new forms of assessment and regular feedback that promotes learning, to the extent that "students must succeed".

the quality of student networked dialogues often proves to be quite poor. Andriessen et al. (2004) explain this by calling attention to the common phenomenon whereby: 'Participants seem to be keen at avoiding conflict, do not really discuss the plausibility and strength of produced information and are not much concerned with the argumentative quality of the resulting text' (p. 107). Their analysis is echoed by Arnseth and Ludvigsen (2006, see also Angeli, Valanides & Bonk 2003; Black 2005; Bonk et al. 1998; Coffin, Painter & Hewings 2006; Innes 2007; Rourke & Kanuka 2007; Veerman 2003; Veerman, Andriessen & Kanselaar 2000) who found that much research on computer-supported collaborative learning (CSCL) reports a lack of discussion, argumentation, and challenging ideas, and that 'Ambiguity, disagreements, or diverging ideas are seldom resolved in any productive manner' (p. 169). These statements reflect a major challenge at a point in time when information and communication technology is promoted as the solution to outdated higher education pedagogy. The same statements also coincide with a central tenet in dialogue theory as well as in my data; multivoicedness, including confrontations with others' contributions and genuine disagreement are as important to learning as consensus, agreement and conformity – and maybe even more so (Johnson & Johnson 2009; Markova 2003; Matusov 1996; Smolka et al. 1995).

The overarching research question I want to pursue in this article is: 'What contributes to productive feedback in a network learning environment?'. More specifically I will investigate what categories or metafunctions of e-feedback can be identified in comments posted by a group of first-year law students and teaching assistants on regular assignments at the Bergen law faculty. I will then discuss the learning potential in different types of feedback on the basis of content analysis, my general theoretical perspectives and specific concepts.

The main body of data was obtained through a micro-ethnographic approach which comprised more than 1600 electronic feedback utterances produced by two small groups of law students in conjunction with mandatory assignments spread over three obligatory courses in the first year of the law degree course. A central point in the analyses of the given e-feedback has been to explore and understand what happens when multiple voices come into contact through regularly given e-feedback. A particular analytic focus is on the multivoicedness afforded by the virtual learning environment (VLE).

RESEARCH CONTEXT: THE STUDY OF LAW

Law is amongst the most popular university studies in Norway, offered at three universities at master's degree level.[3] To achieve a good grade from a law school is (still) important in order to compete successfully for attractive jobs in private businesses, law firms and in the public legal system (Hansen 2001). Accordingly, Norwegian law schools have been marked by a strong individualistic and competitive learning culture, in which intense reading for final high stakes exams has been the predominant way of acquiring a broad set of procedural and fixed knowledge components (Jensen 1997; Karseth & Solbrekke 2006; Åkvåg 2000). Partly due to unacceptably high rates of failure and drop-out during the 1990s,

---

[2] In Norwegian higher education VLE's are commonly used as tools for posting student assignments and peer mediated feedback (Dysthe et al. 2006).

the Bergen law faculty has attempted to alter radically the teaching and learning environment consistent with modern ideas of social-constructivist pedagogy and problem-based learning. Since the turn of the millennium, major transformations have been carried out, amongst them the implementation of group- and problem-based learning, course modularisation, and new formative forms of assessment (see Vines & Dysthe, in press, for a detailed description). As a consequence of a very high teacher-student ratio, a comprehensive corps of trained teaching assistants (TAs) has been built up in order to provide personalised study support for all undergraduate students.[4] The primary role of a TA is to guide undergraduates in mandatory face-to-face small group discussions and to provide electronic feedback on their weekly assignments.

A key disciplinary feature of Norwegian legal education is that students are principally trained in two distinct written genres. In short, 'theoretical tasks' (*teori*) require the student to give an account of valid law within a more or less defined legal area (Hagelien & Vonen 1994). 'Practical tasks' (*praktikum*), on the other hand, are constructed on basis of a given case where the problem to be addressed is pre-defined by a detailed description of litigants' claims and allegations. Normally the students must take the perspective of a judge and apply various and relevant sources of law in order to solve the legal problem at issue.[5] My data material consists exclusively of comments on practical tasks, which are predominantly what law students encounter in their first year. To some degree it is relevant to compare the widespread use of practical tasks in the Norwegian study of law with the Anglo-American case law and its emphasis on the legal case method. However, at the law faculty I have investigated, there has been a deliberate shift onto a problem-based learning model in which 'ready-made' case solutions are downplayed in favour of giving students appropriate tools to explore several possible solutions jointly and discover feasible proposals on complex legal problems. This is in part reflected in the faculty's overall programme objectives, where the development of communicative and argumentative skills are emphasised equally with the acquisition of substantive law. The strong focus on practising academic legal writing helps the students to recognise its important double function; being crucial to the practice of the discipline as well as being tools for acquiring disciplinary knowledge (Duncan & Ritchie 2003; Goodrich 1987; Ricks & Istvan, 2007; White 2003).

The Role of the Virtual Learning Environment

At present more than 1000 written assignments are distributed through the shared VLE every week, covering all undergraduate courses. This demonstrates the main benefit of using a VLE; its effectiveness to organise and keep track of a massive flow of written texts to be

[3] At the University of Bergen 350 law students were admitted in 2004, out of roughly 4000 applicants. The total student numbers are 2200.

[4] Senior students in year 4 and 5 apply for this position and mainly candidates with grades of A and B are recruited. The TAs are trained through a comprehensive in-house and credit-giving training programme, led by an experienced educationist in company with one experienced law teacher.

[5] According to Norwegian processes of law and justice, laws are created by the judiciary and decisional law, and hence make a particularly important legal source. The Norwegian legal system is very similar to those of the other Nordic countries (Denmark, Finland, Iceland, and Sweden) and makes use of an eclectic blend of elements of the Anglo-American common law tradition and the Continental European civil law tradition.

commented on by teacher assistants (TAs) and peer learners across the entire learning community. From an organisational perspective, the faculty reduces its total teaching budget through the use of a VLE, which needs to be achieved in order to finance such close follow-up of every undergraduate student, as the law study programme intends. Another major benefit is that the VLE reduces the time that teachers, TAs and peers spend on writing a lot of comments. In this case the most important and widely used tools in the VLE (Classfronter) are the writing and feedback devices, which are essentially a simple text editor and an easy commentary function. An important feature of the VLE is that the length of comments is not restricted, as distinct from handwritten comments in the margins of student papers.[6] In this way, the design of technology has opened up space for extended responses on students work. Also, the VLE provides the framework for a more complex interaction between a large number of students, and between students, teachers and TAs. The strict structure and time limits built into the law faculty's learning design are, moreover, easy to maintain using a VLE and it can be argued that it would be nearly impossible without such technology. Indeed, the mandatory requirements of writing, group participation and electronically mediated peer commenting make it difficult for any student to avoid the hard work of formulating their emerging understanding of the subject matter. Moreover, assignments and subsequent peer comments can easily be submitted to and read in the VLE from sites that are either off or on campus. This is an important feature of the technology, because there are a limited number of computers on campus and the web-based technology thus makes it possible for students to work from home or elsewhere. I will also emphasise the fact the VLE supports the freshmen's emerging knowledge of various areas of law by making easily available model texts in the form of high-quality student answers, complemented by detailed comments from the TAs. The aforementioned advantages of the technology have been discussed in greater detail elsewhere (Vines & Dysthe, in press). My aim in the present article has been to look more closely into the micro-level aspects of the dialogic dynamics and the productive learning potential of e-feedback.

RESEARCH EXPLORING ADVANTAGES OF E-FEEDBACK

Feedback in academic settings is traditionally conceptualised as providing comments on students' work with the purpose of closing the gap between the expected and the actual performance (Ramaprasad 1983; Sadler 1989). In the early research literature based on behaviouristic theory, 'effective' feedback was understood as feedback that fulfilled this goal, while research based on constructivist theory is often seen to have a wider goal, for instance, enhancing the quality of student learning, fostering students' self efficacy and their ability to self-assess and self-regulate (Nicol & Macfarlane-Dick 2006). A dialogic and sociocultural perspective extends the analysis to involve also the broader social, institutional, and cultural circumstances and the potential influence originating from the whole peer review process, such as reading peers' writings and playing the reviewer or the audience role (Dennen 2008; Dysthe et al. in press; Tannacito 2004; White & Kirby 2005). Many issues identified from

---

Statutory law, customary law, constitutional law, and judge-made law are equally legitimate sources of law in Norway (Miller 2002).

research on traditional paper-based feedback practices will apply to electronic feedback delivery, but as a background to my own study I shall review some recent studies of asynchronous e-feedback in higher education.

Most of the research studies on e-feedback report advantages over traditional feedback, particularly related to peer involvement. For example, in a case study of second language (L2) writers, Tuzi (2004) reports on a close interrelationship between the process and products of response in the sense that many of the ideas students received through e-feedback led to substantial revision of essays, particularly at the larger writing-level units (sentence, clause, and paragraph). Moreover, her study shows that L2 students learned from reading and engaging with each others' writing style, made available by a web-based database. Tuzi's case study also indicates that careful preparation and training in peer response increases the quality and usefulness of peer comments (see also Sljuismans 2002; Zhang 1995). Training is also likely to benefit student reviewers and make them more critical evaluators of their own texts (Ferris 2003; Hyland 2003). In another study from a L2 setting, Tannacito (2004) found that students built very close and supportive communities by participating in electronic peer response groups. Her discovery contradicts Tuzi's assumption that e-feedback leads to a greater sense of anonymity compared with oral and traditional written response. Tannacito's finding of the community-building effects of e-feedback is corroborated by several other studies (e.g. Matusov, Hayes & Pluta 2005; Na 2003). As emphasised by Pilkington (2001, p. 6; cf. Raaheim 2006), in order to facilitate on-task critical student dialogue, it is essential to scaffold a discourse community in which students are confident to communicate. Ware and Warschauer (2006) argue that encouraging students to share paper drafts may be one way of fostering a sense of community in a networked learning environment. When feedback is moved from the individualised and private one-to-one exchanges to the public arena of a network, however limited, one of the major advantages seems to be that students gain access to other ways of solving a particular assignment and to other perspectives. Though it is not always possible to trace how this shift may affect draft revisions, a number of studies shows that many students find electronic teacher and peer feedback worthwhile and beneficial to their social and academic development (e.g. Na 2003; Tannacito & Tuzi 2002; Ware & Warschauer 2006). Several studies on computer-mediated communication also demonstrate the critical importance of teacher's active and critical engagement with students' texts (e.g. Bonk, Wisher, & Lee 2004; Matusov, Hayes & Pluta 2005; Na 2003; Tannacito 2001). While the discursive, community-building aspects were highlighted in the underlying pedagogical designs examined by Na (2003) and Matusov and colleagues (2005), further positive effects of electronic peer feedback are well summed up by Ware & Warschauer (2006): 'Electronic feedback through peer response increases student writing output, enhances student motivation, provides a nonthreatening environment, makes papers more readily available for sharing, and allows instructors greater opportunity to monitor peer response' (p. 116).

---

6 See Barnett (2007) for an excellent discussion of the pro and cons of handwritten comments on hard copy versus electronic typed comments in a law school context.

Some Critical Issues Emerging from the Literature

Peer feedback has long been seen as a way of introducing a dialogic model of feedback, giving more control and agency to students, instead of passive reliance on teacher feedback to fix their writing (Mendoca & Johnson 1994). This shift in perspective is highlighted in the analytical distinction of Dysthe et al. (in press) of an authoritative versus a discursive model of e-feedback. Whilst the authoritative model is rooted in a transmission view of learning and the authority of the expert, the discursive model is based on a different epistemology where new understandings of knowledge are being created through joint or participatory activities. It is therefore regarded as important that students gain access to different and even conflicting 'voices' from both teachers and fellow students, and, at the same time, develop a sense of ownership and agency of the product. Despite substantial empirical evidence that oral, written and computer-mediated peer feedback prove to be worthwhile in higher education and beyond, there are a number of critical issues arising from the literature. A recurrent observation is that students, especially undergraduates, do not understand, misinterpret or disagree with tutor feedback because it suffers from lack of clarity, consistency, specificity and encouragement (Chanock 2000; Hyland 2000; Lea & Street 1998).

Numerous research studies show that students are particularly selective about using peer feedback and commonly value instructor feedback over peer-mediated feedback. For instance, Zhang's (1995) study showed that 75 per cent of 81 college freshmen found teacher e-feedback preferable to e-feedback given by peers. Jacobs et al. (1998; cf. Sadler 1998) argue, however, that asking students to choose between teacher and peer feedback is misleading, as they supplement one another. Empirical support for this claim can be found in Ertmer et al. (2007) who uncovered that, despite students' preference for teacher feedback, the majority indicated that peer feedback influenced the quality of their discussion postings in constructive ways. Arguably, along the lines of Jacob et al.'s (1998) sound advice on judicious use of a combination of feedback sources (teacher, peer, and self-directed), Topping (1998) asserts that: 'While peer feedback might not be of the high quality expected from a professional staff member, its greater immediacy, frequency, and volume compensate for this' (p. 255).

In one of the very few studies of electronic feedback in the study of law, Lindblom-Ylänne & Pihlajamäki (2003) report on how 25 Finnish first-year students made use of a VLE to submit and share written drafts on a critical essay as part of a problem-based course in legal history. Interviews revealed that one group of students were enthusiastic about sharing drafts and found this to be highly beneficial for their own understanding of the subject. The other group felt reluctant to do so because they were frightened and unaccustomed to the technology. Wegerif's (2007) notion of 'communicative anxiety' is relevant here, referring to students, even at master's level (cf. Littleton & Whitelock 2005), who feel very insecure due to the lack of non-verbal communication in online communication, especially when they are expected to display productive critical challenges and creative reflection (Blignaut & Lillejord 2006; Crook, Gross & Dymott 2006). Moreover, productive discourse is not likely to occur if students are primarily trying to avoid conflicts (Carson & Nelson 1996; Johnson & Johnson 2009; Hyland 2003). Arguably, written feedback, given electronically, is sensitive to the possibility of misinterpretation due to the lack of synchrony that allows one to modulate and moderate what is said, and this must be conveyed in any training. Thus, when peer comments are made public through network technologies, the quality is even more important. Not surprisingly, a series of studies have shown that e-feedback works best when it is carefully structured (e.g. Na, 2003) and integrated into the curriculum (Hyland & Hyland 2006). There is reason to believe, furthermore, that productive feedback is also heavily dependent on thorough knowledge of the particular discipline (Gibbs & Simpson 2004). This point is particularly relevant in contexts of peer tutoring since it typically focuses on curriculum content (Topping 1998), so also in the context of my research.

THEORETICAL PERSPECTIVES

This study is informed by dialogic perspectives on learning and communication (Bakhtin 1981, 1986; Linell 1998; Wegerif 2007; Wertsch 1991, 1998), in contrast to previous feedback research which has primarily been informed by behaviouristic and cognitive models (Mory, 2003). The effects of various types of feedback on the quality of individual student essays have been much in focus (see e.g. Faigley & Witte 1981; Paulus, 1999), while contextual factors such as disciplinary characteristics, learning architectures and technological infrastructures have generally been overlooked. Sociocultural and dialogical perspectives have directed my attention to the fact that both teachers and students are deeply influenced by such contextual factors, including when they are involved in giving and receiving feedback. I will, however, limit my attention to a central and recurrent idea in Bakhtin's dialogism, namely that meaning cannot be transferred, but is created through tensions and struggles between multitudes of differing voices coming into contact under constantly changing circumstances. This far-reaching statement implies that genuine meaning differences and transformation should always be sought for in learning intensive interactions. Below I will attempt to unpack and discuss some core assumptions derived from Bakhtin's original writings and later interpreters along these lines of thought.

Bakhtin's conceptualisation of dialogue or dialogicality is multifaceted and takes on a variety of meanings and manifestations. Wegerif (2007) distinguishes between five different but interlinked ways of understanding 'dialogic', all of them traceable in the writings of Bakhtin. For the purpose of this article I will concentrate particularly on what Wegerif refers to as 'dialogic texts as opposed to monologic texts'. One could argue that texts and utterances are not equally dialogical, but depend on the extent to which different voices, within or across text(s) and mind(s), are represented and responded to (Fairclough 2003). Following Bakhtin, writers such as Fairclough (1992), Linell (2007), Morson & Emerson (1990), and Wegerif (2007) suggest that texts and utterances can be positioned in continuum from dialogic to monologic. I ought to stress here that text artefacts do not inherently possess dialogicality, since they are connected to and depend on the complex relationship between producers, utterances, receivers, and contexts. For this reason it is extremely difficult for researchers to develop appropriate coding schemes and analytical models aiming at assessing the dialogic quality of different types and structures of message content in diverse networked learning forums. I shall return to this matter in the section that precedes the analysis.

Bakhtin describe several ways that utterances can be 'dialogised' in the sense that two or more voices become intermingled and hence prepare the ground for new meanings and understandings to come into being. Most important, Bakhtin's accentuation of the active response of the 'addressee(s)', to the extent of becoming a co-constructor of meaning, stands in strong contrast to the long-established transmission model of communication, where the focus is on how well the 'receiver' is capable of deciphering messages as they are fully intended by the 'sender' (Reddy 1977). However, dialogue does not just happen because two or more people exchange information (Sidorkin 1999, p. 48); the productive aspect lies in the tension between conflicting or actively agreeing voices and multiple viewpoints. There is further a firm line to be drawn between productive and reproductive ways of responding, as it appears from Bakhtin's (1981) distinction between active (responsive) and passive understanding. While active understanding demands that we 'assimilate[s] the word under consideration into a new conceptual system, that of the one striving to understand, establishes a series of complex interrelationships, consonances and dissonances with the word and enriches it with new elements' (p. 282), passive understanding affords no further expansion of the dialogue and does not lead to any new insights, because it:

> remains purely passive, purely receptive, contributes nothing new to the word under consideration, only mirroring it seeking, at its most ambitious merely the full reproduction of that which is already given in the word – even such an understanding never goes beyond the boundaries of the word's context and in no way enriches the word. (Bakhtin 1981, p. 282)

It is often argued that Bakhtin denied the existence of purely passive understanding in real living discourse, in the sense that it is 'only an abstract aspect of the actual whole', to use Bakhtin's own words. However, as pointed out by Wertsch (1998, p. 117), by the very discussion of this distinction, Bakhtin allows room for passive understanding as part of language and human communication. Although passive understanding is a very slippery concept, I find the distinction between passive and active understanding a fruitful way of elucidating a pedagogically crucial matter: What motivates and enables learners to produce high quality feedback? The problem with an authoritative model of feedback is that it runs the risk of passive student understanding because it basically focuses on how to use 'feed-back' to inform the students of what needs to be done, make them act accordingly and do the appropriate changes in order for their product to be as 'correct' or up to standard as possible. The important thing, if we are to put forward a dialogic or discursive model of feedback, is that in order to enrich the speaker's or writer's perspective, the response must exceed what the speaker or writer already knows, e.g. about a topic, an object, and so forth. As Vološinov (1986) points out, active understanding happens when the reader (responder) strives to 'match the speaker's word with a counter word' (p. 102). This viewpoint is closely connected with Bakhtin's characterisation of discourse as an arena or a battle between two voices (1984, p. 193).

Central to Bakhtin's construct of human understanding, or recognition (Vološinov 1986), is the tension between what he describes as a 'sharp gap' between the 'authoritative' and the 'internally persuasive' discourse. In Bakhtin's account: 'The authoritative word demands that we acknowledge it, that we make it our own; it binds us, quite independent of any power it might have to persuade us internally; we encounter it with its authority already fused to it' (1981, p. 342). In contrast to authoritative discourse, 'the inner persuasive word is half-ours and half-someone else's' (ibid.). As Matusov (2007) makes clear, Bakhtin defined internally persuasive discourse (or, 'retelling in one's own word') 'as critical stance to a text: he talked about experimenting with the text, questioning the author, imagining alternatives, evaluation of diverse discourses, and challenging the text'.[7] This is why multivoiced or polyphonic dialogue becomes particularly important in academic disciplines where truths are contested and where critical thinking and the ability to argue are more important than giving a 'right' answer. Moreover, Bakhtin's notions of 'appropriation'[8] and 'ideological becoming' placed further importance on the need to empower students to become competent at 'making others' words their own' in a process of selectively assimilating them for their own intentions. This process is to all intents and purposes about a constant struggle with others' internally persuasive discourses and for hegemony among ideological points of view, approaches, directions and values (Bakhtin 1981, p. 345).

According to Bakhtin, every human utterance is polarised between polyphony and dialogue on the one hand, and forces working in the service of dominance and authoritarianism on the other. In law this perspective is prominent, because law is an 'argumentative science' where conflicting voices and interests are an inherent part of doing law. In the discussion part of the article I will return to how the clash of two opposite tendencies, one towards viewing legal education as a site for continual arguing and disagreement; the other towards conformity and uniformity, are played out in the institutionalised practice of giving and receiving e-feedback.

An Illustration of Sequential Multivoiced Feedback

Before I proceed to describe the context and methodological foundation for this study in more detail, I will present a relatively brief example from one of the comment transcripts from the VLE. This makes it possible to catch sight of some facets of the dialogical dynamics involved in sequential multivoiced e-feedback. The following excerpt stems from the end of the first year, just before the exam.

Extract 1

Andrew 2005-06-02 12:21 [1st commentator]
    First, a question about your method: I see that you use a lot of quotations (or references??) to the ruling in the case. Have you any indications that this is the way to do it, -- I mean referring to the specific ruling each time you refer to case law...? I think you give a good account of the purpose, though.

Morten 2005-06-02 12:44 [2nd commentator]
    Nice that you use the wording of the law as a point of departure and present the legal basis. The way you refer to the rulings is also good I think, at least as long as we write with all the supporting material available as we do now. At the exam I am afraid it will be impossible to do the same.

---

7 As all our words come from the mouths of others, initially much is authoritative that later becomes inner persuasive. For sure, there are no clear-cut boundaries between authoritative and inner persuasive discourse.
[8] 'Appropriation' is a much more active and complex term than Vygotsky's 'internalization'.

Henrik 2005-06-04 15:20 [4th commentator – the TA]
> In my opinion one should NOT use a specific ruling in order to anchor a common sense understanding of the wording of the law. That seems a bit artificial. Frankly, this established legal principle that the wording of the law serves as the basis for interpretation of contract, does not need to be confirmed at all. If you wish to stress the wording of the law in particular or another factor for some reason, it should be anchored – for this one gets credit at the exam. (...) In my opinion the wording of the law indicates that the reason why he must retire from his job is irrelevant. It's great that you clarify the purpose of the contract.

In the first comment Andrew questions the methodological relevance of the original author's many references to various rulings. His rather critical appraisal is followed by a general and positive remark. In the subsequent comment, Morten agreed with the way the original author draw on the references from the body of law, in order to solve the legal problem at hand, and consequently he seems to challenge Andrew's underlying criticism. In his final remarks, though, Morten deepened Andrew's concern about the fact that they (the students) did not have access to such detailed sources of information at the final exam. In my interpretation, Morten hinted to the initial author that he should have chosen another approach when account is taken of the exam conditions. The final commentary, given by the TA, adds an important element to the asynchronous micro-dialogue started by the two first commentators. Initially Henrik (the TA) utterly rejected one of the author's arguments, and (indirectly) advised him to use his own words (understanding) when interpreting the wording of the law. Ultimately Henrik told the author and, of course, the other group members, what would count positively towards the grade at the exam. This latter remark deserves emphasis, since the data material comprises numerous accounts of comments about future exams and the exam genre. There is no doubt that through the electronically mediated writing and feedback process, students were given lots of helpful advice in order to succeed at qualifying examinations.

The abovementioned extract is furthermore indicative of other dimensions of e-feedback. A particular communicative feature occurred as a direct consequence of the asynchronism (i.e. delayed responses) built into the technology. More specifically, this has to do with the fact that the first commentator was the only one who engaged exclusively with the initial text, as distinct from the subsequent respondents who were, inevitably, affected also by the words of the previous commentators. The TA usually gave comments at the end of each assignment in order to capture the totality of the argumentation, reflecting an adoption of a long-standing practice carried out by the voice of law professors. Hence, intertextual relationships grew in complexity and unanticipated juxtapositions. This may seem trivial were it not for the constitutive effect this had on students' feedback practice and academic development. Some students reported that it was most labour-intensive to respond as the first commentator, and suggested that some of their peers deliberately avoided submitting their response before anyone else did. However, in order to take an active stance and not merely reproduce what has been picked up in previous comments, this might be experienced as even more demanding – especially if the first commentator did a good job. The fact that 50 per cent of the challenging feedback was given by the first commentator (cf. Table 2) underscores this dilemma.

An important finding from the student interviews reveals that it is common to go back and read through the commented postings in the VLE as part of the preparation for final examinations. This phenomenon underscores a prominent aspect of a Bakhtinian approach to dialogue, in that utterances (texts, rejoinders) are fundamentally dialogic because they draw on past utterances (i.e. submitted comments), are produced for particular purposes in the present and addressed in that production, and are received by others who make meanings and evaluations of the utterance. I would argue, at this point, that asynchronic e-feedback affords rich opportunities for a prolonged dialogue with the material, that does not ebb away after the TA's final comment is submitted and read by the student(s) in the first place.

In summary, the abovementioned transcript depicts some of the complexity of dialogic interactions involved in asynchronous e-feedback: multiple voices coming into contact, agreeing and disagreeing about various aspects of the text produced by the initial author. Any deep and substantial understanding demands that respondents strive to match the author's word with a counter word (Bakhtin 1996; Vološinov 1986), and the greater their number and weight, learners will be more enabled to develop as independent thinkers who use the many voices they meet as raw material for their own meaning-making in the discipline. The next section on students' study structure shows that these law students engage in oral and written interactions every week over their first three years of study. The long-term effect of building such patterns can be documented in improved exam results, while the development of independent thinking is more complicated to trace.

METHODOLOGY

Students' Study Structure

The students I followed started with two introductory courses, followed by courses in administrative law, family and succession law, and contract law in their first year. Legal method was integrated in all the courses. All courses were modularised (most courses were 10 or 15 ECTS credits), culminating with a traditional closed-book exam. The law cases were constructed by experienced teachers (course coordinators), and made electronically available through the VLE in advance of weekly two-hour group discussions (face-to-face). The TAs had regular meetings with the course coordinator, in order to prepare for the given assignments, and were also provided with a teacher-written draft of each case solution in order to assure a certain level of quality in the peer group supervison. Within the next 48 hours after the group discussion, two or three of the students were selected to write up an essay individually on either the whole or smaller parts of the same case that was discussed at the group meeting. Thereafter all group members commented on the different assignments, following a predetermined list in which every student was allocated to a sub-team of commentators. Eventually, within six days, the TA submitted his final comments. The assignments were not graded, but every student had to attend 80 per cent of the group meetings, accompanied by follow-up assignments and peer commenting. Very likely, the unusual amount of writing and commenting required of the students in this study programme, efficiently administered online through the VLE, increased their communication skills and socialised them into disciplinary genre conventions and the fundamentals of legal argumentation.

Participants and Data Collection

Twenty first-year law students and two TAs (senior students in year 4) participated in the study. Both groups, hereafter called group A and group B, consisted of six females and four males, all in their early twenties. Only a few of the participants had any prior experience of higher education. The two TAs were male students in their mid twenties. My primary data consists of a corpus of 1307 peer comments spread over 137 assignments, in addition to 355 TA comments spread over 59 assignments. This corresponds to 54 per cent of the total amount of assignments produced by the two groups in their second semester. For practical reasons I have chosen to analyse the first and final set of the assignments in each of the four courses. All documents have been transferred to Nvivo 2.0, a specialised software programme for qualitative data analysis, to support coding and analysis. Regular observations of the weekly two-hour face-to-face meetings in the two groups, and retrospective in-depth interviews of three students from each of the two groups, provide additional useful information of the context. All interviews were recorded and transcribed before analysis.

Data Coding and Analysis

A review by De Wever et al. (2006) reports on fifteen 'state-of-the art' instruments for content analysis of online asynchronous discussions. These authors show that various units of analysis (e.g. sentences, paragraphs, entire discussions, themes or ideas in a message) have been deployed for a variety of research purposes and theoretical interests. However, in this study I have chosen not to use predetermined (a priori) coding categories, although this is common (cf. Henri 1995; Schellens & Valcke 2005). The case study approach enabled me as a coder to become sensitive to the context in which the feedback messages were shaped, and, thus, informed my decision to develop the coding categories inductively and iteratively through reading the data material repeatedly (Hyland & Hyland 2001). Each feedback comment is treated as the unit of analysis, following Bakhtin's emphasis on the utterance. In essence, the utterance is a social border phenomenon, 'drenched in social factors' (Holquist 2002, p. 61), with regard to its limited occurrence between what is uttered by one writer (speaker, commentator) before someone else takes over (Bakhtin 1986). From a dialogical point of departure one cannot analyse individual postings in isolation, but need to focus on the relationship and alteration between postings (Jeong 2003). My interpretive content analysis approach (Ahuvia 2001; Baxter 1992) seeks to meet this premise in the way I have juxtaposed the different typologies or categories of feedback on a 'higher' discursive or interpretive level, and which goes beyond coding texts into categories and counting the frequencies in each category. Admittingly, since I am not trained in jurisprudence, it is beyond my province to appraise the accuracy and validity of the legal arguments in the content of the data material. However, my interest lies in revealing and elucidating (latent) communicative and dialogic patterns of a new electronic literacy practice that needs to be better understood.

ANALYSIS AND DISCUSSION OF FINDINGS

In this section I will first present and discuss theoretically some core features of the different types or categories of feedback identified from the empirical analysis. Second, I will compare feedback given by peers and by teacher assistants (TAs) in regard to the distribution of the different categories. Third, I shall examine how feedback is influenced by the order in which they are given, on the basis of a distinct content analysis. A theoretically informed discussion of the learning potential in different types and combinations of e-feedback is incorporated into the different parts of the following presentation of findings.

AFFIRMATORY FEEDBACK

The first category I have chosen to call 'affirmatory' feedback. Basically, it consists of fairly short formulated utterances expressing unreserved agreement with the author and/or the arguments of the preceding commentator(s), use of legal sources, conclusions, and so forth. Here are some illustrative examples of the first category:

- Agree!
- Much relevant here.
- I agree with you :) Short and nice explication.
- Great. Precise and to the point.
- A clear and nice solution. Agree with the conclusion.
- A very good and lucid introduction.
- Nothing particular to point out which I disagree with.

Obviously, these extracts indicate that affirmatory feedback varies in terms of length. It is also notable that there are some differences between displays of a response ('I agree') and evaluation ('Good discussion'), even in very short feedback comments. I shall elaborate more on the evaluative aspect in the next section. Affirmatory feedback is furthermore characterised by providing rather unspecified praise of the actual text content and its argumentative structure. This feature appears frequently in combination with a clearly expressed approval for the author's argumentative skills. The following are some examples:

- Seems like a thought-through discussion, Linda ;) Great!!
- I think you argue very well in this paragraph, Ingrid!
- Very good work. You're the best writer in the group. Lucky you :) Good method, good understanding. A good assignment. Have a nice weekend Liv :)

Even though peer respondents frequently attempted to make brief comments of praise and encouragement more specific by recapturing the structure or the essence of definite text passages, when asked to read and reiterate comments given by peers, students clearly expressed negativity towards specific and reiterated praise. Rather, as expressed in a great many comments, students are inclined to blame themselves if they feel unable to come up with any critical response, e.g.:

- I know my comments don't give you much, but there's nothing particular to point out in your assignment.
- This is an appealing assignment! Easy to read and follow, and you have obviously worked a good deal with it. I just cannot find something to put my finger on, good work Jonas :)

Interestingly, I found as many as 98 text passages in the transcripts containing self-critical meta-comments of this kind from peer commentators. I read them as indications of the students' awareness of an implied expectation to produce substantial, critical feedback – an expectation they often fail to live up to.

Why Do Students Write Affirmatory Feedback?

My analysis of the feedback transcripts has revealed four reasons for writing affirmatory feedback comments:

(1) Time pressure ('I'm out of time, so sorry for little constructive criticism'; 'Yes, I agree with you again. I guess that's the punishment for commenting right before deadline.')
(2) Lack of participation in group discussion ('Hi Trude! I haven't been to the group meeting nor done the writing (…) Looks fine this.').
(3) Too difficult or too easy assignment ('Nothing to criticise on 1B... it's not easy to direct constructive criticism at such short answers. :D').
(4) Lack of competence or avoiding risk taking ('Feel I don't have enough insight into the subject to come up with something sensible. So take the comments with a grain of salt :o)'.).

It is noteworthy that several of the students I interviewed specifically said they believed it was common for students to avoid giving comments if they were afraid to make a blunder. Risk taking, in the sense of possibly offering a wrong suggestion, goes against the culture. It is thus much safer to echo what another commentator has said. Arguably, it is often much easier and more socially acceptable to say 'I had no time' than to say 'I cannot think of anything constructive or intelligent to say here', though there is evidence that this happened at times. Some of the interviewees even accused peers of using this type of feedback to cover their own lack of knowledge or commitment.

What is the Learning Potential of Affirmatory Feedback?

Whatever the reason in each particular case, it seems that a lot of peer feedback resulted in shallow and ritualistic ways of giving feedback. One explanation may be that the student did not have anything to say, and therefore used general praise as a safe strategy. This might lead to a discussion about forced nature of e-feedback in the pedagogical regime, as described earlier, and where non-contribution was not legitimate. In any case, affirmatory feedback consisted greatly of praise and clearly expressed agreement with the author, despite the fact that students perceived affirmatory feedback to provide little useful information. One of the male students put it most succinctly when he complained about the affirmatory comments he had got from one of his peers: 'It doesn't help me to hear that 'It was easy to read and to follow your discussions'. I think she should write more specifically what was good.'

From a dialogic theoretical perspective it can reasonably be argued that because this type of feedback does not provide the learner with any alternative suggestions or new perspectives, that could enhance her understanding of the legal issues under consideration, it can possibly maintain, or even produce a passive understanding in the student. Consequently, this may contribute to a lack of engagement in the formative assessment process of sharing and commenting on texts. However, the fact that the students seem to equate feedback with negative critique (i.e., revealing deficits and shortcomings) could be the result of a deficit model that is very prevalent in conventional education. This may lead students not to realise and appreciate the power of positive criticism – finding strengths in the work of others. Indeed, even if affirmatory feedback is likely not to lead to any significant new insight for the original writer, it may help his or her self confidence, if taken seriously and not just seen as ritualistic.

EVALUATIVE FEEDBACK

'Evaluative feedback' is the second main category of feedback identified from the empirical analysis. This category comprises somewhat longer and more substantiated comments compared with affirmatory feedback, and hence the evaluative dimension becomes more prominent. This feedback category picks up and gives more value to certain elements in the author's text. It contains frequent use of 'moderators' such as conjunctions (but, however, etc.), and the style is quite personalised (e.g. I, you, I think etc.). Most typically, the response-giver seemed to produce more dialogised responses by engaging more directly with the text than did 'affirmatory feedback'. Often this was done by pointing out what the commentator believed was missed and, therefore, should be taken into further consideration. Comments of the latter sort might be grounded in intuition or a more or less vague feeling of what is missed out, or by referring to more authoritative voices like the teacher, the textbook author, or the law maker. The following are some typical examples of evaluative feedback:

- You find the main rule as 'point of departure', before your subsequent consideration, well done.
- Good point about showing that there is no statutory basis to excuse things that 'were meant' to be erased, and also that neither Liv's 'instructions' lacks statutory basis...
- Great that you use the statement. I think that the problem-formulation is good. The condition for inspection is that it is a document.
- Excellent that you present the current problem and the legal basis in the introduction.

Evaluative feedback is, not unlike the former category, characterised by a high level of agreement and openly expressed acceptance of the way the author has tackled the assignment and argued his case. Evaluative feedback 'exceeds' affirmatory feedback in two important ways. First, the written comments are repeatedly identifying gaps in the text, which can inform the author whether she is on target or not. Second, evaluative feedback often contains an element of rephrasing the (main) arguments made by fellow students. This may be useful for the writer's understanding as it gives access to another style of writing and way of expressing legal arguments. In this sense, evaluative response appears to be less marked by a 'final language' (Brown & Smith 1997, p. 13) that rules out other ideas about the text.

Is Evaluative Feedback Educationally Productive?

Much of what I have termed evaluative feedback can be understood as 'telling back', i.e. offering a reading of what the writer did. The writer might find that such readings do not match her intentions, as I have reported above. The problem is that evaluative feedback rarely introduces or contributes any new elements likely to enrich the words of the writer, and thus the feedback recipient is easily left 'within her own boundaries', to use one of Bakhtin's phrases (Bakhtin 1981, p. 281) in his exposition of passive understanding. For instance, merely asking for greater clarity by praise, or reformulation of the writer's own words, does not offer much contribution to a highly informative and challenging discourse, at least not from the writer's perspective. This might be true even if the writer might also not be fully aware of the discourse she has produced. I do not dispute, however, that such responses might be productive. Neither do I disregard the possibility of evaluative feedback having a very rich response while saying little. Also, in many educational settings, not at least in the USA where writing centres is a rooted part of university education, it is common to encourage such forms of feedback, especially in preference to authoritative evaluations.

The issue here is not whether to give preferential treatment to disagreement over agreement, or praise over critique; all these dimensions are needed and serve different dialogic functions.[9] The important point is to avoid the double pitfall of reproductive feedback, either in the form of peer response that mainly provides information, concepts and ideas that were already understood by the writer, or by transmission of definite advices from a knowledgeable expert. What, then, is the learning potential of what I have termed evaluative feedback? In fact, I do not think this query can or should be answered in any univocal way, partially because the specific forms of feedback that are productive vary from discipline to discipline (Gibbs & Simpson, 2004), and from individual to individual (Shute 2008). However, in the context of my research in the context of a law school, specific and unmitigated critique is evidently desired in preference to less specific responses. This makes sense because law is an argumentative, text-based subject and thus requires a very high degree of linguistic precision.

CHALLENGING FEEDBACK

In contrast to affirmatory feedback especially, but also evaluative feedback, 'challenging feedback' much more directly confronts the writer by pointing at weaknesses, inconsistencies,

---

9 Thus, we should not assert that disagreement is predominantly active and agreement is passive understanding. Bakhtin, for instance, often emphasised the possible active dialogic nature of agreement.

unheeded circumstances and suggestions in her text. Thus, praise and more or less unconditional support are 'replaced', in the latter category, by palpable critical, substantiated argumentation, which may help the receiver to discover alternative solution routes. Typically, challenging comments are relatively long, consisting of counter-arguments and alternative (methodological and subject-specific) solutions to the legal problems at hand. Pointing out inconsistencies, self-contradictions, paradoxes, wrong or unfortunate formulations, was part of this.

My analysis reveals several examples of confrontational (or disputational) feedback, which I interpret as a special instance of challenging feedback. This kind of feedback occurred particularly where the commentator signalled anticipation towards the author of some kind of active revision to be made (although none of the assignments in the data corpus actually required any kind of amendment in order to be approved). Below I present two separate extracts, the first given by one of the TAs, the second by a student. These were chosen because they exhibit some of the dialogic complexity and learning potential in electronically-mediated challenging feedback.

Extract 3

Henrik 2005-06-04 16:01 [TA comment]
You are placing too much emphasis here on the relationship between §§33 and 36.

I do not agree that 'circumstances that are not covered by §33' rarely 'can be covered by agreement §36'. Unfortunate wording. §33 applies to formation defects. §36 opens for the possibility to test the reasonableness of the agreement's content to a far greater degree.

I do not entirely accept the circumstance hidden v's open reasonability check between §§33 and 36. It is more natural to speak of such differences when one examines the meaning of reasonableness for whether:

a)   an agreement has been entered into (approval)
b)   agreement interpretation (reasonability is also significant here)
c)   agreement's §36 with a so-called open reasonability check.

This extract displays an example of a comment where the TA actively disagreed with the author's argumentation and thus challenged the student to reconsider some particular points in her application of the law. I read this response as quite confrontational in the tone of voice and in the TA's use of personal pronouns to underscore the difference between the student's and his own understanding of the legal problem at hand. The TA not only identified concrete weaknesses in the student's answer, but went on to present some helpful suggestions for where to look for an alternative solution. Perhaps the most intriguing question to consider from a dialogic perspective is whether the writer just accepts the TA's word as the 'authoritative voice' or uses such comments as a thinking-device (Lotman 1988; Wells 1999) to generate new meanings and a renewed motivation to pose new questions.

My research design does not allow me to answer this question thoroughly, but the student interviews clearly revealed that all the respondents found regular and well-thought-out commentaries from the TAs to be of the utmost importance for their learning development and disciplinary understanding.

Extract 4

Title Karsten 2005-02-10 13:01 [Peer comment]

Purview El. §42(2) 'If the other party understands or should have understood that the agreement had a negative impact on what the spouse was entitled to according to the first section, only this spouse will be liable.'

I think that your interpretation is a little incorrect here. An antithetic interpretation would be that 'if the other party does not understand, or had no reason to understand...', both spouses will be liable.

When you then come to the point that it could not be expected that the tailor should have understood that Peder had no right to send the bill to Kari, then both will be liable.

Then Kari will be responsible for the debt...

That is how I have understood the rule, but it is possible that you are correct...

Extract 4 is descriptive of a student who challenges the peer author by presenting an alternative interpretation; although he is not sure if he has got it right himself. Nevertheless, by challenging the initial interpretation, he could possibly widen his own and his fellow student's understanding of the particular problem. In this extract we can also trace another dialogic quality, given in this particular response: 'I think that your interpretation is a little incorrect' and 'That is how I have understood the rule, but it is possible that you are correct', signalled a less authoritative stance compared with the TA's response in the previous example. Nevertheless, the invitation for the author to rethink her positions and arguments are, in my opinion, just as strong as in the response of the TA. However, as will appear from the analysis of the following sections, the two TAs produced a disproportionately high rate of challenging and confrontational feedback, compared with the less experienced students. But as the latter extract indicates, students who engage actively with the author's text, who 'possess' a minimum of necessary technical knowledge, and who dare to contradict the author's words, are indeed capable of producing feedback of comparable high quality.

What Makes Challenging Feedback Productive?

Challenging feedback involves and depends on active, responsive understanding (Bakhtin 1981 p. 280-282), in which meaning is created through tensions and struggle between at least two voices, as displayed in Extracts 3 and 4. Challenging feedback involves conflicting views and distinctions of more than one solution to any instance of a problem under study. This can productively enhance the student's ability to argue and realise that there could be more than one solution to a problem, and direct the feedback receiver to take an equally active stance towards the opinions and arguments expressed by her commentators. Challenging feedback comments are, in other words, productive to the extent that they can generate new thoughts and push the parties to reconsider their initial position(s). This is in fact a prerequisite for what Bakhtin calls the 'inner persuasive word'; when the student does not just accept the 'authoritative word' 'independent of any power it might have to persuade us internally' (Bakhtin 1981, p. 342) but evaluates alternatives and can 'match the speaker's word with a counter word' (Vološinov 1986, p. 102), or actively decide to agree. When I asked one of the male students what he saw as particularly helpful in peer and TA feedback, his answer was:

'The TA is much more experienced and has more knowledge [than us, first-year students]. He looks into problems far more methodically, and he dares to challenge us in a far more critical way.'

One potential problem of challenging feedback occurs if students are not capable of appropriating it for their own purposes, and if the amount of it becomes overwhelming. Indeed, it can be asserted that it is always possible to provide challenging feedback on a given text. The problem may develop that some texts have to arrive at a point where they are seen as 'fit for purpose'. At this point further challenging feedback may not be what is needed or wanted.

A COMPARISON BETWEEN PEER AND TA FEEDBACK

I will now continue to expand the analysis by comparing peer and TA feedback through the counting of the appearance (frequency) of each of the three feedback categories mentioned above. In general, it seems that peer feedback contained a lot of supportive claims about the author's text, most often in the form of affirmatory and in part also unspecified evaluative comments. Even when peers raised critique or suggested alternative answers or reformulations, their core message was easily overshadowed by a tendency to understate substantial critique, for example, by extensive use of moderators such as 'maybe' and 'you could perhaps' (cf. Extract 4) In contrast, the TAs used a more authoritative and instructive language, for example: (you) should, could, must (not), ought (to), etc. This may either lead to superficial agreement or to serious reconsiderations in the students. The TAs seemed also to ask more guided and open questions. Supportive claims were built into a more substantive critique, and praise was never the main ingredient. Feedback from TAs was generally more complex and covered a much broader range of issues. There were, however, many instances also of substantial peer critique, as shown in Table 1 below.

Table 1. Frequency and distribution of feedback

Feedback Category	Peer feedback			TA feedback		
	Feedback comments	Number of papers*	Comments per paper	Feedback comments	Number of papers*	Comments per paper
Affirmatory	433 (33.1%)	96	3.2	37 (10.4%)	22	0.6
Evaluative	478 (36.6%)	105	3.5	78 (22%)	30	1.3
Challenging	396 (30.3%)	105	2.9	240 (67.6%)	48	4.1
Total	1307 (100%)	137	9.6	355 (100%)	59	6.0

* 'Number of papers' refers to numbers of posted assignments, in which each of the three feedback categories was found.

Distribution of the Three Categories in Peer and TA Feedback

Let us then take a closer look at the frequency and distribution of affirmatory, evaluative, and challenging feedback, and how it relates to peer and TA e-feedback.

As Table 1 shows, almost seven out of ten peer comments were either affirmatory (33.3 per cent) or evaluative (36.6 per cent). Challenging comments constituted 67.6 per cent of TA feedback, but only 30.3 per cent of the peer feedback fell into the same category. Additionally, I have analysed the length of peer comments versus TA comments, and I found that the latter were considerably longer than those given by peers. This was particularly the case for challenging comments.[10] These findings are consistent with an earlier study by Tuzi (2004), where the amount of advice, alternatives and criticism was overwhelmingly given by instructors, by a ratio of 10:1, whereas praise, the second most common response type amongst peers, was given far more often by the students than by the instructors (4.5:1).

ORDER OF THE COMMENTATORS

Nearly all the assignments I have analysed received comments by more than one person, and I wanted to find out if there were any systematic variations in the distribution of the three feedback categories, depending on the order in which they were given. In the interviews I was told by some students that they found it far more demanding to submit the first comments, as would be expected, but also that they felt that some of the commentators who followed tended to agree with and repeat what they had arrived at as the first commentator. The results of the content analysis give some empirical support to the students' experience of this unintended effect of the e-feedback system (see below). This finding was partially explained by first-year student Marcus, who stated:

> If you are the second commentator it's easy to believe that the first person has done his part of the job. And you agree with what they have written, and you think: All right, they are more thorough and they have got it right. (Interview, Marcus, 20.06.2005).

If Marcus's statement is descriptive of a common practice or inclination in the learning community, this may reduce the chances for the writer to receive multiple perspectives on what she has written. There are, however, reasons to treat this assumption with care, because students can 'naturally' exhaust their feedback and just add what they think is missing in the previous feedback. In other words, the first feedback is qualitatively different from the following feedback, because the task is different as a consequence of the nature of asynchronous technology embedded in the VLE. The first feedback is about evaluation of the original message. The follow-up feedback is evaluation of the feedback itself. This is unavoidable, even if the students were instructed not to comment on others' comments in order to concentrate on producing the most useful feedback to the person who took on the task of writing the assignment.

---

10 In challenging feedback, the TAs write on average 6.6 paragraphs, while students write on average 2.7 paragraphs. The corresponding numbers for evaluative feedback were 1.9 (peer comments) and 2.6 (TA comments).

Table 2 displays the distribution of affirmatory, evaluative, and challenging feedback in relation to the order in which the feedback was given (TA comments are not included).

Table 2. Order of feedback comments in relation to distribution between affirmatory, evaluative and challenging feedback

Feedback Category	Order of feedback comments			
	1st	2nd	3rd	4th
Affirmatory	42%	42.4%	11.4%	3.7%
Evaluative	43.8%	39.9%	11.8%	3.5%
Challenging	50.0%	35.9%	12.3%	1.8.%

The result from the content analysis substantiates the significant role of the first commentator. Almost half (195 out of 396 comments) of the total amount of challenging student feedback was actually given by the first commentator. The results from Table 2 also indicate that the most general feedback pattern is that the first commentator provides challenging feedback, followed by affirmatory or evaluative feedback by the second and the third commentator. Moreover, the comments from the second and the third commentator seem to be strongly influenced by the first commentator's response, often agreeing with or reformulating first commentator's arguments and perspectives.

To summarise, my analysis strongly indicates that the TAs were far more critical about the author's text than were fellow students commenting. It should be mentioned, though, that the TAs commonly incorporated at least one positive comment about each text segment. Although the TA was the only person to give extensively responses on the others' feedback, inter-textual feedback references were, to a less but still significant extent, utilised in freshmen's comments on each other's writing. The data material also consisted of 'self-directed' written comments, in which the students raised questions, made statements indicating their own insecurity towards the given problem, or simply referred to their own task approach. This finding further underscores that electronically mediated feedback is a multifaceted and sophisticated dialogic activity.

CONCLUSION AND PEDAGOGICAL IMPLICATIONS

In this article I have identified and discussed three different feedback categories from the interchange of written comments between twenty first-year law students and two TAs. I have discussed them in terms of their learning potential and their functions as 'building blocks' in a complex web of different role positions between peers and TAs, disciplinary characteristics of the study of law, the overall learning design of the particular law programme at the Bergen law faculty, and the dialogic dynamics involved in asynchronous multivoiced e-feedback. Taking a Bakhtinian dialogic approach to the emerging pedagogical genre of e-feedback, I have argued that it is crucially important for text respondents to challenge the text of the author actively, in order to provide useful comments on the subject content and trigger new and active understanding. A dialogical perspective seems particularly useful for analysing feedback practices in higher education because this is a context where knowledge claims are always challenged and where new knowledge is created through dialogical confrontations between often opposing viewpoints and paradigms. In this study, I have attempted to demonstrate that productive feedback not only serves a narrow purpose of 'getting it right' for the exam, but of producing independently-thinking future members of the legal profession. Thus, productive feedback is not restricted to whether the writer finds the comments useful or not. Rather, I view it as a discursive learning practice, shaped by the sociocultural circumstances and the overall learning design of the law faculty, in addition to each student's participation in the VLE. Furthermore, my analysis cast light on the wider communicative circumstances when multiple respondents are commenting on the same content asynchronously and sequentially in VLE.

The overall findings suggest that systematic multivoiced e-feedback offers students unique opportunities to develop their own authoritative voice and grow as independent thinkers who are able use the varied voices they meet as raw material for their own meaning-making in the discipline. Here it is important also to underline that this is a long-term goal that may only be accomplished because the feedback system is integrated in the teaching and learning system over the three first years. By comparing and contrasting some of the core differences between affirmatory, evaluative, and challenging feedback I have tried to argue especially for the productive learning aspects of challenging feedback. This does not mean that confirmative and evaluative feedback do not have merits for the writer by providing motivation, reformulation of their own ideas and examples of other styles of writing. They all have their place in peer feedback. A clear finding from the interviews is that the students had most confidence in the feedback from the TAs, a finding which is consistent with previous research (e.g. Zhang 1995), and my interpretive content analysis, in combination with information through in-depth interviews with students, leaves no doubt of the important contributions made by trained TAs who generally give substantial and challenging feedback. The learning potential for advanced students who choose to qualify themselves as a TA in such a study system is considerable, but my main focus in this study has been on the learning process of first-year law students. Because of the extensive quantity of writing exercises and the interactive feedback system, embedded in the law faculty's learning ecology, students at this institution become quite skilled academic writers even during their first year of study. This is confirmed by experienced external assessors and by the fact that the exam results have radically improved since the introduction of the VLE and the new assessment regime (cf. Vines & Dysthe, in press). Without the VLE, given the distribution and organisation of the huge amounts of weekly assignments and comments, it would be practically impossible to achieve timely multivoiced feedback. The transparency afforded by the technology is invaluable in providing students with opportunities of being confronted with other's voices on a regular basis, and thus becomes legitimate participants in an ongoing professional discourse, characterised by distinctive dialogic features and communicative patterns.

In the context of Norwegian legal education, the introduction of e-feedback is in fact a major shift from previous models and changes the concept of what it actually means to be a law student. It represents a break with a long tradition of the law student as a solo performer who focuses on competition and therefore keeps things to herself. The fact that the e-feedback is carefully structured and fully integrated into the curriculum makes it institutionally robust and meaningful for the students. Further actions should be taken in order for students to reap the full benefit of multivoiced e-feedback, for instance, better training in what it takes to give more challenging feedback, and enhance students' awareness about the importance of both giving and utilising challenging feedback in order to gain full benefit of the intensive task it is to write and comment on new assignments on a weekly basis. Closer consideration of the balance between just learning the exam genres and fostering independent thinkers for future work in highly demanding professions will hopefully have a positive effect on student learning, within and beyond legal education.

REFERENCES

Ahuvia, A. (2001). Traditional, interpretive, and reception based content analyses: Improving the ability of content analysis to address issues of pragmatic and theoretical concern. *Social Indicators Research*, 54(2), 139–172.

Andriessen, J., Erkens, G., van de Laak, C., Peters, N. & Coirier, P. (2004). Argumentation as negotiation in electronic collaborative writing: In J. Andriessen, M. Baker, & D. Suthers, (Eds), *Arguing to learn. Confronting cognitions in computer-supported collaborative learning environments*, 79–115. Dordrecht: Kluwer Academic.

Angeli, C., Valanides, N. & Bonk, C. J. (2003). Communication in a web-based conferencing system: The quality of computer-mediated interactions. *British Journal of Educational Technology*, 34(1), 31–43.

Arnseth, H. C. & Ludvigsen, S. (2006). Approaching institutional contexts: Systemic versus dialogic research in CSCL. *Computer-Supported Collaborative Learning*, 1(2), 167–185.

Askew, S. & Lodge, C. (2000). Gifts, ping-pong and loops-linking feedback and learning. In S. Askew (Ed.), *Feedback for learning*. London: Routledge Falmer.

Bakhtin, M. M. (1981). Discourse in the novel. In M. Holquist (Ed.), *The dialogic imagination: Four essays by M. M. Bakhtin*, Austin, TX: University of Texas Press (C. Emerson & M. Holquist, Trans.).

Bakhtin, M. M. (1986). C. Emerson & M. Holquist (Eds.), *Speech genres and other late essays*. Austin: University of Texas Press (V. W. McGee, Trans.).

Bangert-Drowns, R. L., Kulik, C.-L. C., Kulik, J. A. & Morgan, M. (1991). The instructional effect of feedback in test-like events. *Review of Educational* Research, 61(2), 213–238.

Barnett, D. L. (2008). Form ever follows function: Using technology to improve feedback on student writing in law school. *Valparaiso University Law Review*, 42(3), 755–795.

Baxter, L. A. (1992). Content analysis. In B. Montgomery & S. Duck (Eds.), *Studying interpersonal interaction*, 239–254. New York: Guilford Press.

Black, A. (2005). The use of asynchronous discussion: Creating a text of talk. *Contemporary Issues in Technology and Teacher Education*, 5(1), 5–24.

Blignaut, A. S., & Lillejord, S. (2006). Lessons from a cross-cultural learning community. *South African Journal of Higher Education*, 19, 168–185.

Bonk, C. J., Malikowski, S., Angeli, C., & East, J. (1998). Web-based case conferencing for preservice teacher education: Electronic discourse from the field. *Journal of Educational Computing Research*, 19(3), 267–304.

Bonk, C. J., Wisher, R. A., & Lee, J.-Y. (2004). Moderating learner-centred e-learning: Problems and solutions, benefits and implications. In T. S. Roberts (Ed.), *Online collaborative learning: Theory and practice*, 54–85. Hershey: Information Science Publishing.

Brown, S. & Smith, B. (1997). *Getting to grips with assessment.* Birmingham, UK: Staff and Educational Development Association.

Carson, J. & Nelson, G. (1996). Chinese students' perceptions of ESL peer response group interaction. *Journal of Second Language Writing*, 5(1), 1–19.

Coffin, C., Painter, C. & Hewings, A. (2005). Patterns of debate in tertiary level asynchronous text-based conferencing. *International Journal of Educational Research*, 43(7/8), 464–480.

Crook, C. K., Gross, H. & Dymott, R. (2006). Assessment relationships in higher education: The tension of process and practice. *British Educational Research Journal*, 32(1), 95–114.

De Wever, B., Schellens, T., Valcke, M., & Van Keer, H. (2006). Content analysis schemes to analyze transcripts of online asynchronous discussion groups: A review. *Computers and Education*, 46(1), 6–28.

Dennen, V. P. (2008). Looking for evidence of learning: Assessment and analysis methods for online discourse. *AssessmentComputers in Human Behavior,* 24(2), 205–219.

Duncan, S. & Ritchie, D. T. (2003). How judges, practitioners, and legal writing teachers assess the writing skills of new law graduates: A comparative study. *Journal of Legal Education*, 53(1), 80–102.

Dysthe, O., Raaheim, A., Lima, I., & Bygstad, A. (2006). *Undervisnings- og vurderingsformer. Pedagogiske konsekvenser av Kvalitetsreformen. Evaluering av Kvalitetsreformen. Delrapport 7* [Teaching and assessment. Pedagogical consequences of the Quality Reform. Report no. 7]. Oslo: NIFU STEP (Norwegian Institute for Studies in Innovation, Research and Education), University of Bergen.

Dysthe O., Lillejord, S., Wasson B., & Vines A. (in press). Productive e-feedback in higher education – Two models and some critical issues. In S. Ludvigsen, A. Lund & R. Säljö (Eds), *Learning in social practices. ICT and new artefacts – transformation of social and cultural practices*. London: Pergamon.

Faigley, L. & Witte, S. (1981). Analyzing revision. *College Composition and Communication*, 32(4), 400–414.

Fairclough, N. (1992). *Discourse and Social Change*. Cambridge: Polity Press.

Fairclough, N. (2003). *Analysing discourse. Textual analysis for social research*. London: Routledge.

Ferris, D. (2003). *Response to student writing: Implications for second language students*. Mahwah, NJ: Lawrence Erlbaum Associates.

Freedman, S. W. & Sperling, M. (1985). Written language acquisition: the role of response and the writing conference. In S. W. Freedman (Ed.), *The acquisition of written knowledge: Response and revision*, 106–130. Norwood, NJ: Ablex.

Gibbs, G. & Simpson, C. (2004). Conditions under which assessment supports students' learning. *Learning and Teaching in Higher Education*, 1, 3–31.

Goodrich, P. (1987). *Legal discourse. Studies in linguistics, rhetoric and legal analysis*. London: Macmillan.

Hagelien, P. & Vonen, M. (1994). *The Norwegian legal system. An introductory guide*. Bergen: Advokatfirmaet Schødt.

Hansen, M. N. (2001). Closure in an open profession. The impact of social origin on the educational and occupational success of graduates of law in Norway. *Work, Employment and Society*, 15(3), 489–510.

Hattie, J. & Timperley, H. (2007). The power of feedback. *Review of Educational Research*, 77(1), 81–112.

Henri, F. (1995). Distance learning and computer-mediated communication: Interactive, quasi-interactive or monologue? In C. O. Malley (Ed.), *Computer supported collaborative learning*. Berlin: Springer Verlag.

Hewings, A. & Coffin, C. (2006). Formative interaction in electronic written exchanges: Fostering feedback dialogue. In F. Hyland & K. Hyland (Eds), *Feedback in second language writing. Contexts and issues*. Cambridge: Cambridge University Press.

Holquist, M. (2002). *Dialogism: Bakhtin and his world*. London: Routledge.

Hounsell, D. (2003). Student feedback, learning and development. In M. Slowey & D. Watson (Eds), *Higher education and the lifecourse*. Maidenhead, Berkshire: Open University Press.

Hyland, F. & Hyland, K. (2001). Sugaring the pill. Praising and criticism in written feedback. *Journal of Second Language Writing*, 10(3), 185–212.

Hyland, F. & Hyland, K. (2006). Interpersonal aspects of response: Constructing and interpreting teacher written feedback. In K. Hyland & F. Hyland (Eds), *Feedback in second language writing*. Cambridge: Cambridge University Press.

Hyland, F. (2000). ESL writers and feedback: Giving more autonomy to students. *Language Teaching Research*, 4(1), 33–54.

Hyland, K. (2003). *Second language writing*. Cambridge: Cambridge University Press.

Innes, R. B. (2007). Dialogic communication in collaborative problem solving groups. *International Journal for the Scholarship of Teaching and Learning*, 1(1), 1–19.

Jacobs, G., Curtis, A., Braine, G., & Huang, S. (1998). Feedback on student writing: Taking the middle path. *Journal of Second Language Writing*, 7(3), 307–317.

Jensen, K. (1997). Studying law – A risky business. A study among Norwegian Law students. *Young* 5(1), 21–38.

Jeong, A. (2003). Sequential analysis of group interaction and critical thinking in online threaded discussions. *The American Journal of Distance Education*, 17(1), 25–43.

Johnson, D. W. & Johnson, R. T. (2009). Energizing learning: The instructional power of conflict. *Educational Researcher*, 38(1), 37–51.

Karseth, B., & Solbrekke, T. D. (2006). Characteristics of graduate professional education: Expectations and experiences in psychology and law. *London Review of Education*, 4(2), 149–176.

Kissam, P. C. (2003). *The discipline of law schools: The making of modern lawyers*. Durham, N.C.: Carolina Academic Press.

Lea, M. & Street, B. (1998). Student writing in higher education: An academic literacies approach. *Studies in Higher Education*, 23(2),157–172.

Lillejord, S. & Dysthe, O. (2008). Productive Learning Practice. A theoretical discussion based on two cases. *Journal of Education and Work*, 21(1), 75–89.

Lindblom-Ylänne, S. & Pihlajamäki, H. (2003). Can a collaborative network environment enhance essay-writing processes? *British Journal of Educational Technology*, 34(1), 17–30.

Linell, P. (1998). *Approaching dialogue: Talk, interaction and contexts in dialogical perspectives*. Amsterdam: John Benjamins.

Littleton, K. & Whitelock, D. (2005). The negotiation and co-construction of meaning and understanding within a postgraduate on-line learning community. *Journal of Learning Media & Technology*, 30(2), 147–164.

Makitalo, K., Hakkinen, P., Leinonen, P., & Jarvela, S. (2002). Mechanisms of common ground in case-based web discussions in teacher education. *The Internet and Higher Education*, 5(3), 247–265.

Markova, I. (2003). *Dialogicality and social representations*. Cambridge: Cambridge University Press.

Matusov, E. (1996). Intersubjectivity without agreement. *Mind, Culture, and Activity*, 3(1), 25–45.

Matusov, E. (2007). Applying Bakhtin scholarship on discourse in education: A critical review essay. *Educational Theory*, 57(2), 215–237.

Matusov, E., Hayes, R. & Pluta, M. J. (2005). Using discussion webs to develop an academic community of learners. *Educational Technology & Society*, 8(2), 16–39.

Mendoca, C. & K. Johnson (1994). Peer review negotiations: Revision activities in ESL writing instruction. *TESOL Quarterly*, 28(4), 745–768.

Miller, M. C. (2002). Norway. In H. M. Kritzer (Ed.), *Legal systems of the world. A political, social, and cultural encyclopedia, Vol. III*. Oxford: ABC-CLIO.

Morson, G. & Emerson, C. (1990). *Mikhail Bakhtin. Creation of a Prosaics*. Stanford, CA: Stanford University Press.

Mory, E. H. (2003). Feedback research revisited. In D. H. Jonassen (Ed.), *Handbook of research on educational communications and technology*, 745–783. Mahwah, NJ: Lawrence Erlbaum.

Na, Y. H. (2003). *A Bakhtinian analysis of computer-mediated communication: How L1 and L2 students co-construct CMC texts in a graduate course*. Dissertation. Austin, TX: University of Texas.

Nicol, D. J. & Milligan, C. (2006). Rethinking technology-supported assessment in terms of the seven principles of good feedback practice. In C. Bryan & K. Clegg (Eds), *Innovative assessment in higher education*. London: Taylor and Francis.

Paulus, T.M. (1999). The effect of peer and teacher feedback on student writing. *Journal of Second Language Writing*, 8(3), 265–289.

Raaheim, A. (2006). Do students profit from feedback? *Seminar.net: Media, Technology & Lifelong Learning*, 2(2).

Ramaprasad, A. (1983). On the definition of feedback. *Behavioral Science,* 28(1), 4–13.

Ramsden, P. (2003). *Learning to teach in higher education*. London: RoutledgeFalmer.

Reddy, M. (1979). The conduit metaphor – a case of frame conflict in our language about language. In A. Ortony (Ed.), *Metaphor and thought*. Cambridge: Cambridge University Press.

Ricks S. E. & Istvan, L. L. (2007). Effective brief writing despite high volume practice: Ten misconceptions that result in bad briefs. *University of Toledo Law Review*, 38, 1113–1135.

Rourke, L. & Kanuka, H. (2007). Barriers to online critical discourse. *International Journal of Computer-Supported Collaborative Learning*, 1(2), 105–126.

Sadler, R. (1989). Formative assessment and the design of instructional systems. *Instructional Science*, 18(2), 119–144.

Schellens, T. & Valcke, M. (2005). Collaborative learning in asynchronous discussion groups: What about the impact on cognitive processing? *Computers in Human Behavior*, 21(6), 957–975.

Shute, V. J. (2008). Focus on formative feedback. *Review of Educational Research*, 78(1), 153–189.

Sidorkin, A. M. (1999). *Beyond discourse: Education, the self, and dialogue.* New York: State University of New York Press.

Sljuismans, D. (2002). *Student involvement in assessment. The training of peer assessment skills.* Dissertation, Open University of the Netherlands.

Smolka, A. L. B., De Góes, M. C. R. & Pino, A. (1995). The constitution of the subject: A persistent question. In J.V. Wertsch, P. D. Rio & A. Alvarez (Eds), *Sociocultural studies of mind*, 165–84. Cambridge University Press.

Tannacito, T. & Tuzi, F. (2002). A comparison of e-response: Two experiences, one conclusion. *Kairos*, 7(3).

Tannacito, T. (2001). Teaching professional writing online with electronic peer response. *Kairos*, 6(2), 1–7.

Tannacito, T. (2004). The literacy of electronic peer response. In B. Huot, B. Stroble, & Charles Bazerman (Eds), *Multiple literacies for the 21st century*, 175-194. New Jersey: Hampton Press.

Topping, K. (1998). Peer assessment between students in colleges and universities. *Review of Educational Research*, 68(3), 249–276.

Topping, K. (2003). Self and peer assessment in school and university: Reliability, validity and utility. In M. Segers, F. Dochy, & E. Cascallar (Eds), *Optimising new modes of assessment: In search of qualities and standards.* Dordrecht: Kluwer Academic.

Tsai, Y.-C. (2006). *The effects of asynchronous peer review on university students' argumentative writing.* Dissertation, Faculty of the Graduate School of the University of Maryland, College Park, MD.

Tuzi, F. (2004). The impact of e-feedback on the revisions of L2 writers in an academic writing course. *Computers and Composition*, 21(2), 217–235.

Veerman, A. L. (2003). Constructive discussion through electronic dialogue. In J. Andriessen, M. Baker, & D. Suthers (Eds), *Arguing to learn: Confronting cognitions in computer-supported collaborative learning environments,* 117–143. Boston, MA: Kluwer Academic.

Veerman, A. L., Andriessen, J. E. B., & Kanselaar, G. (2000). Enhancing learning through synchronous discussion. *Computers & Education*, 34 (2/3), 1–22.

Vines, A. & Dysthe, O. (in press). Productive learning in the study of law: The role of technology in the learning ecology of a law faculty. In L. Dirckinck-Holmfeld, C. Jones, & B. Lindström (Eds), *Conditions for productive learning in networked learning environments.* Rotterdam: Sense.

Volosinov, V. N. (1986). *Marxism and the philosophy of language.* Trans. L. Matejka & L. R. Titunik. Cambridge, MA, and London: Harvard University Press.

Ware, P. & Warschauer, M. (2006). Electronic feedback and second language writing. In K. Hyland and F. Hyland (Eds), *Feedback and second language writing*, 105–122. Cambridge: Cambridge University Press.

Wegerif, R. (2007). *Dialogic education and technology: Expanding the space of learning.* New York: Springer.

Wertsch, J. V. (1991) *Voices of the mind: A sociocultural approach to mediated action.* Cambridge, MA: Harvard University Press.

White, J. B. (2003). *From expectation to experience. Essays on law and legal education.* Ann Arbor, MI: The University of Michigan Press.

White, T. L. & Kirby, B. J. (2005). 'Tis better to give than to receive: An undergraduate peer review project. *Teaching of Psychology*, 32, 259–261.

Zhang, S. (1995). Re-examining the affective advantage of peer feedback in the ESL writing class. *Journal of Second Language Writing*, 4, 209–222.

Åkvåg, I. M. (2000). *Jusstudentene fra A til Å* [Law students from A to Å]. Master's thesis, Faculty of Law, University of Oslo.

In: Learning in the Network Society and the Digitized School   ISBN 978-1-60741-172-7
Editor: Rune Krumsvik

Chapter 14

THE NEED FOR RETHINKING COMMUNICATIVE COMPETENCE

Aud S. Skulstad

University of Bergen. Norway

ABSTRACT

View of language is fundamental to any second/foreign language teaching method or approach. This chapter discusses how such views have changed in the last few decades in the western world. An important claim that is made is that a redefinition of the term *communicative competence* is needed to take account of the aims of foreign language learning in a networked society and of the recent shift in view of language. Issues related to multimodality, multiliteracies and digital competence are central in the discussion. To illustrate certain problems in relation to the topic, some aspects of Norwegian curriculum guidelines and textbook activities are included in the discussion. The issues are relevant to language teaching in general, but specific examples are selected from the teaching of English as a foreign language.

Keywords: communicative competence, digital competence, digital *Bildung*, genre awareness, multiliteracies, multimodality.

INTRODUCTION

Views of language and language learning are the corner stones of any foreign language teaching method or approach. This chapter will concentrate on views of language and the aims of foreign language learning. Since the late 1970s, developing the learner's *communicative competence* has been the central aim of any second/foreign language programme in the western world. In the past few years, a number of researchers have argued that there is a need for a redefinition of the concept of communicative competence for various reasons (e.g. Skulstad 2002, Leung 2005, Kenning 2006). The present chapter makes the theoretical claim that the concept of communicative competence needs to be redefined to take account of the aims of foreign language learning in a networked society and of new views of language and communication. The task of suggesting a whole new specification of subcompetences of communicative competence is too large for a book chapter of this limited size. Instead, the chapter focuses on why this rethinking is needed. Central here is the projection of a multimodal view of language and the aims of developing the learners' multiliteracies and digital *Bildung*. The chapter points out problems that remain to be solved as to developing a redefined model of communicative competence.

Learners in the network society are sometimes referred to as the New Millennium Learners or Millennials[1]. These terms refer to generations born from the 1980s on. They are "the first generation to grow up surrounded by digital media, and most of their activities dealing with peer-to-peer communication and knowledge management, in the broadest sense, are mediated by these technologies" (Pedró 2007: 244). New Millennium Learners need to develop digital literacy or digital competence. A discussion of the Norwegian national curriculum guidelines of 2006 is interesting, because these guidelines specify that digital competence should be a basic skill in all school subjects in primary and secondary education and training. In this respect, Norway is rather unique compared to other countries. The chapter also includes an examination of two textbook activities which may serve to illustrate the problem of integrating digital competence in subject-related activities.

The next section examines communicative competence in a historical perspective and discusses the view of language on which communicative language teaching (CLT) is based. The third section identifies a new shift as to view of language in a networked society. The fourth section points out specific problems that remain to be solved as to specifying a new model of communicative competence. Included here is a discussion of the concepts of digital competence and digital *Bildung* as part of the overall aim of developing the learner's communicative competence. This section also includes a discussion of a new model of communication which has been proposed by Kenning (2006). In the next section, digital competence in a Norwegian context is discussed. The concluding section sums up the main arguments of the chapter.

COMMUNICATIVE COMPETENCE IN A HISTORICAL PERSPECTIVE

In the mid-1970s communicative approaches to second/foreign language learning emerged. These approaches share a view of language, but there is more variation as to theories of learning. That is also the reason why I prefer to use *approaches* in the plural form (as opposed to "the communicative approach" used e.g. in Brumfit and Johnson 1979, Howatt with Widdowson 2004). Language is seen as communication and the (non-linguistic and non-textual) context is crucial. This means that language is not seen as a system of component

---

[1] This term was first used by Howe and Strauss in their essay *Millennials Rising: The Next Great Generation* which appeared in 2000. This generation was contrasted to the previous one, *Generation X*. Competing terms to *New Millennium Learners* include the *Net Generation* (Tapscott 1999, Oblinger & Oblinger 2005), the *IM* [Instant-Message] *Generation* (Lenhart, Rainie & Lewis 2001), the *Gamer Generation* (Carstens & Beck 2005) and *homo zappiens* (Veen 2003).

parts (phonemes, morphemes, words, structures, sentence types), but as a unified event of utterances, discourses, texts, genres (Howatt with Widdowson 2004: 330).

The aim is to develop the learner's *communicative competence*, a term coined by the American sociolinguist Dell H. Hymes. The American linguist Noam Chomsky had been concerned with the language user's competence, referring to his or her knowledge of the language which enables him or her to produce and understand an indefinitely large number of grammatically well-formed sentences. Hymes called Chomsky's view of competence and performance a "Garden of Eden view" in the sense that the speaker's competence is "an ideal innately-derived sort of power" as a contrast to performance which may be seen as imperfect of "fallen" compared to competence (Hymes 1972). He said that "There are rules of use without which the rules of grammar would be useless" (1972: 278). In other words, he saw the need for a term which took sociolinguistic and sociocultural factors into account. Another important source of influence within CLT was M. A. K. Halliday's notion of *meaning potential*. He stated that "learning the mother tongue consists of mastering certain basic functions of language and developing a meaning potential in respect of each" (Halliday 1975: 33). *Meaning potential* refers to the semantic options that are available to participants in social interaction. His direct influence is seen most clearly in the Council of Europe's Threshold level documents (van Ek 1976, van Ek and Trim 1991) providing extensive checklists of what language activities, topics, communicative functions and notions are likely to be particularly useful to foreign language learners.

The concept of communicative competence has been redefined a number of times by people like Canale and Swain (1980), Canale (1983), van Ek (1986), Council of Europe (2001). Based on Hymes' concept of communicative competence, Canale and Swain (1980) identified three elements of communicative competence: grammatical competence, sociolinguistic competence and strategic competence. Grammatical competence comprises competence as to linguistic aspects such as grammar, lexis and phonology. Sociolinguistic competence refers to awareness of the social context of interaction (status, role, degree of formality, attitude, purpose etc.). Strategic competence refers to strategies employed to avoid breakdown in communication and other potential difficulties, and how to deal with these problems when they occur. A fourth subcompetence was added by Canale (1983), discourse competence. This type of competence implies an awareness of how expression units link to form larger discourse units.

van Ek (1986) specified two more subcompetences of communicative competence: sociocultural competence and social competence. Sociocultural competence includes *Landeskunde*, but it also goes beyond the cognitive domain to include aspects such as attitudes, opinions, value-systems and emotions. Social competence refers to the will (motivation, attitude, self-confidence) and the skill (empathy, ability to handle social situations) to communicate.

In 2001, the Council of Europe made a new specification of what they call the user/learner's competences. They made a binary division into *general competences* and *communicative language competences*. *General competences* are specified as declarative knowledge (knowledge of the world, sociocultural knowledge and intercultural awareness), skills and know-how (practical skills and know-how, intercultural skills and know-how), "existential" competence (attitudes, motivations, values, cognitive styles, personality factors etc.) and ability to learn. *Communicative language competences* are split into linguistic competences, sociolinguistic competence and pragmatic competences. Pragmatic competences include the "traditional" term *discourse competence* and also *functional competence*. The latter term refers to the abilities to use and interpret communicative language functions (e.g. asking the way, thanking somebody) and knowledge of what they call "text design". Included in the term *text design* are aspects such as the rhetorical organization of a specific genre and ability to interpret and use discourse patterns (e.g. problem-solution patterns and question-answer schemata). As I see it, there is a need for a respecification of the foreign language user/learner's competences. Reasons for this will be presented below.

A SHIFT IN VIEW OF LANGUAGE

In the last few years, we have witnessed a shift in view of language. Language is still seen as a unified event of utterances, discourses, texts and genres, but researchers and scholars are now projecting a multimodal view of language. In practice, this means that modern technologies have made other means of communicating beside spoken and written language readily available to the average participant in a communicative situation. A consequence of this fact is that our genre repertoire for consumption and production has been widened. Taking a multimodal view of language means to acknowledge the fact that multiple semiotic resources (written words, sound-tracks, visuals, video-clips etc.) combine and interact to make meaning.

As for the aims of language learning, the term *multiliteracies* is frequently used. It refers to the multiplicity of communication channels and media in the networked society and the increasing cultural and linguistic diversity. The term was coined by "the New London Group" who met in 1994 to discuss the future of literacy teaching (Cope and Kalantzis 2000). Kellner (2002: 163) uses the term *multiple literacies* to refer to "the many different kinds of literacies needed to access, interpret, criticise, and participate in the emergent new forms of culture and society". Buckingham (2006: 275) describes the need for *multiple literacies* in the following way:

> The increasing convergence of contemporary media means that we need to be addressing the skills and competencies – the multiple literacies – that are required by the whole range of contemporary forms of communication. Rather than simply adding literacy to the curriculum menu, or hiving off information and communication technology into a separate school subject, we need a much broader reconceptualisation of what we mean by literacy in a world that is increasingly dominated by electronic media.

First, he makes the important point that the use of ICT should not constitute a separate school subject, but form an integral part of the other school subjects. Second, he points out the need for a reconceptualisation of literacy in the network society. Warschauer (1999: 162-163) specifies some aspects of this new type of literacy. Learners need to

- understand how grammar of text as well as grammar of visual design combine to express meaning
- learn the types of genres and rhetorical structures that are used in particular media

- learn enough about cultural and dialectical differences to choose appropriate communication strategies
- have a clear and meaningful purpose for the reading and writing activities they undertake.

"Grammar of visual design" is a concept which appears in Kress and van Leeuwen (1996). It refers to the ways in which visual elements (depicted elements such as people, places, objects) are combined into a meaningful whole or visual "statements".

It is important to consider the fact that a classroom situation dominated by "old" technologies such as books, pencils, blackboards, maps, overhead projectors etc. also involves a range of modes of representation. Even a printed page is never monomodal: it includes several modes of representation such as linguistic, graphic and spatial (Baldry and Thibault 2006). The introduction of new technologies into the classroom has widened the range of modes.

Schools within the western world have a long tradition for analysing the relationship between different modes of representation in the case of advertisements that appear in the press, on radio, television, cinema or outdoor. As for other multimodal genres, this relationship has been much less systematically treated in schools. Text producers often learn to use multimodal sources for meaning making outside school. Every other year the "Network for IT Research and Competence in Education" (ITU) at the University of Oslo carries out a longitudinal survey of the use of ICT in Norwegian schools. The first survey was carried out in 2003 and the third one, the "ITU Monitor 2007", was published in October 2007. One of the findings in this survey was a discrepancy between the number of pupils using multimedia resources on a regular basis (daily, weekly or monthly) at home versus at school. 499 schools participated in the survey. 31 per cent of the pupils in grade 7 said that they used ICT to produce multimedia texts at school, whereas 43 per cent did this at home. In grade 9 the figures were 30 per cent at school versus 47 per cent at home, and in the second year of upper secondary school the figures were 28 per cent at school versus 47 per cent at home. This is important in the sense that it proves that "most pupils already have the competence to deal with sophisticated learning environments where digital resources are an important asset" (Pedró 2007: 261-262). A problem here is that learners may be seen as digital natives whereas teachers may be seen as digital immigrants of the networked society. Liestøl (2006) discusses one way of overcoming this difference in which both parties may pool their knowledge and abilities. Learners often possess what Buckingham (2006) calls *game literacy*, and language teachers are trained within the analysis of literary texts. Teachers and learners can benefit from each others' abilities by comparing rhetorical strategies and genre aspects in novels by Tolkien or Rawlings, for instance, to strategies and genre variations found in computer games based on the same novels. Liestøl (2006) points out that the results of this type of project work should be presented in the form of multimodal texts that are digitally produced.

SOME PROBLEMS THAT REMAIN TO BE SOLVED

Leung (2005) points out that Hymes' concept of communicative competence was originally developed for ethnographic research. When it was transferred to the context of language teaching and learning it came to be based on abstracted contexts and idealized social rules of use based on native-speaker norms (British English or American English). Computer-assisted means of communication has largely increased the possibilities for communicating with non-native speakers of a foreign language as well as for interacting with native speakers. Leung claims that *communicative competence* should be redefined to take account of new knowledge of language use as documented in research on World Englishes, English as a lingua franca and Second Language Acquisition. A consequence of the increased focus on languages used as a lingua franca and e.g. global English(es) is that Successful Users of English (SUEs) has been introduced as an alternative term to native users of English (Prodromou 2003, O'Keeffe, McCarthy and Carter 2007). What this means is that SUEs may not fully master all the various idiomatic expressions, for instance, as native speakers do, but they may be able to compensate for this by various communicative strategies which still make them into "expert users" of English. A consequence of this fact is that communicative strategies of this type would occupy a more central role in a model of communicative competence.

To some extent it is fair to claim that The Council of Europe's (2001) specification of communicative competence does not reflect to a large extent the fact that learners need to learn to communicate in a networked society. This specification briefly mentions that "Users of the Framework may wish to consider and where appropriate state: which media the learner will need/be equipped/be required to handle a) receptively b) productively c) interactively d) in mediation" (Council of Europe 2001: 95). Their list of media includes "computer", but the specific examples are limited to "e-mail, CD Rom, etc." (ibid.: 94). Kenning (2006: 368) points particularly to the need for taking into consideration "the ways in which technology affects communication processes". Having primarily computer mediated communication (CMC) in mind, Kenning (2006) identifies five variables of communication: space coordinates, time coordinates, range of symbolic cues, interactivity and action orientation. [2]

As for space coordinates, the use of ICT has introduced a more complex element of space in terms of the notion of virtual space (e.g. MUDs (Multiple-User Dungeon programs) and MOOs (MUD Object-Oriented programs)). The element of time coordinates has to do with differences between asynchronous and synchronous communication. In the latter case, the participants may be engaged in several conversations simultaneously and there may be multiple interwoven utterances in the case of multiple participants. The variable called range of symbolic cues refers to the number of semiotic modes applied in a given text. The fourth element is interactivity, and the variables included here are reciprocity and simultaneous feedback. Examples of reciprocal interactions are face-to-face interaction, telephone conversations and chat. Examples of non-reciprocal communication include listening to the radio, watching television, reading newspapers and writing e-mail messages. Simultaneous feedback refers to the feedback received while holding the floor (e.g. facial expressions, "ums", "ahs"). The final variable, action orientation, refers to degree of interpersonal specificity. In other words, it refers to strategies employed to enhance communication with the (imagined) reader or listener. The degree of specificity will be highest when engaging in face-to-face communication with someone one knows very well.

---

[2] Kenning's model represents a modified version of Thompson's (1995) framework of the key elements of communication.

As I see it, Kenning's model seems to work better for analysis of computer-assisted means of communication and as a parameter for selection of learning activities than as a model of communicative competence. The main advantage of this model is that it draws attention to the fact that models of communicative competence need to be broadened to take recent developments in communication in a networked society into account. The greatest disadvantage of the model is that the important variables of cultural and sociolinguistic contexts and genre are blurred.

One way of taking account of the fact that foreign language learners need to communicate in a networked society would be to introduce digital competence as a basic skill in all school subject. As mentioned above, Norway is rather unique in projecting this position in the national curriculum guidelines of 2006. Adding digital competence to subject-related activities opens for certain misinterpretations: it may be interpreted as the ability to operate digital tools. To avoid this misinterpretation, the concept of *Bildung* should be introduced as a central component. This is a concept which does not easily translate into English by means of one single term. One attempt at explaining what it means is the following: "the process and product of personal development guided by reason" (Gundem and Hopmann 1998: 2). The classic concept of *Bildung* absorbed ideas from the European Enlightenment in the works of scholars like Lessing, Kant, Herder, Goethe, Schiller, Pestalozzi, Herbart, Schleiermacher, Fichte, Hegel, Froebel and Diesterweg (Klafki 1998). [3] Klafki (1998) specifies three elements or abilities which *Bildung* aims to promote: self-determination, co-determination and solidarity. In other words, he is concerned with the relationship between *Bildung* and society.

By *self-determination* he refers to the aim of enabling every member of society "to make independent, responsible decisions about her or his individual relationships and interpretations of an interpersonal, vocational, ethical or religious nature" (Klafki 1998: 314). In the networked foreign language classroom this goes hand in hand with the aim of developing the learner's intercultural competence so as to avoid offensive remarks and misunderstandings when using the foreign language as a lingua franca, for instance. Central ideas are that learners should not only learn to operate digital tools technically, but more importantly, they should become able to make independent, responsible decisions about how to use the data and tools in cultural contexts and in interpersonal relationships.

Co-determination refers to the fact that individuals have the right as well as the responsibility to contribute to the cultural, economic, social and political development of the community. In the context of digital *Bildung*, *community* may refer to virtual communities as well as classroom communities.

By *solidarity* Klafki refers to the recognition of equal rights and at the same time recognition of the need for active help for less privileged groups whose opportunities for self-determination and co-determination are limited or non-existent. Relevant here is the relationship of ICT to democracy, social development, equity and social inclusion (see e.g. Warschauer 2006 and 2008).

A redefinition of the concept of communicative competence is not limited to an inclusion of the aspects of multimodality, multiliteracies and digital *Bildung*. The rethinking should also involve important variables of communication. One example is the "classic" variable of

---

3 In the last few decades, Wolfgang Klafki's concept of *der kategorialen Bildung* has become widely quoted (Klafki 2001 [1959]). A discussion of the different traditions and theories of *Bildung* goes beyond the scope of the present chapter.

context which has changed in the case of computer-assisted means of communication compared to offline-communication. In chat rooms, for instance, the participants may be geographically dispersed and their identities may be masked. In such cases their offline culture may be difficult to identify (Danet & Herring 2007). As we saw in Kenning's model above, CMC may also be asynchronous. Consequently, Malinowski's classic terms *context of situation* and *context of culture* need to be reinterpreted to allow for virtual realities and geographically dispersed participants.

The use of new technologies has also led to the emergence of new genres as well as to the use of "genre chains" in the case of hypertext. Hence, the need for developing learners' genre awareness becomes a prerequisite for successful communication. These are merely some illustrations of the rethinking that needs to be made in terms of a respecification of the subcompetences of communicative competence proposed by e.g. the Council of Europe.

DIGITAL COMPETENCE IN A NORWEGIAN CONTEXT

The Norwegian national curriculum guidelines for the 10-year compulsory school and upper secondary education and training of 2006, *The National Curriculum for Knowledge Promotion* (LK06) has added digital competence as a basic skill in all school subjects. In the subject of English, the basic skills are understood as follows: being able to express oneself in writing and orally in English, being able to read English, having skills in mathematics in English, and being able to use digital tools in English. This also illustrates the fact that digital competence is seen as being of equal importance to writing, reading and arithmetic. Report No. 16 to the *Storting* (2003) specifies that the concept of digital competence includes the central aspect of *Bildung* (*danning* in Norwegian) (NOU 2003,16: 77). In LK06, digital competence in the subject of English is explained in the following way:

> *Being able to use digital tools* in English allows for authentic use of the language and opens for additional learning arenas for the subject of English. English-language competence is in many cases a requirement for using digital tools, and using such tools may also help the development of English linguistic competence. Important features of the English subject in digital contexts include being critical of sources and aware of copyright issues and protection of personal privacy (LK06: 3).

The inclusion of critical skills is important.

The specification made in LK06 is very general and the problem of integrating digital skills into subject-related activities is left to teachers and textbook writers. Here is an example from a Norwegian textbook for learners of English in their first year of upper secondary school (age 16-17) which may serve to illustrate potential problems involved:

Presenting cross-curricular material

What is your favourite subject – apart from English, of course? Choose a topic from this subject and present it in English to your classmates either through 1) speaking, 2) writing or 3) computer skills.

A	B	C
SPEAKING	**WRITING**	**COMPUTER SKILLS**
Make an interview with an "expert" on your chosen topic (pair work).	Write a textbook page, include text, illustrations and tasks.	Make a power point presentation, include main points, illustrations and/or sound

(Heian, Lokøy, Ankerheim and Drew 2006: 208).

In the example above, the textbook writers have split the tasks into three different skills: speaking, writing and computer skills. This signals to the learner that computer skills are added as a fifth skill in addition to the four traditional ones: listening, speaking, reading, writing. Instead, it would have been a good idea for the textbook writers to point out that the speaking and writing tasks could also include the use of ICT. In task A, the learners could record the interview and link this audio file to a web page (e.g. home page) or podcast it. In task B, the learners could use word processors which would make it easy to insert photographs and other types of visuals in their texts. The textbook writers also blur the distinction between language skills and genre. In addition, they ignore the central aspects of intended audience and communicative purpose.

Another pitfall is that there may be too much focus on the form of presentation and material. Here is an example from a textbook for the optional programme subject International English (age 17-18):

Making a presentation
Notting Hill Carnival
　　The task is to make a multimedia presentation of the Notting Hill Carnival. Your resources can all be found on the net. You will need pictures, music and information about the Carnival.
　　The Wikipedia article about the Notting Hill Carnival is an excellent starting point for gathering information. A Google Images search will also give you pictures you can use.
　　If you want live videos you can find them on sites like YouTube that allow amateurs to share their work (Skifjeld, Rodgers, Sandor and Løken 2007: 197).

Here the aim is to make a multimedia (multimodal) presentation of a particular type of event. There is no mention of the communicative purpose of the presentation except to find pictures, music and information about the event. Obviously, the learners can make their individual choices of communicative purposes and genre, but to make sure that this important aspect is not ignored in the classroom, the textbook writers should either list examples of communicative purposes to choose from, or remind the learners that they need to make such decisions before they start their text production. There is no mention of genre. The learners could choose to make a TV commercial for the event, to make a news report from the Carnival last year, to make a travel report attracting people from abroad, and so forth. In the case of hypertexts, the learners may also choose to link different types of genres such as report, narrative, diagram etc. Ideally, the use of different semiotic modes such as pictures, video clips and music should emerge from a genuine communicative purpose. To become able to communicate successfully in a foreign language the learners must have a particular role, purpose, genre and intended audience in mind, and make choices of semiotic resources which match those genre-specific variables and communicative purposes. Only then can they develop genre awareness.

CONCLUSION

As we have seen, the call for a redefinition of communicative competence is based on an acknowledgement of the recent shift to a multimodal view of language and on the fact that foreign language students need to learn to operate in a large number of multimodal genres, and to consume and produce texts which are heterogeneous in terms of types of discourses, genres and semiotic resources. Students also need to learn what resources for meaning making that are available, and which consequences the choice of these resources may have for the consumer's interpretation of the text. In other words, both the view of language and the aims of language learning have changed.

The present chapter has discussed some of the problems that need to be solved in order to arrive at a redefined concept of communicative competence. I have also shown two examples of textbook activities which have served to illustrate pitfalls as to implementing the aim of developing digital competence. These textbook activities show that the important aspects of communicative purpose, genre, intended audience and role of digital material are sometimes ignored. I believe that the relevance of these two textbook examples goes beyond a Norwegian context because they illustrate the problem of integrating digital competence in subject-related activities. To succeed in doing so, the aim of developing digital competence should be included in the specification of communicative competence and in a rethinking of the classic variables of communication such as context, situation and culture. In addition, increasing numbers of learners are gaining access to computers and the Web. This fact has made it easier to design activities where the learners can communicate with real readers for genuine communicative purposes – a feature which no constructed textbook activity can match.

In addition to the changes as to view of language and aims of foreign language learning, the learners themselves may be seen to have changed as to their cognitive characteristics. New Millennium Learners are used to

a)   accessing information mainly on non-printed, digital sources,
b)   giving priority to images, movement, and music over text,
c)   feeling at ease with multi-tasking processes, and
d)   gaining knowledge by processing discontinued, non-linear information
                                                                (Pedró 2007: 255).

For language teachers, the cognitive characteristic of giving priority to images, movement, and music over text may not sound very promising for the future of language teaching and learning. However, as I see it, one should not view this primarily in terms of a competitive relation between visual image and verbal text, but accept that the concept of text also within the category of school genres is widened to include a number of semiotic resources for meaning making beside written and spoken language. Similarly, some people are worried about the literacy skills of New Millennium Learners who use texting language to a large extent with its characteristics of pictograms and logograms, initialisms, omitted letters, non-standard spellings, shortenings and genuine novelties (Crystal 2008). Rather than banning texting language from the classroom, the foreign language learners could be asked to translate SMS language to formal written English, or to discuss when it would be appropriate to use texting language and when not.

In the networked classroom, where each learner often has his/her own laptop, we frequently find learners who do not cope with the multitude of semantic options, and they end up using cut-and-paste techniques in their text production. A stronger focus on digital *Bildung* may compensate for this problem. Learners should be trained to develop critical skills in their selection of semiotic resources and their production of multimodal texts. They should also develop critical skills as to their consumption of texts, genres and media (Zammit 2007). Both the concepts of communicative competence and digital competence need to be redefined in terms of a more overt inclusion of the important aspects of genre awareness, critical skills and digital *Bildung*.

REFERENCES

Arnseth, H. C., Hatlevik, O., Kløvstad, V., Kristiansen, T. & Ottestad, G. (2007) *ITU Monitor 2007:Skolens digitale tilstand* [ITU Monitor 2007: The Schools' Digital Conditions]. Oslo: Universitetsforlaget.

Baldry, A. & Thibault, P. J. (2006) *Multimodal Transcription and Text Analysis*. London/Oakville: Equinox.

Brumfit, C. J. & Johnson, K. (Eds.) (1979) *The Communicative Approach to Language Teaching*. Oxford: Oxford University Press.

Buckingham, D. (2006) Defining digital literacy. *Digital kompetanse*. [*Nordic Journal of Digital Literacy*], 263-276.

Canale, M. & Swain, M. (1980) Theoretical bases of communicative approaches to second language teaching and testing. *Applied Linguistics*, 1, 1-48.

Canale, M. (1983) From communicative competence to communicative language pedagogy. In Richards, J. & Schmidt, R. (Eds.) *Language and Communication*. London: Longman, 2-27.

Carstens, A. & Beck, J. (2005) Get ready for the Gamer Generation. *TechTrends*, 49, 22-25.

Cope, B. & Kalantzis, M. (Eds.) (2000) *Multiliteracies: Literacy Learning and the Design of Social Futures*. London/New York: Routledge.

Council of Europe (2001) *Common European Framework of Reference for Languages: Learning, Teaching, Assessment*. Cambridge: Cambridge University Press.

Crystal, D. (2008) *txtng: the gr8 db8*. Oxford: Oxford University Press.

Danet, B. & Herring, C. (2007) Introduction. In Danet, B. & Herring, C. (Eds.) *The Multilingual Internet: Language, Culture and Communication Online*. Oxford: Oxford University Press, 3-39.

Ek, J. A. van (1976) *The Threshold Level for Modern Language Learning in Schools*. Strasbourgh: Council of Europe. (Published by Longman in 1977.)

Ek, J. A. van (1986) *Objectives for Foreign Language Learning*. Vol. 1: Scope. Strasbourg: Council for Cultural Co-operation.

Ek, J. A. van & Trim, J.L.M. (1991) *Threshold Level 1990*. Strasbourg: Council of Europe Press.

Gundem, B.B. & S. Hopmann (1998) Introduction: Didaktik meets curriculum. In Gundem, B.B & Hopmann, S. (Eds.) *Didaktik and/or Curriculum*. New York: Peter Lang, 1-8.

Halliday, M.A.K. (1975) *Learning How to Mean: Explorations in the Development of Language*. London: Edward Arnold.

Heian, B., Lokøy, G., Ankerheim, B. & Drew, I. (2006) *Experience*. English for the first year of upper secondary school. Oslo: Gyldendal.

Howatt, A.P.R. with Widdowson, H. G. (2004) *A History of English Language Teaching*. Second Edition. Oxford: Oxford University Press.

Howe, N. & Strauss, W. (2000) *Millennials Rising: The Next Great Generation*. New York: Vintage Original.

Hymes (1972 [1971]) On communicative competence. In Pride, J & Holmes, J. (Eds.) *Sociolinguistics: Selected Readings*. Penguin Books, 269-293.

Jewitt, C. (2006) *Technology, Literacy and Learning: A Multimodal Approach*. London/New York: Routledge.

Kellner, D. M. (2002) Technological revolution, multiple literacies, and the restructuring of education. In Snyder, I. (Ed.) *Silicon Literacies: Communication, Innovation and Education in the Electronic Age*. London: Routledge, 154-169.

Kenning, M. M. (2006) Evolving concepts and moving targets: communicative competence of communication. *International Journal of Applied Linguistics*, 16, 363-388.

Klafki, W. (2001 [1959]) Kategorial dannelse: Bidrag til en dannelsesteoretisk fortolkning av moderne didaktikk [*Der kategorialen Bildung*: Contributions to a Theoretical Interpretation of Modern Didactics in the Light of *Bildung*]. Translated by A. Gylland. In Dale, E.L. (Ed.) *Om utdanning: Klassiske tekster* [On Education: Classic Texts]. Oslo: Gyldendal, 167-203.

Klafki, W. (1998) Characteristics of critical-constructive Didaktik. In Gundem, B.B. & Hopmann, S. (Eds.) *Didaktik and/or Curriculum*. New York: Peter Lang, 307-330.

Kress, G. & van Leeuwen, T. (1996) *Reading Images: The Grammar of Visual Design*. London/New York: Routledge.

LK06 (2006) *The Knowledge Promotion*. Oslo: Ministry of Education and Research. Retrieved February 5th, 2008, from http://www.utdanningsdirektoratet.no/templates/udir/TM_Artikkel.aspx?id=2376

Lenhart, A., Rainie, L. & Lewis, O. (2001) *Teenage Life Online: The Rise of Instant-Message Generation and the Internet's Impact on Friendship and Family Relationships*. Washington DC: Pew Internet & American Life Project.

Leung, C. (2005) Convivial communication: recontextualizing communicative competence. *International Journal of Applied Linguistics*, 15, 119-144.

Liestøl, G. (2006) Sammensatte tekster – sammensatt kompetanse [Multimodal texts – compound competences]. *Digital kompetanse*. [*Nordic Journal of Digital Literacy*], 277-305.

NOU 2003: 16, *I første rekke. Forsterket kvalitet i en grunnopplæring for alle* [Report No. 16 to the *Storting*, First Priority. Improved Quality in Basic Education for All Pupils]. (Kvalitetsutvalget).

Oblinger, D. & Oblinger, J. L. (Eds.) *Educating the Net Generation.* Washington DC: Educause.

O'Keeffe, A., McCarthy, M. & Carter, R. (2007) *From Corpus to Classroom: Language Use and Language Teaching.* Cambridge: Cambridge University Press.

Pedró, F. (2007) The New Millennium Learners: challenging our views on digital technologies and learning. *Digital Kompetanse* [*Nordic Journal of Digital Literacy*], 2, 244-264.

Prodromou, L. (2003) In search of the successful user of English. *Modern English Teacher*, 12 (2), 5-14.

Skifjeld, K., Rodgers, D., Sandor, C., Huseby, E., & Løken, K. D. (2007) *Global Paths. Internasjonal engelsk, studiespesialiserende programfag* [Global Paths. International English, programme subject in Programme for Specialization in General Studies]. Oslo: N. W. Damm & Søn.

Skulstad, A.S. (2002) Developing genre awareness in the "online era". In A.M. Simensen (Ed.) *Teaching and Learning Foreign Languages: Issues and Ideas.* Acta Didactica. Oslo: Unipub, 141-160.

Tapscott, D. (1999) *Growing Up Digital: The Rise of the Net Generation.* New York: McGraw-Hill.

Thompson, J. B. (1995) *The Media and Modernity: A Social Theory of Media.* Cambridge: Polity Press.

Veen, W. (2003) A new force for change: homo zappiens. *The Learning Citizen*, 7, 5-7.

Warschauer, M. (1999) *Electronic Literacies: Language, Culture, and Power in Online Education.* London: Lawrence Erlbaum Associates.

Warschauer, M. (2006) Networking the Nile: technology and professional development in Egypt. In Inman, J. & Hewett, B. (Eds.) *Technology and English Studies: Innovative Professional Paths.* Mahwah, NJ: Lawrence Erlbaum, 163-177.

Warschauer, M. (2008) Whither the digital divide? In Kleinman, D.L, Cloud-Hansen, K.A., Matta, C. & Handesman, J. (Eds.) *Controversies in Science and Technology: From Climate to Chromosomes.* New Rochelle, NY: Liebert, 140-151.

Zammit, K. (2007) Popular culture in the classroom: interpreting and creating multimodal texts. In Mc Cabe, A., O'Donnell, M. & Whittaker, R. (Eds.) *Advances in Language Education.* London/New York: Continuum, 60-76.

In: Learning in the Network Society and the Digitized School   ISBN 978-1-60741-172-7
Editor: Rune Krumsvik   © 2009 Nova Science Publishers, Inc.

Chapter 15

INTERGENERATIONAL ENCOUNTERS – DIGITAL ACTIVITIES IN FAMILY SETTINGS

Pål Aarsand[1] & Liselott Assarsson[2]

1) Uppsala University, Sweden
2) Växjö University, Sweden

ABSTRACT

This chapter focuses on how families use digital technology in everyday life, and draws upon video recordings and interviews with children and adults in Swedish middleclass families. The study is inspired by discourse psychology and the ideas of governmentality in order to understand what counts as digital competence and how it is produced. We argue that digital competence is produced within families, but what counts as valid knowledge varies across activities. While traditional socializing practices often operate according to the adult as an expert and the child as the less knowledgeable, the present study shows that this knowledge relation is not static but is continuously negotiated in terms of who is to be positioned as the expert or novice. In addition, it is argued that because digital competence is seen as important knowledge in the network society, it is reason to believe that parents are willing as well as able to accept that children enter the position as experts in digital activities. Simultaneously, this means that adults act as responsible parents that create their own as well as their children's digital competence.

CHILDREN AND DIGITAL ACTIVITIES

'Becoming old too early from playing videogames'

(Aftonbladet 18th of June 2008)

'He chased young girls – 42-year-old pretended to be 12 year old on the web'

(Aftonbladet 11th of April 2008)

'18 year old stabbed to death – inspired by a computer game'

(Expressen 4th of August 2008)

Children's digital activities are a reoccurring topic discussed in the Swedish media. In newspapers, magazines and on the news bills, children's use of internet and digital games are often emphasized as highly problematic. The examples above are headings of articles from two of the biggest evening papers in Sweden. They all illustrate how digital activities; gameplay and participating in online communities, are seen as problematic when young peoples everyday lives are discussed. In articles like these, gameplay typically occurs together with violence, obesity, addiction, and lack of a social life, while online communities occur together with rape, paedophiles, murders, drugs, and bullying. In these descriptions, young people's digital activities are presented as risky behaviour. Yet, participating in online communities and playing digital games are part of children's everyday lives, particularly when they are at home (Erstad, Kløvstad, Kristiansen, & Søby 2005, Livingstone & Bovil 2001, Medierådet 2006). Thus, children's game playing as well as their participating in online communities may be considered a family issue.

While the media debate tends to describe children's digital activities as problematic, the political rhetoric focuses on how to make the citizens users of digital technologies. More precisely, there has been and still is an increasing debate about the necessity to become the digital literate citizen (e.g. European Commission 2005a, 2005b, Swedish Ministry of Enterprise, Energy and Communications 2007, Swedish National Agency for Improvement 2005). The European Union presents *digital competence* along more traditional basic competences such as writing, reading, and numeracy (Commission 2005a), and argues that digital competence, as one out of eight basic competences, is something that 'all individuals need for personal fulfilment and development, active citizenship, social inclusion and employment' (p. 13). Moreover, that digital competence has to be developed to a level that equips young people for adult life. In the political discourse, digital competence is considered important with regard to the individual's flexibility in the labour market (e.g. Ministerial Declaration 2006) as well as to make a nation succeed in the global economy (Commission 2005b). The necessity to develop digital competence is not made an object of discussion, rather it is seen as an inviolable fact. In northern European countries such as England, Sweden, Finland, Denmark and Norway, the educational system has become a central instrument for the governments to create digitally competent citizens. This turns digital competence into a topic for everyone involved in education, either as students or as parents. However, even though digital competence is high on the political agenda, 'it is not clear what is meant by this term, especially when we try to link in-school and out-of-school activities' (Erstad 2006 p. 418). When we look at the digital activities among school-aged children, it is obvious that most of these, in regard to the amount of time, as well as in variation of activities, take place outside educational settings (Drotner 2001, Erstad et al. 2005, Facer, Furlong, Furlong & Sutherland 2003, Kløvstad & Kristiansen 2004). Yet, there is little work on how computer activities in the homes of families are carried out.

DIGITAL COMPETENCE AND GAPS

Among scholars, digital competence has often been discussed in terms of *literacy*. Depending on the research field and the scholars' backgrounds, different prefixes have been used to describe and understand digital competence. Frequently used combinations include media literacy (e.g. Livingstone 2002), digital media literacy (Buckingham 2003), critical media literacy (Kellner 2002), digital literacy (Tyner 1998), information literacy (Eisenberg, Lowe, & Spitzer 2004), visual literacy (Jewitt 2005), and computer game literacy (Gee 2003). The variety of research foci underlines several central aspects of digital competence. First of all digital text consists of more than written words. Second, reading and writing texts demand competence in handling multiple modalities (Jewitt 2005, Manowich 2001), and third, there are different digital text genres (Bolter & Grusin 2000) that are not necessarily supported by the same digital technology (soft and/or hardware).

The question of digital competence and literacy has been discussed in relation to what has been called the *digital divide* (Aarsand 2007, Buckingham & Scanlon 2005, Facer & Furlong 2001, Gee 2003, Livingstone & Bober 2005, Papert 1996, Selwyn 2004, Tapscott, 1998). There is a gap between those who know how to act in a digital environment and those who do not. The research on the digital divide has been investigated as an asymmetrical knowledge relation between different socio-economic groups, ethnicities, genders, geographical places, and generations. In research on families, knowledge gaps between adults and children have traditionally been studied as socializing practices where children are seen as less competent actors who learn how the practices work (Fasulo, Loyd & Padiglione, 2007, Rogoff 2003, Kremer-Sadlik & Kim, 2007). When it comes to digital activities this asymmetrical knowledge relation has often been described as running the opposite way, where the child is considered as the most knowledgeable (Gee 2003, Papert 1993, Tapscott, 1998). David Buckingham (2005 p. 33) points to one central discussion in relation to the ongoing debate on digital divides when he writes, 'barriers to media literacy are primarily barriers to access (…). These barriers may be of different kinds: economic, institutional, social and personal'. Lately, the discussion of the digital divide has turned away from focusing on access to and ownership of digital technology to peoples' use and relationship with digital technology (e.g. Aarsand 2007, Facer et. al. 2003, Holloway & Valentine 2002, Selwyn 2004). Neil Selwyn (2004) argues that the questions that must be asked are how people engage with digital technology and what consequences this has on the short term and the long term. To be digitally competent does not necessarily indicate anything about the person's moral standards. The digitally competent citizen is able to enter relevant information on the web to, for instance write a thesis, but the same competence makes him/her able to access websites with child pornography and prostitutes. This ambivalence has made digital activities the topic for ethical discussions concerning 'preferable' ways of using digital technologies like the internet and digital games.

The present study of children's digital activities is conducted in Swedish families and focuses on interactions between adults and children. As an extension of the question of access to digital activities, we study how families deal with digital activities, how use is encouraged or prohibited *in situ*. Further on, we will discuss possible implications this may have in terms of digital competence. Inspired by the discussion above, we have used *digital competence* as an empirical concept to study what counts as legitimate and preferable ways of acting in digital activities in family settings.

NEGOTIATING DIGITAL ACTIVITIES

Digital activities in families can be seen both as the outcome of social organization of families and as ongoing negotiations about how these activities are understood and related to by the members of the family. To investigate digital activities in family life and how they create conditions for the production of digital competence, we have been inspired by discourse analysis and actor network theory (ANT). From discourse analysis, we have used the concepts of 'subject positioning' (Davids & Harré 1990, Goffman 1974, Potter & Wetherell, 1987) and 'governmentality' (Foucault 1991, Rose 1989), while from ANT we have use ideas regarding 'network' and 'agency' (Latour 1999, 2005).

Politics of Families

The meaning of the notion of families varies (Hertz & Marshall 2001). Despite of that, it has been claimed that 'the prime intimate social unit is the family; family members ideally provide secure environments that promote an openness to learn about how one should treat other people, build relationships, enact social identities, and at the same time, how one should apprehend and creatively reconfigure objects in the world' (Kremer-Sadlik 2007 p. 5). In short, the family can be seen as a social unit where members learn how to access and act in social life, which includes everything from how to handle artefacts, expectations from the school/job, to how one deals with strangers in online communities. As such, families can be considered as political bodies that are organized through different activities and the everyday negotiations that take place (Ochs & Taylor 1992). For instance, children's homework, how long the children are allowed to use the Playstation, and how to arrange furniture are issues discussed. In these negotiations, the participants learn how and what to negotiate as well as expectations, norms and rules of how to behave and evaluate actions. In short, how to act in social life is guided by rules negotiated in the situation at hand (Goffman 1974), as well as regulations and notions of normalities that circulate in the society (Rose 1989). In families, parents and children, have to deal not only with different ideas of what constitute digital competence, but also with images of internet and digital games.

The social and the cultural context are of importance in the politics of families; '…, it (the social and cultural context) inheres in each of us, maintained and reactivated constantly by the images that surround us – in advertising, on television, in newspapers and magazines, in the baby book' (Rose 1989 p. 213). Images and ideas of children and their digital activities in media and in political discourses underline the importance of knowing how to handle digital technology and environments "correctly". However, it is not enough to claim that the surroundings, in terms of images and ideas, has implications. Bruno Latour (2005) argues that we should trace the appearance of actors (actants), humans as well as objects, that make a difference to the activity. According to Michel Foucault's line of reasoning, the modern society and the subject could be discussed in terms of *governmentality* (Foucault 1991).

Governmentality means to govern with a certain mentality in order to shape the conducts of others. In advanced liberal democracies, governing takes place in an indirect way by structuring the field of possible action (Foucault 1982). Thus, the state is not the only unit governing; subjects govern each other and even govern themselves. Through acts of subjection, one governs oneself and regulates the conduct in line with certain expectations mediated through different channels, all shaping norms of how to act in different social practices. Thus, govermentality can be seen as an approach to everyday life and all power relations that the subject is part of, either in relation to other subjects or in relation to oneself. In short, how to be a responsible parent in relation to your children's digital activities depends on the expectations that operate in the situations, which shape patterns of possible/impossible and preferred/non-preferred actions. This disciplining process is not to be seen as oppressive, rather it could be considered a process in which the subject gets created and creates itself in relation to norms of how to act. The approach of governmentality is a way to understand what rationalities of governing are applied to digital activities in family settings, and why certain positions seem to reoccur in family interaction while others are never observed.

Negotiations, govermentality, and agents actualise the notion of *power*. In the present text, we argue that power is a way of understanding how actions modify other actions within the relationship between adults and children, as well as between social settings, such as family, school, and media. In other words, power is seen as relational and productive (cf. Foucault 1982). Thereby, power is understood as an assemblage of relations between agents that constitute fields of possible/impossible actions. Power and knowledge are intertwined (Foucault 1980); power needs knowledge about the object it operates on, and similarly as power defines what is considered to be legitimate knowledge. Power/knowledge becomes central to understanding how adults and children engage in digital activities.

Subject Positioning and Family Settings

We are members of the society, we are members of families and we participate in several activities every day. These activities include being parent, daughter, partner, employee, soccer player, child, and student. The identity position one takes and/or get positioned into may be of a relatively stable character, but it may also vary within the activity (Aronsson 1998, Antaki & Widdicome 1998, Goffman 1981).

In the question of how digital activities are carried out as possible consequences of family politics, we use identity in terms of *subject positioning* as an analytical tool. The concept of subject positioning describes how subjects relate to other participants, activities, and discourses (Bamberg 1997, Davies & Harré 1990, Edley & Wetherell 1997). Being positioned or entering a subject position means gaining access to conceptual repertoires, and ways of seeing and understanding the activities, where the participants are offered resources to deal with what happens (Lagenhove & Harré 1999). One is not fixed to a position, rather one engages in different activities, relations and subject positions. How to act, or where and when to act is not something the subject solely does by him/herself, rather '…they are patterns that he finds in his cultures and which are proposed, suggested and imposed on him by culture, his society and his social group' (Foucault 1988 p. 11). The subject's position and the meaning of this position are negotiated in the ongoing activity by using patterns and meanings that can be found in other activities as resources. For instance, what it means to be a father, president, pupil, mother, brother, or teacher is related to similar patterns across activities and practices. In terms of govermentality, it could be claimed that how to act in these subject positions is proposed, suggested, and imposed, as well as adjusted to, negotiated and challenged by the subject.

Various relations are being actualized within the family; the relations between adults, the relations between children and the relations between children and parents. The relations between parents and children is not necessarily an asymmetric knowledge relation where the parent is considered the expert and the child the novice (cf. Rogoff 2003, Lave & Wenger 1991) or, as it has been claimed in regards to the use of digital technology, the other way around (cf. Tapscott 1998). Rather, we see the knowledge relation as negotiations concerning what counts as valid knowledge in the situation. Regarding informal learning, Barbara Rogoff (2003) has by her notion of 'guided participation' shown how the cultural frames matter when it comes to how the expert structures participation of the novice. To understand the relation between subject positions, such as expert and novice, we have used the idea of guided participation.

DESIGN AND ACHIEVEMENT OF THE STUDY

The data form part of a larger study of the everyday lives of middle-class families in the USA, Italy, and Sweden. Since the middle-class succeeds in the educational system (cf. Bernstein 1980, Bourdieu 1984, Willis 1977), there is reason to believe that it identifies and relates to the demands raised in the educational system. This makes middle-class families suitable for studying rationalities that guide digital activities in family lives. In the present study, middle-class is defined by economic criteria. In total, three criteria were used for selecting families: (i) two adults working full time (ii) who own their own house, and (iii) who have at least two children, including one who is between 8 and 10 years old. The Swedish dataset includes 19 children between 5 and 13 years of age, and about 300 hours of video footage. Each family was filmed during an ordinary week, starting when they woke up in the morning, stopping when the children went to school, and resuming when they came home until they went to bed in the evening. Moreover, the different family members' activities were documented (every ten minutes) and coded using activity logs, which have provided us with a general overview of the data. In addition, children and parents were interviewed about their everyday life as a family.

All of the families had at least one computer, which was located in a communal space of the house. Furthermore, playing computer- and videogames, as well as using the internet were reoccurring activities (Aarsand & Aronsson, accepted). Despite the fact that children were the generation group that used the digital technology most frequently, intergenerational encounters in relation to digital activities occurred on a regular basis. A guiding question has been: how are digital activities accomplished in intergenerational encounters in families? Also, what rationalities of governing are constructed? What is considered digital competence, and how is this distributed among the family members?

On the basis of the activity logs and viewings of the footage, instances in which children and adults were engaged in computer activities were identified. All the chosen sequences have been transcribed in a simplified version of the conventions of conversation analysis

(Appendix 1). The children have been given pseudonyms, while the parents are called mother and father in order to keep the actors given name. The sequences were initially analyzed in Swedish before they were translated into English.

DIGITAL COMPETENCE, ACCESS AND POSITIONING

To become a digitally competent citizen, we must have experience in using digital technology. However, having a computer in your home is not the same as having access (Aarsand & Aronsson accepted, Facer et. al. 2003, Holloway and Valentine 2003, Selwyn 2004). Access is studied here as 'the ability to *manipulated* technology (and related software tools) in order to locate the content or information that one requires' (Buckingham 2005 p. 6).

In the present text, focus is placed on intergenerational encounters and the organization of digital activities. Two interrelated aspects have been of analytical interest; first, what is displayed as valid knowledge in terms of legible or illegible digital competence, and second, how this is carried out in relation to the subject positions negotiated by the family members. We will highlight three different types of digital activities and intergenerational encounters that regularly occurred in the families; gameplay (computer games and console games), talk about digital games, and internet activities.

Getting the Game Started

Accessing digital environments to get experience and to learn how they work is not without its problems. In the first example, we will see how an asymmetrical knowledge relation is established and sustained in order to make playing a computer game a possible activity Mikaela tries to start the computer game, 'Bob the Builder', on her own without succeeding. The excerpt begins when she has just called her father for help. Afterwards, he leaves Mikaela to play the game alone.

Excerpt 1

Participants: Father, Mikaela (5)
Place: Hall
Activity: Starting game

1	Father	Nope then we got to do like thi:s ((bends down and switches the computer
2		off and on))
3		(2)
4	Father	We reboot it
5		(3)
6	Father	Now you may wait a while then (.) then you may try it out by <u>yourself</u>
7		afterward then we will start it (.) here we will only look here wait
8		(3)
9	Mikaela	I want to[um:::

10	Father	[Wait na: wait a little we are not going to do it now because it
11		may lock itself
12		(22) ((PC starts))

...

43	Father	A:: wait until (.) wait until it is like usual again so you know when you
44		push that that personal
45	Mikaela	Who?
46	Father	That blue one next to the arrow has to disappear before you can push the
47		Button
48	Mikaela	Now? ((a window concerning the Internet connection appears on the
49		screen))
50	Father	Now, you can push those that one ((pointing at the screen))
51		(2)
52	Mikaela	Where?
53	Father	That one! ((the finger is still placed at the screen))
54	Mikaela	((Presses cancel))
55	Father	Like tha::t
56		(12) ((The screen turns dark))
57	Father	I am going to turn on that one ((turning on the speaker))
58		(4)
59	Father	Did it stopped?
60		(5)
61	Father	Now you will see that 'Bob the Builder' is coming

The father starts by evaluating Mikaela's previous act (line 1) before he tells her what to do to get the game started (line 4). Mikaela has already positioned the father as the expert by asking him to help her to start the game. The father enters the expert position simultaneously as he places Mikaela in a less knowledgeable position by confirming that she did not handle the problem correctly (line 1). During the first lines, the father talks loudly without addressing Mikaela; 'Nope then we got to do like thi:s' (line 1) and 'We reboot it' (line 4). This loud talking can be seen as making what he is doing visible as well as labelling the activity by telling her what it is called. The use of 'we' indicates that getting started is a common problem that they are going to solve together.

The father demonstrates how to solve Mikaelas starting up problems while he tells her that it takes time to reboot the computer (lines 6 and 7) and that she can do it by herself afterwards (line 6). Mikaela reacts to this utterance by taking the initiative to do it by herself: 'I want to um::' (line 9), an initiative that is immediately turned down by her father who starts to argue even before she has finished her sentence that the timing is wrong (line 10). The importance of timing is important to learn. Restarting as well as starting the computer is part of entering a computer game, and it is not like turning on the light. It takes some time, and it has to be finished before touching the keyboard. Thereby, knowing how to start a computer game also means knowing the exactly moment to press the keys. The computer becomes an actor that structures the sequenciality of the activity, which is verbalised by the father. Knowing how the computer will react and how to manipulate it is portrayed as important knowledge. To legitimate this knowledge, the father relates to Mikaela's experiences of the computer shutting down just a few minutes ago, which also may be the reason why Mikaela accepts his argument.

The fact that Mikaela has asked her father for help and the fact that he tells her what to do and when to do it, legitimates him as the expert in the situation (lines 6-7 and 10). When the father is positioned and positioning himself as the master, it implies that Mikaela is positioned as the novice in the situation. It can be seen how the father gradually explains more carefully how she is to act and, maybe more importantly, when to act in order to start the game. The question of time becomes the main topic. This lesson of sequenciality can be seen as the outcome of what the father displays as what-to-know-about-computers-as-actors. According to the father, Mikaela has to wait until the screen looks as usual (line 43). When the father uses the term usual, it indicates that he expects Mikaela to know what the screen looks like. By telling Mikaela that the blue box has to disappear, the father prepares for Mikaela what is to come (lines 46-47), and when the question of connecting to the internet appears on the screen (line 48), he simultaneously points at the screen and tells her when to push the button (line 50). This is followed by a two second pause where Mikaela tries to figure out which button the father is talking about (line 52). The father, who still is pointing at the screen, repeats that she has to push 'that one' (line 53). When she finally pushes the right button, the father declares the operation finished by saying; 'like that' (line 55) before he finishes by turning on the speakers.

In short, this episode shows how the technical problem of getting the computer started is solved and turned into a learning situation within the family. The father is called in to help Mikaela, and he uses this as a learning occasion where he shows Mikaela how she may solve similar problems in the future. The knowledge relation between the father and Mikaela is unchallenged in the sense that the father is the expert throughout the situation without being questioned. He is the one who deals with the technical aspect of making Mikaela get access to the game. He turns the computer off and on, he turns the speakers on and he tells her which and when the different icons have to be 'pushed'. To access a game you need to have some basic technical knowledge, like how to turn the computer on, how to set up a computer game, and how to read the text and icons that appear on the screen. This last part becomes even more important when the player does not know how to read. The present example, shows how this phase of entering the game is explained in detail by the father who tells Mikaela what is valid and legitimate knowledge in these situations. As such, the father is structuring (cf. Rogoff 2003) and disciplining Mikaela's participation and contribution to getting the game started. This school like situation becomes fruitful for both parties; the father gets Mikaela's attention and, she becomes able to enter the game.

To be noticed, the father arranges the scene for Mikaela to play 'Bob the Builder', but he never displays any interest to enter the game. When the game starts, he leaves the room, at which point game is made to be Mikaela's activity, both by the father and by Mikaela herself.

Tales of Successful Playing

Digital competence is actualised differently depending on the activity, place, and persons involved. The next example will show how parents are positioned, as well as enter the position, as novices in relation to their children in a discussion about a computer game. We enter the situation on a Saturday morning at breakfast. The mother has just finished a

discussion with Sara about her taking sugar in the church before Sara introduces the topic of
cheating while playing the computer game 'the Sims'.

Excerpt 2

Participants: Felicia (10), Sara (8), Father and Mother
Place: Kitchen table
Activity: Talking game

17 Sara	Do you remember that episode (.) when Madelen saw us?
18	(2)
19 Felicia	That we were cheating
20	(1)
21 Sara	[Hi hi
22 Felicia	[Hi hi
23	(1.5)
24 Mother	How did it come that she saw you? ((looking at Felicia))
25	(3)
26 Felicia	And every time Madelen is out in the bathroom then we start cheating
27	(2)
28 Father	Oh yeah >why's< that? (.) is it to see if she notices anything?
29 Sara	[No!
30 Felicia	[It is to get more money because Madelen knows how to cheat but she does
31	not use the cheat and before that she has always wanted to cheat
32 Father	M::: so now you are using it, to get
33 Felicia	=If I'd been able to cheat I would have cheated a whole lot more
34 Sara	Then I would have gotten a whole lot of money
35 Felicia	They have a two-storey house full of thing[s and
36 Mother	[I don't get the thing with cheating
37 Father	=What do you do to get more money?
38 Sara	Well, then you cheat ((turning to her father and points with her finger))
39 Felicia	Then you push on that the sum before big letter L Alt and C >then a grey
40	square< comes, where you should write in something later on and then you
41	>push Enter, then you bring the square back again< and then
42	you should push >exclamation mark comma exclamation mark and then you
43	could push Enter< at any time, whenever you want, but when it says dunk
44	dunk then you have to push (.) push Enter
45	(3)
46 Mother	Like I don't understand a thing e:: I don't understand what you do
47 Felicia	=You get more money
48 Mother	Really?

* Madelen is a friend of the girls.

Sara starts by asking her sister if she remember when Madelen witnessed them (line 17),
a question that is followed by a two second pause before her sister Felicia says, 'that we were

cheating' (lines 19). This is followed by a second pause before both start laughing simultaneously. Sara does not jump into a discussion of cheating as such, but starts by asking if her sister remembers a particular episode (line 17). By not telling what Madelen saw, Sara suggests 'cheating' as a topic for discussion around the breakfast table. If cheating is unproblematic in gaming, then it is reason to believe that there should not be a problem that Madelen witness them cheat because it is considered to be part of the game. However, after Felicia says 'that we were cheating?' the girls start laughing indicating, that Madelen saw something she was not supposed to. In short, the girls introduce cheating as part of the game but also as an ethically problematic act.

When the mother asks how Madelen came to know that they were cheating, Felicia waits for three seconds before she tells their parents that this is something that takes place every time Madelen leaves for the bathroom. The fact that cheating takes place when she is out of sight also indicates that this is not something that the girls have agreed upon, rather the opposite cheating is not expected from their co-player. When the father asks whether or not this is to see if Madelen discovers the cheating, he discloses that he does not know what this cheating is about. Cheating is not a friendly act to see whether the other player notices it, rather it is about succeeding in the game. This turns cheating into a 'trick of the trade', a question of computer game competence. Felicia's answer to the father's question is not just an explanation about the purpose of cheating in the Sims (i.e. to get more money), it is also an account were she downgrades the act as morally problematic. They cheat because Madelen knows how to cheat, despite fact that she did not do it this time. Furthermore, Felicia's claims that cheating is something Madelen always has wanted to do is as an extreme case formulation to underline the attractiveness of knowing how to cheat while playing the Sims, a stance that she fully aligns with both through their telling about what they did and through her claims (line 33).

The girls' explanation of why they cheat does not help their mother in understanding why they do it; thereby, the mother enters the position as the less knowledgeable, the novice who asks questions concerning the game practice (lines 36 and 46). The father, who is a good student, listens to the girls and recognises that cheating is not about fooling the co-player, but it is about getting money. He even asks what they do to get more money (line 37), in which Sara repeats that it is all about cheating, while Felicia enters the position as the play technical expert, explaining which key to push when. The mother, who has not listened carefully to their explanation or does not understand how cheating may be part of the game, returns to the question; why cheat (line 46). Felicia simply says, 'you get more money' (line 47), but the mother does not seem to be convinced (line 48).

The potential problem with introducing cheating is that it is considered unethical in, for instance, sports or tests at school. Despite of this cultural convention, the girls argue that these actions are needed to succeed in the game and being a knowledgeable gamer. Put differently, the knowledge of cheating is legitimated by being part of playing the game successfully, which is supported by their parents' questions and displayed interest for why and how to cheat. Similarly, Felicia and Sara are the experts on the Sims in this talk about the game. The adults never challenge the expert position or ask critical questions about the game, thereby letting the girls 'own' the story. The type of questions and the displayed lack of knowledge concerning gameplay indicate that this is an activity that is seen as a 'child activity'. Moreover, the parents' interest in Sims may be understood as involvement in their children's everyday lives (cf. Aarsand & Aronsson accepted), but it may also be understood as part of the rationality that is seen in the debate about computer games and virtual environments in the media, as well as in educational policy.

Surfing and Searching the Web

In the above examples, we have seen how children and adults act as expert versus novice in relation to different computer activities. In the first excerpt, the adult was the expert, whereas in the second one, the children were experts in relation to their parents. In the next example, there is no such agreement when it comes to the distribution of positions, which, in turn, poses the question of who is the expert and what is to be seen as valid knowledge. We will meet Jessika and her father while they are searching for pictures of horses on the internet. The father has just turned on the laptop that is placed on top of the kitchen stove, and he controls the keyboard.

Excerpt 3

Participants: Father, Jessika (10)
Place: Kitchen
Activity: Web surfing/searching

55	Father	You are going to look for animals, right?
56	Jessika	°Mm::° gooogle (.) g o o g l e ((spelling))
57		(2)
58	Jessika	And then, I can do it by myself
59		(2)
60	Jessika	I believe that [xxx
61	Father	[but what do you mean pictures of animals (.) pictures on
62		horses or what?
63		(3)
64	Jessika	Pictures (.) no but (.) horse like horses
65		(2)
66	Jessika	I have been looking at dogs for sale (.) I think it was the three [those that
67		sat like this while they looked up into the air ((shows with her arms))
68	Father	[Mm::
69	Jessika	One was white
70	Father	Mm::
71	Jessika	And then it was hihi a grey and then it was a black one hi hi
72	Father	Mm::
73	Jessika	And then they all sat on a row white grey and black hi hi they were so
74		cute
75	Father	Mm:: there is a really good page over here that we are going to look at
76		where I you can find some really nice pictures
77		(2) ((Both are turning their gaze to the screen))

78	Father	We will see (.) Eureka's page is it named
79	Jessika	>Can we look at Hooks?<
80	Father	Here we will see no now we will look at that part then then you have to
81		go to bed you know
82	Jessika	Yes but I also want to take a look by myself
83	Father	Eureka.se ((pointing at the screen))
84		(3)
85	Jessika	I want to see it by myself ((crawling in between the fathers arms))

The father starts by stating that Jessika is looking for animals (line 55). Jessika confirms this and says at once, 'Google', and then she spells it (line 56). Despite the fact that Jessika asks for help to get started, she seems to know one of the most successful searching engines at the moment. Further on, Jessika tells her father that when he finds "Google", she can take it from there (line 58). The father does not react to her statement; instead, he focuses on what kind of pictures she is interested in. Jessika tells her father that she is interested in pictures of horses and that she has been looking at pictures of dogs for sale (lines 66-77). Telling about the dogs, Jessika reveals that she knows how to use the Web and, she even manages to find subjects of interest to her. The father reacts with minimal response to Jessika, which makes her keep talking (lines 68, 70, 72, 75), but he does not comment or connect to anything of what she says. Rather, he introduces his 'own' search engine, 'Eureka', as an alternative to 'Google' (lines 75-78). In the discussion of the search engine, the father uses *we* instead of 'I', or 'you' (lines 78, 80). When he says, 'We will see (.) Eureka's page is it named' (line 78) Jessika responds by asking if she is allowed to do the searching by herself. The father responses by saying, 'we will see no now we will look at that part then then you have to go to bed you know' (lines 80-81). In this utterance he says *we* twice, underlining that searching on the Web is not something that she is going to do on her own, rather it is something that they will do together. At the end of this utterance, the father even brings in his identity as a responsible parent as a resource by telling his daughter that she has to go to bed once they have looked at this page. To note, this appears after she asks to be allowed to search the internet by herself. Jessika responds by saying, 'Yes but I also want to take a look by myself' (line 82), an utterance that is neglected by her father who continues to demonstrate his suggestion, 'Eureka'. Then Jessika declares; 'I want to see it by myself' and moves in between her fathers arms that both are placed on the computer's keyboard (line 85).

After the father's technical support is finished, the father and Jessika do not agree about who is to be in control of the search engine. Jessika suggests using 'Google', but this is turned down by her father who introduces an alternative. It could be argued that where to search becomes important for the father, and Jessika is not allowed to search for information at any place she likes on the Web. Valid information is found by using Eureka, not by using Google. Moreover, when this is accepted by Jessika, and she wants to investigate this search engine by herself, the father introduces another criterion, searching on the internet is something that they do together. This means that the father is the one who decides where to search as well as the one who is in control of the search engine. The father acts as the one who knows how to search, as well as the one who decides how this activity progresses. At the same time, Jessika does not act as if she does not understand how to search, rather, during this episode Jessika intensifies in her demands of getting the control of the search engine. She starts by telling her father that she knows how to search (line 58). When the father does not respond positively to her suggestion of which page to look at, she tells her father that she wants to have a look by herself (line 82), and finally, she both verbally and physically states that she wants look by herself (line 85). In short, this negotiation of control of the search engine, as well as how searching is to be done, shows how digital competence is created in the meeting between Jessika and her father. In the end, the valid information of searching competence consists of using the correct search engine and that this is done together with another (adult) person.

In contrast to Excerpt 1, where the child was encouraged to continue on her own when the father had finished the technical adjustment of the computer, the opposite may be seen in this example. One explanation as to why there seems to be two lines of reasoning may be that the internet is a different medium than digital games, and information searching is a completely different activity than gaming. In the mass media, the use of digital technology has often been followed by a moral panic (Critcher 2003, Drotner 1999) that has often claimed that parents do not know what their children do on the Web or when playing computer games. When looking at the present examples of children at such a young age, it could be argued that the parents are the one who have chose and bought the games (cf. Buckingham & Scanlon 2005). Thereby, the parents actually control which games the children are allowed to play. In contrast, the internet offers no such control, except when it comes to Web pages that have been investigated by the parents in advance.

GOVERNING THE CITIZEN OF THE FUTURE

Digital competence is a central concept in relation to the debate on lifelong learning, where it is discussed as one out of eight basic competences (European Commission 2005a). According to national and international policy texts, the subject has to be or become digitally competent. Developing digital competence or digital literacy is discussed as a necessity in order to participate in the future society, or, what sometimes has been referred to as part of being a flexible and active citizen (cf. Edwards 1997). Becoming a digital competent citizen is not only related to education or being a child or a youngster. Rather, becoming a digital competent citizen means that one learns from activities in different settings throughout the lifespan. Two stances seem to be central: first, that the subject is a learner from the cradle to the grave. Second, the educational system alone does not seem to manage creating the digital competent citizen; it needs to be supplemented with knowledge and experience from other arenas. We know that handling digital environments is mostly learned outside the formal education system (Drotner 2001, Erstad et al. 2005). This means that learning digital competence is seldom regulated or guided by an official curriculum, such as formal pedagogical practice. The family, as one of the arena where digital competence is developed, facilitates, structures, and restricts the creation of digital competence in lines with social and cultural expectations.

Negotiating Digital Competence

The formation of digital activities and the development of digital competence deal with images and ideas, possibilities and restrictions created and mediated through discussions in media and academia, as well as in discussions with colleagues and friends. These images and ideas refer to 'how to be a parent', 'what is a happy childhood', and what is meant by 'digital competence'. Digital activities in families deal with images that underline the necessity of digital competence, and also with images that connect children's use of computers to violence, sexism, and health problems. On the one hand, children and adults need to develop digital competence. On the other hand, these activities are framed as problematic and even dangerous. Since parents are legally responsible for their children, they also have the responsibility to raise, cultivate, and discipline their children in order to become active citizens in the future society. More precisely, the parents are positioned as responsible in terms of producing the digitally competent citizen. A certain pattern seems to be created and established, in which specific ways to act are made possible and desirable, whereas others are made more or less impossible and unthinkable. This means that considerations concerning what is 'normal' and accepted is negotiated and created, for instance how to write an e-mail, how and where to search for information, as well as what kinds of digital places and activities are considered inappropriate. In terms of governmentality, different mechanisms and procedures operate in order to shape and discipline the human conduct (Foucault 1991, 1997). The normal and accepted work as guidelines of how, what, and when to participate in digital activities. These guidelines have consequences when it comes to the kind of digital competence developed both by children and adults. In particular, we have highlighted how digital competence is produced in terms of what counts as valid digital knowledge in the families.

In the present data, we see how the families engage in digital activities in everyday life. The parents take the responsibility of their children seriously; they have bought the equipment needed (computers, software, games, as well as internet connection), and they have invested time in learning how to handle the technology. Every family in our data has at least one computer with internet connection at home, which indicates that not having a computer is not an option. The necessity of possessing, or the impossibility of not possessing, a computer could be discussed in terms of rationality of governing, a regime of knowledge and truth, shaping human behaviour (Foucault 1980, 1991). This means that to have access to a computer is taken for granted. The appearance of computers and internet in homes of families is an important component that makes the production of digitally competent citizens possible. Access to computers and internet was focused on when digital competence and digital divides were discussed throughout the 1990's, but access to the technology is no longer considered a problem. Rather, the challenge is now discussed along the line of how to make people competent users of information and communication technology. The three examples in this text indicate that parents create possibilities for their children to access digital environments. In the first example, it could be seen how the father helps his daughter to access a computer game. The second example shows how the children actually have experience that goes beyond what the parents know about this particular digital activity. At the same time, this example shows how the children make parts of gameplay accessible and understandable for the parents. A similar pattern can be seen in the last example where the daughter questions her father's position as an expert based on her own searching/web-surfing experience. Once again, it shows that the child has digital experience and, thereby, has been accessing digital environments. The last two examples not only show that the children are digitally competent, but it also shows that their knowledge is considered legitimate. In addition, children's display of digital competence is an acknowledgment of the parents' success of making their children access and relate to digital activities. Common to these examples is that digital activities are made accessible and are encouraged by adults and children. Notably, the positive view of digital activities in these families is similar to the view that appears in educational policy documents.

Intergenerational Encounters and Power/Knowledge

Intergenerational encounters are of importance in the production of digital competence in families. Focusing on three different digital activities, the text demonstrates variations concerning who is positioned as the most knowledgeable, as well as what counts as knowledge. The examples show how digital activities are encouraged, whether the participant is in the position of the expert or the novice. It is not given that it is either children or adults that are experts on digital activities, moreover who enters this subject position depends on what kind activity, when and together with whom. Discussing the expert-novice relation also actualizes the question regarding power/knowledge. In the present examples of established asymmetrical knowledge relations (excerpts 1 and 2), the one who displays competence is the one who gets to decide what is worth knowing. Displaying competence also involves positioning oneself and others in the ongoing activity. For instance, how to cheat is important competence needed when playing the Sims; timing is a necessity to get a game started. The participants establish these as truths based on arguments and claims brought forward by the more knowledgeable part that, further on, strengthens her/his position as an expert. Power/knowledge works in a slightly different way in situations where the participants do not agree upon who is the most competent actor. In the third excerpt, there is a disagreement about who is to be the expert when it comes to deciding where to search for information and the progression of the activity. Unlike the other examples, the parent and the child do not accept how they are positioned. In short, the father is not willing to let his child enter the position as the expert and the child does not recognise him as the expert. To maintain the asymmetrical knowledge relation, the father actualizes the positions parent and child as resources to exercise power. Being a father means being the one who makes decisions about his children, the one who sets the agenda, and, thereby, the one who structures the activity. In other words, when the father's knowledge is questioned, he uses another subject position, 'the responsible father', as a resource to exercise power in the present activity.

Pedagogicalization of Families' Leisure

Children's and parents' positioning in computer activities seem to differ depending on the activity and what is considered as competence. In the present excerpts, children were positioned as experts in relation to digital games and gameplay. One could ask what make the parents display such a positive interest towards digital games and gameplay. One way to understand this is that games such as 'Bob the Builder' and 'The Sims' are not part of the moral panic that has followed the increased interest for digital games among children and adults. Rather, these are examples of games that may be categorized as *edutainment*. It could be argued that playing these games is an attractive activity because they are believed to be contributing to learning and development. Gaming becomes a preferred activity where possibilities of learning are introduced to children at the same time as they are having fun. In short, as responsible parents they are expected to give access to and let their children play certain kind of games. Another aspect of this is that parents are usually the one who buy the digital games (Buckingham & Scanlon 2005), which can be seen as an acceptance and allowance for children to use them. This also means that the good and responsible parents are active consumers that orient to and make choices on a media market (cf. Biesta, 2004). Several researchers have argued that edutainment may be seen as a way of *pedagogicalization* of children's leisure (Buckingham & Scanlon 2005, Popkewitz 2003), which is part of the rationality of governing the digital citizen. Compared to digital games, in which parents have a possibility of getting to know what the child may encounter, this becomes impossible with the internet. The only way to control what the child see and meet is to join the child in the activity, or by surveillance (cf. Facer et. al. 2003, Holloway & Valentine 2003).

According to the ideas of lifelong learning, the subject is characterized by being problem-solving, active, flexible and self managed (Popkewitz 2003). In addition, adults, as well as children are responsible for developing their own competence (Nicoll & Fejes 2008, Sipos Zackrisson & Assarsson 2008). Since digital competence is considered to be important knowledge in the future society, combined with the notion of children being computer-literate (cf. Tapscot 1998, Gee 2003), there is reason to believe that parents are willing and able to position their children as experts in these particular activities. Despite the fact that digital competence seems to be part of families' socializing practices, the traditional relation concerning 'who knows' and 'who is to learn' is negotiated in the ongoing activity. When it comes to digital activities in family settings, the question of which actor is shaping the other can be raised. Why have the parents bought and learnt how to handle computers with internet connections? Why seem digital games to interest parents? Is it the parent guiding the child, or the child guiding the parent? In other words, the rationalities of governing seem to presuppose both children and adults disciplining each other in order to produce 'the network society citizen'.

ACKNOWLEDGEMENTS

The study is financed by the Swedish research council and done on data gathered in the Swedish part of the project "Everyday Lives of Working Families in Italy, Sweden and the US" founded by the Sloan foundation. Thanks to Tatyana Plaksina for helping us with the English language.

APPENDIX 1. TRANSCRIPT CONVENTIONS

Symbol	Meaning
?	Inquiring intonation
=	Contiguous utterances
↑	Raising intonation
:	Prolongation of preceding vowel
…	Lines left out
(2)	Pause 2 seconds
(.)	Pause shorter than 0.2 second
Xxx	Something was said but the transcriber could not discern its content.
Wo[rd	The bracket indicates the onset of over lapping speech
<u>Word</u>	Underlined means stressed word (or part of it)
°Word°	Quiet speech
WORD	Loud speech
Word	Italics mean spoken English
((laughing))	Comments made by the researcher
>Word<	Embeds faster speech than surrounding speech

REFERENCES

Aarsand, Pål André (2007). Computer- and Video games in Family Life: the digital divide as a resource in intergenerational interactions. *Childhood, 14*(2), 235-256.

Aarsand, Pål & Aronsson, Karin (accepted) Computer gaming and territorial negotiations in family life. *Childhood,*

Antaki, Charles & Widdicombe, Sue (1998). *Identities in talk.* London: Sage.

Aronsson, Karin (1998). Identity-in-interaction and social choreography. *Research on Language and Social Interaction, 31*(1), 75-89.

Bamberg, Michael G. W. (1997). Positioning Between Structure and Performance. *Journal of Narrative and Life History, 7*(1-4), 335-342.

Bernstein, Basil (1980). *Codes, modalities and the process of cultural reproduction: a model.* Lund: The Department of Education.

Biesta, Gert (2004). Against learning: reclaiming a language for education in an age of learning. *Nordic Journal of Education, 24*(1), 70-82.

Bolter, Jay D. and Grusin Richard (1999). *Remediation: understanding new media.* Cambridge: MIT Press.

Bourdieu, Pierre (1984). *Distinction: a social critique of the judgement of taste.* Cambridge: Harvard University Press.

Buckingham, David (2007). Children and consumer culture. *Journal of Children and Media, 1*(1), 15-24.

Buckingham, David (2005). *The Media Literacy of Children and Young People: a review of the research literature.* London: Ofcom.

Buckingham, David (2003). *Media education: literacy, learning, and contemporary culture.* Cambridge, UK Malden, MA: Polity Press.

Buckingham, David, & Scanlon, Margaret (2005). Selling Learning: Towards a political economy of edutainment media. *Media, Culture and Society 27*(1), 41-58.

European Commission (2005). *Proposal for a recommendation of the European Parliament and of the council: on key competences for lifelong learning.* Brussel: European Commission.

European Commission (2005b). *i2010 – A European Information Society for growth and employment. Communication from the commission to the council, the European parliament, the European economic and social committee and the Committee of the regions.* Retrieved 15.08.2008 from: http://eur-lex.europa.eu/LexUriServ/LexUriServ.do?uri=CELEX:52005DC0229:EN:NOT

European Commission (2006). The Ministerial Declaration on eInclusion. *ICT for an Inclusive Society Conference*. Riga: European Commission.

Critcher, Chas. (2003). *Moral panics and the media.* Buckingham: Open University Press.

Davies, Bronwyn & Harré, Rom (1990). Positioning: The Discursive Production of Selves. *Journal for the theory of social behaviour, 20*(1), 43-63.

Drotner, Kirsten (1999). Youth, media and modernity: senses in a changing landscape *(Unge, medier og modernitet: pejlinger i et foranderligt landskab).* Valby: Borgens Forlag.

Drotner, Kirsten (2001*).* Media for the future: children, youth and the new media landscape *(Medier for fremtiden: børn, unge og det nye medielandskab).* København: Høst.

Edley, Nigel, & Wetherell, Margaret (1997). Jockeying for Position: the construction of masculine identities. *Discourse Society, 8*(2), 203-217.

Edwards, Richard (1997*). Changing places? Flexibility, lifelong learning, and a learning society.* London: Routledge.

Eisenberg, Michael B., Lowe, Carrie A., & Spitzer, Kathleen L. (2004). *Information literacy: essential skills for the information age.* London: Libraries Unlimited.

Erstad, Ola (2006). A new direction? Digital literacy, student participation and curriculum reform in Norway. *Education and information technologies 11*(3-4), 415-429.

Erstad, Ola , Kløvstad, Vibeke, Kristiansen, Tove , & Søby, Morten. (2005). ITU Monitor 2005: on the way to digital competence in primary education *(ITU Monitor 2005: på vei mot digital kompetanse i grunnopplæringen).* Oslo: Universitetsforlaget.

Facer, Keri, Furlong, John, Furlong, Ruth & Rosamund Sutherland (2001). Home is where the hardware is: young people, the domestic environment and 'access' to new technologies. In Jo Hutchby and Jo Moran-Ellis (Eds.), *Children's technology and culture: the impact of technologies in children's everyday lives*, pp 13-27. London: Routledge/Falmer.

Facer, Keri, Furlong, John, Furlong, Ruth, & Sutherland, Rosamund. (2003). *Screenplay: children and computing in the home.* London: RoutledgeFalmer.

Fasulo, Alessandra, Loyd, Heather & Vincenzo Padiglione (2007). Children's socialization into cleaning practices: a cross-cultural perspective. *Discourse & Society 18(*1), 11-33.

Foucault, Michel (1997). On the Government of the Living. In Paul Rabinow (Ed.) *Essential works of Michel Foucault 1954-1984. Ethics: subjectivity and truth,* pp. 81-86. New York: The New Press.

Foucault, Michel (1979 [1975]). *Discipline and punish: the birth of the prison.* New York: Vintage Books.

Foucault, Michel (1980). *Power, knowledge: selected interviews and other writings 1972-1977.* New York: Pantheon.

Foucault, Michel (1982). Afterword: the subject and the power. In Hubert L. Dreyfus & Paul Rabinow (Eds.), *Michel Foucault: beyond structuralism and hermeneutics* (pp. 208-226). New York: Harvester Wheatsheaf.

Foucault, Michel (1988). The ethic of care for the self as a practice of freedom. In J. Bernauer & D. Rasmussen (Eds.). *The Finale Foucault*. Cambridge, MA: MIT Press.

Foucault, Michel (1991). Governmentality In G Burchell & C. Gordon & P. Miller (Eds.), *Studies in Governmentality with Two Lectures and an Interview with Michel Foucault*. London: Harvester Wheatsheaf.

Gee, James Paul (2003). What video games have to teach us about learning and literacy. New York: Palgrave Macmillan.

Goffman, Erving (1981). Forms of talk. Philadelphia: University of Pennsylvania Press.

Goffman, Erving (1974). Frame analysis: an essay on the organization of experience New York: Harper and Row.

Hertz, Rosanna and Marshall, Nancy L. (2001). Working families the transformation of the American home. Berkeley: University of California Press.

Holloway, Sara L. and Valentine, Gill (2003). Cyberkids: children in the information age. London: Routledge.

Jewitt, Carey (2005). Technology, literacy and learning: a multimodal approach. London; New York: Routledge.

Kellner, Douglas (2002). New Media and New Literacies: Reconstructing Education for the New Millennium. In Leah Lievrouw & Sonia Livingstone (Eds.), Handbook of New Media (pp. 90-104). London, Thousand Oaks, New Delhi: Sage Publications.

Kløvstad, Vibeke , & Kristiansen, Tove (2004). ITU Monitor: the school's digital conditions (*ITU Monitor: skolens digitale tilstand 2003*). Oslo:ITU.

Kremer-Sadlik, Tamar & Kim, Jeemin Lydia (2007). Lessons from sports: children's socialization to values through family interaction during sports activities. Discourse & Society 18(1), 35-52.

Lagenhove, Luk van & Harré, Rom (1999). Positioning theory: moral contexts of intentional action. Malden, Mass.: Blackwell.

Latour, Bruno (1999). Pandora's hope: essays on the reality of science studies. Cambridge: Harvard University Press.

Latour, Bruno (2005). Reassembling the social: an introduction to actor-network-theory. Oxford: University Press.

Lave, Jean and Wenger, Etienne (1991). Situated learning: legitimate peripheral participation. Cambridge: Cambridge University Press.

Livingstone, Sonia M. (2002). Young people and new media: childhood and the changing media environment. London: Sage.

Livingstone, Sonia & Bober, Magdalena (2005). UK children go online: finale report of key project findings. London: London School of Economic.

Livingstone, Sonia M. and Bovill, Moira (2001). Children and their changing media environment : A European comparative study. Mahwah, N.J.: Lawrence Erlbaum Associates.

Manovich, Lev (2001). The language of new media. Cambridge: MIT Press.

Medierådet (2005). Youth and Media: facts about children and youth's use and experience of media *(Unga och Medier: fakta om barns och ungas använding och upplevelser av media)*. Stockholm: Kultur departementet.

Nicoll, Kathy and Fejes, Andreas (2008). Mobilizing Foucault in studies of lifelong learning. In Kathy Nicoll and Andreas Fejes (Eds.), Foucault and lifelong learning: governing the subject, pp 1-18. London: Routledge.

Ochs, Elinore, & Taylor, Carolyn. (1992). Family narrative as political activity. Discourse and Society, 3(3), 301-340.

Papert, Seymore (1996). The connected family: bridging the digital generation gap. Atlanta: Longstreet Press.

Papert, Seymour. (1993). The children's machine: Rethinking school in the age of the computer. New York: BasicBooks.

Popkewitz, T. (2003). Governing the child and pedagogicalization of the parent: A historical excursus into the present. In Marianne. N. Block, Kerstin Holmlund, Ingeborg Moqvist and Thomas S. Popkewitz (Eds.), Governing Children, Families, and Education: Restructuring the welfare state Gover, pp. 35-61. New York: Palgrave Macmillan.

Potter, Jonathan and Wetherell, Margaret (1987). Discourse and social psychology: beyond attitudes and behaviour. London, Sage.

Rogoff, Barbara (2003). The cultural nature of human development. New York: Oxford University Press.

Rose, Nikolas. (1989). Governing the soul: the shaping of the private self. London: Routledge.

Selwyn, N. (2004). Reconsidering political and popular understandings of the digital divide. New Media & Society 6(3): 341-362.

Sipos Zackrisson, Katarina, & Assarsson, Liselott. (2008). Adult learner identities under construction. In Andreas Fejes & Katherine Nicoll (Eds.), Foucault and Liflong Learning: Governing the subject. London: Routledge.

Swedish National Agency for Improvement (2005) Strategy for IT in the School (Myndigheten för skolutveckling. Strategi för IT i skolan). Stockholm: Myndigheten för skolutveckling.

Swedish Ministry of Enterprise, Energy and Communications (2007). Policy for the IT Society - Recommendations from the members of the IT Policy Strategy Group. Stockholm: Näringsdepartementet.

Tapscott, Don. (1998). Growing up digital the rise of the net generation. New York: McGraw-Hill.

Tyner, Kathleen R. (1998). Literacy in a Digital World: teaching and learning in the age of information. London: Lawrence Erlbaum.

Willis, Paul E. (1977). Learning to labour: how working class kids get working class jobs. Farnborough: Saxon House.

In: Learning in the Network Society and the Digitized School   ISBN 978-1-60741-172-7
Editor: Rune Krumsvik   © 2009 Nova Science Publishers, Inc.

Chapter 16

IF INNOVATION BY MEANS OF EDUCATIONAL TECHNOLOGY IS THE ANSWER - WHAT SHOULD THE QUESTION BE?

Ingrid Helleve[1] and Rune Krumsvik[2]

University of Bergen, Norway

ABSTRACT

This chapter considers action research as a presupposition for implementation of educational technology in teacher education. The study is based on the author's experiences as a teacher educator in a local part of the innovative PLUTO project in Norway in the early 2000s. Through action research I learned what student teachers look upon as productive learning in teacher education and what consequences their experiences had for my future design and guidance of online learning communities.

INTRODUCTION

Innovation by means of educational technology is a challenge for teachers and teacher educators alike. Fullan's (1982) famous study about innovation in school reveals the many obstacles that occur in innovation processes and shows the potential complexities of succeeding with an innovation. A Norwegian study on innovations around ICT-use in Norwegian teacher education (NIFU/STEP 2008) revealed the same tendency and the acknowledged obstacles facing teacher educators in their attempt to implement the innovation.

This chapter also focuses on innovation in teacher education and highlights some of the experiences that a group of student teachers and I as a teacher educator had when we participated in an innovation project in teacher education in Norway in the early 2000s. The data collection is effected within the local part of the national teacher education programme, PLUTO (Programme for Teacher Education, Technology and Change) and is named INVITIS (2000-2003) (ITU, 2003a) (Innovation by Means of ICT in Education of Language Teachers) which was carried out at the University of Bergen in 2001 to 2003 (ITU, 2000-2003b). This chapter discusses how action research can be a support for teachers and teacher educators. I will first explain how the INVITIS project was organised and describe my input as an action researcher. I will also give an account of the theoretical underpinning the subject, pedagogy, and its organisation. The empirical data are based on interviews with a group of student teachers and my own experiences as an action researcher. The aim of the chapter is to highlight some of the challenges I met as a teacher educator during this period and what I learned from listening to the students' experiences. The main research question was: How did the student teachers experience the ICT-supported innovation project and what could I possibly learn from their experiences?

BACKGROUND

Owing to national legislative reforms, higher education, and notably teacher education, in Norway has been transformed in the last few years. One example is the Parliamentary Proposition 27 (2001-2002), the so-called 'Quality Reform' (MER, 2001), concerning higher education in general. Another example is the National Law for Teacher Education (MER, 2002). Both these reforms propose greater use of assessment for learning purposes (formative assessment), and a closer follow-up of students at all levels, combined with more active learning processes. Information and communication technology (ICT) is expected to strengthen the learning environment in significant ways. Altogether this has meant a major change in the traditions of teaching and learning; a new view of learning as constructing knowledge rather than simply transmitting information. The 'Action Plan for ICT in Norwegian Education' for the period 2000 to 2003 supports this view. Combined with increased focus on ICT in education, the plan acknowledges previous difficulties, and emphasises the need for knowledge and experience so that ICT can become an integral part of education. What the plan seems to call for is what Koschmann (1996) calls 'Computer Supported Collaborative Learning' (CSCL) and Krumsvik and Almås (in press) call 'Digital Didactic', each of which is a change from a behaviouristic and cognitive view of ICT in education to a socio-cultural perspective. These theoretical foundations became an important part of both PLUTO and INVITIS. In the next two paragraphs I will describe how the project was designed and organised.

INNOVATION BY MEANS OF EDUCATIONAL TECHNOLOGY

Several studies in the last thirty years show a common tendency within innovation in school and education: it implies a larger complexity than in other organisations. Huberman and Miles's (1984) and Fullan's (1982) studies reveal this complexity, and it is vindicated by the fact that change in schools takes a long time. The same tendencies have been found within the ICT area in education, Cuban (1986) and Tyack and Cuban (1998) arguing that top-down implementation of ICT in school very seldom has transformational potential. Krumsvik (2006) found the same tendencies in the Norwegian ICT PILOT project. The study also revealed that action research with teachers as the driving force dismantled some of the well-known obstacles in ICT-initiated school development. Some of these preliminary findings and experiences from the design of PILOT were used as a backdrop for implementation of ICT in teacher education in Norway and this project was named PLUTO. PLUTO was initiated by the Department for Education and Research. The main aim was to develop new pedagogical and organisational models for designing and guiding learning environments of which ICT was supposed to be an essential part. The University of Bergen was one of eight participating teacher education institutions. The aim of the INVITIS project was to develop an alternative online model for the education of language teachers. This model was to establish a platform for language teachers' abilities to become creative and innovative in the traditional classroom. The project was initiated and planned by a group of four teachers of language didactic from January 2001. I joined the project in August 2002, one and a half years after it had started. As a teacher educator I was expected to join the research group, to plan and organise innovation of pedagogy by means of educational technology for a group of twenty students, and to do action research on the project.

The student teachers attended a one-year teacher education programme (PGCE) at University of Bergen. Most of them had graduate-level qualifications in at least two different subjects. So far they had encountered the traditional way of study, with lectures and final exams. This is also what they expected to meet when they entered teacher education. The course was divided between twelve weeks of theoretical education in pedagogy and didactics in two subjects at the University and fourteen weeks of school practice.

The local research group was expected to gain as much information as possible concerning the possibilities and advantages of using ICT in teacher education. As a result, many different activities were planned. Since I joined the project after it had started, there was little time for me to prepare and plan activities. The fact that this was my first such venture meant that I was a little uncertain of my ground.

THE ORGANISATION OF INVITIS

The students who joined the INVITIS project were going to become language teachers. The four teacher educators in language didactic had planned different activities. The students were introduced to different LMS (learning management platforms) comprising LUVIT, the MOO-system and Lingo-forum. In the two languages they were supposed to make portfolios and to participate in asynchronous and synchronous discussions. Among other activities they analysed pupils' texts and published plans for their lessons in practicum. Another activity was supervision by means of e-mail. In French they used pedagogical computer-games and communicated online with a group of French teachers. In addition to the interactive use of LMS, the students were offered courses in how to use PowerPoint and make web pages.

My responsibility was to arrange and organise pedagogy. The different themes, such as classroom management, were dealt with in lectures to the whole group of 80 students, in face-to-face discussions in seminar groups and in portfolios where the students gave feedback to each other.

Table 1. Seminar- and basic group activities

		Face-to-face meetings	Online activities
Seminar group	20 students	Met once or twice a week during the theory period	Asynchronous discussions
Basic group	4-5 students within the seminar group	Practicum at the same school	Compile portfolio + give and receive feedback from peers

The semester started with an introductory week for the seminar groups. During the theoretical part of the study the students met face-to-face once or twice a week. They were meant to gain basic confidence, to become familiar with the main goals of teacher education and the INVITIS project, and to learn how to use the technology. In order to prepare for the online collaboration, students in the basic groups had to write texts and give feedback to each other face-to-face. Participation in seminar groups as well as online activities was compulsory. Based on a procedure decided by the teacher educator, each student gave feedback to two peers on each assignment in the portfolio. Face-to-face as well as online discussions took place either between the members of the seminar groups or in the subject-related groups. As a participator from the research team I was supposed to do action research on the innovative activities.

ACTION RESEARCH

Bridget Somekh (2002, cited in Krumsvik, 2006) claims that action research is the research approach that is most suitable for teachers and schools in an innovation period because it is based on the values and context where it takes place. Accordingly it fits in with everyday practice and focuses the participants' concern. Action research here is understood as 'a particular way of researching your own learning' and 'self-reflective practice, or as learning in and through action' (McNiff, 2002, p.15). McNiff defines the term as a process of improving one's own understanding of how to improve social situations. Knowledge is understood as something people *do*. There are no fixed answers. Rather, answers are transformed into new questions. According to McNiff, a research report is required. This report should make visible the systematic investigation- process you have gone through in order to better understand your own behaviour and reasons for behaviour. The report should be a support for your continuing development and work.

A classic definition of action research is: '...a form of self-reflective enquiry undertaken by participants in social situations in order to improve the rationality and justice of their own practices, their understanding of these practices, and the situations in which these practices are carried out' (Carr & Kemmis, 1986, p.162). Somekh (2007) claims that the process of innovation is projected through two ideas. First, that the interrelationship between multiple levels of human activity co-construct change. Second, that there is an active, intervening position for the researcher in supporting this process. Innovation depends on social processes between interrelated phenomenal levels of the educational, cultural systems. Action research is sometimes criticised for being characterised by ideological theories and personal values more than other scientific paradigms. The scientific status of action research has been questioned because of the danger of the researcher's getting lost in details, a danger that is impossible to see from an inside position. According to Zimann (2000), all social science is based on personal interests and a strong engagement in realising emancipative ideals. What is important is that the researcher paves the way for others to reach these ideals through reports from the action research process. Another important issue is to discuss questions concerning the research in different contexts of interpretation (Kvale, 2001).

I joined the INVITIS project after it had begun. This meant that I participated in an innovation process of which I did not have the full ownership. Another problem during this period was that I found little or no time for systematic reflection. What I had to do was to organise and guide the learning activities for the students. What was good was that I shared the vision in PLUTO and INVITIS concerning the change in teaching and learning activities in teacher education. I believed that student teachers should participate in small groups where they had the possibility to take part in collaborative reflective dialogues. What I was more uncertain about was how these processes could possibly be supported by ICT.

THE IMPORTANCE OF REFLECTION IN TEACHER EDUCATION

The change in teaching and learning activities is based on a socio-cultural perspective on learning. This perspective is also called socio-historic, socio-interactive and situated (Vygotsky, 1978; Lave & Wenger, 1991; Cole, 1996; Cole & Wertsch, 1996; Wenger, 1998; Säljö, 2000; Wertsch 1998; Rogoff, 1998; Valziner & Van der Veer, 2000; Dysthe, 2001). The foundation of this theory is that knowledge is created in social collaboration, and that language is a basic element in the learning process. A situated perspective indicates that the context is decisive for learning. According to the socio-cultural perspective on learning, the possibility to reflect is of essential importance for teachers if they are to learn from their experiences (Schön, 1987; Calderhead, 1989; LaBoskey, 1994; Korthagen et al., 2001; Korthagen & Vasalos, 2005). Reflection is necessary in order to promote sound professional behaviour and growth in competence for teachers and student teachers. What the authors also argue is that reflection should be structured and based on different levels. In addition to observable levels such as environment, behaviour and competences, they argue for reflection on personal beliefs. This is a difficult process because beliefs are often deep-rooted and persistent and consequently difficult to change (Calderhead & Robson, 1991; Korthagen & Vasalos, 2005). Given this fact, perhaps the most important task for teacher educators is to select learning activities that invite students into processes that promote deep reflection. Yrjö Engeström (1998) uses the concept 'zone of possibilities' as an equivalent to Vygotsky's 'zone of proximal development', indicating that when people co-operate they are not only acquiring existing knowledge, they also renew it. Through collaboration, peers create a common zone of development. Rommetveit (1979) uses the expression 'a temporarily shared world' (p. 100). The 'interpretive zone' is also used (Wasser & Bresler, 1996; Hoel, 2002) to refer to the common interpretative processes we enter when we are engaged in collaboration with other people. The individual's personal zone, as well as the group's common zone, develops according to the process of interaction.

Collaboration by means of educational technology has changed our notions of what learning actually is. The search for a solution to this question may explain the growing popularity of the term *productive learning* (Lillejord & Dysthe, 2008). This term illuminates the relationship between learning as a process and learning as a product. Learning as an inter-subjective activity means to see something in a new perspective. This perspective on learning goes beyond an information-sharing understanding by focusing on a co-construction of knowledge. The core of Bakhtin's notion of dialogue is that meaning is created in the tension between different voices, that answers give rise to new questions and that dialogue is an end in itself. '..meaning opens up between incommensurate perspectives in a dialogue' (Bakhtin, 1986, p.162). Learning is not only accomplished through the interactions of the participants, but also consists of those interactions in the inter-subjective space. Given that learning is dependent on collaboration in common 'zones' or inter-subjective space, the main task for a teacher educator is to create possibilities for reflective dialogues that enhance creativity and argumentation.

ACTIVITIES THAT SUPPORTS COLLABORATIVE REFLECTION

Teamwork can develop in different directions. Normally we distinguish between two different concepts: co-operation and collaboration. Co-operation is product-oriented and the group members divide the work between themselves. Collaboration, on the other hand, means that the students work together on all the different parts of a shared exercise (Bruffee, 1999). Through collaborative activities the students should have the possibility to learn through argumentation and creativity. Argumentation in this context means a language-based activity, and is looked upon as epistemic as well as semiotic. It is an epistemic activity since it involves the expression of knowledge (Andriessen et al., 2003).

Compiling portfolios for learning purposes is intended to encourage student teachers' reflective processes (Klenowski, 2002; Smith & Tillema, 2003). The primary aim of using portfolios in teacher education is to encourage students to reflect upon teaching, become more conscious of the theories and assumptions that guide their practices, and to engage in collaborative dialogues about teaching. Implementation of portfolios should contribute to personal knowledge and insight into performance, and support competence development (Smith & Tillema, 2001). Compiling a portfolio is an interaction of collaboration with peers and the feedback process (Anderson & DeMuelle, 1998; Darling-Hammond & Snyder, 2000; Klenowski, 2002; Dysthe & Engelsen, 2003; Elminn & Elminn, 2005).

A Space for Collaboration

In addition to awareness around learning activities, another important task for teacher educators is to create and offer suitable meeting-places for the students where collaborative activities can take place. The theory of a community of learners acknowledges the socio-cultural perspective of learning, emphasising active discovery, reflectivity, meta-cognition and collaboration. A community of learners is characterised by its members building on each other's ideas and taking multiple viewpoints into consideration. (Brown, 1994; Matusov,

2001; Mintrop, 2001; Darling, 2001; Sumison & Patterson, 2004; Leite, 2006). According to Ludvigsen and Hoel (2002), there are four principles for design of a community of learners that are often recognised in an innovation process. First, there is a connection between individual and collective responsibility. Second, the students participate in a learning community when they share and produce collective knowledge. The third principle is that students should experience different ways of working in groups. Finally, the teacher is responsible for designing and guiding the learning activities.

The way the students were organised in seminars and basic groups in pedagogy was based on the theoretical foundation I have described so far. What was new to me was designing for online collaborative learning processes. The online activities I planned were asynchronous discussions for the seminar groups and compiling portfolios through feedback from peers for the basic groups. The activities were mediated by LMS (Learning Management System). As a mediating artefact, the LMS should be able to create new meeting-places for collaborative activities. LMS is a broad term used for a wide range of systems that organise and provide access to online learning services for students, teachers and administrators. These systems usually include access control, provision of learning content, communication tools and organisation of user groups (Paulsen, 2002).

DEVELOPING RESEARCH QUESTIONS FOR A GROUP OF STUDENTS

Even though I was supposed to be an action researcher, I was so occupied with organising and teaching that little time was left for systematic reflection. This was a frustrating experience. As a parallel to my own frustration I found that some of the students complained about the online activities in which they had to take part. Many of them were frustrated. They also complained about all the different ICT-supported activities they had to do. One of the students even told me she thought of quitting teacher education because of the INVITIS project. This made me curious to understand what I as a teacher educator could possibly learn from their experiences. Action research requires systematic investigation (McNiff, 2002). Accordingly I decided to hold interviews with the students after graduation in order to learn as much as possible. The main research question I wanted an answer to was: How did the student teachers experience the ICT-supported innovation project and what could I possibly learn from their experiences?

Methodology

In qualitative research, one of the main aims is to understand as much as possible of the frames, the structures and the connections among people in order to analyse and understand (Merriam, 1998; Kvale, 2001). The research questions are suitable for qualitative interviews owing to their suitability to probe complex social phenomena.

The sample was part of the INVITIS project and included approximately 20 students each semester with two languages as their teaching subjects. All the students were female. The selection was non-probability (Merriam, 1998) and based on purposeful sampling and typical sampling (Patton, 1990). Two groups of students, numbering ten in all, were interviewed after their study; five students in the first group (A) and five in the second (B). Group A graduated in June 2003; group B in December 2003. They were all female students between 25 and 30 years old. All the interviews were semi-structured with several pre-arranged questions. The semi-structured design ensured that all the respondents were confronted with the same set of core questions. In addition to the core questions, follow-up questions were formulated. These offered the interviewees the opportunity to introduce unexpected ideas and thoughts. All interviews were fully transcribed before the structural phase of the analysis.

In order to increase the internal validity of the study, Kvale's seven stages of analysis were used to examine the interviews (Kvale, 2001). The researcher condensed the views expressed by the interviewees into shorter formulations. Through meaning categorisation the interviews were coded into categories. First, they were categorised according to the positive as well as negative experiences the students mentioned. Further, in order to answer the research questions, the following categories were chosen.

- What the students looked upon as the most important learning activities during teacher education
- How they experienced participation in an innovation project
- If, and eventually how, the educational technology had been a support to their learning process

Kvale (2001) raises new questions on interview statements from different interpretation contexts and the validity of these interpretations is related to different validity communities. Therefore, as a starting-point for such internal validity issues, Kvale's three contexts for interpretation are used: self-understanding (the interviewee), critical understanding based on common sense (the general public) and theoretical understanding. In the first context we find it essential to have an understanding of the informant's everyday reality and be faithful to their understanding of the same reality (Kvale, 2001). In the second context, the interpretation has a broader framework of understanding than the interviewer's own. It means that we as researchers may be critical about what is being said and can focus either on the content of the statement or on the person behind the statement (Kvale, 2001). The last understanding is used to interpret statements in a theoretical framework, where we have used different theoretical 'lenses' to handle such issues. Concerning the first community, one of the students has read the draft of this paper and acknowledged the content. Second, the study is published in a journal meant for teachers (Helleve, 2004). Third, the draft of the paper has been read by other researchers in the research community. The study has also been presented at two international peer-review conferences (Helleve, 2007, a, b). The feedback I received from these contexts of interpretation gave me new insight and contributed to learning.

With regard to generalisation, the study is tied to naturalistic generalisation (Stake, 1995) and reader or user generalisability (Firestone, 1993), with thick description (Geertz, 1973). As regards the ethical part of the research, the Norwegian Social Science Data Services have accepted an application.

What Did the Students Experience?

In the following, the findings are presented in the same order as the questions were asked.

The Most Important Learning Activities

Looking back at teacher education, what are the students' opinions about the learning activities they met as a result of the ICT project? They all agree that practice in schools was the most important learning activity, but also other activities were appreciated. Productive learning was regarded as the possibility to reflect upon theory and practice with peers face-to-face as well as online. With regard to the campus activities and the face-to-face collaborative activities, the students agreed that the reform was an improvement. Compared with listening to lectures aimed at a group of eighty students, they highly valued the new learning activities based on their own contribution.

> 'Practicum was most important. Or to meet the pupils. And to write portfolios and get feedback. I have never done that. But I think I have learned a lot from it' (Student 2).

They all saw that becoming a teacher requires participation and personal engagement. Most of all, they appreciated collaboration with three or four other students in the basic groups, and the regular meetings in the seminar groups where they were supposed to contribute themselves and to discuss topics from lectures, pedagogical theory and their own practicum. Some students mentioned that the seminar group was comparable to a class in school, and therefore it became a model for their future classrooms.

> 'I think it is important to get to know each other and experience being a class. Not public lectures. I think it is important to learn in a social context, I mean socio-cultural learning' (Student 5).

They also appreciated the assessment for learning purpose where they compiled their own presentation portfolio, and the close relation they established as peers in the basic groups. Many students claimed that they learned more from other students than from anything else during teacher education.

Experiences as Students in an Innovation Project

When graduating, all the ten students felt positive about parts of the ICT project. They saw the value of knowing something about educational technology when they entered school as novice teachers.

> ' I did not profit that much from the ICT-supported activities. It had little to do with my situation. But still I think it is important and it is important to handle it. I think it is important in school' (Student 3).

Their enthusiasm, however, varied. They all described the frustration they experienced around the organisation of INVITIS when they started as student teachers. Their expectations included traditional university education with lectures and a school exam. Instead they were asked to compile portfolios and to collaborate face-to-face as well as online. One of the students said that she was very close to dropping teacher education for that reason (Student 2).

Another important reason for frustration was the fact that the students experienced little if any ownership of the ICT project. They were told what to do, but seldom *why* they were supposed to collaborate online. Consequently, they did not see the relation between their future work as teachers and the aims of the INVITIS project. A third reason for confusion was that too many different online activities were going on at the same time. The students were asked to collaborate in basic groups and seminar groups in pedagogy, in addition to all the other different activities connected with their two teaching languages. They had to use synchronous as well as asynchronous forums and chats. Some students even had to try different LMS. A fourth reason was the technological problems the students experienced. Some of them knew the technology beforehand, and some had even studied computer science, but for many students, this was the first time they were asked to collaborate online. Additionally, the situation was much the same for the teacher educators, and the students recognised their teachers' uncertainty. A fifth provocative factor, according to some of the students, was the fact that the online activities were compulsory.

> 'I thought many of the assignments we had to do were ridiculous, because we had to do it and the assignments were obligatory. But there were no demands as to the content. There was no product' (Student 6).

This provoked them for at least two reasons. The first reason was that as traditional university students they were used to a great deal of personal autonomy. All the obligatory assignments made them feel like small pupils. Accordingly, the second provocative element was the theoretical lectures where the teacher educators spoke about the value of pupil autonomy in schools. The student who was about to leave the study said:

> 'What I reacted most aganist was that we heard a lot from the teacher educators about pupils' autonomy and pupils' interests and how important it was to speak to them, take them seriously and listen to them. But as students we experienced quite the opposite. So I felt no kind of motivation' (Student 2).

But perhaps the most serious obstacle was the fact that few of the schools they visited practised any kind of ICT facilities in their education. None of the schools were yet using portfolios, let alone digital portfolios. Few, if any, schools used LMS or any kind of ICT-based equipment in their own classes. When the students looked at what they had learned from the project, most of them mentioned the value of learning how to use PowerPoint and how to make homepages. They used these learning activities in the schools in which they practised, and even got credit for it from pupils as well as teachers.

If and How the Educational Technology Had been a Support to their Learning Process

By the end of teacher education some of the students saw that there were qualitative differences making ICT and LMS suitable for productive learning processes not just for distance learning but also for campus students. The activities they mentioned are portfolios with feedback from peers and asynchronous discussions. Not synchronous discussions and chats. What seemed to characterise these activities was that they encouraged collaboration and deeper reflection. Through the reflective process the students became more open to other students' ideas and also to getting new ideas themselves. With regard to the asynchronous discussions, one student said:

> 'I have become much more positive about the ICT-supported activity even though I still think it should be used with intelligence. To share texts and thoughts has been very nice. I used to be very negative. It was impossible for me to understand why we could not sit around a table and discuss. But now I see that a virtual discussion is something quite different from a face- to-face discussion' (Student 5).

An important reason was that the online discussions and feedback processes paved the way for deeper reflection because there was a distance in time and space. Students did not have to respond immediately, but could wait and think before they pressed the button. Other groups of students were in this way favoured because in face-to-face discussions one or two students often dominate the discussion. Online discussions gave them time for reflection before they had to react to the other students' utterances. One student said:

> 'It is another process. You get more time for reflection when you participate in the asynchronous discussions. It is something else to write. You have to think more. I often write my answers to the discussion immediately, but I wait a while before I send it. In the meantime I do some housework before I press the button' (Student 9).

The distance in space also meant that they had to imagine the other person without actually seeing her. This means that the students experienced the computer's "transparent abilities", making it easier to understand the other students' opinions. The utterances were not isolated, but linked together over time like a chain of thoughts, possible to trace backwards. This gave them an opportunity to go deeper into the text, grasping the other students' thoughts and feelings. The students state that the fact that they first had to read the other students' texts or statements before responding was an important distinction between face-to-face and online feedback. The reading and writing process meant that they had to go deeper into the essence of utterances. Another fact linked to this was that what is written in an online context is impossible to erase. The text leaves the writer and becomes the group's property. One student said:

> 'You stress your words more because you know they will be standing there for ever' (Student 9).

Because the students knew each other well, online collaboration seemed to contribute to an extra dimension in their understanding.

In pedagogy the starting-point for the virtual discussions was a topic related to pedagogical theory and practice initiated by the teacher educator. This could be either an open question or an article everybody had to read. One student mentioned the question, 'What is learning, in your opinion?', as an example of a suitable discussion topic. She argued that there was no correct answer to this question, but still everybody had their own theories and opinions. Another fact mentioned by one of the students was that everybody had to participate in the online discussions. In face-to-face discussions one or two students often dominate. The student teachers who were going to teach French in school communicated with a group of French teachers through an asynchronous forum. This was an activity from which they learnt a lot.

As time went on, the students realised that the closed space or room in the LMS functioned as a sort of treasure-chest; all the texts and feedback from others were stored within the computer. But, as one of the students said, this was something she had to experience herself when she was compiling her own presentation portfolio. She concluded:

'It is very nice to have this archive there. It is like a property chest. You can enter the "room" whenever you want and the archive expands all the time. Perhaps the teacher educators told us when we started as student teachers, but I did not understand it. We thought it was silly, but gradually we understood that we could find something there'(Student 1).

In summary, some students saw that asynchronous text-based activities had potential for productive learning which supported face-to-face collaboration. Discussions and feedback from peers encouraged reflective processes that made them more conscious of their own opinions and beliefs and other students' points of view. The process of writing and reading other students' texts paved the way for deeper reflection as well as speech. Because of the transparent abilities of the educational technology, they found it easier to understand their peers' thoughts and feelings. Asynchronous discussions favoured other students more than face-to-face discussions. Together the students in a group built a knowledge base in the closed room.

What Did I Learn from the Student Teachers' Experiences?

To be a teacher educator means to be in a continuing process of designing and guiding students' learning. Acting on the principles of action research, I intended to learn as much as possible from their experiences when I interviewed the students. When I joined INVITIS I shared the vision of the national as well as the local project about student teachers' participation in small groups with possibilities for reflective dialogues. What I was uncertain of, was if and how educational technology could support productive learning for student teachers. So what did I learn?

I was convinced that the way we had organised teaching and learning activities in seminar and basic groups was the proper way of doing it. Reflection on theory and experiences from practicum seems to be the next most important factor for the students after practicum. What the interviews showed me was that student teachers' attention is related to the activities going on in practicum and that there should be a connection between the learning activities they experience as students and teachers during PGCE.

'I think it was important to try formative assessment. I have never tried that myself, and it is an advantage to experience it yourself before you use it as a teacher. That is also the fact for many of the activities we tried in the groups like performing a play. If you have tried it, then I think you will try it in your own classroom'(Student 5).

Further, I learned the importance of students and teacher educators sharing the aims of the activities. The students had many complaints concerning the way the INVITIS project was organised. One of their main objections was that they felt no ownership of the project. They did not understand why they had to do all the activities connected to the project and they saw no link between their aims of becoming teachers and the use of all the ICT-supported activities. This might partly depend on the fact that I as a teacher educator shared their questions, and partly on the fact that I also lacked ownership of the project. Evaluation of the PLUTO project shows that there was resistance to the use of ICT among teacher educators as well as teachers during this period (Rambøll, 2004). I do not think that was true for me. I was curious to find out how educational technology could possibly support productive learning processes.

Educational Technology as a Support for Learning?

Though limited in its generalisability, this study shows that, given the right conditions, LMS can give student teachers an extra dimension for a productive learning process by offering a new kind of room for collaboration; a virtual community of learners (Matusov, 2001; Mintrop, 2001; Darling, 2001; Sumison & Patterson, 2004; Leite, 2006). The closed space in the LMS is like an ordinary room. When the door is closed, no one other than the persons inside can listen or see. Some of the students in this research experienced online learning processes to be qualitatively different from face-to-face collaboration and an important supplement.

What the students argue is that asynchronous text-based forums are better suited for productive learning activities than synchronous forums and chats. This corresponds with other researchers' results concerning online learning (Palloff & Pratt, 1999; Salmon, 2000; Collison et al., 2000; Wallace, 2002). Reading a text and responding through writing are qualitatively different from face-to-face meetings. The texts that are published, and the statements that are written, remain forever as a kind of collective property. Naturally, the students first realised this at the end of the study when the archive had grown into what they called a 'property chest' and they were supposed to compile their presentation portfolio. Unlike an ordinary room where you have to wait for the others, the virtual room invites you to enter whenever you want. In an asynchronous forum, you can take the initiative to give feedback to another person's text whenever you want. The distance in time and space is an important difference between face-to-face and virtual meetings, and consequently encourages a deeper reflection process. Campus students should have the possibility of utilising the strengths of face-to-face as well as online collaboration.

Listening to the student teachers, I learned that a learning community might as well be an online community with qualities additional to those of a face-to-face community. For example, the teacher is no longer the centre of communication. Perhaps the most important job for the teacher is to design the learning process for the students (Palloff & Pratt, 1999; Wallace, 2002). Peer learning is important in order to encourage meaningful learning which involves student teaching and learning from each other. Students should be encouraged to share ideas, knowledge and experiences, thus engaging in interdependent learning (Keppel et al., 2006).

In addition to sharing aims with the students, there are other assumptions that are important to notice when a teacher is designing an online community for student teachers. The community should be based on trust and connectedness between the students. This corresponds with other researchers' findings (Light & Cox, 2001; Thurston, 2005).These assumptions are confidence, assignments that challenge different points of view, and the presence of a teacher. First the students underline the importance of confidence.

> 'Discussions were important because the whole environment becomes part of it. But you have to know each other because you cannot read the language of the body when you are online' (Student 7).

With regard to the construction of the digital portfolio by means of feedback from peers, the students stressed the importance of being a small group. Regardless of the background, confidence is fundamental in human collaborative work where people are supposed to learn (Giddens, 1991; Hargreaves, 2002). The social basis is even more important in online collaboration than in face-to-face contexts because the students are unable to see each other. If the aim is to participate in reflective dialogues you have to trust the other members. Accordingly, students need to be connected to each other and to the content being studied (Palloff & Pratt, 1999; Salmon, 2000; Collison et al., 2000; Light & Cox, 2001; Wallace, 2002; Thurston, 2005). Building learning communities like basic and seminar groups in face-to-face contexts as done in this project forms a foundation of trust and confidence between the online collaborators. In distance learning the students often miss the opportunity of knowing each other. On-campus students often meet face to face. This gives teacher educators an important chance to establish trust and confidence between the students before they start their online collaboration. Combined with learning how to handle the technology the students should learn about the purpose of compiling portfolios and how to give feedback to other students. Through the introductory week and seminar meetings, they learned to trust each other. Looking back, they saw the need to know each other before they started their online collaboration. In process writing they had to show their unfinished texts. One of the students said:

> 'It is better to show a written text you are proud of. Even worse when you have to publish it by pressing a button, and send it into the computer. But you get used to it' (Student 1).

They felt more vulnerable when publishing unfinished texts; perhaps still more vulnerable when they met the other students every day. It also seemed to be important to learn about process writing and to give feedback to the others in face-to-face contexts first.

The second assumption for the teacher is to design for assignments that can challenge the students' different opinions in collaborative text-based feedback and discussions (Helleve, 2003, 2007). Open questions like, 'What is learning, in your opinion?', which have no definitive answer, invite the students to reflect and argue. The third assumption concerns the position of the teacher in online learning education. In ordinary classrooms the teacher acts as a visible instructor and a central part whatever the learning activities are. In an online classroom on the other hand, the teacher is an embodied person (Wegerif, 2007). The students, however, wanted the teacher to be present:

> 'I missed a teacher who could conduct the process. We were fumbling. We thought maybe we had misunderstood the articles, and when we gave feedback it was perhaps not as fruitful as it might have been' (Student 9).

The student claims that they missed the teacher educator's participation. What they actually seem to miss was the teacher's guidance, a teacher who could tell them if they were on the wrong path. They wanted to know that the teacher was caring for their learning process and watching the collaborative work going on.

To sum up, I learned that for student teachers the learning activities should be connected to the activities taking place in practicum. The students should have the possibility of using the same activities in the theoretical part of teacher education as in practicum and also have the possibility to reflect upon the use of these activities. What I further learned was that I should share my aims for the activities with the students. They should understand *why* they were supposed to do things. For future teachers this meta-consciousness of their own learning is important (Loughran, 2006). In this case I, as a teacher educator, also felt uncertain of the goals of the project. Probably my confusion strengthened the students' confusion. My conclusion is that online activities like portfolios and asynchronous discussions seem to be well-suited to reflective dialogues taking place within the closed space of an LMS. The activities can contribute to productive learning for student teachers, given.. The closed space of an LMS can function as a community of learners, given certain assumptions. I learned that it is important to care for as much confidence as possible for the group in face-to-face contexts before the online collaboration starts; further, to arrange for assignments that can spark discussion and argumentation, and to be present as a teacher even if the students are online.

Through a systematic visualisation of the students' experiences I have shown what I learned as a teacher educator. I think my experiences underline what was argued initially in this article about ICT-supported innovation in education. Education is complex. Designing for ICT-supported learning has significantly increased the challenges teachers have to face. Research shows that top-down implementation of ICT in education seldom has transformational potential (Cuban, 1986; Tyack & Cuban, 1998). This study illustrates what happened when neither I as a teacher educator nor the students shared the aims of the ICT-supported innovation project.

ACTION RESEARCH AND INNOVATION IN EDUCATION

The aim of this chapter was to highlight some of the challenges I as a teacher educator and a group of student teachers faced when participating in an ICT-supported innovation project in the early 2000s. Through this chapter I wanted to show what I learned from my own and a group of student teachers' experiences and the main research question was: How did the student teachers experience the ICT-supported innovation project and what could I possibly learn from their experiences?

When I joined the INVITIS project as a teacher educator I recognised that I had many different roles and that there were different expectations connected with those roles. I was participating in a local project that was part of a national project. PLUTO was meant to be a change agent for learning activities in teacher education. Furthermore, I joined a research group and a local project that had been in operation for eighteen months. Action research places the participants at the heart of any attempt to adopt an innovation within a social situation (Somekh, 2007). In this position I was supposed to be an innovative teacher, to carry out action research and to teach the students. I was pressed for time and found that I was not able to honour all the different roles. Looking back, I can see that this frustration probably made me still more alert and that this attention contributed to an analytical understanding (Solberg, 1996). Through the interviews with the students as part of my action research I understood more of my own position as a teacher educator in an innovation process as well as the challenges all teacher educators have to face when they are designing for productive learning activities.

Somekh (2007) argues that the difficulty of understanding the process of innovation is that we need to derive meaning from the activities we are engaged in, but can only attempt this in terms of our own experiences. Further, she argues that through methods like interviews and observations action research generates new insight into the relationship between self and others and often the unintended consequences of actions. The 'Programme for Digital Competence (2004-2008)' (MER, 2003) states that ICT should be an integral part of Norwegian schools' development and way of working, and this is underlined in the National Curriculum Plan from 2006, 'Knowledge Promotion', indicating that digital competence should be one of five basic skills for all pupils (MOK, 2006). This means that designing for innovation by means of educational technology will be an ongoing challenge for Norwegian teachers and teacher educators (Krumsvik, 2006, 2007). Educational technology develops fast. Some of the challenges that are discussed in this chapter may no longer be urgent in teacher education. With reference to the chapter heading, if the answer from policymakers is that education should be supported by ICT, I think the question should be: how can we make sure that teachers can be involved through action research? In the light of my own experiences I want to argue for action research as a way of integrating research and action in a cyclical process of enquiry, action, reflection and evaluation. Through this process of listening to the student teachers' experiences I learned a lesson for future design of online learning communities that I could not possibly have learned otherwise.

REFERENCES

Anderson, R. & DeMuelle, L. (1998). Portfolio use in twenty-four teacher education programs. *Teacher Education Quarterly, 25*(1), 23-32.

Andriessen, J., Baker, M., & Suthers. D. (2003). *Arguing to learn.* London: Kluwer Academic Publishers.

Bakhtin, M. (1986). *Speech genres and other late essays.* Austin: University of Texas.

Brown, A. (1994). The advancement of learning, *Educational Researcher 23*(8), 4-12.

Bruffee, K. A. (1999). Collaborative learning. Higher education, interdependence, and the authority of knowledge. Baltimore/London: John Hopkins University Press.

Calderhead, J. (1989). Reflective teaching and teacher education. Teaching and Teacher Education, 5(1), 43-51.

Calderhead, J. & Robson, M. (1991). Images of teaching: Student teachers' early conceptions of classroom practice. *Teaching and Teacher Education, 7*(1), 1-8.

Carr, W., & Kemmis, S. (1986). *Becoming critical: Education, knowledge and action research.* Basingstoke: Falmer Press.

Cole, M. (1996). *Cultural psychology. A once and future discipline.* Cambridge, MA: Harvard University Press.

Cole, M. & Wertsch, J. V. (1996). *Contemporary implications of Vygotsky and Luria.* Worcester, Mass.: Clark University Press.

Collison, G., Erlbaum, B., Haavind, S., & Tinker, R. (Eds.). (2000). *Facilitating on-line learning: Effective strategies for moderators.* Madison, WI: Atwood Publishing.

Cuban, L. (1986). *Teachers and machines: the classroom use of technology since 1920.* New York: Teachers College Press.

Darling, L. (2001). When conceptions collide: constructing a community of inquiry for teacher education in British Columbia. *Journal of Education for Teaching, 27*(1), 7-21.

Darling-Hammond, L., & Snyder, J. (2000). Authentic assessment of teaching in context. *Teaching and Teacher Education, 16*(5-6), 523-545.

Dysthe, O. (2001). Sosiokulturelle teoriperspektiv på kunnskap og læring [Socio-cultural Perspectives on Knowledge and Learning; in Norwegian]. (pp. 33-73). In: O. Dysthe (Ed.). *Dialog, samspel og læring* [Dialogue, Interaction and Learning; in Norwegian]. Oslo: Abstract Forlag.

Dysthe, O. & Engelsen, K. S. (2003). *Mapper som pedagogisk redskap. Perspektiver og erfaringer.* [Portfolios as pedagogical tools. Perspectives and Experiences; in Norwegian]. Oslo: Abstract forlag.

Ellminn, R., & Elminn, B. (2005). *Å arbeide med portfolio* [To work with portfoilio; in Norwegian]. Oslo: Interface Media A/S.

Engeström, Y. (1998). Den nærmeste udviklingssone som den basale kategori i pædagogisk psykologi [The zone of proximal development as the basic element in pedagogical psycologi; in Norwegian.]. (pp.1-26) .In: M. Hermansen (Ed.). *Fra læingens horison* [From the horizon of learning; in Norwegian]. Århus: Klim.

Firestone, W.A. (1993). Alternative arguments for generalizing from data as applied to qualitative research. *Educational Researcher, 22*(4), 16-23.

Fullan, M. (1982). *The meaning of educational change.* Toronto : Ontario Institute for Studies in Education.

Geertz, C. (1973). *The interpretation of cultures- Selected essays by Clifford Geertz.* New York: Basic Books.

Giddens, A. (1991). *Modernitet og selvidentitet* [Modernity and self-identity; in Danish]. Köbenhavn: Hans forlag.Reitzels Hargreaves, A. (2002). Teaching and betrayal. *Teachers and Teaching. 8*, 393-407.

Helleve, I. (2003). Samspel med data? [Interaction with the Computer; in Norwegian]. *Nordisk Pedagogikk, 4,* 161-170.

Helleve, I. (2007 a). In an ICT-based context: Why was our group "The magic group"? *European Journal of Teacher Education, 30*(3), 267-284.

Helleve, I. (2007 b). *What do student teachers look upon as the most important support for their reflection process?* Paper presented at NERA (Nordic Educational Research Association) Nordic perspectives on lifelong learning in the new Europe (15th-17th of March). Turku, Finland.

Hoel, T. L. (2002). Interaksjon og læringspotensial i samtalegrupper på e-post [Interaction and learning potential in e-mail based groups; in Norwegian]. (pp. 125-146).

In S. Ludvigsen & T. L. Hoel (Eds.), *Et utdanningssystem i endring. IKT og læring* [The change of an educational system. ICT and learning; in Norwegian]. Oslo: Gyldendal. Norsk forlag.

Huberman, A.M., & Miles, M.B. (1984). *Innovation up close: How school improvement works*. New York: Plenum Press.

ITU. (2000-2003a). The INVITIS project[INVITIS-prosjektet]. Retrieved October 23, 2004 from: http://www.itu.no/filearchive/fil_Sluttrapp_INVITIS.pdf

ITU. (2000-2003b). The PLUTO-project[PLUTO-prosjektet]. Retrieved October 23, 2004 from: http://www.itu.no/Prosjekter/1079504497.79/view

Keppel, M., Au, E., Ma, A., Chan, C. (2006). Peer learning and learning-oriented assessment in technology-enhanced environments. *Assessment & Evaluation in Higher Education, 31*(4) 453-464.

Klenowski, V. (2002). *Developing portfolios for learning and assessment*. London: Routledge Falmer.

Korthagen, F., Kessels, J., Koster, B., Lagerwerf, B., & Wubbels T. (2001). *Linking practice and theory; The pedagogy of realistic teacher education*. Mahwah, NJ,: Erlbaum.

Korthagen, F. & Vasalos, A. (2005). Levels in reflection: Core reflection as a means to enhance professional growth. *Teacher and Teaching, 11*(1), 47-71.

Koschmann, T. (1996). *CSCL: Theory and practice of an emerging paradigm*. Mahmah. New Jersey: Erlbaum.

Krumsvik, R.J. (2006). *ICT in the school. ICT-initiated school development in lower secondary school*. Ph D thesis. Bergen: University of Bergen.

Krumsvik, R. (2007). *Skulen og den digitale læringsrevolusjonen*.[The school and the digital learning revolution; in Norwegian]. Oslo: Universitetsforlaget.

Krumsvik, R., & Almås, A. (In press). The digital didactic. In R. Krumsvik (Ed.), *Learning in the network society and the digitized school*. New York: Nova Science Publisher.

Kvale, S. (2001). *Det kvalitative forskningsintervjuet* [The qualitative research interview; in Norwegian]. Oslo: Ad Notam.

LaBoskey, V. K. (1994). *Development of reflective practice: A study of pre-service teachers*. New York: Teachers College Press.

Lave, J., & Wenger, E. (1991). *Situated learning*. Cambridge: Cambridge University Press.

Leite. L. (2006). Prospective physical science teachers' willingness to engage in learning communities. *European Journal of Teacher Education, 29*(1), 3-22.

Light, G. & Cox, R. (2001). *Learning and teaching in higher education*. London: Chapman.

Lillejord, S., & Dysthe, O. (2008). Productive learning practice- a theoretical discussion based on two cases. *Journal of Education and Work, 21*(1), 75-89.

Loughran, J. (2006). *Developing a pedagogy for teacher educators. Understanding teaching and learning about teaching*. London: Routledge.

Ludvigsen, S. & Hoel, T.L. (2002). *Et utdanningssystem i endring.* [A change in the Educational System; in Norwegian]. Oslo: Gyldendal Norsk Forlag.

Matusov, E. (2001). Intersubjectivity as a way of informing teaching design for a community of learners' classrooms. *Teaching and Teacher Education, 17*(4), 383-402.

McNiff, J. (2002). *Action research. Principles and practice*. London: Routledge Falmer.

MER. (2001). (Undervisings-og forskningsdepartementet) (UFD). The Quality Reform[Kvalitetsreformen]. Retrieved October 23, 2007, from: http://odin.dep.no/kd/norsk/dok/regpubl/stmeld/045001-040003/hov003-bn.html).

MER. (2002). [Undervisings-og forskningsdepartementet] [UFD]. The Quality Reform – Concerning new teacher education [Kvalitetsreformen – om ny lærerutdanning]. Retrieved October 23, 2007, from:
http://odin.dep.no/kd/norsk/dok/regpubl/stmeld/045001-040003/hov003-bn.html.

MER (2003).[Undervisings-og forskningsdepartementet] [UFD]. The Program for digital competence 2004-2008[Program for digital kompetanse 2004-2008]. Retrieved October 23, 2008, from: http://odin.dep.no/kd/norsk/satsingsomraade/ikt/045011-990066/dok-bn.html

Merriam, S. B. (1998). *Qualitative research and case study applications in education.* San Francisco: Jossey-Bass.

Mintrop, H. (2001). Educating students to teach in a constructivist way - Can it be done? *Teachers College Record, 103*(2), 207-239.

MOK. (2006). The Knowledge Promotion. The new national curriculum. Retrieved October 23, 2008, from: http://odin.dep.no/kd/english/topics/knowledgepromotion/bn.html

NIFU/STEP. (2008). *Digital kompetanse i norsk lærerutdanning* [Digital competence in Norwegian teacher education; in Norwegian]. Report 28/2008. Oslo: NIFU/STEP.

Palloff, R. & Pratt, K. (Eds.) (1999). *Building learning communities in cyberspace: Effective strategies for the online classroom.* San Francisco: Jossey-Bass.

Patton, M. Q. (1990). *Qualitative Evaluation Methods.* (2nd Ed.). Thousand Oaks, CA: Sage.

Paulsen, M. F. (2002). *Online education systems: Discussion and definition of terms.* Retrieved May 2, 2008, from
http://home.nettskolen.nki.no/~morten/pp/Nordisk%20LMS%20analyse.ppt#413,6.

Rambøll (2004). *Evaluering av IKT satsingen i lærerutdanningen* Sluttrapport [Evaluation of the ICT investment in teacher education. The final report; in Norwegian]. Oslo: Utdannings- og forskningsdepartementet.

Rogoff, B. (1998). Cognition as collaborative process. In W. Damon, D. Kuhn & R.S. Siegler (Eds.), *Handbook of Child Psychology* (pp. 679-729). Toronto: John Wiley.

Rommetveit, R. (1979). On the architecture of intersubjectivity. In: R. Rommetveit & R. M. Blakar (Eds.), *Studies of language, thought and verbal communication.* New York: Academic Press.

Säljö, R. (2000). *Lärande i praktiken* [Learning from practice; in Swedish]. Stockholm: Bokförlaget Prisma.

Salmon, G. (2000). *E-moderating: the key to teaching and learning online.* London: Kogan Page.

Schön, D.A. (1987). *Educating the reflective practitioner.* San Francisco: Jossey-Bass.

Solberg, A. (1996). Erfaringer fra feltarbeid [Experiences from fieldwork; in Norwegian]. pp. 130-144. In H. Holter & R. Kalleberg (Eds.), *Kvaltative metoder i samfunnsforskning* [Qualitative Methods in Social Science; in Norwegian].Oslo: Universtitsforlaget.

Smith, K. & Tillema, H. (2001). Long-term influences of portfolios on professional development. *Scandinavian Journal of Educational Research, 45*(2), 183-203.

Smith, K. & Tillema, H. (2003). Clarifying different types of portfolio use. *Assessment & Evaluation in Higher Education, 26*(6), 625-648.

Somekh, B. (2007). *Pedagogy and learning with ICT.* London: Routledge.

Stake, R.E. (1995). *The art of case study research.* Thousand Oaks, CA: Sage.

Sumison, J. & Patterson, C. (2004). The emergency of a community in pre-service teacher education program. *Teaching and Teacher Education, 20*, 621-635.

Thurston, A. (2005). Building online communities technology. *Technology, Pedagogy and Education, 14*(3), 353-369.

Tyack, D. & Cuban, L. (1998). *Tinkering toward Utopia.* Cambridge, MA: Harvard University Press.

Valziner, J. & Van der Veer, R. (2000). *The social mind.* New York: Cambridge University Press.

Vygorsky, L.S. (1978). *Mind in society. The development of higher psychological processes.* Cambridge, MA: Harvard University Press.

Wallace, R. M. (2002). On-line teaching as moderating in a community of learners: An essay review of three books. *Teaching and Teacher Education, 18*(2), 363-369.

Wasser, J. D., & Bresler, L. (1996). Working in the interpretive zone: Conceptualizing collaboration in qualitative research teams. *Educational Researcher, 25*(5), 5-15.

Wegerif, R. (2007). *Dialogic education and technology.* Lausanne: Springer.

Wenger, E. (1998). *Communities of practice. learning, meaning and identity.* Cambridge: Cambridge University Press.

Wertsch, J. (1998). *Mind as action.* New York: Oxford University Press.

Zimann, J. (2000). *Real Science.* Cambridge: Cambridge University Press.

In: Learning in the Network Society and the Digitized School   ISBN 978-1-60741-172-7
Editor: Rune Krumsvik   © 2009 Nova Science Publishers, Inc.

Epilogue

PRODUCTIVE HORIZONTAL LEARNING AND DIGITAL TOOLS

Sølvi Lillejord and Olga Dysthe
University of Bergen, Norway

This publication clearly shows that the power to change educational practices is not in the tools or technologies human beings use, but in *how* people choose to use and utilise available technologies. As the introduction of new technologies often reveal deeper structural problems in organisations, many educational institutions are today struggling with how to establish social practices that are productive (Lillejord and Dysthe 2008) to the process of promoting literacy in general and digital literacy in particular. While the expectation is that new technologies will contribute to renewing educational practice, educators often find themselves caught in traditional patterns of institutionalised practices that limit or inhibit the potential for change inherent in new technologies. The question is then, how can technology be used to change educational processes that are not productive?

During the last decennia, the social aspect of learning and learning processes have been emphasised in education research. A fundamental understanding in social learning theories is that human beings are not only being made social by others through processes of socialization; they are *born* social (Bråten 1998). From birth we start interacting with others, communicating with and learning from others. Since early 1900, the understanding of learning as cultural *practices* has been developed and refined in pragmatism and sociocultural theories, where learning is basically understood as interactional, contextual and situated activities. While social perspectives on learning historically challenged the cognitive views with their emphasis on the individual learner, social perspectives on learning today are themselves being challenged on how to account for individual learning. As the articles in this publication show, the developments of new technologies and interactions with ICT as a mediating tool have contributed to a reconceptualisation of individual and social learning. This may be so because information and communication technologies have a unique quality of directly addressing the individual while at the same time establishing networks between individuals. Hence, ICTs open for the development of *hybrid* educational structures where students are not only being "told" from above, but also learn from each other.

Social learning theories are concerned with explaining learning and development as *interaction* between the individuals and their environment. This group of theories assumes that learning is always social; it is something we engage in as individuals among fellow human beings. Whether this fundamental understanding of how we learn is reflected in institutional practices – and in what way – are returning question in educational research. Etienne Wenger notes in the introductory chapter that learning may, from a social perspective be perceived as *horizontal* or networked practices and that technology has a particular potential of enhancing horizontal and social interactions. The strength of the articles in this volume is that they contribute to our understanding of how this may be implemented in a variety of ways.

This tension between vertical and horizontal learning is for instance exemplified by Roger Säljö and Jan Wyndham through two analytical models of educative communicative patterns in mathematics classrooms. The traditional communicative pattern is that the teacher is using the white board to "go through" the subject matter to be learned. During this process of "going through", the teacher explains concepts and theories and instructs the students before he or she gives the students assignments to exercise individually and shows them procedures for solving the problem. This model for educational practice is referred to by Wenger as the provider – recipient – model. As the expert provider, the teacher is handing over the knowledge to be learned to the (receiving) students. This model is vertical, not horizontal, and it aligns with the point made by Simonsen and Assarson when they describe an educational tradition placing the teacher in the parents' position, perceiving "the adult as the expert and the child as the less knowledgeable". In this vertical and often monological educational tradition, the teacher interacts with each student individually, neglecting the learning potential in the horizontal interactions.

The second model of learning in the mathematics classroom described by Säljö and Wyndham is where the students are placed in groups and engage in *talking* mathematics and collaborate in problem solving. In order to understand the problem and discuss strategies for problem solving, the students engage in multivoiced and dialogical inquiry. This horizontal, peer-to-peer interaction introduces a new discourse of non-linear learning in education. And this is also where new digital tools may support the development of a broader understanding of instructional practice than the one underpinning the vertical model.

The articles in this volume document that the technology-driven shift from a vertical to a horizontal model poses challenges at all levels of educational institutions as well as for education in general. While the majority of the chapters present and discuss examples from schools, Ola Erstad shows how the establishment of learning networks *between* schools involves interactions at all levels: Central authorities, local authorities, school leaders, teachers and students. Rune Krumsvik and Ingrid Helleve discuss face-to-face and web-based actions and interaction from a student teacher perspective and Federica Olivero is analysing educational processes in postgraduate courses. The move from a vertical to a horizontal educational practice is also illustrated in Arne Vines' analysis of how technology facilitated the shift from vertical and monological feedback from teacher (tutor) to horizontal peer feedback in law. Another example of horizontal learning is provided by Thomas De Lange and Sten Ludvigsen, showing how students use multiple electronic resources in collaborate team based learning in secondary school. Also, as shown by Aud Solbjørg Skulstad, focusing on multimodality and multiliteracies may be a way of creating new kinds of horizontal communication among learners in foreign language classrooms.

Obviously, the question is not to abandon the vertical model altogether, but to use the potential of technology to create more space for the horizontal model. Bridget Somekh and Caty Lewin draw on 25 years of work that show how digital technologies may be used to transform students' learning environment. Technology driven distributed collaboration between peers and teachers is one way of challenging the vertical model, and as Krumsvik and Almås argue in their article, there is an obvious need to rethink the learning potential in traditional didactic models.

In order to create educational change and promote productive learning practices, both practical empirical research and conceptual work is necessary. The articles in this volume will provide useful resources for both researchers and practitioners in how to use technology as a tool for the promotion of horizontal learning processes.

REFERENCES

Bråten, S. (1998) (red.) Intersubjective Communication and Emotion in Early Ontogeny. Cambridge University Press.

Lillejord, S. & Dysthe, O. (2008): Productive learning practice – a theoretical discussion based on two cases. *Journal of Education and Work*, Vol.21, 1: 75-89.

INDEX

G

H

I

S